MUSLIMS ON THE
AMERICANIZATION PATH?

MUSLIMS ON THE
AMERICANIZATION PATH?

Edited by
Yvonne Yazbeck Haddad
John L. Esposito

OXFORD
UNIVERSITY PRESS

2000

OXFORD
UNIVERSITY PRESS

Oxford   New York
Athens   Auckland   Bangkok   Bogotá   Buenos Aires   Calcutta
Cape Town   Chennai   Dar es Salaam   Delhi   Florence   Hong Kong   Istanbul
Karachi   Kuala Lumpur   Madrid   Melbourne   Mexico City   Mumbai
Nairobi   Paris   São Paulo   Singapore   Taipei   Tokyo   Toronto   Warsaw

and associated companies in
Berlin   Ibadan

Copyright © 1998 University of South Florida

First published in 2000 as an Oxford University Press paperback
198 Madison Avenue, New York, New York 10016

Oxford is a registered trademark of Oxford University Press.

Library of Congress Cataloging in Publication Data
Muslims on the Americanization path? / edited by
Yvonne Yazbeck Haddad and John L Esposito.
p. cm.
Included bibliographical references.
ISBN 0-19-513526-1
1. Islam—United States.   2. Muslims—United States
I. Haddad, Yvonne Yazbeck.   II. Esposito, John L.
BP67.U6M88   2000
297'.0973—dc21   98-6046

9 8 7 6 5 4 3 2

Printed in the United States of America
on acid-free paper

Contents

Contributors

KHALED ABOU EL FADL teaches at the University of Texas at Austin in the Department of Middle Eastern Languages and Cultures and the University of Texas Law School. Previously, he taught at Yale Law School and at Princeton University.

ERNEST ALLEN, JR., is a professor of African American Studies at the W.E.B. Du Bois Department of Afro-American Studies at the University of Massachusetts, Amherst. A contributing editor to *The Black Scholar*, he is currently writing a book regarding the convergence of Islamic, Pan-Asian, and Masonic influences on African American life during the Great Depression.

CAROL L. ANWAY has spent many years as a school counselor and as an author of Christian-education resources on children, families, and women for her denomination. She is the author of *Daughters of Another Path: Experiences of American Women Choosing Islam*.

ROBERT DANNIN is an adjunct professor of Metropolitan Studies at New York University's College of Arts and Sciences. He received his doctorate in anthropology and ethnolinguistics from the School of Advanced Studies in Social Science, Ecole Pratique des Hautes Etudes, Paris. His ethnographic and ethnohistorical research with Jolie Stahl will be published in *Black Pilgrims to Islam*.

YUSUF TALAL DE LORENZO is the secretary of the Fiqh Council of North America, and has recently been involved in the development and administration of a Master's level program for Muslim military chaplains. He has served as Director of Naleemiah College in Sri Lanka, as the Advisor on Islamic Education in Pakistan, and as a professor at the International Islamic University in Islamabad. He has published articles and book chapters in Urdu, Arabic, and English. His most recent publications include *Imam Bukhari's Book of Muslim Morals and Manners*, and *A Compendium of Legal Rulings on the Operation of Islamic Banks*.

JOHN L. ESPOSITO is Professor of Religion and International Affairs, Georgetown University, and Director of the Center for Muslim-Christian Understanding: History and International Affairs at Georgetown University's Edmund A. Walsh School of Foreign Service. He is also Editor-in-Chief of the *Oxford Encyclopedia of the Modern Islamic World*. Among his publications are *The Islamic Threat: Myth or Reality?*; *Islam and Democracy* (with John O. Voll); *Islam: The Straight Path*; *Islam and Politics*; *The Contemporary Islamic Revival* (with Yvonne Haddad and John O. Voll); *Voices of Resurgent Islam*; *Islam in Asia: Religion, Politics, and Society*; and *Women in Muslim Family Law*.

ELISE GOLDWASSER lives with her family and tends her garden in Durham, North Carolina. Her current research project is on racist stereotypes in the circus. She is also writing children's stories in Hebrew and Arabic.

YVONNE Y. HADDAD is Professor of History, Islam, and Christian-Muslim Relations at the Center for Muslim-Christian Understanding at Georgetown University. She is past president of the Middle East Studies Association and a former editor of *Muslim World*. Her published works include *Contemporary Islam and the Challenge of History*; *Islam, Gender and Social Change*; *Islamic Values in the United States* (with A. Lummis); *The Contemporary Islamic Revival* (with J. Voll and J. Esposito); *The Islamic Understanding of Death and Resurrection* (with J. Smith); *The Muslims of America*; *Mission to America* (with J. Smith); *Muslim Communities in North America* (with J. Smith); and *Christian-Muslim Encounters* (with W. Haddad). She is an associate editor of the *Oxford Encyclopedia of the Modern Islamic World*.

OMAR KHALIDI is a senior research scholar and reference librarian for the Aga Khan Program in Islamic Architecture at the Massachusetts Institute of Technology. He obtained his Ph.D. from the University of Wales, and is the author of *Indian Muslims since Independence* and *Hyderabad: After the Fall*. His research interests include ethnicity, diasporas, and nationalism.

MOHOMMED A. MUQTEDAR KHAN is a Ph.D. candidate in international relations at Georgetown University. His areas of interest include Islam, international relations theory, and American foreign policy. He has published articles in *Islam and Christian-Muslim Relations*, *American Journal of Islamic Social Sciences*, *Middle East Policy*, *The Muslim World*, *The Diplomat*, *Middle East Insight*, *Islamic Horizons*, *The Message*, *Counter Terrorism Chronicle*, and *Saudi Gazette*.

KATHLEEN M. MOORE is an assistant professor in the Department of Political Science at the University of Connecticut. Her research interests include religion, law, migration, and the construction of identities. She is the author of *al-Mughtaribun: American Law and the Transformation of Muslim Life in the United States*. Currently, she is writing a book on the emergence of a "minoritarian" legal culture among Muslims living in the "diaspora."

GREG NOAKES, an American Muslim, is the news editor of the *Washington Report on Middle East Affairs*. He has a B.A. in history from the University of Virginia and an M.A. in Middle Eastern Studies from the University of Texas at Austin. In addition to a regular "Issues in Islam" column in the *Washington Report*, he has written on Islamic affairs for *Aramco World*, *The Message*, *The American Muslim*, *Traces*, *Islamic Horizons*, *al-Mustaqbal al-Islami* and the *Middle East Affairs Journal*, among other publications.

YUSUF NURUDDIN is currently working on a manuscript entitled "Islam and the African American Experience"; the essay in this volume has been excerpted from that work. Nuruddin has taught in the Social and Behavioral Sciences Department of Medgar Evers College (CUNY) and the African American Studies Department of John Jay College (CUNY). Born in the Bedford-Stuyvesant section of Brooklyn and educated at Columbia, Harvard, and Yale, he has been a practicing Sunni Muslim for over twenty years. He is a contributor to the book *Muslim Communities in North America*, and the editor of the forthcoming *Timbuktu: A Journal of Contemporary African-American Muslim Thought*.

ESMAIL SHAKERI teaches political science and Islamic studies at Huron and King's Colleges, University of Western Ontario. His Ph.D. is from the Department of Political Science, University of Toronto. His current research interests include ethics, human rights, and democracy in the international Islamic discourse, the Muslim minority in Canada, and the rivalry between Islamic states in the newly independent Central Asian republics.

MUSLIMS ON THE
AMERICANIZATION PATH?

Introduction

Muslims in America or American Muslims?

JOHN L. ESPOSITO

Islam is the fastest growing religion in America and in Europe. There are, for example, more Muslims in America than in Kuwait, Qatar, and Libya. It has been common to speak of Islam *and* the West, but today any consideration of that topic must include Islam *in* the West. Islam is the second largest religion in France, the third in Britain, Germany, and North America. Even if Muslim immigration and the rate of conversion were not to grow, birth rate alone ensures that in the first part of the twenty-first century, Islam will replace Judaism as the second largest religion in the United States.

Integral to the experience of Muslims, like all religious or ethnic minorities in America, is how to deal with the question of integration or assimilation. The majority of Americans have yet to realize that Muslims are "us," but many Muslims have not solved the problem of the relationship of their faith to national identity either: will they remain Muslims in America or become American Muslims? The identity of the community, or more specifically, the need to form a new identity in America, raises many questions. Can Muslims become part and parcel of a pluralistic American society without sacrificing or losing their identity? Can Muslims be Muslims in a non-Muslim state that is not governed by Islamic law? Is the American legal system capable of allowing for particular Muslim religious and cultural differences within the Constitution's broader universal claims? Do the secular and/or Judeo-Christian values of American society make this impossible? Is there a contradiction between demanding equal rights and access and insisting on maintaining a distinctively separate identity?

The American Path Option:
Between Tradition and Reality

Although the Muslims of America are indeed on the path to Americanization, what that means and what it will yield remain uncertain. The variety
of Muslim experiences in America covered in this volume exemplify some
of the major themes in the development of Muslim communities today: the
push and pull, tension and conflict, between tradition and change; the reconciliation of religious, political, and social identity; the relations of law to
society; the role of religion in cultural identity.

The Muslims of America are far from homogeneous in their composition and in their attitudes and practices. Islam in America is a mosaic of
many ethnic, racial, and national groups. The majority are first- or second-
generation immigrants or African-American converts. Their problems, like
those of other religious minorities, center on assimilation or integration
and the preservation and practice of religious faith in an American society informed by Judeo-Christian or secular values, the relationship of religious tradition to the demands of current realities, and gaining a place in
American politics and culture. The situation is complicated by the historical relationship between Islam and Christianity, especially between the
West and Muslim societies, which includes everything from memories of
the Crusades and European colonialism to what many perceive as the distorted image of Islam projected by Orientalist scholarship and the media,
and finally to the hegemony and anti-Islamic policies of the West, in particular the United States.

Yvonne Y. Haddad, in "The Dynamics of Islamic Identity in North
America," analyzes questions of language, community, and faith in the
American immigrant experience, the significant differences within the
Muslim community and the problems encountered in an American society often brought up on stereotypes that breed fear and distrust. Islam in
North America reflects the diverse backgrounds of the community from
immigrants in pursuit of political, religious, or economic freedom to native-
born African-Americans seeking social justice. The identity of immigrants
has been shaped by the Muslim societies in which they were raised and
by their interaction with American society and with Muslims from other
traditions. Haddad suggests that, living as a minority in a dominant culture often hostile to Islam, Muslims are often alienated and powerless. They
are confused and challenged by an America in which, despite separation
of church and state, Christian values are assumed to be integral to American identity and values. The tendency to contrast American "national culture" with Islamic values further complicates the process of assimilation.

Finally, the idea inculcated by the media in the post-cold war period that
Islam has supplanted the Soviet Union as the threat to its survival and the
tendency to equate Islam with extremism and terrorism, combined with the
American policy tilt toward Israel and its inconsistent record not only in

the Middle East but also in Bosnia and Chechnya further disillusion and alienate many.

Haddad contends that some Islamic leaders have encouraged immigrants to return to their homelands and work for the establishment of Islamic governments. Others also discourage assimilation, but advocate the creation of Islamic communities within the broader non-Islamic society. Still others encourage engagement and peaceful coexistence, emphasizing the common religious and social values and interests between Islam and Christianity. While the isolationists practice their faith privately and worry about losing their children to the attractions of Western culture, the socially engaged build institutions (mosques, schools, professional and social associations) to establish a place for Islam in the American religious and cultural landscape. But the majority dissociate themselves from the issue of Islam's presence in North America. In contrast, African-American Muslims are visible and active in asserting their Muslim identity when they focus on the problems facing inner-city America in particular: racism, poverty, crime, violence, and drugs. These differences among and within Muslim communities raise questions of interpretation, law, and cultural identity.

The primary question facing Muslims in America is whether or not they can live Muslim lives in a non-Muslim territory. Especially for immigrants raised in Muslim-majority countries, this is a particularly vexing question. In "Striking a Balance: Islamic Legal Discourses on Muslim Minorities," Khaled Abou El Fadl examines how Muslim minorities are dealt with in Islamic law and discourse. Muslim jurists had in the past encouraged Muslims to migrate from non-Muslim areas, lest they inadvertently contribute to the strength and prosperity of non-Muslim states. But, although ideally Muslims should live in a Muslim territory, Islamic jurisprudence does allow for them to live outside the Dar al-Islam provided they can fulfill their religious obligations without hindrance.

Some religious leaders have counseled emigration from non-Muslim territories back to Muslim lands, others have defined the conditions under which Muslims can live permanently as loyal citizens in non-Muslim lands and still preserve their faith and identity. They continue to differ, debating questions such as whether they should vote, whether they are bound by Islamic (divine) or secular (man-made) laws, and whether they should participate with non-Muslim neighbors in community life and fully accept and defend a non-Muslim homeland.

Islamic law provides the ideal blueprint for society, delineating what can and can not be done. Formulated in the early centuries of Islamic history, classical law provided guidance to Muslim courts and individual believers down through the centuries. Since the late nineteenth century, however, Islamic reformers have called for a bold reinterpretation (*ijtihad*) of Islamic law to address the challenges of modern life. But the weight of tradition remains formidable. A popular belief is that, the early Muslim jurists having defined and delineated the parameters of Islamic law, the obligation of

the community was simply to follow it—the door that led to further interpretation had been closed. This static notion of Islamic law was promoted
by many among the ulama (religious scholars) and remained convincing until
it was vanquished by rapid and significant systemic change. Then prescient
Muslim intellectuals realized that such dramatically changed circumstances
required fresh responses. Across the Muslim world, a minority of Islamic
reformers called for a bold reinterpretation of Islamic theology and law. The
majority of the ulama who, despite Islam's lack of clergy, had appropriated
the trappings of a clerical class, including distinctive dress and the claim
that they were the true guardians and interpreters of Islam, adamantly clung
to the doctrines of the past (taqlid).

The problems of Muslims living both in America and Europe have been
compounded by the challenges of life as a Muslim minority in a non-Muslim
country, and this in turn presented a challenge to human and textual resources. In "The Fiqh Councilor in North America," Yusuf Talal DeLorenzo
shows how the Muslims of North America have had to broaden the definition of the scholar qualified to reinterpret Islamic law (mujtahid) and the
mufti (scholar qualified to give definitive rulings on specific issues) as well
as the law itself in order adequately to address the new realities of life in
North America.

As in many parts of the Muslim world, so in North America Muslims have
realized that the complexities of modern life often require disciplinary skills
that are beyond the limits of a single individual. Thus, for example, medical ethics requires expert knowledge not only of religious texts but also of
the sciences and, perhaps, economics as well. In addition, the realities of
life in the West are often quite different, indeed alien to, those of traditional
Muslim societies. Many in North America have concluded that legal decisions can only be rendered by those who have had firsthand experience of
this new world. As with imams, so too with legal scholars, the Muslims of
North America have had to develop an indigenous core of experts since they
could no longer simply import personnel and interpretations from the old
country.

The Fiqh Council of North America was established to provide just such
an indigenous Muslim response. A group of scholars representing a cross-
section of expertise was constituted to respond to the questions posed by
Muslims in North America. DeLorenzo gives examples of some of the questions that have arisen in areas ranging from economics and medicine to
marriage and the family and the responses of American muftis. Economic
problems have centered on how to deal with interest in banking, mortgages,
insurance, car loans, and the like. Islamic organizations face questions such
as how to invest their funds; Muslim stockbrokers and financial advisers
have had to convince clients that their services are Islamically acceptable.
Lawyers and their clients face similar issues regarding property, estates, and
pension plans. As in many parts of the Muslim world, gender issues have
included problems in marriage, dower and divorce compensation, inherit-

ance and bequests. Unique to the Muslim-minority experience in the West, however, has been the decision not to recognize as Islamically valid a marriage or divorce that has not gone through the secular courts.

For many decades the Muslims of America have remained relatively invisible, but by now they constitute a significant minority whose concerns can be effectively addressed through the political system. But to what extent can or should Muslims participate in the political system of a non-Muslim state in which Islamic law plays no part? Can Muslims vote? Can they fight and die in defending their new country? What if they are called upon to fight and kill fellow Muslims on behalf of a non-Muslim state?

In "Muslims and Identity Politics in America," Mohommed A. Muqtedar Khan analyzes this struggle in terms of the identity politics of self and the internal other (other nationalities and sects) and the self and the external other (non-Muslims). He demonstrates the extent to which identity issues and identity politics prevent American Muslims from interacting and cooperating across national and sectarian lines. This phenomenon is reflected in professional associations, universities, and mosques where national and sectarian backgrounds can determine attendance and participation at lectures and in other programs. These divisions carry over into politics where many are more united and involved in political developments in their countries of origin than those in the United States. As a result national American Muslim organizations often have to struggle to survive financially and to achieve any sense of common platform and strategy. In contrast, American-born Muslims who have grown up divorced from the socialization of the Muslim world's politics tend to be more open, inclusive and less sectarian than their immigrant forebears.

Many American Muslims remain keenly involved in international Muslim politics (Palestine, Afghanistan, Bosnia, Chechnya). Their disenchantment with United States policy stems from what some regard as the American "double standard" in its promotion of democracy and use of sanctions. This American anti-Islamic attitude can be seen not only abroad but in anti-terrorist legislation and media coverage of Islam and Muslims at home. Thus, while freedom and prosperity attract many Muslims to America, American foreign policy towards the Middle East and the media's demonization of Islam often alienate them once they arrive. However, Khan argues, just as Muslims in Muslim countries in the twentieth century have come to identify both with Islam and their national identity, so too in the next generation, many more will subscribe to an Islamic as well as an American identity, as African Americans have already done.

Differences of national origin remain strong because of continued ties and involvement with politics back home, and these often hinder cooperation among American Muslims. Tensions between Saudi Arabia and Iran or Pakistan and Bangladesh are echoed in America and demonstrate the extent to which sectarian and national differences continue to divide American Muslims.

North American Pluralism and the
Challenge of the Veil

The contested issue of the status of women has often been symbolized in the wearing of the *hijab* in Muslim countries and in the West. It became a political issue in more secular Muslim countries, such as Tunisia and Turkey, because it was regarded a sign of a "fundamentalist threat." It has also been at the center of some controversy in Europe and North America as a threat to the secular state. In a celebrated case, the French government banned its wearing by school children. The ensuing debate saw France, in the name of preserving its secular government, declare that, if Muslims were to become good French citizens, they must integrate not just assimilate. France rejected multiculturalism for integration. (Ironically, when French scholars needed a term for Islamic activists, Islamists, or fundamentalists, they hit upon "integrism" as the proper term for the union of religion and politics in Islamist ideology.)

In both the United States and Canada, multi-cultural societies that pride themselves on maintaining an individual's freedom of choice and religion, Muslim women who choose to wear the hijab have experienced discrimination. Kathleen Moore and Esmail Shakeri provide studies that describe the many facets of this issue. The hijab debate encompasses not only questions about the status and role of Muslim women, but also about the rights of members of religious-minority communities to define their identity vis-à-vis the dominant majority community.

In the United States, which prides itself both on maintaining the separation of church and state and on its positive valuation of diversity, Muslim women who wear hijab have encountered problems in the workplace and in the courts. In "The Veil and Religious Liberty: Anti-Discrimination Law and Muslim Women in the United States," Moore takes issue with those who have maintained that judicial interpretations of the religion clauses in the U.S. Constitution have been more generous than they once were toward the religious practices of minorities. Recent appellate-court decisions, she maintains, involving Orthodox and Hasidic Jews, Native American Indians and Sikhs, and Muslims have often appeared to belie the liberal guarantee of nondiscrimination and equal protection.

Muslims in America often find themselves in the position of other religious minorities who argue that the state's application of the same rules to all citizens must be balanced by the state's refraining from interfering in "private" social spheres where individuals should be free to practice their faith with its religious and cultural differences. Moore's study of the American Muslim experience, specifically as regards religious discrimination cases involving veiled women in the workplace, explores the question of whether there are judicially defined limits within which cultural and legal pluralism can develop in American society. Based on this study of employment cases involving religious discrimination, Moore argues that American constitutional law as currently constructed is incapable of solving the problem of the observant Muslim who wears the veil in a secular state.

Given global migration patterns, the remarkable number of Muslim minority communities that have come into existence, and the rapid growth of Islam in Europe and America, issues of law and religion will become increasingly significant both in and of themselves and because they will reflect or inform the attitudes of the broader society. In the twenty-first century, Moore maintains that the successful resolution of workplace discrimination requires broader political and social changes and not just changes in the law. Many of these changes are examined in the Canadian context by Esmail Shakeri in "Muslim Women in Canada: Their Role and Status as Revealed in the *Hijab* Controversy," where debate over wearing the hijab has also surfaced. There controversy centered on the attempt by the school board in Montreal to ban wearing the hijab in school. However, as Shakeri demonstrates, much of the public discourse was influenced by what the hijab symbolized or represented to many of its opponents (Western feminists, journalists, academics, politicians) for whom Islam is an alien, oppressive, extremist, or terrorist religion. The Canadian debate reflects the tensions between text or norm and context, both Muslim and Western values and social conditions, educated Canadian-born Muslim and non-Muslim (Western feminist) women; a policy of integration vs. assimilation; accommodationism and isolationism; majority norms and minority rights; the veil as a symbol of the oppression and subservience of women vs. freedom and liberation.

Problems facing Muslim women in North America involve not only immigrant or first- and second-generation Muslim women, but also the growing number of American converts. That Islam is the fastest growing religion in America is due in part to the number of American women who have embraced Islam in recent years. They face the same problems of faith and identity, of dress and employment, but in their case it is often compounded by the reactions of their families, neighbors, and friends. In "American Women Choosing Islam," Carol Anway, who has studied (mainly Christian) women who convert to Islam in the United States and Canada, discusses the results of a study of these converts. Anway analyzes why they converted, their family background, religious quest, and the impact of their conversions on their lives as well as their parents and relatives. For many, Islam provided answers to the doubts they experienced as Christians. Far from questioning the compatibility of Islam with American values, these converts often found a congruence between their new faith and traditional American ideals, including commitment to family, community, education, and discipline, though they often also found themselves caught up in the process of integrating their Western heritage with new beliefs and cultural practices.

The African-American Experience

A significant number of Muslims in America are African Americans, who are among the oldest members of the American community. While all Muslims in America may be called Muslim or refer to their religion as Islam, the experience of African-American Muslims has been very different from that of Muslims who were born and raised in Muslim countries or in an immigrant Muslim milieu. Most are descendants of slaves, were raised as Christians, and are members of a community whose religious and political identity has been affected by the struggle for freedom and equality.

The earliest African-American Muslim communities were in fact a response and reaction to the "negro, black, or African-American" experience. Early leaders such as Noble Drew Ali and W. D. Fard, with their syncretic version of "Islam" (the Moorish Science Temple and the Nation of Islam), emerged in the 1920s and 1930s, but perhaps most influential was Elijah Muhammad and the Nation of Islam. The spiritual descendants of Elijah Muhammad, from Muhammad Ali and Malcolm X to Warith Din Muhammad (Elijah Muhammad's son) and Louis Farrakhan, epitomize the diverse currents that account for much of the African-American Muslim experience. Today, they are in the midst of a period of transition from what some have called proto-Islam to more traditional or mainstream Islam as African-American Muslims continue to struggle with issues of faith, identity, and destiny, including the relationship of their adopted faith to Christianity, to race, to black liberation, to traditional Islam, to their African heritage, and to American citizenship. At the same time, their interaction with immigrant Muslim communities challenges the ability of Muslim Americans to transcend the divisions of race and ethnicity.

Three studies provide critical perspectives on the history and development of the African-American Muslim identity, its formative experience, its relationship to traditional Islam, its African heritage, and the American experience, and the dilemmas of co-existence in a multi-ethnic context.

Understanding the origins and causes of the conversion of African Americans to Islam is provided in "Identity and Destiny: The Formative Views of the Moorish Science Temple and the Nation of Islam," in which Ernest Allen compares the influences and beliefs of the Moorish Science Temple of America and the Nation of Islam. While there were theological differences between them, the fundamental existential questions were the same: Why do black people suffer? How can this suffering be brought to an end? Both offered a paradigm that emphasized the (material as well as spiritual) here-and-now and not just the hereafter, and both preached individual initiative and responsibility, family life, hard work, and frugality. The Bible, Qur'an, Freemasonry, theosophy, the Ahmadiyya movement, and especially the creative imaginations of their founders joined to form a world view that offered a sense of history, identity, meaning, and value to their followers.

African-Americans are heirs to a triple cultural heritage: African, Islamic, and Western. Yusuf Nuruddin in "African-American Muslims and the Question of Identity: Between Traditional Islam, African Heritage, and the American Way," discusses how they are the source both of alienation and integration, and of conflicting ideologies (nationalism/separatism and integration/assimilation), manifested today in the tension between Westernization, re-Africanization, and re-Islamization. Nuruddin demonstrates the relationship between the African-American nationalism espoused by a small but vocal minority and African-American Islamic movements which, as Ernest Allen indicated, sought to restore or revive a "lost" culture.

While most discussions of the origins of African-American Islam or of Islam in the African-American community focus on the role of early charismatic figures and their syncretistic, heterodox forms of Islam, Yusuf Nuruddin argues that what he regards as more orthodox Islamic influences preceded these heterodox movements, among them Marcus Garvey, Edward Wilmot, Noble Drew Ali, and the Ahmadiyya, who provided a bridge between black cultural nationalism and (Islamic) pan-Africanism to the black supremacist Nation of Islam.

First came the black nationalist/separatists; then the radical (though not anti-nationalist) Islamic separatists, the ostensible followers of Sunni Islam who call for jihad against all unbelievers—African-American Muslims who did not agree with them and European-American Christians alike. Next were those who adopted a more assimilationist, ecumenical outlook, such as Warith Din Muhammad, and finally a number of responses, including Louis Farrakhan and others, who are trying to reclaim leadership from both Islamic separatists and assimilationists by reasserting the separatist legacy of the Nation of Islam and, at the same time, aligning themselves with a more traditional or orthodox Islam. At the same time, a variety of secular cultural nationalists, including American and continental African authors and artists, have launched an Afrocentric crusade against all variations of Islam.

Nuruddin then discusses the debate that rages today among major African-American and African scholars and artists over Afrocentricity vis-à-vis Islam. Some wish to continue to recognize and integrate their triple heritage and legacy; others reject the legacy of both Western and Islamic culture. The problems are compounded when there are interactions between the African-American and immigrant Muslim communities or international Islamic organizations like the World Muslim League (Rabita al-Alam al-Islami). They reveal the continued tension and at times conflict between faith and race/ethnic identity, between the normative universality of Islam and the realities of Muslim communities.

Robert Dannin, in "Understanding the Multi-Ethnic Dilemma of African-American Muslims," analyzes the impact of multi-ethnic Muslim communities on African-American Muslims, drawing his examples from international politics (the Gulf war) as well as local mosques. Thus, for example, when the Saudi-based and -funded Rabita sought worldwide consensus for the Saudi-American coalition against Iraq, the initial show of unity among African-American Muslims was shattered when Operation Desert Shield became Desert Storm in 1990. Warith Din Muḥammad and Louis Farrakhan assumed polar opposite positions based upon religious and ethnic considerations, and, as Dannin notes, those divisions remain.

African-American Muslims, however, share a common challenge with immigrant Muslims and Muslims worldwide: How is one to be Muslim and African-American simultaneously? Despite the shared beliefs and rituals that unite Muslims, the transnational unity of Islam disintegrates in the face of ethnic, linguistic, and nationalist differences and conflicts. The result, Dannin argues, is an endless crisis of identity. On major religious holy days or the annual pilgrimage to Mecca, Islam appears to be multi-racial and multi-ethnic; but inter-racial and inter-ethnic tensions remain common at the local level, in mosques and in community politics. This dilemma is seen quite vividly in relations between new Muslims of African descent and new American Muslims of Middle Eastern and South Asian backgrounds. Their interaction or lack of it is often based on ethnic (e.g., African-American vs. Arab) and cultural differences, especially religious attitudes, values, and practices that a particular group regards as religious doctrine.

Americanization and the Preservation of Cultural Identity

Despite the fact that Islam is the third largest religion in the United States and that by now most American Muslims have been born and raised in the United States, the American media continue to view Islam through the prism of the Iranian revolution, regarding it as a retrogressive religion given to extremism and terrorism. Greg Noakes, in "Muslims and the American Press," analyzes the quality of media coverage and the reasons for the tendency to misunderstand and distort the nature and function of Islam. Noakes maintains that the media's propensity for the "sensational," the explosive headline events, acts of violence, and religious extremism capture the headlines at the expense of the faith and practice of the vast majority of Muslims. The contentious terminology used to describe events and movements in the Muslim world, terms like "fundamentalism" and "ethnic cleansing," add to the problem, as does the focus on idiosyncratic or retrograde cultural practices such as female circumcision and the slave trade.

Noakes finds that key among the factors affecting coverage are political sensibilities (vis-à-vis the Arab-Israeli conflict, Kashmir, Bosnia, for example), the realities of domestic lobbies and advertising revenue, and the limited number of expert analysts in the media and the ideological/political biases of the few who exist. While these factors can be countered, he maintains, deep-seated differences and biases are more intractable: "It is clearly impossible to put an end to fourteen centuries of mutual fear and distrust overnight." Noakes argues that this distrust combined with a basic ignorance of Islam and Muslims among Americans affects the media's ability to cover Islam and Muslims adequately. The situation is compounded by the tendency of the media to focus on the explosive or violent act, to give primacy to those events that impinge on American interests and overlook or minimally cover equally significant ones that do not, the shrinking resources of especially the print media, and the tendency of many reporters and editors not to regard religion (unless it involves acts of terrorism) as hard news.

The failures or limitations of American media reporting on Islam and Muslims have an impact on the sensibilities and sensitivities of American Muslims. Although critical of the media, Noakes also challenges the American Muslim community to recognize that complaint must be accompanied by action, from protest and participation (e.g., becoming professional journalists) to self-criticism and a recognition that positive coverage of Muslims will be seriously affected so long as religious violence and terrorism do occur in the name of Islam.

For the majority of Muslims in America, the multi-ethnic experience has reinforced the extent to which economic security and Muslim identity are interrelated. Elise Goldwasser's "Economic Security and Muslim Identity: A Study of the Immigrant Community in Durham, North Carolina," examines the impact of economic and social factors on the development of the Islamic community there, which reflects the unity and diversity of the American Muslim (and for that matter, the broader Muslim) experience. Many in the Eritrian community which has gathered there struggle to survive, handicapped by lack of English and marketable skills. At the same time another group of highly educated English-speaking Muslims enjoys prosperity. As Goldwasser demonstrates, although both groups are united in their commitment to the Islamic faith, they differ in their application of Islam to everyday life. Unlike the Eritrian laborers, the prosperous Muslims can easily preserve their Islamic identity and accommodate its practices from prayer and fasting to medical treatment and burial. They have been able both to accept and at times to resist the dominant non-Islamic culture.

Goldwasser maintains that financial security is the key variable to these differences in response to American culture. The economically less secure Eritrians opt for cultural assimilation; the Muslim professionals choose not to assimilate to a culture they regard as too materialistic, sexually permissive, and violent. Drawing on specific examples, she describes the challenges and responses of the Muslims in Durham to issues of faith, family, and professional life.

Few things symbolize Islam and the Muslim community more than the mosque, the center for community prayer throughout the ages. Today, mosques also reveal the very issues of faith and identity faced by many

Muslim communities: the relationship of tradition to change and to religious and multi-ethnic identities. Omar Khalidi, in "Approaches to Mosque Design in North America," discusses the history of immigrant mosque building. Especially in the beginning, the mosque was whatever building was available; since the primary purpose of immigration then was economic and the immigrant's stay presumably temporary, limited resources required creative, unorthodox responses to a temporary need. More recently new mosques have been built by more prosperous communities; these buildings are often as totally foreign to North America's religious and cultural landscape as Islam itself. In the architecture of Muslim countries mosque design is integrated and coherent; in North America it displays a range from the derivative to innovative. Mosque buildings in North America often provide not only a prayer hall but a school, community and conference rooms, library, and recreational center.

Khalidi compares and contrasts a number of mosques and Islamic centers built in the last two or three decades to highlight some of the underlying questions of identity and aesthetics: can one effectively transplant a Middle Eastern pattern onto an American landscape? How and where have the old or traditional and the new been blended successfully? Failures result when mosques are not appropriate to site or context; lack of respect for the role of the professional architect among immigrants has not helped. Imitative and unimaginative buildings passing for "authentic" Islamic architecture have cropped up in the United States from coast to coast. Khalidi's discussion of the differences of opinion that arose between an advisory committee of immigrant Muslims and a committee of consultants (mostly non-Muslim architects and scholars of Islamic architecture) who were appointed to decide on a design for an Islamic cultural center in Manhattan underscore the relationship between architectural production and the cultural politics of identity.

Khalidi's descriptions of several mosques highlight the range of identity responses from the transplanting of traditional designs to the creation of a contemporary, entirely North American mosque architectures. The older communities tended to construct architecturally nondescript buildings that would not attract attention; more recent immigrant communities like to stick to a design that is either traditional in a particular Muslim country, or a stereotyped "typical" traditional mosque; more adventurous communities are willing to try something new. From the vantage point of what will best meet the needs of Muslims, Khalidi concludes that the design should fulfill Islamic requirements but minimize ethno-national cliches, and find a fit between tradition and the local environment. This kind of solution will best meet the needs and demands of the next generation of American Muslims.

Muslim communities have existed for more than fourteen centuries. Islamic history has demonstrated an enormous diversity of cultural adaptations as Islam has interacted with other cultures and peoples from North Africa to Southeast Asia. While in the past the vast majority of Muslims lived in Muslim societies, today record numbers of refugees and immigrants live as minorities in non-Muslim countries. As a result old religious and cultural paradigms have had to yield to new realities. The threadbare distinction between Islam and the West is no longer useful.

For observant Muslims, the challenges loom large. Some may choose to live in denial that they are permanent residents or citizens of the West. Others will choose to jettison their tradition and totally assimilate into the local society. For still others, the more complex way will be to blaze a new trail, redefining faith and identity within contemporary contexts and realities, a subtle process, not of assimilation, but of selective cultural accommodation. The challenges for Muslims on the path to Americanization will continue to be primarily those of identity, pluralism, and participation as they continue to define and redefine their faith and identity as a Muslim minority in and of the West.

PART I

THE AMERICAN PATH OPTION

Between Tradition and Reality

1

The Dynamics of Islamic Identity in North America

YVONNE YAZBECK HADDAD

The immigration of Muslims to Europe and North America during this century has ushered in a new era in the relationship between Islam and the West, conditioned in part by the Muslim experience of "the West" in the form of European colonialism until mid-century and "American neo-colonialism" since the 1950s. As a result the dynamic between the two is seen by Muslims as being that between conqueror and conquered, powerful and powerless, dominant and weak. This has also influenced the ways in which Muslims have formed questions of identity as they strive to negotiate a secure place for themselves and their children in Western societies.

This chapter will attempt a preliminary exploration of the dynamics shaping Islamic identity in North America. It will look at the elements that formed the variety of identities prior to emigration, the immigrant experience in America, and the options immigrants find as they struggle to make their home in an environment that they as Muslims find hostile.

The American experience has provided the Muslims with a variety of encounters and challenges and presented them with a bewildering array of options as they struggle to adapt to life in the United States. At first glance their experience may be seen as similar to that of other immigrants, raising the familiar questions of what of the old identity should be salvaged, what given up, and what renegotiated or invented as the community seeks to find a niche for itself. A closer look shows that there are some profound differences. While some of what they experience can be ascribed to changing times or political considerations, increasingly many see their marginalized situation as deliberate and specific, the product of longstanding tendencies in American society to fear and distrust Islam. Thus, while Muslims may be facing the same problems earlier generations of immigrants had encoun-

tered—what language to teach their children or how to implant and perpetuate the faith of the forebears—they are also burdened with the question of
whether their children and grandchildren will be accepted in the United
States, and whether Islam can ever be recognized as a source of enlightenment, a positive force contributing to a multicultural, pluralistic America.

The Question of Muslim Identity

One of the most important characteristics of the Muslim community in North
America is its diversity.[1] It includes immigrants who chose to move to the
United States for economic, political, and religious reasons from over sixty
nations of various ethnic, racial, linguistic, tribal, and national identities.[2]
It also includes émigrés and refugees forced out of their homeland, who still
retain allegiance to it and are reluctant to relinquish the intention of returning to it to help restore the order they left behind.[3] It also includes a large
number of converts, both African American and white, who through the act
of conversion have opted out of the dominant American cultural identity,[4]
and a significant number of Muslims whose forebears immigrated between
the 1870s and World War II and who are in varying degrees already integrated and assimilated.[5] The majority of Muslims in America today, however, are foreign born, socialized and educated overseas, and come from
nation states whose identity has been fashioned by European colonialism.

Since the creation of the nation state, the question of identity has been
part of nation building and has received a great deal of attention in Muslim
states carved out of chunks of imploding and crumbling empires. Following the European model, these nation states focused their efforts on creating a loyal constituency out of the diverse populations that constituted the
former empires with their different linguistic, tribal, ethnic, sectarian and
religious allegiances. The intellectuals in these states believed that finding
the proper vision, ideology, constitution, or constellation of ideas could
initiate modernization and development, propelling these nation states into
parity with the West.[6]

These ideologies have varied, depending on prevailing circumstances,
with each producing a generation committed to a different vision guaranteed to provide the salvation and modernization of their nation. The immigrants to the United States who came throughout this century, therefore, have
not only reflected diverse national identities, but in many cases have also
promoted allegiances to different ideologies that they believed held the key
to revitalization of their home countries. At the turn of the century, the elites
in various Muslim countries placed their trust in nationalist ideologies. They
drew on an identity of shared history, language, and culture in order to create a shared vision and commitment to helping bring about independence
from colonial hegemony. This gave way in the middle of the century to support for socialism as various regimes looked to its implementation for rapid

development. Socialism transcended national identities and emphasized a specific economic and social doctrine. Beginning in the mid 1970s, the ideology that has been most attractive has been Islamism, an ideology based on the hope of restoring the transnational Islamic empire, grounded in Islamic history and law. Its vision is of a shared destiny to be initiated through representative government administered by Islamic elites committed to providing economic and social justice.

An interesting development in the mid-twentieth century is the increasing importance of the United States as a center for Muslim intellectual reflection and ferment. Having replaced Europe as the dominant power in the Third World, the United States began to attract to its universities a large number of students seeking technical and professional training. The American government, confident of the validity of the American way of life and seeking to fashion the leadership of the Third World, encouraged the education of foreign nationals in the benefits of capitalism and the evils of Marxism. Many of the graduates of American universities then decided to stay in the United States. In the process, American campuses as well as some of the mosques and Islamic centers associated with them became the locus for reflection on and experimentation with a variety of Islamic world views. In the United States, Muslim students from many nations have been able to forge links of friendship and common purpose, providing the nucleus for an international network of leaders committed to the creation of an Islamic state or an Islamic world order.

At the other end of the spectrum is a different set of American institutions that have become major centers of Muslim reflection and identity, namely the prisons of America, both state and federal facilities. They continue to be an important locus of the African-American conversion to Islam that began in the early decades of this century. While there are no statistics on the number of converts or the scope and effectiveness of conversion in the penal system, some scholars estimate that by the second decade of the twenty-first century the majority of African-American males will have converted to Islam.[7] While students from abroad living on American campuses often discover Islam and turn to the task of reshaping Islamic societies worldwide, prison alumni focus their efforts at home, helping reshape America from the bottom up. They seek the redemption of African-American society through the teaching of responsibility, family values, and accountability. In the process they are hoping to save their children from a future of violence and the drug-infested ghettos of America.[8]

The earliest immigrants to found mosques before the Second World War and, for the most part, their children and grandchildren appear to have fitted comfortably into America. They tried both to fit into the new culture and to interpret it in ways that tended to emphasize the respect Islam had for Jesus and his mother Mary and to quote verses from the Qur'an emphasizing the commonalities between the two faiths. To the immigrants who have come since 1960, however, this kind of accommodation seems too high a price to pay. They are critical of their coreligionists who appear to have diluted the importance of Islamic traditions, rituals, and distinguishing characteristics, going so far as to refer to the mosque as "our church," to the Qur'an as "our Bible," and to the imam as "our minister."

The more recent immigrants are neither poor nor uneducated; on the contrary, they represent the best-educated elite of the Muslim world who see themselves as helping develop America's leadership in medicine, technology, and education. They have been influenced by a different socialization process, and while they appreciate, enjoy, and have helped create America's technology, they want no part in what they see as its concomitant social and spiritual problems. Confident that Islam has a solution to America's ills, they have no patience for the kind of accommodation that they see as compromising the true Islamic way. As the executive secretary of the Council of Masajid in North America put it:

> In spite of the most spectacular progress in science and technology, man still finds himself in the wilderness of despair. One thing that has constantly eluded his grasp is happiness and peace of mind. Even technology, which is his creation, at times threatens to destroy him and to blot out all his works, as if he never lived on this earth. . . . Man finds himself in a "blind alley" and there are no exits in it. Should he abandon all hope and resign himself to perish in a nuclear-chemical-biological conflict? Islam's answer is an emphatic NO! For a Muslim there can be no surrender to despair.[9]

Muslim Identity in the American Context

Perceived by some Muslim leaders as "the mother of all issues" (umm al-masa'il), the question of Muslim identity and its meaning and ramifications in the context of the United States has been the focus of several national conferences sponsored by the Islamic Society of North America, as well as the topic of numerous lectures, sermons, and books by Muslims in North America (both immigrant and convert) and foreign intellectuals who choose to reflect on the subject. The quest for a relevant Muslim identity is part of the American experience, as each generation of immigrants has brought a certain sense of self which appears to undergo constant revision and redefinition in the context of the American melting (boiling?) pot. This identity is influenced by what the immigrants bring with them as well as their American experience: how America defines itself as well as American foreign policy in various Muslim countries, the place the immigrants choose to settle, how they are treated in their new environment, the diversity of the community with which they associate, their involvement in organized religion, their relations with older generations of immigrants and/or African-American Muslims, and involvement in interfaith activities. In the last decade and a half, it has also been profoundly influenced by what Muslims feel is a hostile American environment in which they are being held accountable for the activities of others overseas.

America, although a nation of immigrants, is nonetheless not particularly fond of them, no matter where they come from or what they believe in. It expects its social institutions, whether the workplace, the armed services, the schools, the churches, or the courts, to assimilate these strangers and forge them into Americans. Overall, those of European heritage have had a better chance of assimilation than people of Asian origin, who were entirely excluded from the mix until the repeal of the Asian Exclusion Act.[10] There is in any case a general American tendency to view the survival of immigrant foreign culture as a relic of the past that must inevitably give way to assimilation and modernization as defined by the Protestant ethos that is claimed to be the foundation of America.

Efforts in the nineteenth century to create an America which was Protestant by choice rather than by mandate made life particularly difficult for atheists, Jews, and Catholics. By the middle of the twentieth century, the United States found it convenient to reinvent itself as a triple melting pot, a mix of Protestants, Catholics, and Jews with no apparent place for other religions. In recent years, Americans increasingly have begun to use the term "Judeo-Christian" to define themselves, a "politically correct" term that for some appears to draw an obvious and tight line of religious acceptance around two major religions, regarding others as transient, permanently marginalized, or destined to disappear into the larger groups.

What is defined as the Judeo-Christian tradition can appear to those of other faiths as an exclusive club, the monopoly of two groups that regard others as outside the polity or subsume them only when they conform to the policies and desires of the dominant groups. It is part of America's heritage as a country founded on the pious hope for a righteous society to see itself as being against those who it believes do not share that vision. Thus, throughout the history of America different groups have played the role of outsider, non-participant, even enemy, in response to which Americans can reaffirm their identity as a nation standing for the right and the good. Currently, Muslims appear to be the victims of the apparent need to create such an enemy, one that can be defined as the antithesis of the national character and a threat to the righteous order.

This reality plays an important role in the shaping of American Muslim identity. The identity of the community and the awareness that it constitutes a powerless minority are enhanced in the American milieu. Muslims believe that the professed separation of religion and state is violated every time a leader affirms that America is a Judeo-Christian country. They ask why it is acceptable for an American president to call for the implementation of Christian values while denouncing all efforts to build a moral and just Islamic society. And they wonder why America seems to support the concept of a "Jewish state" in Israel while Muslims are urged to be civilized and renounce their "extremist" hope for an "Islamic state." Furthermore,

Muslims are keenly aware that American social life is organized to a great degree around churches and other religious organizations. They watch the parade of religious programs on television which call for commitment to Christian values and wonder why Americans affirm the necessity of pluralism, of secularism, and of national identity only when they address Muslims.

At the same time the American principle of the separation of church and state is welcomed, since it provides for toleration of a variety of religious institutions and identities. Muslims as a minority find that the guarantee of freedom of religion provides opportunities for new experiments and developments in ideas, institution building, and propagation, unequaled in the countries from which they came. By the same token, those committed to an Islamist perception of reality, members of the Muslim Brotherhood and their sympathizers, adhere to the belief that it is God's intent that government should be regulated by the religious decrees of the Qur'an, that there should be no separation between religion and state, and that the only government sanctioned by God for such a task is one devoted to Islam.[11]

Also influential in defining Islamic identity in North America have been the vicissitudes of American foreign policy towards Arab and Islamic countries during the last forty years, policies that continue to trouble and alienate the majority of Muslim citizens. The dramatic acceleration of interaction between American society and the Muslim world does not appear to have had any significant positive influence on policy makers, who continue to ignore Muslim sensibilities especially in regard to such things as American support for the state of Israel, despite the latter's documented violation of the civil, political, and human rights of its Christian and Muslim citizens; American support for India, despite its record of violently suppressing the right of Kashmir's population to self determination; and American reluctance to support what are perceived as the just causes of people in Azerbaijan, Bosnia, and Chechnya, among others. Proclamations by the State Department of its advocacy of human rights, pluralism, and minority rights as an important foundation of American policy in the world are increasingly viewed by Muslims as hypocritical.

"Target Islam"[12]

There is a growing concern among Muslims both in America and overseas regarding American tolerance for negative depictions of Islam and Muslims.[13] Anti-Muslim sentiment generally increases in the wake of what Muslims believe to be the unbalanced coverage given events overseas by the American press. Media treatment of the hostage-taking in Iran in 1979 and the TWA hijacking in Lebanon in 1985, for example, seem to have brought out deep-seated prejudices in American society. More recently, the press had a heyday with the World Trade Center bombing and some in its corps insisted that the Oklahoma City bombing showed the modus operandi of Middle Eastern terrorists even after investigation proved it to be the work of Christian Americans.[14]

As a consequence of such biased coverage, Muslims have reported a series of attacks on mosques and other Islamic institutions. In addition to the vengeful acts of some isolated Americans inflamed by media reports about Islam, Muslims fear the more organized hostile activities of certain groups. Most obvious, perhaps, is the Jewish Defense League (JDL),[15] an American urban terrorist organization which, according to FBI reports, is the second most violent group in the United States. The JDL threatened several American mosques and other Islamic targets in 1985, and is suspected of having bombed the Arab-American Anti-Discrimination Committee (ADC) offices on the West Coast which killed Alex Odeh.[16] More recent hate crimes by other groups include the bombing of a mosque in Texas and the burning of mosques in Indiana and California.

The negativism toward Islamists comes from various sources. Only one group, the Christian right, is motivated by religious conviction. Others engaged in negative propaganda include officials of the American government seeking support from various sectors of American society. What seems to be an anti-Muslim, anti-Arab, anti-Islam wave sweeping across the United States accelerated beginning in 1980, encouraged by President Reagan's confrontational style and his Manichaean world view.[17] Since then, some American leaders have increasingly described Muslims as outside the "national character" or the "shared American culture," with the insinuation that their values are not mainstream. Questions are raised about whether their religious practices and cultural preferences are compatible with the American way of life, especially when it comes to dress, roles for women, sexuality, child rearing, use of free time and alcohol, attitudes toward gambling, education, private hygiene, occupation, and scruples about financial transactions that involve interest. Muslims protest that these attitudes not only deprive them of power and status but also deny them a voice and a presence.

Casting Islamists as the enemy of humanity, tolerance, and civilization is also a theme in the chorus repeated daily by officials of Arab governments seeking legitimacy and American support against opposition political groups in their own countries. These opposition groups are generally looking to democratize the authoritarian political regimes that rule in various Muslim states and to hold the corrupt officials accountable to the people. Often they are trying to implement a more equitable and just social and economic order that aims at ameliorating the conditions that exist in these states; they are concerned with the welfare of the people rather than the profit of the Western corporations. They believe that the kind of government they want cannot be created unless it is formed by those initiated into the Islamic consciousness and committed to implementing an Islamist world view.

Among those who see "Islamic extremism" as the enemy are members of the Israeli government and their American defenders.[18] Since the fall of the

Soviet empire, Islamist literature has taken note of the intensified and sustained emphasis on the supposed threat of Islam in the speeches of Israeli leaders in their effort to portray Israel as the guardian of American and Western interests in the Middle East and to maintain the high subsidies given to it by the United States.[19] The Islamist press notes that Muslims have been depicted as a cancer that should be combated by the combined forces of the Clinton administration and Israel.[20] Also perpetuating the image of Islam as the enemy are so-called experts on foreign policy who need a threat in order to sell their expertise. Observing that the fall of the Soviet empire eliminated the enemy against which the United States could place itself, they eagerly pointed to the threat of Islam as filling that vacuum.[21]

Americans, conditioned to respond to a world they feel is threatened by malevolent forces that they are somehow mandated to overcome, are quick to see Islam as the next challenge which must be met. For some, the opposition to Islam is subtler. Recent pieces on the editorial pages of our newspapers suggest that Americans should distinguish between good Muslims and bad Muslims, condemning the Islamists and cooperating with the moderates. The moderates are identified as people like Taslima Nasreen and Salman Rushdie, both of whom are seen as apostates by many Muslims. While some may find this an improvement over wholesale condemnation, it is nonetheless difficult for many to accept. As one Muslim put it: "It used to be that the only good Arab was a dead Arab; now it has shifted to the only good Muslim is the one who wants to assassinate his religion."

While Muslims in America have ample reason to fear "Judeo-Christian" prejudice incited as a result of events overseas, they are also concerned about deliberate falsifications of Islam that are perpetrated by those who appear to have declared Islam to be an "enemy faith." The community is also afraid of becoming a target of Christian missionary assaults by church groups who seek to induct Muslims into the Christian faith through conversion. The demonization of Islam is also perpetrated by Christian fundamentalists who have revised their theology to include Muslims among the villains hastening Armageddon and bringing about the imminent end of time when Jesus will come to initiate the rapture. Muslims are depicted on Christian television programs as war mongers, bent on destroying Israel.[22]

While some segments of the American press have managed to create the image of the Muslim as the consummate terrorist, Muslims surveying the history and experience of the Muslim community worldwide often see themselves as the victims of circumstance as well as conspiratorial forces of hatred. They trace this victimization back to the Crusades and the Reconquista, through the age of imperialism, and see it reinforced in contemporary events such as

> the brutal massacres at Sabra and Shatila Refugee Camps in Lebanon, the one-sided Gulf War in which Muslims were pitted against Muslims, the continued repression of the Palestinians in the face of Arab

disunity, the indiscriminate slaughter and torture of Bosnian Muslims by Serbians, the persecution of Kashmiris and the Hindu savagery against Muslims in India, the slaughter of Rohingas in Burma, the Civil War and famine in Somalia, the demolition of the Babri Mosque in India, Soviet aggression and internal strife in post-Communist Afghanistan, turbulence in Central Asia, the Kurdish problem, and the suppression of democracy in Algeria, to name only a few.[23]

Muslims as Minorities

A new genre of Islamist literature has developed over the second half of this century by popular authors such as Abu al-A'la al-Mawdudi[24] of Pakistan and Sayyid Qutb[25] of Egypt that has had some influence on Muslims trying to find their identity in the American context. Both addressed Muslims living in Islamic nations deemed secular, but who were committed to the vision of the Islamist future and willing to work for the realization of Islamic government. They encouraged Muslims who felt themselves to be persecuted because of their political stance not to remain living in oppressive environments but to emigrate to a more congenial place, enhance their Islamic consciousness, and organize in order to return to their homelands to overthrow un-Islamic nationalist and socialist governments. This vision tapped into the powerful imagery of the struggle of the early believers in Medina under the leadership of the Prophet Muhammad.

The focus of al-Mawdudi's attention was the community of Muslims living in India. He insisted that minorities deserve to suffer the consequences of belonging to a minority faith and that they must expect to be mistreated and marginalized.[26] In order to guarantee their security and the freedom to practice their faith, Muslims should find areas governed by Islam to live in. Although they may venture into other regions of the world as diplomats or traders, if their right to practice their faith is threatened, they should return to a Muslim country. Qutb focused on Nasserist Egypt and encouraged Islamists to separate themselves, raise their Islamic consciousness, and return to eradicate un-Islamic governments that have assumed power over the Muslims. He viewed Islam as a divine imperative cast in the world to topple all man-made institutions and governments.[27]

Younger Islamists in non-Muslim societies, aware of the changing circumstances of life for a growing number of Muslims who find themselves needing to emigrate in search of a livelihood, have proposed other solutions. Moroccan Islamist Ali Kettani, for example, insists that Islam seeks the health and well being of the community, conditions that can only be guaranteed by social and political empowerment.[28] Muslims therefore must not accept minority status as a permanent condition in which they accommodate and acquiesce to those in power since that will perpetuate their weakness. They must perceive their "minorityness"[29] as a challenge to be transcended.

The experience of the Muslim immigrant community in Medina during the formative period of Islam provides a choice between two models, each based on the example of the Prophet. According to the first, the immigrant community must prepare to return from whence it came in order to cleanse the oppressive system it left behind, just as the Prophet did when he returned to Mecca. Emigration in this case becomes a matter of refuge, of empowerment, of organization, and of planning focused on the domain of Islam. According to the second, extrapolating from the hijra from Mecca to Medina, relocation and settlement are permanent and unceasing effort is required to Islamize the society in which one lives. The final goal is to create an Islamic state in the land of immigration.

The realization that immigrants in the West currently are in no condition to take over the rule of the countries in which they live, or to utilize the power of these countries in the interest of bringing about an Islamic state, led Kettani to recommend that they instead live in special enclaves. There they could establish a truly Islamic community based on the brotherhood of Islam, an organization that is not elitist, sectarian, partisan in politics, or divided into racial or professional distinctions. Such enclaves, if governed by Muslims through the principle of *shura* (consultation), would not be ghettos but specially created communities empowered to foster and maintain Islam. Their social, economic, political, and cultural life would be centered on the mosque and the Islamic school. These enclaves would protect the community from the dangers of assimilation and disintegration. Only through the maintenance of control over their children's education would Muslims be able to insulate themselves from the pressure to discard their Islamic identity and integrate into society. Thus for Kettani, maintaining cultural distinctions such as language, dress, and Islamic names (he condemned the practice of adopting anglicized names) was crucial. He conceded that while it may be necessary to learn the majority language in order to communicate with the hegemonic culture, Arabic as the language of the Qur'an must be taught and Islamic dress be worn by members of the community as a sign of distinction.[30]

For Muhammad Abdul-Rauf, former imam of the Islamic Center in Washington, D.C., isolating the community through fear was unnecessary for two reasons. First, he trusted the tenacity and ability of Islam to survive powerful cultural influences just as it has successfully resisted them in other places during the fourteen centuries of its existence. Second, he did not believe that the United States was about to crush the Muslims. Although "largely dominated by the Judeo-Christian tradition," he says, "the hospitable American melting pot"[31] will make it possible for Islam "not only to survive intact in America but also to flourish in honor and dignity."[32] In support of this Abdul Rauf quoted from the speech President Eisenhower made at the opening of the Islamic Center in Washington in June 1957: "We shall fight with all our might to defend your right to worship according to your conscience."[33]

A few American-born Muslims in the United States have looked to another incident in the life of the Prophet and the first Muslim community,
namely the emigration of the Muslims from Mecca to Ethiopia in search of
security, as a model for determining Muslim roles and identity in a Christian environment. As developed by a Muslim Sunday school teacher[34] based
on lessons on the life of the Prophet, this model shows that the Muslim
community in its formative period was saved from total annihilation by the
Christians of Ethiopia who refused to deliver the Muslims to their enemies
by sending them back to Mecca. Unlike the Medinan model, this Ethiopian
model teaches the common brotherhood of Christianity and Islam and advocates cooperation and mutual support. It focuses on the protection that
the Christian Ethiopians provided for the Muslims, on coexistence, and on
dialogue. As the teacher put it to her class, "But for the protection of Islam
by the Christians, there might have been no Muslims or Islam today." While
there is no consensus on what is the ideal model to be followed in the North
American context, variations of this "interactive-cooperative" model are
attractive to many American-born Muslims.

Islamic Identity and the American Experience

The American experience forges as well as forces a new Muslim identity
that is born out of both the quest to belong and the experience of being permanently depicted as "the other." As one young Muslim said, "I cannot be
a white Anglo Protestant, but I have to be something. Everyone has an identity. People keep asking: 'What are you?' 'What do you believe?' 'Why does
Islam oppress women?' 'Why do you marry four wives?' 'Why does your
religion teach violence?' Suddenly, you begin to realize that you do not know
what a Muslim is and you begin to search for yourself."

There is no unanimous Muslim understanding of the American challenge
or of how to respond to it, what strategy to employ, or what kind of identity
to foster. Questions persist as to whether as Americans, Muslims should
participate in the political arena, support a particular party or candidate,
vote, or run for office. Other questions that surface periodically are whether
to build umbrella political organizations or organize political-action committees and negotiate coalitions with other interest groups; whether to risk
participation in interfaith activities or refrain from such activity as undermining Muslim unity; whether to relinquish authority in running the mosque
to a trained leadership, and whether this leadership should be American
home-grown or dependent on religious leaders trained overseas who bring
ideas that are not compatible with the reality of the American context.

Three of the most influential Islamic thinkers in the United States in the
last two decades—the late Fazlur Rahman, the late Isma'il al-Faruqi, and
Seyyed Hossein Nasr[35]—are foreign-born emigres whose ideas have influenced numerous students who have come to the United States in search of

higher education from Pakistan, Iran, Malaysia, Indonesia, and the Arab world.[36] Fazlur Rahman was dedicated to redefining a modernist Islam that would make Islamic jurisprudence relevant to modern life. His ideas have had an international impact, especially in Indonesia and among a growing number of Muslims in the United States who are disenchanted with the ideas of Islamist organizations such as the Muslim Brotherhood and the Jamaat-i Islaami. He promoted the concept of the commonality of the three faiths of Judaism, Islam, and Christianity and found no impediments to amicable relations among their members.

The ideas of Seyyed Hossein Nasr have had a wide international impact, especially among intellectuals in the United States who are interested in Sufism and who find in its focus on privatizing religion and emphasis on the relation with the divine a superior Islamic identity for North America. Nasr has participated in various forums of inter-faith dialogue and has written and spoken extensively on what he sees as some of the impediments to mutual understanding. He has also advocated a separate track of Christian-Muslim discussions, arguing that participants in the Christian-Jewish dialogue appear to have reached a level of consensus that makes it very difficult for Muslims as newcomers to join in the conversation.

Isma'il al-Faruqi was especially interested in the leadership potential of the community in the United States and labored to organize intellectual institutions to provide committed Islamic leadership, not only for the immigrant community, but for the whole world of Islam. He is credited with organizing the American Association of Muslim Social Scientists and with establishing the International Institute of Islamic Thought as well as the American Islamic College. His ideas helped maintain the mosque movement that has flourished in North America since the 1970s, and have been adopted by a large number of Muslim immigrants who have found in them the way to a superior identity as well as a strategy for survival.

In order to combat the feeling of defeatism and weakness that may overwhelm the Muslim student and/or immigrant, Isma'il al-Faruqi recommended the appropriation of an Islamic ideology. Muslims are not in the United States as beggars, he said, but as contributors to the building of a just society. Faruqi stressed that the adoption of an Islamic ideology or vision frees one from the sense of guilt at having left the homeland and achieved some measure of success in a new place. It also liberates one from the need to be grateful to the adoptive country because success belongs to God. Meanwhile, the Muslim will help address the ills of American culture by posing the challenge of Islam. "The Islamic vision," he said, "provides the immigrant with the deepest love, attachment, and aspiration for a North America reformed and returned to God." When this transformation has taken place, immigrants and converts alike will find their lives taking on a new meaning and significance "whose dimensions are cosmic. . . ."[37]

From this perspective, Islam is a unique order of life established by God for humanity, where religion and politics must be intertwined to ensure justice and freedom. It provides special cohesiveness and communal support to a community going through a troubled time in which it sees itself rejected, the object of hate and fear. For many Muslims, America seems to have been hijacked by special interest groups, as a result of which it has departed from the values and the vision that previously had merited God's blessing. Thus, it is in need not only of salvation but also of radical transformation that can restore it to its mission as a country living in obedience to God. The answer is the kind of Islamic vision articulated by Faruqi. The Muslim who opts for this vision identifies with a universal ideology of brotherhood that does not discriminate between human beings according to race, color, language, or national origin; its goal is the conversion of the world. In this way distinctiveness and separateness are experienced not as the result of rejection by the host culture, but as a divine blessing made necessary because America has deviated from a moral life devoted to God.

A Time for Constructive Engagement

Operation Desert Shield/Desert Storm had a profound effect on the Muslim community worldwide.[38] For North American Muslims it was particularly disturbing since it pitted their adopted country, the United States, and the large coalition of the international community it had orchestrated against one Muslim nation and in alliance with another. The majority of American Muslims were greatly disappointed that the American government did not work hard to find a negotiated solution to the conflict, opting instead to devastate the state of Iraq. But even more distressing was the division of the Muslim world into two camps with many lining up in support of the American intervention. The lack of support by immigrant American Muslims for Kuwaiti and Saudi policies led the Gulf nations to cut off aid to various Muslim organizations in North America. This action brought a suspension of many Islamic activities and proved to many Muslim Americans that Gulf support for Muslims in the United States had perhaps been motivated less by their Islamic commitment than by their national political interests.

The cutoff of aid in the 1990s led the Muslim community to reassess its mission and its goals as well as to generate resources to maintain the institutions it had so diligently established during the preceding two decades. The Gulf war also made the Muslim community fully cognizant of its lack of political power in the United States and its inability to influence American policy. Its weakness became evident when new immigration laws were passed by the American Congress restricting the immigration of people from Muslim countries and when various segments of American society launched a relentless campaign against Islam and Muslims. This drove some Muslims to seek security by further isolating themselves from the dominant society; others took refuge in further Islamization, while still others continued the quest for a negotiated place on the American scene.[39]

Concern over the marginalization and demonization of Muslims in American society, as well as what was seen as the failure of the models projected by the leadership of the 1970s and 1980s, led to the formation of the North American Association of Muslim Professionals and Scholars (NAAMPS) in April 1993. At its first annual conference a variety of concerns were discussed and participants began to reassess the goals that had been followed in the previous two decades and to indulge in some self-examination.

Addressing the annual conference, Fathi Osman, the former editor of the London-based magazine *Arabia*, called for a clear vision "to eliminate wishful thinking and ambiguity . . . [for] confidence is not sufficient if it is not grounded in fact and reality."[40] He urged his listeners to undertake a periodic reassessment of priorities in an effort to remain relevant and effective. The Islamist manifesto must not be viewed as carved in stone but should be revised every three to five years.[41] "Unless Muslims can convince the technologically advanced, materially rich and militarily superior world that Muslims and Islam have something to offer and to contribute," said Osman, "no one will listen to us, however theoretically logical and rhetorically superb our talk may be."[42] Osman perceived the unique role for Muslims in the United States as being to provide a practical model that could help Muslim countries overseas where "the masses are illiterate and the rulers are tyrants" and where "Islamic educational institutions are sticking to the past and use books written centuries ago. In this country we have a fresh climate. The challenge is to pioneer a new experience." This can be achieved by beginning a constructive participation with scholars from all disciplines to find a way to solve problems.[43]

There was agreement that the boundaries that separate Muslims from the larger society must be breached and that the Muslims must identify new ways for the community to relate to other Americans. Addressing the same conference, Maher Hathout of the Islamic Society of Southern California recommended that they start by learning how to listen to Americans as well as talk to them. It cannot continue to be a one-way operation in which the Muslims are explaining what they are about. There is a need to change the rhetorical apologetic and defensive message that has been adopted by Muslims until now, affirming an idealized Islam that has no relation to the condition of Muslims. By separating Islam from the Muslims, apologists have been able to project a perfect system and believe in it. The discrepancy between the projected ideal and the real conditions of Muslims is a source of embarrassment not only because Muslims fail to embody and demonstrate the efficacy of Islamic teachings, but, more important, because in so doing they cast doubt on the vision itself. Those observing reality, whether outsiders or Muslim children, can see the discrepancies.[44]

Muhammad Ahmadullah Siddiqi then accused Muslim intellectuals in North America of living in the past, busily directing their efforts toward peripheral issues, unable to realize the changes taking place in American society in this era of globalism and pluralism.[45] It was their ignorance of

American reality that had made them marginal on the American scene. Siddiqi suggested that they had so far adopted one of three kinds of responses. The first was isolationist, separating itself from the dominant environment. They were responsible for their marginality because of their negative attitude and lack of concern for their neighbors and the future of their children.

> As a result some Muslims still believe that they have nothing to contribute to this society, and their only duty is to save themselves from the evil that prevails in this Dar ul-Harb (the land of non-believers). They create an island and live in that without caring about how they and their religion are perceived by the next-door neighbor, a nonbeliever. The most they worry is about their children, whom they are unable to restrict to the island. So they frighten them with the monstrous West; however, to their dismay most of these children sooner or later suffer miserably by losing an identity as a Muslim, because of them Islam is not relevant in this developed society.[46]

The second response is to build institutions, mosques, and Islamic organizations as a symbol of Muslim presence in North America. Eager to make the minaret a prominent feature of the American skyline, those who follow this line sometimes do not question their sources of funding. Siddiqi criticizes them for accepting contributions from oil-rich Muslim countries. "For them it does not matter whether their donors are the legitimate representatives of the people they rule or whether they help strengthen the forces of the status quo."[47]

A third response, and the one adopted by the majority of Muslim professionals and intellectuals in this country, is not to be concerned with how Islam manifests itself in American society. They go about their business in isolation from the other two groups, in some cases dissociating themselves from them. Meanwhile, "the Muslim presence in North America is defined by what Muslims do and say in other parts of the world, with modern media emphasis on portraying conflict and chaos."[48]

The agenda Siddiqi sets for Muslim intellectuals is derived from a mix of issues facing the community that need redefinition by involved Muslim intellectuals. These include the relationship with non-Muslims, family values, public morality, Islamic education, Islamic economics, politics, science and technology. Like other Muslim scholars he starts with the need to ground all intellectual endeavors in an understanding of the Qur'an, the Sunna, and the Islamic intellectual heritage. His emphasis, however, is on contemporary interpretation.[49]

For many contemporary Muslim thinkers a better understanding of the reality of America must involve participation in the political process and an awareness that using American methods of pressure and lobbying may be more effective than relying on the foreign organizations Muslims had hoped would be able to work for Islamic causes. For example, Salam al-Marayati writes how he came to realize that his small political-action group had perhaps become more powerful than the Organization of the Islamic Conference which represents the governments of about fifty Muslim nations.

> We can be more powerful than the Organization of the Islamic Conference. At the Organization, when we called them to see what they were doing, they told us that they have to go to the United Nations before they can do anything about Bosnia. The Organization of the Islamic Conference is politically castrated. And it is our job to guide our community to an independent pathway. We can be more powerful than so many other Islamic groups because we live in a free society and we can organize politically and we can represent to help ourselves here and help others elsewhere. But we must invest in the political career.[50]

Hathout also calls for a change in the approach to interfaith relations. He notes that the current apologetic strategy that addresses the theological divide between Christianity and Islam and attacks a variety of Christian doctrines that Muslims find offensive such as the Trinity and the infallibility of the Bible have not been helpful.

> We say how stupid Christians are to believe in the Trinity. But what do we achieve by saying such a thing other than making them angry? Instead of talking about how stupid the Trinity is, why don't we talk about how oneness of God is the light and the solution? Why do we try to make a career in proving that the Bible is nonsense? Why don't we spend time in showing that the Qur'an is the light and solution, and delivers people from slavery to liberty?[51]

Another issue of concern to the Islamic movement is commitment to human rights and democracy. "We should support oppressed people not because it is being said and used like a slogan, not because it was man-made, but because every human being has these God-given rights," says al-Marayati.[52] Islamic groups should not be given a blanket endorsement simply because they are Islamic, but must first be given an honest assessment.

> Just because somebody raises the flag of Islam, or says he is a Muslim, does not mean that we should go to their [sic] defense. If somebody does something wrong, then it is our Islamic duty to say that it is wrong. The Qur'an enjoins us to stand up for justice, even if it is against yourself, your family, or your friends. So we base the analysis of these movements on human rights and democracy. . . . We are politically, financially, and even ideologically independent from these other groups, like the Ikhwan, or Hizbut Tahreer, or Jamaat-e-Islami, and other groups that are active.[53]

Al-Marayati insists that Muslims must seek engagement with the larger society and attempt to break out of their isolation.

> We can get trapped into the false choice of assimilation or isolation. We cannot say that we are Muslims so we have to be isolated from the rest of the society. What good is our message, if we cannot deliver it to the world, to the humanity, or to the public? Contrarily, we cannot

assimilate and lose our Islamic identity because we want to be involved in some ethnic group, or we think that is the American thing to do. That is not the right thing to do. Yes, we can be Muslims, offer Islamic values, and be American citizens all in one.[54]

Some Muslims find the development of the ethnic mosque an objectionable and unhealthy development, part of the Americanization process which has historically divided the various immigrants into their constituent national identities on the path of assimilation. As Hathout puts it:

> Most of our institutions in America, unless they change fast, will fall into major errors. Most of our centers are institutions to deal with homesickness, not headquarters for driving and guiding the Islamic movement in America. Egyptians miss Egypt, so they form a part of Egypt here in Los Angeles, where they can come together. So it is with Pakistanis, and Palestinians, and so forth. Indeed, you can walk into a center and say that this is an Indian center, a Pakistani center, or an Egyptian center. From people to food to virtually everything—you can see, you can feel it in the air—these were not built here for America after all. They are built so that I do not feel lonely. I am scared out there and I need my buddies to come together the way we used to huddle back home.[55]

Hathout also objects to the development of ethnic mosques since some of their advocates defend their existence as a means of grounding their children in the faith and culture of their ancestors. He sees such efforts as counterproductive for, while the ethnic mosques may provide comfort for the immigrants, they are an alienating experience to many of their children.

> While we huddle together as Pakistanis or Egyptians or Iranians or whatever else, our children are, whether we believe it or like it or hate it or not, American kids. The question should be whether they will be Muslim-American kids or just American kids. Anyone who believes that he will raise an Egyptian boy in America is wrong; the maximum we can do is to have a distorted Egyptian kid. The grandchildren will be without doubt American.[56]

According to Siddiqi, the crisis of Muslim intellectuals persists because they continue to believe that they hold a key to the future, that it is their mission to create a workable ideology that can set the world straight. Right thinking—and increasingly, some think, right planning and execution—will provide the remedy for underdeveloped Muslim nations to embark on the path to achieving parity with the West. The quest for the right paradigm for initiating the revitalization of society needs to include a reconciliation between contemporary scientific advances and social and political thought, on the one hand, and the Islamic value system, on the other.[57] Muslim intellectuals in North America are in a unique situation that makes it possible for them to be pioneers in the effort to revitalize Islamic societies. They are not under the constraints that scholars in most Muslim countries are. Some believe therefore that it is their responsibility to invest their time and energy in developing an Islamic vision and specific agenda for Muslims here in North America, one that can be emulated by Muslim specialists in the rest of the world.[58]

At the 1993 NAAMPS annual meeting there was a call to reassess the mission of Islam in North America. The speakers proposed that rather than seek to convert the whole nation, the Muslims should strive to illuminate it with the light of Islam. The Islamist groups in the United States had decided to center their interaction with American society on an effort to convert the American population to Islam. Osman wondered whether the time may have come to work with them rather than against them. "I would like the younger generation of Muslims to focus on 'change' rather than conversion. We are always obsessed by the conversion of individuals to Islam, as if one billion Muslims in the contemporary world is not enough. We want to change the lives of Muslims as well as the lives of non-Muslims for the better."[59]

> Muslims should gain the confidence of other people by their positive contributions to the growth of the contemporary civilization, which is universal, and by participating in the concerns of all their fellow human beings. This surely does not mean being lost in mere imitation of others. Muslims should have their own understanding and stands, but with regard to the interests of humanity at large and restricted to their own selves, however numerous and extensively distributed all over the world they may be. There are areas of cooperation where Muslims should not hesitate to work with others without compromising on their differences. Sometimes Muslims talk about social justice in a totalitarian way which is rejected by the world. We should be careful about our words and pay attention to the limitation of our audiences. We have to consider the importance of modern thinking and not try to underestimate or ignore it because of its shortcomings. We may not agree with many contemporary ideas and thinking, but we cannot also rule out that they have also led to achievements. If our thinking is so oversimplified that it considers every modern institution as superficial and every emphasis of human right as hypocritical, then how can we be a partner in this world and how can we benefit from these international institutions and documents for our peoples and for the whole world?[60]

Immigrant-Convert Relations: An African-American Complaint

The conversion of Americans to Islam, regardless of color, has encouraged the community to seek growth through the propagation of the faith. The convert is a valuable commodity, an important visible validation of Islam and its efficacy for life in America. His testimony to the faith manifests publicly Islam's claim to universality. Converts through conviction often eschew identity with American culture and in the process condemn it as inferior to Islam. This provides a confirmation for immigrant Muslims that what they are struggling to preserve is inherently right, legitimating their efforts to protect from erosion what they understand to be Islamic cultural identity. The importance of missionary work and the appeal of conversion have led several overseas organizations to provide missionaries to help convert Americans. The conversion of whites to Islam has reaffirmed the mission of Islam to transform the world to a degree that for some has made the definition of a Muslim synonymous with *da'iya* (missionary).

The conversion of African-Americans to Islam has been both an inspiration and a challenge to the immigrant Muslim community. During the early part of this century, African-Americans sought to shed an identity shaped by the experience of slavery and to reconstitute the link to their roots. As this process continued, the African-American rejection of this identity has been not so much an act bearing the "earmarks of masochism,"[61] an accusation levied against other black converts, as an effort to find meaning and an authentic existence. In taking a Muslim name, the convert sheds dependence on the former master; appropriates a distinctive culture of her/his own choice, not to play with the exotic, but to adopt a legitimate identity that binds one to a culture and tradition that has made its contribution to civilization. S/he is no longer the product of the cotton fields rendered obsolete by machinery, but a servant of God with a glorious history and a noble ancestry.

At the heart of the matter is the desire to be free to choose what one believes is compatible with one's own identity and to create one's own culture. Some in the African-American community have become increasingly sensitive to immigrants who insist on including regional cultural preferences as an essential part of the definition of Islam and set themselves up as arbiters of Islamic norms and of what it means to be Muslim. Unlike immigrants who are drawn to Americanization and struggle to resist its seduction, African-Americans in many cases have rejected its imperialist and racist culture. Initially, African-Americans paid special attention to the cultural aspects of Islam, assuming Islamic names, donning Islamic dress, and appropriating a variety of imported Islamic cultural norms. They tended to take seriously anyone who claimed to have particular knowledge of Islam, with the result that they made changes in dress, in food, in greetings. Then they were told by others that these were local cultural definitions, not part of the essential culture of Islam. Many African-Americans grew tired of hearing various immigrant groups insist that theirs was the only Islamic way. One former imam from the American-Muslim Mission referred to the struggle for cultural identity in the African-American community by saying, "We have become cultural chameleons."

Imam Warith Din Muhammad, the leader of the African-American Muslim community since 1975, who transformed the majority of his father's followers in the Nation of Islam into Sunni orthodox Muslims, has been resisting absorption by the immigrant groups insofar as that means subservience to a foreign leadership or agenda. At one time he called his organization the American Muslim Mission, placed American flags in the *masajid* (mosques) and allowed his followers to enlist in the armed services, emphasizing its American identity. While he has decentralized the organization he heads and delegated authority to the local *masajid*, insisting that all Muslims are one and should worship together, he has also maintained an independent perspective on American foreign policy. For example, he supported American intervention in the Gulf, while most immigrants did not.

Black Muslim sects continue to flourish in the ghettos of urban America, attracting members to such groups as the Nation of Islam,[62] Ansaaru Allah,[63] and the Five Percenters,[64] as well as gangs such as al-Rukn[65] of Chicago fame. While Louis Farrakhan, the leader of the Nation of Islam, appears to have amicable relations with leaders of Muslim nations designated by the American government as "harboring terrorists," immigrant Muslims have dissociated themselves from his teachings and regard him as advocating heresy. Isa Muhammad, the leader of Ansaaru Allah, flirted with Arabs and Muslims during the 1980s, hoping for aid in establishing schools and institutions. When none was forthcoming, and when his sectarian teachings were condemned as heretical, he attacked Arabs and Sunnis as racist, revised the Islamic components of his teachings, and moved his organization out of its Brooklyn headquarters.[66] A recent development, viewed with mixed feelings ranging from curiosity to apprehension by leaders of the Sunni community, is the attraction by a growing number of blacks to revolutionary Shi'ite Islam and in some cases to Sufi groups.

In the proceedings of the NAAMPS conference, Professor Aminah Beverly McCloud of DePaul University expressed concern that the immigrants not only are confident that they are the carriers of true Islam, but see themselves as the only experts who can judge its activities in the United States. She noted that, although the majority of American converts to Islam are the product of African-American rather than immigrant *da'wa* (missionary) activities, immigrants persist in regarding themselves as the authority on issues of conversion and do not consult with African-Americans on da'wa methods and goals. She also takes the immigrants to task for being ethnically bound and exclusively concerned with issues of injustice and suffering in the communities from which they emigrated, to the total disregard of the reality of America. Their humanitarian concerns and relief efforts appear to be directed primarily towards Muslims in other countries while they ignore the poverty and deprivation around them.[67]

McCloud also faults immigrants for not living up to the ideals of Islam that they preach. Immigrants like to insist that "there is no racism in Islam or ethnicity is second place in Islam, when in fact there is no racism in Islam but there is plenty among Muslims, and ethnicity is a priority when it comes to who is really Muslim."[68] She accuses them of innate racism, preferring the conversion of whites to Islam and totally disregarding African-Americans, Hispanic-Americans, and Native Americans. Their tribalism manifests itself most often in social gatherings of Muslims where groups separate themselves according to ethnicity or language. "What does it take for African-American or Hispanic-American Muslims to be Muslims? They have surely sacrificed a lot in this land of negotiable freedoms in their striving for Islam. They are also not likely to become white anytime soon."[69] McCloud accuses the immigrants of an inability to unite on issues and, by appearing to be intimidated by America, of opting to live marginal lives. Both the American system that has taken advantage of Muslim division and the Muslims themselves are held responsible for their ineffectiveness. Tribalism and division into ethnic groups have weakened the community. While they proclaim brotherhood under Islam, they have separated into ethnic and ideological units.

Another area of debate between African-American and immigrant Muslims is whether or not individuals are free to interpret the scripture. African-Americans generally come from an evangelical background where the individual's encounter with the word of God is an individual effort that may precipitate a unique experience or interpretation. Immigrants for the most part have difficulty in accepting this and fear that individual interpretation not supported by the consensus of the community and heritage may lead to deviance and to new sectarian movements.

The diversity of the Muslim community in North America and the cultural differences it represents have raised the question of whose cultural definition is truly Islamic—Arab, Pakistani or whatever. Can the immigrants feel comfortable enough to make room for an African-American definition? Will the immigrants trust the African-American Muslim community to create an Islamic world view relevant to their life in the United States, or will they trust the Qur'an to transform the lives of new believers, in new ways without immigrant mediation of what is acceptable and allowed? In the final analysis will they trust God to be at work among the new believers bringing about the salvation of a minority long oppressed and the redemption of a people long victimized? Or will they insist that God works in the world only in the ways identified and codified by Muslim authors centuries ago?

For the Muslims in North America, the need to define themselves by religious identity and increasingly by ethnicity is in a sense a product of the Americanization process. The current culture is in flux, with strong sentiments supporting the definition of America as a Judeo-Christian nation and others advocating a pluralistic society. Initially, it may appear that the Islamist identity that has flourished among certain groups in the mosque movement since the 1970s is a foreign import of self-imposed boundaries that constrains the Muslims within a dogmatic and ideological definition. A closer look reveals that it is also in a very important way a reflection of what obtains in American society at large, enhanced and reinforced by an America increasingly paranoid about Islam and the Muslim presence.

For many immigrants and their children, Islam has become a survival mechanism. Identity is negotiated among the members of the group in response to marginalization and anti-Muslim diatribes by various sectors of American society. Commitment to an ideal Islam that confronts all cultural institutions seen as deviating from the moral imperatives revealed by God in the world as man-made and consequently deficient, if not evil, will probably continue in the foreseeable future to garner the support of some of the Muslim immigrants and the converts who are disenchanted with the American reality. The appeal of this ideology rests in its affirming the nobility of the identity of the individual in a culture that degrades it and in preserving the integrity and integration of the group that is relentlessly depicted as the "other" or as a threat to the polity. Given the experience of prejudice in the American context, Islam will for some continue to serve as a haven of refuge and for others as the efficacious instrument guaranteed by God to transform America, redirect it from its present course of evil, and in the process redeem it and utilize it for the salvation of the world.

While there is no apparent shortage of leadership potential in the community given the high ratio of highly educated professionals and intellectuals who see themselves as the vanguard of the revitalization of Islam, nor any apparent shortage of ideas of what needs to be done, two major problems are the lack of consensus on what needs to be done and the lack of expertise in forging one, owing to a lack of experience among the immigrants in participatory democracy. As Maher Hathout puts it, "We really do not know what we want to do," a fact that leads to "contradictions in our performance."[70]

If the American system of religious pluralism is grounded in consensus rather than insistence on difference, Muslims question why there is deference to one group that can call itself distinctive with special rights because it is chosen by God. If the American system of pluralism calls for acceptance of other ways to salvation and the abandonment of proselytizing, why are the Muslims targeted by Christian groups for conversion? One strategy is to insist on exclusiveness and provide a haven for members where they not only celebrate their distinctive cultural heritage, but also arm themselves against competing views. Others seek ways of blending in; sometimes abandoning the faith, they adopt a theology of separateness. Demonization by the press reinforces their assurance of the truth of the message they have received. Their hope is that somehow America can both realize and admit its nature as a multicultural and multireligious society and that finally it can be proud of its identity as Christian, Jewish, and Muslim.

Notes

1. For studies illustrating the diversity of Muslims in North America, see Yvonne Yazbeck Haddad and Jane I. Smith, eds., *Muslim Communities in North America* (Albany: State University of New York Press, 1994); cf. Yvonne Yazbeck Haddad, *The Muslims of America* (New York: Oxford University Press, 1991).

2. Yvonne Yazbeck Haddad, "Maintaining the Faith of the Fathers: Dilemmas of Religious Identity in the Christian and Muslim Arab-American Commu-

nities," in *Arab-American Communities*, ed. Ernest McCarus (Ann Arbor: University of Michigan Press, 1994).

3. See, for example, studies on Iranians and Lebanese, Georges Sabbagh and Mehdi Bozorgmehr, "Secular Immigrants: Religiosity and Ethnicity among Iranian Muslims in Los Angeles," *Muslim Communities*, ed. Haddad and Smith, pp. 445–74; Linda S. Walbridge, "The Shia Mosques and Their Congregations in Dearborn," ibid., pp. 337–58.

4. See, for example, E. E. Essien-Udom, *Black Nationalism* (Chicago: University of Chicago Press, 1962); Eric C. Lincoln, *The Black Muslims in America* (Boston: Beacon Press, 1961); Akbar Muhammad, "Muslims in the United States: An Overview of Organizations, Doctrines, and Problems," in *The Islamic Impact*, ed. Yvonne Yazbeck Haddad, Byron Haines and Ellison Findly (Syracuse: Syracuse University Press, 1984), pp. 195–218.

5. For a comparative study of five mosques on questions of integration and assimilation, see Yvonne Yazbeck Haddad and Adair Lummis, *Islamic Values in the United States* (New York: Oxford University Press, 1987).

6. For a discussion on the subject, see Yvonne Yazbeck Haddad, "Current Arab Paradigms for an Islamic Future," in *Religion and the Authority of the Past*, ed. Tony Siebers (Ann Arbor: University of Michigan Press, 1993).

7. According to Professor Ernest Allen, University of Massachusetts, Amherst.

8. See, for example, the writings of Warith D. Muhammad, *Challenges that Face Man Today* (Chicago: W. D. Muhammad Publications, 1985); and *Focus on al-Islam* (Chicago: Zakat Publications, 1988).

9. Dawud Assad, "Holy Prophet," *Majallat al-Masajid* 2, no. 2 (February 1981): 4.

10. Immigrants coming from the Middle East and Asia in the 1870s generally did not receive a warm welcome. In a Georgia court, for example, questions were raised about their eligibility and qualifications for citizenship, and there was a discussion about whether they fit the criteria of citizenship at the time restricted to "caucasians and negroes."

11. For studies on Islamist thought, see, for example, John L. Esposito, ed., *Voices of Resurgent Islam* (New York: Oxford University Press, 1983); Richard P. Mitchell, *The Society of the Muslim Brothers* (London; Oxford University Press, 1969); Yvonne Yazbeck Haddad, "Islamic 'Awakening' in Egypt," in *Arab Studies Quarterly* 9, no. 3 (1987): 234–59; Yvonne Yazbeck Haddad, "Muslim Revivalist Thought in the Arab World: An Overview," *The Muslim World* 76, nos. 3–4 (1986); Bassam Tibi, "The Worldview of Sunni Arab Fundamentalists: Attitudes toward Modern Science and technology," in *Fundamentalisms and Society: Reclaiming the Sciences, the Family and Society* (Chicago: University of Chicago Press, 1993), pp. 73–102; and the two articles in Martin E. Marty and R. Scott Appleby, eds., *Fundamentalisms Observed* (Chicago: University of Chicago Press, 1991): John O. Voll, "Fundamentalism in the Sunni Arab World: Egypt and the Sudan," pp. 345–402; and Mumtaz Ahmad, "Islamic Fundamentalism in South Asia: The Jamaat-i-Islami and the Tablighi Jamaat," pp. 457–530.

12. For a book by a former Israeli agent deemed as targeting Muslims, see Yossef Bodansky, *Target America: Terrorism in the U.S. Today* (New York: S.P.I. Books, 1993).

13. See, for example, Ahmad Yusuf, "al-Hajma al-Sihyoniyya `ala al-Muslimin

fi al-Wilayat al-Muttahida. Mawjat al-Tahrid al-Thalitha: al-Jihad fi America," *Filastin al-Muslima*, January 1995, pp. 38–40.

14. Besides producing the controversial documentary "Jihad in America" aired on PBS, Steven Emerson testified before the House International Relations Committee where he asserted, "Radical Islamic networks now constitute the primary domestic—as well as international-national—security threat facing the FBI and other law enforcement agencies"; "Testimony of Steven Emerson: Subcommittee on Africa, House International Relations Committee, U.S. House of Representatives," April 6, 1995, p. 4. He was one of the first journalists to ascribe the Oklahoma City bombing to Muslim terrorists as vindication of his analysis and assessment. He has also published an article and is in the process of writing a book on the subject: Steven Emerson, "The Other Fundamentalists," *The New Republic*, June 12, 1995, pp. 21–30.

15. Raphael Merguii and Philippe Simonnot, *Israel's Ayatollahs: Meir Kahane and the Far Right in Israel* (London: Saqi Books, 1987).

16. Robert I. Friedman, "Who Killed Alex Odeh? FBI Probe of JDL Bombers Gets No Help From Israelis," *The Village Voice*, Nov. 4, 1987.

17. In an interview with *Time* magazine, President Reagan said, "Lately we have even seen the possibility of, literally, a religious war—the Muslims returning to the idea that the way to heaven is to lose one's life fighting the Christians and the Jews" (*Time* 116, no. 20 [November 17, 1980]: 37). In responding to Reagan's accusation the Council of Masajid adopted a unanimous resolution expressing indignation over the "slanderous travesty and fallacious distortion of the teachings of Islam." The resolution affirmed that Islam is the "religion of peace and stands against injustice and tyranny," and stressed that in fact Islam makes a special point of urging its followers to be polite and kind to Christians and Jews (see S. 3:64). The president's statement was further condemned because it was perceived as potentially inciting violence against Muslims in the United States. The document continued, "We regard this matter as transcending politics and a flagrant violation of Muslim rights as enshrined in the U.S. Constitution." ("Mosque Council Condemns Reagan's Attack on Islam," *Majallat al-Masajid* 2, no. 2 (February 1981): 17–18.

18. Daniel Pipes, "Fundamentalist Muslims," *Foreign Affairs*, Summer 1986, pp. 939–59; Daniel Pipes, "The Muslims Are Coming! The Muslims Are Coming!" *National Review*, November 19, 1990, pp. 28–31; Bernard Lewis, "Islam and Democracy," *The Atlantic*, February 1993, pp. 87–98; Martin Kramer, "Islam vs. Democracy," *Commentary*, January 1993, pp. 35–42.

19. The late Israeli Prime Minister Yitzhak Rabin is reported to have told American Jewish young people that the United States must support Israel in order to combat the Islamists, the enemies of peace who also threaten America. In an address to the American Israel Public Affairs Committee Annual Conference on March 21, 1993, Rabin said: "Thank you very much for your decision to go [to Capitol Hill] and to try to convince the senators, the congressmen in the need in Israel in this period. . . . to ensure that the United States will support these efforts by Israel, as the president said, by minimizing our risks, by military aid, economic aid, understanding of the threat of the Islamic extremist terror groups not only to Israel. . . . It's a threat to all moderate regimes. . . . The United States has to continue to support and to prove to the region, to the peoples, to the countries, that its readiness to assist those who seek peace and ready to bring eco-

nomic and social reform and to try to contain ... the dangerous trend of the Islamic fundamentalistic [sic] terrorist organization and the country that backs them" (as quoted in Ahmad AbulJobain, Islam Under Siege: Radical Islamic Terrorism or Political Islam? (Annandale, VA: United Association for Studies and Research Inc., 1993), Occasional Papers Series No. 1, June 1993.

20. Other Israeli leaders have expressed similar sentiments. Haim Hertzok is reported to have said that while the world today is concerned about the atom bomb and weapons of mass destruction in the region, a more sinister and dangerous development is the growth of Islamic fundamentalism. Shimon Peres told a White House audience that the United States must increase its aid to Israel because it is engaged in a war against Islamic extremism (al-Mujtama' 1078 (December 1993): 6.

21. See Yvonne Yazbeck Haddad, "The 'New Enemy'? Islam and Islamists after the Cold War," in Altered States: A Reader in the New World Order, ed. Phyllis Bennis and Michel Moushabeck (New York: Olive Branch Press, 1993), pp. 83–94; cf. John L. Esposito, The Islamic Threat: Myth or Reality? (New York: Oxford University Press, 1995); Patrick J. Buchanan, "Is Islam an Enemy of the United States?" New Hampshire Sunday News, November 25, 1990.

22. Donald E. Wagner, Anxious for Armageddon (Scottdale, Pa: Herald Press, 1995); Grace Halsell, Journey to Jerusalem (New York: Macmillan and Company, 1982); Grace Halsell, Prophecy and Politics (Westport, CT: Lawrence Hill Books, 1986); see also Dwight Wilson, Armageddon Now (Tyler, TX: Institute for Christian Economics, 1991); Hal Lindsey, Countdown to Armageddon (New York: Bantam Books, 1980).

23. Mir Maqsud Ali, "Resurgence of Islam: A Dream or a Reality?" in Islam: A Contemporary Perspective, ed. Mohammad Ahmadullah Siddiqi (Chicago: NAAMPS, 1994), p. 33.

24. Abul A'la al-Mawdudi, The Process of Islamic Revolution (Lahore: Islamic Publications, 1977).

25. Sayyid Qutb, Milestones (Cedar Rapids, IA: Unity Publishing Co., n.d.).

26. Yvonne Yazbeck Haddad, "The Challenge of Muslim 'Minorityness': The American Experience," in The Integration of Islam and Hinduism in Western Europe, ed. W. A. R. Shadid and P. S. van Koningsveld (Kampen, The Netherlands: Kok, 1991).

27. Yvonne Yazbeck Haddad, "The Qur'anic Justification for an Islamic Revolution: The Views of Sayyid Qutb," Middle East Journal 38, no. 1 (January 1983); Yvonne Yazbeck Haddad, "Sayyid Qutb: Ideologue of Islamic Revival," in Voices of Resurgent Islam, ed. Esposito.

28. M. A. Kettani, Muslim Minorities in the World Today (London, 1986), pp. 9–13; for a more extensive discussion of Kettani's arguments, see Haddad, "The Challenge of Muslim 'Minorityness,'" pp. 134–53.

29. The term was coined by Syed Z. Abedin in his foreword to Kettani's book, Muslim Minorities, p. xiii.

30. Ibid., pp. 9–13.

31. Muhammad Abdul-Rauf, "The Future of the Islamic Tradition in North America," in The Muslim Community in North America, ed. Earle H. Waugh et al. (Edmonton: University of Alberta Press, 1983), p. 271.

32. Abdul-Rauf, "Future of the Islamic Tradition," p. 272.

33. Ibid., p. 277. A slightly different version quotes President Eisenhower

as saying, "Americans would fight with all their strength for your right to have your own church and worship according to your own conscience. Without this, we would be something else than what we are." Muhammad Abdul-Rauf, *History of the Islamic Center* (Washington, D.C.: The Islamic Center, 1973), p. 75.

34. The teacher was opposed by some of the parents who found her ideas subversive, and she was relieved of her duties.

35. Al-Faruqi and Rahman are both now dead; Nasr teaches at George Washington University in Washington, D.C. For studies on the three thinkers, see the following articles in Haddad, *Muslims of America*: John L. Esposito, "Ismail R. Al-Faruqi: Muslim Scholar-Activist," pp. 65–79; Jane I. Smith, "Seyyed Hossein Nasr: Defender of the Sacred and Islamic Traditionalism," pp. 80–95; and Frederick M. Denny, "The Legacy of Fazlur Rahman," pp. 96–110.

36. Isma'il al-Faruqi was from Palestine, Seyyed Hossein Nasr from Iran, and Fazlur Rahman from Pakistan.

37. Isma'il R. al-Faruqi, "Islamic Ideals in North America," in Waugh et al., *Muslim Community in North America*, pp. 259–70; cf. Muhammad Shafiq, *Growth of Islamic Thought in North America: Focus on Isma'il Raji al-Faruqi* (Brentwood, MD: Amana Publications, 1994).

38. Yvonne Yazbeck Haddad, "Operation Desert Shield/Desert Storm: The Islamist Perspective," in *Beyond the Storm: A Gulf Crisis Reader*, ed. Phyllis Bennis and Michel Moushabeck (New York: Interlink Books, 1991).

39. A similar pattern appears to be taking place in Britain as Muslims begin to reassess the problems the community faces. A leading Islamist in Britain wrote that some of the existential problems Muslims face in the West are the product of Western society itself, while others are of its own making, the product of the Islamist vision which was developed in and for a different environment. The Islamist intellectual output was judged to be culpable because its vision was fashioned to deal with the realities of the home countries, where Muslims constitute the majority population. Were Islamists whose works are being advocated and utilized in the minority populations of the West aware of this, they would have been disturbed and would condemn such an application, especially with what pertains to their writings about the West. Their efforts had been aimed at a local population describing the role of Western imperialism and its conspiracy in an effort to wake up the Muslim community from its sleep, to expose the traitors in their midst who had agreed to be the means through which imperialism realized its agenda in Muslim countries (al-Tamimi, "Nahwa Muntalaqat," p. 44).

40. Mohammad Fathi Osman, "Towards a Vision and an Agenda for the Future of Muslim Ummah," in *Islam: A Contemporary Perspective*, ed. Mohammad Ahmadullah Siddiqi (Chicago: NAAMPS, 1994), p. 13.

41. Ibid., p. 14.

42. Ibid., p. 15.

43. Ibid., p. 22.

44. Maher Hathout, "Islamic Work in North America: Challenges and Opportunities," in *Islam: A Contemporary Perspective*, ed. Siddiqi, p. 64.

45. Mohammad Ahmadullah Siddiqi, "Towards an Islamic Vision and Agenda for the Future," in *Islam: A Contemporary Perspective*, ed. M. A. Siddiqi, p. 25.

46. Ibid.

47. Ibid.

48. Ibid.

49. Ibid., pp. 27–28: the list includes the following: "1. A contemporary understanding of Qur'an and Sunnah. 2. The status and scope of the efforts of Muslim scholars in past time and space. 3. Muslims' relationship with non-Muslims, particularly in North American context. 4. Islam and contemporary social, cultural and family related issues in North America. 5. Islam and the modern political thoughts and political systems. 6. Islam and contemporary economic system. 7. Muslims' education in North America. 8. Muslims' stand with respect to dictatorship, monarchy, human rights, and violence. 9. Islamic moral system vis-à-vis the current state of morality in North America. 10. Islam and science in the technical context."

50. Salam al-Marayati, "Formulating an Agenda of Political Actions for North American Muslims," in *Islam: A Contemporary Perspective*, ed. Siddiqi, p. 68.

51. Hathout, "Islamic Work," p. 64.

52. Al-Marayati, "Formulating an Agenda," p. 69.

53. Ibid., p. 70.

54. Ibid.

55. Hathout, "Islamic Work," p. 62.

56. Ibid., p. 62.

57. Siddiqi, "Towards an Islamic Vision," p. 27.

58. Ibid., p. 27.

59. Osman, "Towards a Vision," p. 15.

60. Ibid., pp. 16–17.

61. A designation used of the Harlem-based Black Hebrews by Israel J. Gerber, *The Heritage Seekers* (Middle Village, NY: Jonathan Publishers, 1977), p. 176.

62. This is a splinter group from the original Nation of Islam that acknowledges the leadership of Louis Farrakhan. See Mattias Gardell, "The Sun of Islam Will Rise in the West: Minister Farrakhan and the Nation of Islam in the Latter Days," in Haddad and Smith, *Muslim Communities*, pp. 15–50.

63. For the teachings of this sect, see the writings of the founder, Isa Muhammad, *The Message of the Messenger is Right and Exact* (Brooklyn: Isa Muhammad, 1979); *Racism in Islam* (Brooklyn: Isa Muhammad, 1982); *Al-Imam Isa vs the Computer* (Brooklyn: Isa Muhammad, 1982); Dwight York (alias Isa Muhammad), *365 Questions to Ask the Orthodox Sunni Muslims* (Brooklyn: [Isa Muhammad], 1989).

64. A splinter group from the Nation of Islam who believe that only five percent of humanity will be saved on the Day of Judgment and that they will be drawn exclusively from members of their community. See Yusuf Nuruddin, "The Five Percenters: A Teenage Nation of Gods and Earths," in Haddad and Smith, eds., *Muslim Communities*, pp. 109–32.

65. The courts convicted members of the gang of conspiracy to commit terrorist activities. It was shown at their trial that they were in contact with Qadhafi of Libya.

66. For a study of the Ansaaru Allah community, see Yvonne Yazbeck Haddad and Jane Idleman Smith, *Mission to America: Five Islamic Sectarian*

Communities in North America (Gainesville: University Press of Florida, 1993), pp. 105–36.

67. Aminah B. McCloud, "Racism in the Ummah," in *Islam: A Contemporary Perspective*, ed. Siddiqi, pp. 73–80.

68. Ibid., p. 76.

69. Ibid., p. 77.

70. Hathout, "Islamic Work," p. 62.

2

Striking a Balance

Islamic Legal Discourse on
Muslim Minorities

KHALED ABOU EL FADL

Muslims in America, though a growing and increasingly diverse community, are nonetheless still a small minority living in an ostensibly Christian
country. One of the most vexing questions for Muslims, particularly those
who consider themselves religious or "practicing," is how to live as persons
of faith in a challenging and sometimes hostile environment. Muslim beliefs are generally not understood in the United States, and Muslim practices are not supported by the social, professional, and economic structures
of American society.

The problems arising from being in the minority have been debated throughout the history of Islam. Debates have centered on how to define the dar al-
Islam (abode of true faith), in relation to the dar al-harb, or dar al-kufr,
the area where Islam is neither the dominant religion nor the basis for the
communitys government or legal structure. Muslim jurists have questioned
whether Muslims should even try to live outside the abode of Islam and, if
so, how Islam should or could be practiced there. They have debated whether
the laws of Islam are applicable in a non-Muslim country, and the criteria that
should be used in living a pious life under these circumstances. At the core
of these distinctions are attempts at determining when justice and righteousness can be served and when one is in a situation of true oppression.

In this essay I will look at several responses to such questions, focusing
on the views of the modern Egyptian jurist Rashid Rida (1865–1935) and
comparing them to those of other Muslim authorities over the centuries. The
issues raised in these continuing discussions have direct ramifications for
American Muslims as well as for the many other Muslim communities living in the West. Regardless of whether one designates the United States and
countries of the West as a part of dar al-harb, or as part of any other abode,

the fact remains that Islam is not the dominant faith or the determiner of either the civil or personal code in these countries. This presents Muslim minorities residing in them with powerful challenges in which Islamic doctrinal imperatives must be reconciled with specific social realities. Although every historical situation is in many ways unique, much of the rich Islamic discourse on Muslim minorities is directly relevant to the contemporary situation of Muslims living in the West. As the discussions of Rashid Rida and other Muslim jurists demonstrate, the Islamic response to the challenge of residence in non-Muslim lands has been vibrant, innovative, and diverse. If history is any indication, the responses of Muslims living in America promise to be no less vibrant or innovative and, definitely, no less diverse.

When Bosnia-Herzegovina was ceded to Austro-Hungarian control in 1909 the Muslims of Bosnia, a large population, fell subject to non-Muslim rule. An Ottoman jurist, visiting one of the main mosques in Bosnia, announced that all Muslims must immediately remove themselves and migrate to the abode of Islam, i.e., to territory where a Muslim sovereign was in power. Since Bosnia was now ruled by non-Muslims, the Ottoman jurist declared, all Muslim acts of worship and all marriages are invalid, and for Muslims to continue living in Bosnia would be to live in sin. An unidentified Bosnian official wrote to Rashid Rida, the most prominent jurist of the time in Egypt, asking him to respond to the Ottoman jurist.

Rida responded with a scathing attack: he accused the Ottoman jurist of ignorance, narrow-mindedness, and of corrupting the religion of Islam[1] and producing a point-by-point refutation. He argued that the Prophet himself had allowed Muslim converts to live outside the abode of Islam; he had not demanded that every Muslim convert migrate to the Muslim city-state in Medina. Furthermore, Rida argued, there is no distinction between a prayer or marriage performed in the lands of Islam and rites performed elsewhere, and a Muslim may live a perfectly pious life in non-Muslim lands. The only difference would be that the variety of Islamic civil and criminal laws applied in Muslim lands would be inoperative in non-Muslim territories.[2]

Nothing in Islam, Rida asserted, prevented a Muslim from living in non-Muslim territory. The real question was whether the non-Muslim territory would allow Muslims to practice their religion. In other words, it was not Islam's theology or law that stood in the way of Muslims residing in non-Muslim territory; rather, the material issue was the amount of freedom afforded by the non-Muslim territory to Muslims for the practice of their religion. If they were kept from practicing their religion altogether, then it was advisable for them to search out a safe place that afforded them the religious freedom they required. However, Rida went on, this analysis applies only if the Muslim population residing in the non-Muslim territory consisted of isolated individuals unable to organize or resist oppression. If there was a sizable Muslim population, then instead of choosing to escape to safety, it was Islamically incumbent upon them to stay where they were and resist oppression.

Rida cites the important opinion of a medieval Muslim jurist, al-Mawardi (d. 1058), as his authority for the proposition that if Muslims are able to manifest and practice their religion in a non-Muslim territory then it is incumbent upon them to remain there because the territory has effectively become a part of the abode of Islam. It was also always possible that one or another of the non-believers would convert to Islam through contact with the Muslim population.[3] In the final analysis, Rida argues, Muslims must serve justice and righteousness and must resist oppression wherever they reside. If and only if it becomes impossible to do so must they emigrate and find a place where such service might be possible.[4] Whether in the particular case of Bosnian Muslims it would be possible was something that the Bosnian Muslims themselves would have to determine.

The issues that confronted Rashid Rida in this *fatwa* were not novel, and his response to them was by no means unusual either. Muslim minorities have lived in non-Muslim territories since the first century of Islam, and after the eleventh century vast Muslim populations had come under non-Muslim rule. Consequently, an extensive juristic discourse has been generated, dealing with the legality of this residence and the obligations and duties of these Muslim minorities.[5]

Today, one-third of the 1.2 billion Muslims in the world live in countries where non-Muslims are the majority.[6] This ought to remind us of the fact that the age-old juristic discourse on the legality of residing in non-Muslim territories, while obviously relevant, is somewhat artificial. The continued practice of so many Muslim minorities throughout Muslim history is as much an articulation of Islam as is of the juristic writings of Muslim scholars.[7] While the writings of Muslim jurists are of considerable normative value,[8] it would be a serious methodological error to equate the positions of Muslim jurists with what Muslim minorities in specific historical contexts actually believed or practiced.

Most of the legal sources of Islam were written by jurists who, like Rashid Rida, lived most of their lives in Muslim lands among clear Muslim majorities. These sources play a significant role in the social and theological discourse that defined Islam in a particular age and place. But they do not play the only role, and not even the most important role, in deciding what Islam has to say about a particular issue relating to Muslim minorities. It is the Muslim minorities themselves, through their continuing historical practices, who play the defining role in the discourse. Rashid Rida acknowledged this fact when he asserted in his *fatwa*, that ultimately it was the Bosnian Muslims "who are the best judges of their own affairs."[9] In other words, it was the Bosnian Muslims themselves who could best judge whether their continued residence under Austrian sovereignty was consistent with their religious obligations.

Muslim jurists dealing with the problems of Muslim minorities have attempted to articulate the moral parameters within which they should conduct themselves. Consistently they have defined these parameters in light of the doctrinal sources of Islam, namely the Qur'an and Sunna. But throughout Islamic history these parameters have been constantly redefined, rearticulated, and recast in light of the specific historical circumstances Muslims confronted at a particular time. This is especially true of the development of the juridical discourse on the hijra of Muslims from non-Muslim lands to Muslim territory.

The Qur'an (4:97–100) does not command Muslims to live in Muslim territory. It does, however, require that people conduct their affairs according to God's revelations (5:44) The Qur'an commands that Muslims escape oppression by migrating in the cause of God:

> As for those whose souls are taken by the angels (at death) while in a state of injustice against themselves, they will be asked by the angels: "What state were you in?" They will answer: "We were oppressed in the land." And the angels will say: "Was not God's earth large enough for you to migrate?" . . . Whosoever migrates in the cause of God will find many places of refuge and abundance on the earth.[10]

The command to escape oppression is not conditioned on finding a territory that follows the Shari'a or any similar specification. The text seems to call for an escape from oppression in an absolute sense.

The Prophet of Islam, Muhammad, had escaped oppression in Mecca by migrating to Medina where he established a thriving Islamic city-state. After organizing a polity in Medina the Prophet had allowed nomads who converted to Islam but did not wish to migrate to Medina to remain in their homeland. The Prophet did, however, emphasize the merits migrating and joining him and his companions in Medina.[11] From a tactical point of view, not only did the young city-state in Medina need the support of all the converts it could muster, but from an ideological perspective, what could be better for a new Muslim than to live near the Prophet and his companions, where he or she could be instructed in the new religion?

With the spread of the Islamic empire early Muslim jurists continued to emphasize the merits of residing among Muslims. Those who convert to Islam should not continue to live among unbelievers, but should join their fellow Muslims in Muslim lands. Sahnun (d. 854) and Malik (d. 796) strongly disapproved of Muslims living in non-Muslim lands because it was not acceptable for a Muslim to be subject to non-Muslim laws. Some jurists emphasized the inherent risks involved in residing in non-Muslim lands. In Muslim lands, the argument went, converts to Islam would enjoy greater safety since they did not run the risk of forcible conversions or of being enticed away from Islam. However, jurists such as al-Shafi'i (d. 819–20) argued that Muslims may reside in non-Muslim territory as long as they do not fear enticement away from their religion. Others, such as Ja'far al-Sadiq (the sixth Shi'i imam d. 765), emphasized the substantive quality of the territory over its formal categorization. In all circumstances, lands in which real justice and knowledge are to be found are superior to lands that are formally associated with Islam.[12]

For the first five centuries of Islamic history, Muslim jurists continued to express a variety of unsystematic views that ranged from the rejectionist to the accommodating. However, the nature of the discourse changed materially in the sixth/twelfth century, when vast Muslim territories fell under non-Muslim control, and with this overwhelming historical reality Muslim jurists were forced to develop a systematic argument regarding the legality of residing in non-Muslim territories. The Western territories of the Islamic empire came under siege by the Christians and in the seventh/thirteenth century the Mongols overran the eastern territories. The majority of Maliki jurists, whose school was widespread in Spain, Sicily, and Crete, responded to the continued political conflict with Christianity by adopting an uncompromising position. Abu al-Walid Ibn Rushd (d. 1122), for example, argued that no Muslim should accept the degradation of living under non-Muslim rule. Every Muslim should immediately emigrate from non-Muslim territory to the security of Muslim lands.[13] The Maliki position was first and foremost politically motivated. In light of the humiliating defeats suffered in Andalus, Sicily, and Crete, a decision to continue residing under non-Muslim rule was perceived as treason against the dignity of Islam. This is, for example, apparent in the polemics of one of the most influential Maliki jurists, al-Wansharisi (d. 1508). In an extended diatribe against Muslims who chose to continue to reside in Marbella after it fell to Christian control, al-Wansharisi warned the Muslim population that it was bound to lose its language and culture. Regardless of any momentary security that this population might enjoy, they were bound to be betrayed and forced to convert to Christianity. More important, al-Wansharisi argues that by refusing to migrate to Muslim lands, this Muslim population effectively declared the superiority of the abode of non-Muslims to the abode of Islam.[14] Although the views of Ibn Rushd and al-Wansharisi are representative of the majority opinion prevailing among North African Maliki jurists, they were not universal: some Maliki jurists, such as al-Mazari (d. 1141) did not share them.[15]

After the sixth/twelfth century, Hanbali and Shi'i jurists argued that it was always preferable that Muslims reside in Muslim lands. This is not because the Shari'a was applied in Muslim territory—as a factual matter, it was not being applied by various Muslim dynasties at that time—but living in non-Muslims territories involved inevitable risks: for example, a Muslim could inadvertently contribute to the material strength of non-Muslims which could then be used against Muslims. Nevertheless, these schools argued, if Muslims are physically secure and are able freely to practice their religion in non-Muslim lands, they may continue to reside among non-Muslims. In such a situation, migration is recommended but not mandated. However, in all circumstances, if the Muslim minority suffers from some type of physical or financial hardship making migration to Muslim lands difficult, then the Muslim minority is excused until the hardship is removed.

The most sophisticated responses to the question of Muslim residence in non-Muslim territory came from the Hanafi and Shafi'i schools. The approaches of these schools was a direct response to the Mongol invasions, when a vast territory from the abode of Islam fell to the Mongols and large Muslim populations found themselves under non-Muslim rule. Even the jurists articulating the responses, though from the heart of the abode of Islam, were under Mongol domination, so their theories very much reflected their reality.

These Hanafi and Shafi'i jurists argued that, depending on circumstances, migration from non-Muslim lands could be required, recommended, permitted, or prohibited. If Muslims residing in non-Muslim lands cannot practice their religion they must migrate to where they can. However, if Muslims are able to practice their religion and they hope to serve Islam in the non-Muslim territory in which they reside, it is recommended that they continue residing there. If, however, Muslims can openly practice their religion and are able to maintain a degree of autonomy and independence, it is mandatory that they continue residing in the non-Muslim territory in which they live because the territory is then considered, at a moral level, to be a part of the abode of Islam and because these Muslims are now in a position to serve Islam.[16]

Muslim jurists effectively reconstructed the theological and legal discourse in light of the historical realities confronting them. Whether they chose to grant legitimacy to the residence of Muslim minorities outside Muslim territories or chose to oppose it, both responses were historically specific. Of particular importance is that Muslim jurists renegotiated and reformulated the concept of dar al-Islam in light of these historical realities. Dar al-Islam was never precisely defined in Islamic discourse. For example, Abu al-Hasan al-Ash'ari (d. 936), writing in the fourth/tenth century, identified six different conceptions of dar al-Islam.[17] Others argued that dar al-Islam is where the Shari'a is faithfully applied; still others, that it is where a Muslim ruler is in power and others added that the ruler must be just and truly pious. It is clear that over the centuries Muslims developed a variety of positions depending on circumstance.[18] In particular, Hanafi and Shafi'i jurists reconstructed the discourse on dar al-Islam so that a territory could be ruled and controlled by non-Muslims and still remain a part of the abode of Islam.

The Qur'anic injunction on migration cast the whole earth as a possible refuge from oppression. Arguably, the injunction was sufficiently broad to permit a historically specific discourse on the obligations of Muslim minorities, but in fact a large number of Sunni and Shi'i jurists simply insisted that a Muslim must migrate from any land in which corruption and injustice are widespread. These jurists argued that territory formally designated as a part of the abode of Islam may be plagued by corruption and injustice and in such a case a Muslim must be in a constant search for just lands. The formal designation of the territory is immaterial.[19]

The obligation of migration, either from corrupt and unjust lands or from non-Muslim territory, continued to engage Muslim thinking well into the twentieth century and continued to respond to historical realities confronting Muslim jurists at specific times. For example, it served as a doctrine of opposition to indigenous Muslim governments and colonial powers.[20] Rida's fatwa is itself a product of colonialism. Rida issued his fatwa in late 1909. Bosnia was annexed by Austria in 1908, and Austro-Hungarian control was recognized by the Ottoman government in a treaty signed in February 1909. At that time, most Muslim countries were under colonial occupation. If one considered that colonial territory was no longer part of the dar al-Islam and that migration from this land was therefore incumbent upon Muslims, the question then became: where were these Muslims supposed to go? The Ottoman jurist who advised Bosnian Muslims to leave Bosnia implied that the migration should be to Ottoman territory, and in fact, a sizable Muslim population had already migrated to Ottoman territory. Rida was not willing to accept this solution because he was not willing to accept the legitimacy of the Ottoman caliphate and in fact entertained the idea of replacing it with an Arab one.[21] These considerations are apparent in the impatient and hostile language Rida uses in responding to the Ottoman jurist in his fatwa.

Although Rida implies that despite the loss of Ottoman sovereignty Bosnia remains a part of the abode of Islam, he does not argue the point or present it in any systematic fashion; he merely cites the opinion of the eleventh-century Shafi'i jurist al-Mawardi. In this context, his primary concern is to empower Bosnian Muslims against the religious authority of the Ottomans. However, in 1927, when Rida is asked whether Syria and Lebanon under French occupation are to be considered a part of the abode of Islam, Rida unequivocally says no.[22] Then he argues that, despite the fact that Muslims constitute the majority of the population in greater Syria, Muslim sovereignty is lacking in this territory, and therefore it cannot be considered a part of the dar al-Islam. Rida admits that some have argued that if Muslims are able to practice their religion in a territory, then it is to be considered a part of the abode of Islam. However, Rida states, according to this argument France and Britain should become a part of the abode of Islam because Muslims are able to freely practice their religion there. According to Rida, France, Britain, China, India, and Syria and Lebanon are all not to be considered a part of the abode of Islam, and such absurd conclusions must be avoided. The abode of Islam is where Muslim sovereignty exits and the laws of the Shari'a are fully enforced.[23]

Strictly speaking, then, according to Rida's restrictive definition of the abode of Islam, no Muslim country in his time would qualify. But Rida again insists that Muslims do not have to migrate from territory that is considered to be non-Muslim. Chinese, Indian, Syrian and Lebanese Muslims should remain where they are. His argument would have been served had he maintained that Muslim minorities do not have to migrate because wherever they can freely practice Islam, therein exists the abode of Islam, i.e., had he adopted the post–twelfth-century Shafi'i position. The question then becomes, why did Rida insist that countries such as Syria were not a part of the abode of Islam?

In a case in Syria, Rida was asked by an Islamic philanthropic foundation whether it would be Islamically permitted for it to build a hotel, lease it out, and use the proceeds to benefit indigent Muslim children. Rida realized that the foundation was concerned that the tenants of the hotel would probably sell alcohol in it and thus the foundation would be indirectly implicated in a sinful act. Rida starts out by stating that a landlord is not responsible for the acts of tenants and that the foundation may engage in the transaction in question because Syria and Lebanon (*al-Shams*) are not a part of the abode of Islam. Consequently, the civil and criminal laws of Islam do not apply in these territories. Despite the fact that Syria has historically been at the heart of Muslim lands, at the present time, Rida contends, a Muslim sovereign is not in power and the rule of Shari'a is not in force, and hence it is not a part of the abode of Islam.

For the same reason the civil and criminal laws of Islam have no application in these territories. In non-Muslim territory, Rida argues, Muslims are only bound to follow the laws pertaining to acts of worship (*'ibadat*) such as fasting, almsgiving, and praying; they are not bound by Islamic commercial or criminal laws. In these areas, Muslims are bound by the laws of the non-Muslim host state. Rida qualifies this statement somewhat by arguing that Muslims may not sell alcohol directly, for example, by opening a bar, because the laws pertaining to not drinking or selling alcohol are a part of the ritualistic laws of Islam.

Muslims living in non-Muslim territory, Rida continues, must be able to serve their interests and maintain their strength. If Islamic commercial laws are observed in non-Muslim territory, then Muslims are going to become financially dependent and powerless. Shari'a, Rida maintains, is founded on the principle of defending the welfare of the people. This principle is so fundamental that Muslims are committing a sin if they burden themselves with Islamic laws that have no applicability in non-Muslim lands.

Rida further argues that these same principles dictate that Muslims may borrow and lend money with interest in non-Muslim territory. Rida remains opposed to usurious transactions which he perceives to be economically oppressive, however; Islamic moral injunctions apply to every Muslim regardless of residence. Consequently, Muslims may not cheat, lie, or oppress others, but depositing money in bank accounts that earn interest, which is arguably prohibited by Islamic civil law, does not apply in non-Muslim lands. Therefore, Rida concludes, the philanthropic organization may build and lease out the hotel, even to people who will sell or serve alcohol.[24]

Rida applies this same analysis to the question of whether Indian Muslims may be employed in the British-Indian civil service where they will apply non-Muslim laws. Here he uses more or less the same line of reasoning. He insists that at the foundation of Shari'a is the purpose of serving the interests of people. If Muslims living in India exclude themselves from civil service and other governmental employment, they are bound to become weak and powerless. However, under all circumstances, Muslims cannot assist in oppressing other Muslims. Therefore, there is no prohibition against seeking governmental employment even if this entails applying non-Muslim laws. But Muslims must be careful not to enforce oppressive laws or cooperate in persecuting others.

Significantly, Rida argues that Islamic laws pertaining to prayer, fasting, and the like are binding on a Muslim everywhere. But Islamic civil and criminal laws are all based on ijtihad (juridical reasoning and opinion). This ijtihad is context-specific; therefore it has no applicability in non-Muslim lands where it was not designed to apply. In short, Muslims are not committing a sin when they help implement non-Muslim laws in non-Muslim lands.[25]

Shafi'i jurists after the sixth/twelfth century had argued that Muslim lands conquered by non-Muslims became part of the abode of non-Muslims in appearance only; in law it was still part of the abode of Islam. Rida inverts this argument. He insists that colonized Muslim lands and all Muslim lands where the caliphate is not in force and where Islamic law is not applied are Muslim in appearance only. In law, these lands are not a part of the abode of Islam. Pre-modern Shafi'i jurists were responding to their own historical reality. By insisting that conquered Muslim territory remain a part of the abode of Islam, they preserved the integrity of the vast Muslim lands conquered by the Mongols. Rida was responding to a different historical reality. The sickly Ottoman caliphate could not be accepted as the fulfillment of the Islamic political ideal. Therefore, Rida insisted that the Ottoman Empire was accepted as a caliphate as a matter of necessity (darura). The ideal of a true Islamic government must be preserved and maintained, and after colonialism, this ideal will be fulfilled by the creation of a state that fully implements the Shari'a and adapts the law of the Shari'a to the challenges of modernity. In the meanwhile, Muslims confronting the challenges of modernity in an unaccommodating age must not be hampered by inapplicable Shari'a laws. Rida persistently argues that it is imperative that Muslims be able to empower themselves economically because this is a necessary condition for achieving independence and for the well-being of Islam. Furthermore, to argue that Muslims may reside in non-Muslim territory only if they are able safely to practice their religion and then deny them the very means for political and economic empowerment is an inherent contradiction. Muslims cannot securely practice their religion unless they are sufficiently empowered to resist attempts at denying them their religious freedom. They cannot attain this position unless they are able to serve in non-Muslim governments and engage in commerce. Otherwise, the permission granted to Muslims to reside in non-Muslim territory becomes meaningless.

In summary, Rida formulates a three-pronged argument: (1) most lands where Muslims reside are not a part of the abode of Islam and, therefore (2) the civil and criminal laws of Islam are not binding; (3) consequently, within certain moral bounds, Muslims may do whatever is necessary to become politically and economically empowered.

Rida did not invent the doctrines which he espoused. He took doctrines that had already emerged from Islamic legal history and recast them to suit his own situation. So, for instance, pre-modern Hanafi jurists had consistently argued the limited applicability of Islamic law. According to the Hanafi school, certain Islamic prohibitions apply regardless of territory. For example, murder, theft, adultery, fornication, and the drinking of alcohol are prohibited in Muslim and non-Muslim territory alike. But these prohibitions are only at the moral level. If one commits any of these acts in non-Muslim territory that person is liable before God on the final day. However, a Muslim state does not have the jurisdiction to punish these violations, even if the violator returns to Muslim territory and admits to the crime. The jurisdiction of Islamic law is only territorial, and hence a Muslim state can only punish infractions committed on its territory. The Hanafis went further and argued that certain Islamic laws do not apply, even at a moral level, in non-Muslim territory. All commercial Islamic regulations have no applicability outside the domain of Islam. Consequently, Muslims residing in non-Muslim territory are bound only by the laws of the host state, and may engage even in transactions that involve *riba* (usury).[26]

Rida consistently cites the Hanafi school in support of his arguments. However, he is well aware that the other Muslim legal schools disagreed with the Hanafi position. In fact, the Shafi'i, Hanbali, Maliki, and Shi'i jurists had all consistently argued that the laws of Shari'a are applicable in the abode of Islam and in the abode of non-Muslims. Al-Shafi'i (d. 819–20), for example, writes:

> There is no difference between *dar al-harb*, the abode of war and *dar al-Islam* as to the laws that God has decreed to His people. . . . [The Prophet] has not exempted any of his people from any of his decrees, and he did not permit them anything that was forbidden in *dar al-harb*. What we are saying is consistent with the Qur'an and Sunna, and it is what rational people can understand and agree on. What is allowed in *bilad al-Islam*, the lands of Islam, is allowed in *bilad al-kufr*, the lands of non-Muslims, and what is forbidden in *bilad al-Islam* is also forbidden in *dar al-kufr*, the abode of non-Muslims. So whoever commits an infraction is subject to the punishment that God has decreed and [his presence in] *bilad al-kufr* does not exempt him from anything.[27]

Jurists from these legal schools had argued that if a Muslim violates Islamic law in non-Muslim lands, that Muslim is subject to punishment upon returning to the abode of Islam. In other words, the abode of Islam has extraterritorial jurisdiction to punish violations of Islamic law if the violator is Muslim and if the violator returns to Muslim territory. The Shafi'i jurist al-Shirazi (d. 1414–15) stated, "Because the prohibitions are the same in both territories, there is no reason for the penalties to be different in any sense."[28] The Shafi'i jurist al-Mawardi argues that God's commands as to murder, adultery, theft, or fraud are equal to His commands as to prayer and fasting. If one argues that there is no jurisdiction to punish Islamic criminal infractions committed outside the domain of Islam this is an implicit admission that the Islamic laws pertaining to worship, such as fasting and praying, are not binding upon Muslims in non-Muslim territory either. This implication, al-Mawardi argues, must be avoided.[29]

The position of these legal schools poses a serious problem for the debate on residence in non-Muslim territory. If Muslims residing in non-Muslim territory are bound to apply Islamic law in all its details then their residence is a legal impossibility. In other words, if Muslims are supposed to apply Islamic law in all its particulars the argument permitting Muslims residence in non-Muslim territory becomes meaningless. This does not pose a problem to the majority of Maliki jurists. As stated earlier, they opposed residence in non-Muslim territory and mandated migration in any case. But the Shafi'i, Hanbali and Shi'i jurists did permit such residence, and the question then becomes how to get around this apparent inconsistency.

The argument in favor of the universal applicability of Islamic law was always made in the context of a polemic refutation of the Hanafi position that Muslims residing in non-Muslim territory may deal in *riba* (usury or interest). The majority of Muslim jurists rejected that, arguing the universality of Islamic law. But non-Hanafi jurists did not argue that Islamic law is to be enforced by Muslims wherever they reside. Rather, these jurists argued that Islamic law has universal jurisdiction. The distinction is subtle but important. A Muslim who commits a criminal infraction is liable in an Islamic court upon returning to a Muslim jurisdiction; it is irrelevant where the infraction was committed. But that does not mean that an Islamic state has the ability to enforce Islamic laws in non-Muslim territory nor that Muslims residing in non-Muslim territory are bound to enforce Islamic law in its totality.

It is unclear how much of Islamic law needs to be implemented by a Muslim minority in order for its residence to be considered legal. In other words, when Muslim jurists argued that Muslims may reside in a non-Muslim territory that permits them the freedom to practice Islam, what exactly did that mean? Muslim jurists used vague expressions such as *iqamat amr al-din* (establish the affairs of religion), *izhar al-din* (manifest one's religion), and *al-qiyam bi wajibat al-Islam* (discharge one's religious obligations) to describe how much religious freedom needs to exist before the residence of a Muslim in non-Muslim lands would be considered legal. These expressions seem to relegate all determinations of the legality of a residence to a case-by-case basis. How much religious practice is sufficient before the residence of a Muslim minority can be considered legal will depend on the specific circumstances and each case is bound to turn on its facts.

Rashid Rida had advised the Muslims of Bosnia that they were the best judges of their own affairs. Perhaps a similar attitude lay behind the obscurity of Muslim jurists on this point: they were intentionally vague as to how much of Islamic law needed to be practiced before the residence of Muslim minorities could be considered legal because it was impractical to articulate strict and specific standards on the point. When Shafi'i jurists were presented with actual cases in which a Muslim minority was able to practice certain aspects of religion but unable faithfully to discharge other obligations, these jurists still insisted that migration from the non-Muslim territory in which the minority resided was not necessary. In one such case the Muslims of Malibar informed the Shafi'i jurist Ibn Hajar al-Haytami (d. 1566–67) that they were able to pray and fast, but unable to offer protection to Christians who converted to Islam. If they sheltered Christian converts, oppressive measures would surely follow. The question was, should they offer shelter to converts and suffer the consequence, which was likely to be expulsion from their homes? Ibn Hajar responded that, under the circumstances, they were not obligated to offer shelter and should continue to reside in Malibar.[30] One of the most fundamental moral obligations of a Muslim is that of assisting and protecting other Muslims. The Prophet is reported to have said, "A Muslim is the brother of a Muslim; he does not wrong him, nor does he surrender him to his enemy. He who relieves the need of a Muslim will find that God will relieve one of his needs. . . . "[31] Yet, the public interest of the Muslim minority in Malibar required an exception to this moral obligation, and such an exception could not be obtained without considering the specific circumstances of that particular minority.

Rida relies heavily on the notion of public interest in attempting to delineate the obligations of Muslims residing in non-Muslim territory. We noted earlier that Rida's discourse is not without precedent in Islamic legal discourse. In fact, under the heading of "the spread of corruption" (*'umum al-fasad*), Muslim jurists often discussed a situation where it becomes impossible for a Muslim in a certain territory (Muslim or non-Muslim) to observe the dictates of Islamic law without suffering material harm. In other words, the laws or practices in the territory in which the Muslim resides are sufficiently contradictory to Islamic law that if one would insist on observing Islamic legal injunctions, this would inevitably lead to material harm. The example often given by the jurists is that of a Muslim who wishes to purchase a house without engaging in Islamically prohibited financial dealings. That Muslim is confronted with a choice: purchase the house and violate Islamic law or respect Islamic law, not purchase the house, and be forced to rely on rentals or the like. The response given by Muslim jurists to this situation is not clear-cut. It depends on whether not owning a house is bound to render Muslims powerless and dependent. As in many other cases, Muslim jurists delineated the principles, but left their application to be worked out on a case-by-case basis. For example, the jurist Abu Bakr al-Kindi (d. 1162) argues Muslims residing in un-Islamic territories (meaning either non-Muslim or corrupt Muslim territory) may plant and farm even if they have to pay unjust taxes. They may also seek employment with non-Muslims in order to avoid poverty and need. A Muslim may engage in these acts even if this involves withstanding some oppression and indignity. Al-Kindi, however, does not explain how much oppression and indignity oversteps the bounds of legality and necessitates migration.[32]

There is a further dimension to the argument. The Qur'an repeatedly commands Muslims to keep their promises and uphold their covenants.[33] Muslim jurists had assumed that a Muslim entering or residing in non-Muslim territory would necessarily do so only under a promise of safe conduct (*aman*). Under this agreement the non-Muslim state promises to protect the Muslim resident and the Muslim resident promises to obey the commands of the host state and refrain from acts harmful to it. All Muslim jurists agree that the requirement of compliance with the terms of the safe-conduct agreement is strict. If a Muslim does not wish to abide by the terms of the agreement then he or she may not enter or reside in the non-Muslim territory in the first place. If there is no explicit agreement of safe conduct then Islamic law implies that such an agreement is inherent in the very permission granted to enter or reside in the territory. In addition to the terms that might be specified in a safe-conduct agreement, Islamic law implies certain terms by law, which include prohibitions against treachery, deceit, fraud, and theft; the Muslims also may not violate the honor or usurp the property of non-Muslims. A Muslim must faithfully discharge all contractual obligations and repay all debts. It is a sin to violate any of these provisions. Most jurists also agree that the Islamic state has the power to prosecute a Muslim for violating the implicit or explicit terms of an aman. So, for example, if a Muslim has injured a non-Muslim or refused to repay a debt and escaped to Muslim territory, the Muslim state can obtain compensation for the victims and send the money to the non-Muslim state.

The Hanafi school agrees that a Muslim commits a sin by violating the terms of aman, but denies that a Muslim state has jurisdiction to prosecute or enforce the terms of an aman agreement because the infraction occurred outside the territorial domains of an Islamic state, and the state has no jurisdiction there. If a Muslim obtains the aman while still in Muslim territory, however, or obtains the aman through official avenues then, as far as the law is concerned, this aman was obtained through the authority of the Muslim state, the Muslim state is then a party to it as a surety or as a guarantor. In this situation, the Hanafis argue, the Muslim state does have jurisdiction to prosecute or compel compliance with the conditions of the aman.[34]

Once again, Muslim jurists explicate the general principles that should guide Muslims when residing in non-Muslim territory, but do not resolve the tensions that arise in practice. They do not, for example, explain when the terms of a safe conduct become sufficiently inconsistent with Islamic obligations to preclude residence in a non-Muslim territory. Nor do Muslim jurists explicate the proper equilibrium between the need to manifest one's religion in non-Muslim territory and the command to abide by the terms of the agreement of safe conduct.

The failure of Muslim jurists to prescribe detailed and specific rules for governing the conduct of Muslims in non-Muslim territory is neither surprising nor unusual. Islamic juridical discourse on Muslim minorities responded to and interacted with the historical realities confronting the Muslims at particular times. From the discourse of Muslim jurists responding to the Christian and Mongol invasions in the sixth/twelfth and seventh/thirteenth centuries to the discourse of Rida responding to a colonial situation, Muslim jurists reconciled their Islamic conceptual categories to the political and social demands of the age. Of course, the discourse does not end with Rida. Mahmud Shaltut (d. 1963), the rector of al-Azhar, for example, argued that migration in the contemporary age primarily means spiritual migration. It is the migration of souls and hearts in support of Muslims resisting oppression around the world. Shaltut does not question whether or not Muslims may reside in non-Muslim territory. In Shaltut's view the real issue addressed by the Qur'anic verse on migration is resistence to oppression, whether actively or spiritually.[35] Again, Shaltut's categorization is not without precedent; it developed from and builds on an already existing discourse in Islamic history. Like jurists before him, Shaltut employs terms and concepts already existing in the Islamic heritage while reconstructing and recasting the Islamic legal discourse.

This process of reconstructing and recasting the Islamic legal discourse on Muslim minorities has not been the exclusive business of Muslims. Several Orientalist scholars, guided by their own reconstructions of Islamic history, have joined the discussion. These scholars have argued that from its very beginning Islam and the state were inseparable. The state's primary function is to implement Islamic law, and therefore the legitimacy of the state is entirely dependent on its religious role. But even more, Islamic law and the religion of Islam is one and the same. Islamic law defines the proper religious life for a Muslim, and consequently a religious Muslim must live under the rule of Islamic law. This conception, it is argued, emerged at the time of the Prophet of Islam and has dominated Muslim thinking ever since. Therefore, Raphael Israeli argues, "Either Islamic law and institutions are given full expression and dominate state life or, failing that, if the state is non-Islamic, Muslims should try to reverse the situation or leave."[36] The clear implication of this argument is that life in a non-Muslim state presents the religious Muslim with an irresolvable contradiction. Wherever a Muslim resides, his or her first allegiance is to Islamic law, and residence in a non-Muslim territory is perceived as a necessary but temporary evil. This is particularly the case when a religious Muslim is forced to reside in a Western secular democracy.[37]

A report issued by the House Republican Research Committee's Task Force on Terrorisms and Unconventional Warfare stated the following:

> Islam is a communal way of life, and the vast majority of emigrants
> and their European-born children live together isolated from, and

hostile to, the society around them. The Muslim communities demand to be allowed to retain *all aspects of Islam* including laws unacceptable in the West . . . and argue for making Islamic law superior to the civil law of the land. For Muslims, the mere acceptance of the Western law of the land means a contradiction of Islam's tenet that the *Sharia* is the world's supreme law [emphasis in the original].[38]

This argument ignores the complexity of the Muslim historical experience and present sociological reality. One suspects that it was constructed largely from assumptions about the doctrinal sources of Islam. To the extent that it is in fact a doctrinal argument, it presents an essentialist view of the Islamic juridical discourse on Muslim minorities, which provides elements to be considered, not a law to be applied or even clear theoretical postulates to be dutifully executed. What emerges from the Islamic discourse on Muslim minorities are several competing and, at times, conflicting arguments for consideration. The first is the necessity of observing Islamic morality and escaping oppression. The Qur'an commands those who are oppressed to resist by migrating to more just lands and the Qur'an (5:44, 49) commands believers to govern themselves by what God has decreed. The second element is the natural desire of a devout Muslim to show deference and respect to Islamic legal injunctions and rules. Muslims cannot reside in an area that denies them the right to practice their religion or discharge their Islamic obligations. But what if the area in which a Muslim is free to pray and fast is oppressive and unjust in every other regard? What if a Muslim is oppressed in the very territory that claims to be the abode of Islam and claims to apply Islamic law?

The third element is that an integral part of Islamic morality is that people be able to serve their interests and escape suffering. The preservation of the mundane interests of Muslims is not a regrettable compromise to be indulged in as a necessary evil. As Rida had argued, it is very much an integral part of the Islamic moral vision. As the Qur'an (2:185) states: "God wishes ease and not hardship for you." The question then becomes: What happens if Muslims residing in non-Muslim lands can observe certain Islamic laws only at great personal cost?

Added to these three considerations is the moral requirement that Muslims abide by their promises. If Muslims enter or reside in a territory, they must abide by its express terms of residence. Even more, Islamic morality requires a promise to refrain from harming the host state and to observe the commands of the host state. But competing with this injunction is the well-established Islamic principle that no one may obey a human being if it involves disobeying God.

What is the proper balance to be struck between the command to escape oppression, uphold Islamic law, serve the public and individual interest of Muslims, and observe implicit and express promises made to a non-Muslim state? Striking the proper balance between competing considerations is nothing unusual; it is at the very heart of any rich and sophisticated legal discourse and the Islamic legal discourse on Muslim minorities is both. The balance cannot be struck in an abstract ahistorical context, and it cannot be struck by the jurists of one historical epoch and set in stone for all ages to come. Even more, the balance is not represented or encompassed by the absolutist visions of some Orientalist writers. A balance reached by Muslims in one historical period, in a specific locality, only informs the choices of future participants. This balance is being struck time and again by Muslim minorities around the world today.

Notes

Author's note: I am grateful to my wife Grace Song who read several drafts of this chapter and provided many helpful suggestions.

1. Rashid Rida, *al-Fatawa* (Beirut: Dar al-Kitab al-Jadid, 1970), 2: 778.
2. Ibid.
3. Ibid. p. 775.
4. Ibid. pp. 776–77.
5. For further information on this juristic discourse, see Khaled Abou El Fadl, "Islamic Law and Muslim Minorities: The Juristic Discourse on Muslim Minorities from the Second/Eighth to the Eleventh/Seventeenth Centuries," *Islamic Law and Society 1*, no. 2 (1994): 140–87; Khaled Abou El Fadl, "Legal Debates on Muslim Minorities: Between Rejection and Accommodation," *Journal of Religious Ethics* 22, no. 1 (1994): 127–62.
6. Syed Z. Abedin and Saleha M. Abedin, "Muslim Minorities in Non-Muslim Societies," *Oxford Encylopaedia of the Modern Islamic World* (Oxford: Oxford University Press, 1994), 3:112.
7. Some scholars insist that only in the modern age have Muslims voluntarily migrated to non-Muslim lands and that this situation is very different from any previous historical condition; see Bernard Lewis, *Islam and the West* (Oxford: Oxford University Press, 1993), p. 56. Whether Lewis's assertion is accurate or not, I believe that this is a distinction without a difference.
8. As is evidenced by the tragic migration of Indian Muslims to Afghanistan in 1920, see Gail Minault, *The Khilafat Movement* (New York: Columbia University Press, 1982).
9. Rida, *al-Fatawa*, 2: 777.
10. Translation is from Ahmed Ali, *Al-Qur'an* (Princeton: Princeton University Press, 1988). Slight changes have been made to reflect my understanding of the original.
11. Abou El Fadl, "Islamic Law and Muslim Minorities," pp. 143–47.
12. Abu Abd Allah al-Shafi'i, *al-Umm*, ed. Muhammad al-Najjar (Beirut: Dar al-Ma'rifa, n.d.), 4: 161; Muhammad al-Hurr al-'Amili, *Wasa'il al-Shi'a*, ed. Ahmad al-Rabbani al-Shirazi (Beirut: Dar Ihya al-Turath al-'Arabi, n.d.), 11:75–77.
13. Abu al-Walid Ibn Rushd, *al-Muqaddimat al-Mumahhidat*, ed. Muhammad Huji (Beirut: Dar al-Gharb al-Islami, 1988), vol. 2:151–54; Abu al-Walid Ibn Rushd, *al-Bayan wa'l Tahsil*, ed. Muhammad Huji, (Beirut: Dar al-Gharb al-Islami, 1988), 4:170–71.
14. Ahmad al-Wansharisi, *al-Mi'yar*, ed. Muhammad Hajj (Beirut: Dar al-Gharb al-Islami, 1981), 2: 121–24, 130–32, 140–41.
15. See Abou El Fadl, "Islamic Law and Muslim Minorities," pp. 149–56.

16. The development and details of these juridical positions are discussed in ibid., pp. 157–64.

17. Abu al-Hasan al-Ash'ari, *Maqalat al-Islamiyyin*, ed. Muhammad 'Abd al-Hamid (Beirut: al-Maktaba al-'Asriyya, 1990), 2:154–55.

18. See Abu Mansur al-Baghdadi, *Kitab Usul al-Din* (Beirut: Dar al-Hilal, 1980), p. 270; Abou El Fadl, "Islamic Law and Muslim Minorities," p. 161.

19. See ibid., pp. 153, 163.

20. See Rudolph Peters, *Islam and Colonialism: The Doctrine of Jihad in Modern History* (The Hague: Mouton, 1979).

21. See Albert Hourani, *Arabic Thought in the Liberal Age, 1798–1939* (Cambridge: Cambridge University Press, 1962; rpt. 1993) p. 240. On the migration of Muslims from Bosnia to Ottoman territory, see Noel Malcolm, *Bosnia: A Short History* (New York: New York University Press, 1994), pp. 139–40.

22. Rida, *al-Fatawa*, 5:1918.

23. Ibid. and see 6: 2302–4; 4: 1520–22; 1: 231–36, 372–73.

24. Ibid., 5: 1917–21.

25. Ibid., 1: 231–136; Rida applies the same analysis to Muslims in China; ibid., 6: 2302–4; as to the question of depositing money in banks, see ibid., 4: 1520–22.

26. See Abou El Fadl, "Islamic Law and Muslim Minorities," pp. 173–74.

27. Al-Shafi'i, *al-Umm*, 7: 354–55.

28. Abu Ishaq al-Shirazi, *al-Muhadhdhab* (Cairo: Mustafa al-Babi al-Halabi, 1971), 2: 310.

29. Al-Mawardi, *Kitab Qital Ahl al-Baghy min al-Hawi al-Kabir*, ed. Ibrahim Sandaqji (Cairo: Matba'at al-Madani, 1987), pp. 214–16.

30. Ibn Hajar al-Haytami, *al-Fatawa al-Kubra al-Fiqhiyya* (Beirut: Dar al-Kutub al-'Ilmiyya, n.d.), 4: 52–53, and see Abou El Fadl, *Islamic Law and Muslim Minorities*, pp. 158–61.

31. Reported in Muhyyi al-Din al-Nawawi, *Riyad al-Salihin* (Beirut: Dar al-Khir, 1993), p. 102.

32. Abu Bakr al-Kindi al-Sammadi al-Nazawi, *al-Musannaf* (Oman: Wazarat al-Turath al-Qawmi, 1983), 10: 273; Abu al-Ma'ali al-Juwayni (Imam al-Haramayn), *Ghiyath al-Umam*, ed. 'Abd al-'Asim al-Dib (Cairo: al-Maktabat al-Kubra, 1401), pp. 475–522; Abu Hamid al-Ghazali, *Shifa'al-Ghalil*, ed. Hamad al-Kabis (Baghdad: Matab'at al-Irshad, 1971), pp. 245–46.

33. For example, Qur'an 17:34; 2:177; 9:4; 23:8.

34. See Abou El Fadl, "Islamic Law and Muslim Minorities," pp. 175–78.

35. Mahmud Shaltut, *al-Fatawa* (Cairo: Dar Shuruq, 1980), pp. 432–34.

36. Raphael Israeli, "Muslim Minorities under Non-Islamic Rule," *Current History* 78, no. 456 (April 1980): 159–60, quoted in Daniel Pipes, *In the Path of God* (New York: Basic Books, 1983), p. 68, also see p. 46; on Islam and the state, see Bernard Lewis, "The Return of Islam" in *Religion and Politics in the Middle East*, ed. Michael Curtis, (Boulder, CO: Westview Press, 1981), p. 11.

37. See Daniel Pipes, "The Muslims are Coming," *National Review* 42, no. 22 (November 19, 1990): 28–31, and ibid., "Fundamental Questions about Muslims," *Wall Street Journal* 30 October, 1992.

38. House Republican Research Committee, "Iran's European Springboard?" unpublished report by the Task Force on Terrorism and Unconventional Warfare, 1 September, 1992, p. 11.

3

The Fiqh Councilor
in North America

YUSUF TALAL DELORENZO

A *fatwa* is generally understood to be an answer that is given by a scholar, or mufti, to a question on an issue of religious significance, or on a point of religious law. The first fatwa was issued by the Prophet (upon him be peace), and the practice was followed later by his companions and the jurists of succeeding generations. A fatwa differs from the ruling of a *qadi* (judge) in that the fatwa ruling is essentially an interpretive one, whereas the qadi's ruling becomes a binding legal judgment. Owing to its interpretative nature, then, the institution of fatwa is closely linked to *ijtihad* (legal interpretation), though many *fatawa* (plural of fatwa) are based on *naql* (precedent) or the ijtihad of others. However, when resort is had to ijtihad for the production of a fatwa, it becomes an effective instrument for addressing innovation and change in society, and thus an essential part of the dynamics that guarantee the continued relevancy of the Shari'a to Muslims of all times and in all places. Finally, as a fatwa is usually not binding, the word *mufti* is often translated as jurisconsult.

The Fiqh Councilor

In the contemporary North American context, the fiqh councilor may be any one of several different entities. Where the term councilor is used to mean mufti, the fiqh councilor may be either an individual councilor, if his or her fiqh deliberations are undertaken without the help of others, or a council member, if his or her fiqh deliberations are undertaken in concert with other fiqh councilors. The other sort of fiqh "councilor" is not a councilor at all, but a counselor, and counseling is most often a function undertaken by a local imam, respected elder, or director of an Islamic center,[1] unless, of course, we are speaking of legal counsel, in which case the fiqh "counselor" would be a member of the bar. Obviously, such a play on words is only suggestive of comparative functions. However, the assumption on the part of many people is that a fiqh councilor must also be a fiqh counselor, and that, in terms of the classical definition of a mufti, that clearly is not the case.[2] (It might, however, apply to the definition of a qadi.[3]) But our concern here is with North America and the role, both actual and ideal, of the American fiqh councilor, or mufti. Suffice it to say by way of definition that Islamic law and American civil law represent the framework within which the American fiqh councilor operates.

While it might be possible to discuss this homonym and the issues it raises at length, it will be more beneficial to consider what characterizes an American mufti. In all candor, it may have been proper twenty years ago to describe an American mufti as a bearded and robed shaykh with a green card. While this description may still hold true for some of the imams and teachers at Islamic schools in the United States and Canada, the idea seems to have taken hold among American Muslims that the institution of *istifta'* or fiqh consultation is one that is best supported by those who fully understand and appreciate the special characteristics of the North American Muslim community and the circumstances in which it strives to develop.[4]

As the community grows to include more ethnically and culturally diverse elements, the phenomenon of the "imported" mufti becomes more problematic. Immigrant and indigenous American Muslims of whatever ethnic or cultural background have often been disappointed by the lack of appreciation for local conditions and circumstances on the part of such "imported" muftis.[5] Likewise, community leaders and members alike have come to realize that the legal responsum or fatawa obtained, so to speak, through the mail from muftis in Muslim-majority countries often fail to address the crux of the issues presented to them for consideration. Quite often, the responses of foreign muftis raise more problems than they solve.[6] This is to be expected, for unless there is a clear understanding of the context of a legal question, there is little likelihood that the solution offered will be an adequate one.

At this juncture, it might be well to turn for a moment to reflect on the nature of Islamic law within the context of the universality of Islam's message. While the notion of the validity of Islam in all times and places is one that is familiar to modern Muslims, it has become more like a catchall, with its correlative, "Islam is the answer," and thus more repeated for effect than actually understood. It is possible to generalize that Muslims over the centuries have only rarely considered the ramifications of Islam's universal validity. Rather, for the most part, Muslims have rested comfortably with notions of a particularized historical and geographical Islam, a corollary of which was the assumption that the legal codes, maxims, and thought of the earliest periods, *khayr al-qurun*, remain applicable today in the same ways as they were back then. Taken to its logical conclusion, such thinking would lead to echoing the catchall that Islam is for all times and places with the statement that the fiqh of Abu Hanifa is likewise for all times and places; or to the declaration that Hanbali, or *salafi* fiqh is the answer![7] Rather, the imperative of the Shari'a is that Muslims continue to review and revise the law in keeping with the dictates of their changing circumstances. Given the incredible changes that have taken place this century in the way people live their lives, a great deal of review is clearly required.

In the past twenty years, the North American Muslim community has turned increasingly to local experts for solutions to their fiqh-related problems. The experts consulted have not always had the sort of fiqh quali fications traditionally required of muftis, but their understanding of local conditions, coupled with backgrounds in Arabic or Islamic studies, have placed them in the position of being called upon to give opinions on sensitive issues. With the rise in interest in Islamic studies in American academia, however, a number of Muslim scholars with fiqh credentials have come to American universities for graduate studies, postgraduate work, or to fill teaching posts in new or expanding departments. At the same time, American Muslims, especially converts and second-generation converts (the children of converts), have sought in increasing numbers to obtain advanced fiqh education abroad at Islamic universities[8] and traditional Islamic institutions.[9]

All of these developments have made it possible for the community to draw upon a wider range of fiqh expertise and experience. Even so, it is clear that as the community grows and branches out in North American society, so also will its requirements for considered fiqh advice expand. Moreover, these requirements have already outstripped the traditional schools of, and approaches to, fiqh. The need, then, is clear. The community must develop its own institutions for understanding and interpreting Islam at the most basic levels (in the form of "Sunday schools" for children), at the formal elementary and secondary levels (in the form of private schools and academies), and at the graduate and postgraduate levels, as well. In particular, there is a real need for specialized fiqh studies which combine mastery of the classical disciplines (Arabic, rhetoric, logic, *tafsir*, recitation, hadith, fiqh, *usul*, *kalam*, etc.) with an understanding of the social sciences, the humanities, and the complexities of the human condition in the modern world.

Origins of the Fiqh Council of North America

In recent years, national organizations like the Islamic Society of North America, the Islamic Circle of North America, and, most recently, the Muslim community under the leadership of Warith al-Din Muhammad, have perceived a need to form committees of scholars to advise on matters related to fiqh and the community. Out of one such committee grew the Fiqh Council of North America, an independent body of fiqh councilors. From this perspective, and in light of the experience gained over the past six years of association with the Fiqh Council of North America, I will speak in what follows of the role of the fiqh councilor, as a scholar of fiqh working in concert with other such experts in the context of contemporary North American society.

The classical jurists of Islam were almost unanimously agreed on the point that only a mujtahid is qualified to issue a fatwa.[10] They went on to explain that a mujtahid may be either restricted or unrestricted in terms of the scope of his legal considerations. While admitting that all expertise has its limits, the classical jurists held that the unrestricted mujtahid needs to be familiar with the entire range of legal issues, while the restricted mujtahid needs only to have knowledge of the issues which pertain to his field of specialization.[11] In modern times, given the way that human knowledge and interests have literally exploded in every direction, it is less than realistic to suppose that anyone, however gifted, could acquire the sort of knowledge necessary to make him or her an unrestricted mujtahid. By way of example, fiqh scholars today are discovering that Islamic banking is becoming such a vast and complex field that in the future it will require the expertise of several specialized fiqh scholars, each specialty so demanding that no single *faqih* (legal scholar) could possibly be expected to excel in more than one.[12]

It is in the light of the classical definition and understanding of a mujtahid, including the formal conditions or *shurut*, coupled with modern realities, that the idea of fiqh scholars working together as a council has taken on new life. In fact, this is not a new idea or phenomenon. Rather, it seems to be an idea that was forgotten.[13] Within the context of a council in which varying kinds of expertise may be pooled, so to speak, the modern faqih may find both credibility and accreditation. Clearly, all of these elements are essential to the working of Islamic law as a social force. This is particularly true when we consider the process of istifta' as one in which consultation takes place between qualified experts on religious law and people for whom adherence to that law is an essential part of their faith.

The Fiqh Council of North America was organized to answer the increasing need on the part of the growing Muslim community in North America for considered Shari‘a-based advice and counsel. The council originated as the Fiqh Committee of the Muslim Student Association in the 1970s, and was charged primarily with the task of setting the dates for the lunar months of Ramadan and Shawwal, the dates which determine when Muslims are to begin and end their month of fasting. Membership on the committee at that time was limited, as was the scope of the issues it dealt with. Moreover, no formal criteria were established for the way it functioned or to ensure the qualifications of its members. When the MSA flowered into the Islamic Society of North America in the early 1980s, the Fiqh Committee followed. Other than the name, however, very little changed. The membership did not increase in any significant way, and the chief function of the council remained the setting of dates for Ramadan and the two 'Id holidays. On 10 March 1988, however, the ISNA Fiqh Committee decided to reorganize as the Fiqh Council of North America. The reason for this move was "to create a larger and more authoritative body of Muslim scholars (ulama) to effectively confront the many legal issues facing Muslims in North America."[14] In the years since then the membership of the council has been increased, statutes dealing with membership, meetings, and procedures have been drafted and approved, and the scope of its activities has expanded considerably.

Today, the council's functioning extends to the needs of individuals and organizations within the community and to those with whom they interact, Muslim and non-Muslim alike. By way of example, over the past year the council has dealt with questions submitted by individual Muslims, by local and national Muslim organizations, by the Departments of Justice and Defense, by non-Muslim trial lawyers, by immigration lawyers, and by journalists with interests as varied as biological engineering and third-world politics.

The Objectives and Practices of the Fiqh Council of North America

In what follows, the role of the fiqh councilor will be defined through the objectives and practices of the Fiqh Council. I will not deal with the matter of *shurut* or qualifications required of individual councilors, as the answer, while well documented in the classical works, is ultimately a subjective one. Suffice it to say here that the most important qualifications, after the obvious academic and linguistic ones, are that the councilors have no political agendas of their own, respect but not be bound by the opinions of the classical imams, and have at least five years of residence in North America. At the macro level, the Fiqh Council aims at participating, through its academic expertise, in the process of facilitating Islamic ways of life[15] in the secular, non-Muslim environment of North America. It intends to do this by providing institutions and individuals with jointly considered legal advice and opinions that are based on the Qur'an and the Sunna. The council's primary objectives, as outlined in its bylaws, are:

1. to consider, from a Shari'a perspective, and offer advice on specific undertakings, transactions, contracts, projects, or proposals, guaranteeing thereby that the dealings of American Muslims fall within the parameters of what is permitted, in the ethical or legal sense, by the Shari'a;
2. to consider issues of relevance to the community and give, from a Shari'a perspective, advice and guidelines for policy, procedure, and practice. Such advice may take the form of position papers, fatawa, research papers, sample forms for legal agreements, or whatever else is deemed effective;

3. to consult, on issues requiring specialized knowledge and experience, with professionals or subject specialists;
4. to establish and maintain working relationships with Shari'a experts worldwide, including muftis, university professors, researchers, Shari'a court justices, and members of national and international fiqh councils and academies;
5. to assist local and national organizations in the resolution of conflicts;
6. to advise in the appointment of arbiters, and review arbitration proceedings and decisions for their consistency with Islamic legal principles;
7. to commission research on relevant Islamic legal issues;[16]
8. to maintain and develop a comprehensive Shari'a library;
9. to anticipate and serve the particular needs of women and of minority groups in the community: youth, prisoners, recent converts, etc.;
10. to develop a fiqh for Muslims living in non-Muslim societies.

The organization of the Fiqh Council centers on questions of procedure and function. Of these, function may be reduced to two major areas: provision of formal fatawa and advice based on the Shari'a of Islam, and the promotion of fiqh scholarship on problems and questions of contemporary significance. The means for accomplishing these may include the circulation of specific questions for the consideration of members, holding regular meetings, publication, commissioning research, consultation with subject specialists and experts, constituting specialized subcommittees, and organizing seminars, conferences, lectures, and training programs. Other means include submission of legal or amicus curiae (friends of the court) briefs to American courts of law on subjects of relevance to Islamic law.

With regard to procedure, the most important points are that the council will consider questions jointly, by applying their varied specializations, experience, and perspectives. It is for this reason that questions must be submitted in writing. Moreover, the council will only consider questions for which no satisfactory answers exist, either for the reason that it is a completely new one, or because the answer posed by the classical scholars seems clearly inapplicable, i.e., that their ijtihad has become outdated. Obviously, then, the council will not consider cases for which clear and unambiguous Shari'a rulings already exist.[17]

The second point of significance in the matter of procedure is that the council will maintain subcommittees of experts in various fields. The task of these subcommittees is to consider questions within the realm of their expertise and advise the council of their findings. For example, the council has worked with a committee of Muslim astronomers for a number of years who have advised and informed the council on subjects relevant to the sighting of the crescent and the beginnings of the lunar months.[18]

Theoretical Considerations

In terms of its philosophy, the council's bylaws state that it will base its decisions on evidence derived from the two most reliable sources of revelation: the Qur'an and the authentic Sunna. In doing so, it will employ the principles and methodologies of *usul al-fiqh* and will consider, where relevant, the various opinions of earlier Muslim jurists. All legal schools will be considered equally as intellectual resources to be drawn from in the process of giving contemporary interpretations to the texts of revelation. In other words, the issue of *madhhab* or affiliation to one legal school of thought or another is one which the council considers valid only in regard to questions of worship or *'ibadat*. Yet, even within that restricted area, new developments have brought about questions that the traditional imams never considered. For example, does possession of a credit card qualify one as having the means to undertake the hajj, even if one is not in possession of the requisite amount in cash?[19]

Among the most important approaches of the council in its treatment of new problems and questions that apply particularly to the Muslim communities of North America is its policy of giving additional consideration, in the light of the higher purposes or *maqasid* of the Shari'a, to the circumstances imposed upon Muslims by the non-Islamic environment that surrounds them. In classical terms these circumstances are called the *ahwal al-mahkum 'alayhi*, and are mentioned only briefly, if at all, in the major works of *usul*. While decisions made by the council are the result of collective scholarship and consideration, members do have the right to write dissenting opinions. As a part of the process of istifta', the *mustafti* (questioner) has the right to accept whichever opinion s/he feels is the more valid. This is partly a function of the questioner's knowing better what his or her particular circumstances or *ahwal* might be.

Let us move on to discuss another matter for the consideration of the fiqh councilor in North America. Since the traditional fiqh of Islam is essentially the fiqh of the historical Muslim state and its Muslim majority, it pays little or no heed to the fiqh of Muslim minorities except in the form of *nawazil* issued at times of crisis, such as during the Mongol invasions, or the Crusades, or in the Moorish period of Andalusian history. The fiqh of these periods, however, was never developed or analyzed, as it was considered to have come about under adversity and therefore fell under the category of legal exception by virtue of necessity. It is therefore essential that the councilor strive to interpret the teachings of Islam in a way that is consistent both with the higher principles of the Shari'a[20] and with the circumstances of Muslims living in predominantly non-Muslim societies. Such fiqh might be known as the fiqh of Muslims in non-Muslim environments, and its applications in today's world are probably without limit. A center for the study of Muslim minorities has been established in Jedda, and recently there have been a few published attempts to look at Muslim minority issues from a fiqh perspective.[21] This is undoubtedly a field that is rich with possibilities for research.[22] Even so, the matter of greater significance to the fiqh councilor is consideration of the principles involved in dealing with fiqh and fiqh-related issues from this particular perspective. Certainly, the traditional works of usul, if they mention the subject at all, mention it only in relation to other matters.

Something of the scope of the task before the fiqh councilor can be garnered from the following passage from an article by the political scientist B. A. Roberson entitled "Islam and Europe: An Enigma or a Myth?":

> Today, Islamic law is being asked to address a full range of modern problems and issues. Nor is Islam unchanging. This is the result of the continual evolution of diverse interpretations, many having emerged long after the era of Muhammad. A resulting characteristic of Islam has been to present a strong sense of the unity of core ideas while at the same time giving rise to intermittent fragmentation via new or revised interpretations. What is not always acknowledged in current analysis is the political, social, and economic conditions in the past and present that have contributed not only to Islam's unifying and sometimes fragmentary effect, but also to its content.[23]

In sum, then, the American fiqh councilor is as much a pioneer on this continent as a guide to the future of Islam. As the Muslim community in North America continues its expansion, the issues that confront it will continue to be the focus of concern on the part of Muslim social scientists and fiqh specialists alike. The success of the fiqh side of that undertaking will depend in part on some of the issues discussed here. But for the entire undertaking to meet with success, it will be necessary that Muslim legal professionals, social scientists, community leaders, and fiqh experts engage in meaningful discourse at several different levels, and by means of a terminological apparatus with which to talk about issues of fiqh and usul in plain English.[24]

To my way of thinking, the best possible forum for such an exercise is the fiqh council, in the generic sense, though I would certainly hope that the Fiqh Council of North America would be the body to set such a discourse in motion. Eventually, however, the clear need is for the process to lead to the establishment of institutions of higher learning in which ways and competencies may be developed for the renewed viability of fiqh, particularly in the North American context.

APPENDIX

A Selection of Representative *Fatawa*

In the following excerpts from fatawa written in response to actual questions addressed to the Fiqh Council, some of the points brought up are open

to debate and do not necessarily represent the opinion of all the Fiqh Council members. The examples are, however, a fairly representative selection
of both the kind of questions that are asked and of council responses. Some
responses are very straightforward and to the point; others deal with issues
that underlie the actual question(s). Some of the examples, like the ones
dealing with dower, are indicative of how fiqh and society are subject to
change.

I. Marriage, Dower, and a Woman's Right to Seek Compensation

First example: In reference to your questions about your marital status, your
right to your dower, your right to seek compensation from your ex-husband,
and your right to custody of your son, the Islamic legal perspective on each
issue is as follows:

Insofar as your marriage is concerned, the Fiqh Council of North America
has determined that no Muslim marriage may be terminated[25] unless it is
terminated through the court system of the state in which the Muslim is
resident. This is an issue which has been discussed extensively by the Fiqh
Council and, owing to the many ways in which the traditional Islamic formula for divorce has been abused by Muslims (and for many other reasons),
the Council has given its opinion that divorce by Muslims living in the United
States will not be recognized unless the divorce is recognized by the state.
In this way the rights of all concerned, husbands, wives, children, and other
relatives, may be protected; including religious rights, conjugal rights, property rights, custody rights, etc.

Having said that, however, there is the question of whether or not an Islamic pronouncement of divorce, as described in the fatwa from al-Azhar,[26]
constitutes legal grounds for divorce. This issue, from an Islamic legal perspective, is very clear. This is the traditional, religious formula for divorce
and, morally, no Muslim woman could resume normal marital relations with
a man who had made such a pronouncement to her. Ethically, no court
should require her to do so. If a state recognizes "irreconcilable differences"
as grounds for divorce, then the pronouncement of a religious form of divorce such as the one described, should certainly qualify as sufficient and
legal grounds.

Secondly, in regard to your dower, you are entitled to all of it. At the time
of your marriage, and in accordance with Islamic law and practice, you were
promised a dower for a specific amount to be paid in a specific manner. When
you entered into the marriage contract that amount became your right. When
you are divorced, the entire amount, if it has not already been paid, is to be
paid to you. If partial payment has been made, then you are to receive the
remaining amount. Your marriage was a contract, and the terms of that contract stipulated the payment of a dower (variously termed *sadaq* or *mahr*).

In all likelihood, there is even a clause in your marriage contract which gives, in writing, the details of the dower to be paid.

The third issue is the matter of whether or not you have the right, from an Islamic legal perspective, to seek compensation from your husband, either in the form of alimony, or maintenance, or child support, or whatever. In this matter, the higher principles of Islamic justice, principles dealing with the welfare of the individual, may be cited as overruling the limited rulings of past times. The concern of Islamic law, before all else, is justice; and not the opinions of jurists who lived under circumstances very different from our own. Thus, if the dower was considered sufficient for the future of a divorced woman under a social system in which the extended family provided every manner of social service, including counseling, moral support, shelter, and so on, it cannot be viewed as sufficient in twentieth century American society. In this country, the so-called nuclear family is more often dysfunctional, or simply unable to support more than itself; and the existence of an extended family is so rare as to be of no consequence in legal considerations. This being the case, many women are quite literally dependent on their husbands for all of their needs, and for those of their children. Then, if a Muslim divorces his wife, he must be held responsible for her, and her children's, welfare. If the woman remarries, then he may be absolved of responsibility for her. But, in regard to his children, he will remain responsible until they have become adults and are able to provide for themselves. This is the meaning of the Qur'anic verse at 4:34: Men have responsibilities to women (men are protectors and maintainers of women).

Finally, it is Allah who knows best.

Second example:

1. Should the court grant Ms. _____ her sadaq?

Answer:

Yes, the court should grant Ms. _____ her sadaq.

At the time of her marriage, and in accordance with Islamic law and practice, Ms. _____ was promised a sadaq for a specific amount to be paid in a specific manner. When she entered into the marriage contract with her husband, the sadaq became Ms. _____'s right. Then, at the time of her divorce, her husband was required to pay her in accordance with the terms agreed upon in the marriage contract. As one dollar had already been paid as an advance, Ms. _____'s husband is responsible for paying the deferred portion of the sadaq, i.e., the full sadaq minus one dollar.

The Qur'anic teaching on this matter is that every bride is entitled to receive a sadaq from her husband. With very few exceptions, the sadaq is to be paid in full either at the time of marriage, or when divorce takes place. So substantial is this obligation that if the husband should die before paying the sadaq, the responsibility for payment will pass on to his estate or to his heirs.

This circumstance in this case should not be confused with *khula'* or the procedure by means of which a wife may seek divorce from her husband in exchange for monetary consideration, which generally takes the form of her returning her sadaq or, if she has not taken possession of it, of her canceling the husband's obligation to pay it. Clearly, Ms. _____ and her husband did not enter into such an understanding.

Nor should the doubt arise that the husband's obligation to pay sadaq in full or in part[27] will be canceled for the reason that the two marriage partners have been separated at the insistence of the wife, or because of her. The example given by the classical jurists is when the judge rules to annul or dissolve the marriage between the two parties on the basis of the wife's request [based on] the presence of a defect or an incapacity in her husband such as would render him incapable of giving her children.[28] Since Ms. _____ herself initiated divorce proceedings in this case, the doubt might arise that the husband's obligation to pay sadaq has been canceled, either completely or partially. Yet, it is clear to me that the obligation remains and, as there is open admission on the part of both partners that the marriage was consummated, the obligation remains in full, i.e. the husband is still obligated to pay the entire sadaq (minus the one dollar paid as an advance at the time of the marriage).

In deliberating over this question, the matter to be taken into consideration is whether in fact the two marriage partners were separated at the insistence of the wife, or because of her, or whether there were other circumstances involved. The example given by the classical jurists is of a woman who discovers that her husband has a physical defect which renders him incapable of giving her children, and then seeks dissolution of the marriage through a judge. In such an instance, the wife is not herself threatened with any sort of harm or subject to any sort of liability other than that she has a right to children and her husband is incapable of meeting his obligation in that regard. As her right is a legitimate one, the judge will dissolve their union but, at the same time, the husband's obligation to pay the sadaq will be cancelled. If intercourse has taken place, then in consideration of the wife's having made herself available to him, the husband will be obligated to pay her half of her sadaq.

In the case of Ms. _____, however, the matter is different. While it may be argued that Ms. _____ did seek dissolution of the marriage through the courts, and that she did so on the basis of a defect she discovered in her husband, there are other circumstances in her case which, upon consideration, will be seen to change the nature of the case. In fact, the defect she discovered in her husband was sexually communicated to her. Moreover, the nature of that affliction is such that it constitutes a real threat to any children Ms. _____ might conceive. Furthermore, as a transmittable disease, the affliction effectively rules out the possibility of Ms. _____'s ever remarrying within the community of her culture and religion. For Ms. _____ the choice was between remaining with the man who had thus maimed her and deprived her of the chance of ever having children, or initiating divorce procedures through the courts.

In the example given by the classical jurists, the wife seeks divorce ostensibly for the reason that she may begin life anew with another husband, one capable of giving her a family and thus fulfilling her life. Under those circumstances, when it is understood that the woman will in all probability remarry and receive a full sadaq from her new husband, there is no harm to her if her first husband is not required to pay her a full sadaq or, if intercourse has not taken place, any sadaq at all. In Ms. _____'s case, however, the probability of fulfillment, like that of remarriage, is effectively nil. In order that justice be served in her case, it is essential that the court award her the full amount of the sadaq agreed upon in her Muslim marriage contract.

II. Muslim Marriage Contract and Ceremony

In answer to your questions about the Muslim marriage ceremony, the following may be of benefit . . . and Allah knows best!

A. You are right in assuming that a "non-clergy" Muslim can perform the necessary ceremony. This is because Muslims are intended by Allah to be their own "clergy," and are not to rely on the intervention or intercession of others in matters related to Islam. Another reason for this is that marriage, while certainly a sacred trust between husband and wife, is actually a transaction or 'aqd and any Muslim who is legally competent may undertake it for him or herself (or, if they should so choose, then by means of a *wali*).

B. The exact words of the 'aqd in Arabic are (*qabiltu*) or "I accept." These are the only words that need to be said by the two parties to the contract. Moreover, these need not be said in Arabic. The English equivalent, "I accept," is a perfectly acceptable alternative. As in any contract, the essential ingredients are an offer by one party and acceptance by the other. (If the other party rejects the offer, then obviously there will be no transaction.) This means that the marriage contract may technically (as long as all the other conditions are satisfied) take place directly between the two parties. The way of the Prophet, however, was that a third person undertake to lead a ceremony, and ask each of the two parties (or their representatives), in front of witnesses, if s/he accepts the offer to enter into a contract of marriage.

C. Enclosed you will find the Arabic text of the *khutbah* (sermon) recited by the Prophet, upon him be peace everlasting. You will also find the English translation of the same. The khutbah for marriage is like the khutbah for *jumu'ah* (Friday congregational prayer) in that each contains elements of both *dhikr* and *tadhkir*, where tadhkir follows dhikr in importance. It is for this reason that the Arabic text of the khutbah (which is dhikr) should be recited, even though this is technically not essential, because it contains an element of worship. The English translation (or any translation) is important as the khutbah carries a message (tadhkir) of importance for those listening to it, and especially those entering into the transaction.

III. The Wearing of Dreadlocks

The context in which the hadith related by Muslim on the authority of Ibn Abbas (no. 996 in the Siddiqi translation) was revealed is difficult to know. This, unfortunately, is the case with many hadith. However, we do know that, in matters of dress and appearance in general, the Prophet, upon him be peace, often ordered the Muslims to do other than what the non-believers were doing. Such commandments should be understood as a part of the Prophet's efforts to instill within the growing Muslim community a sense of its own identity, and not merely, as many traditional readings of the texts suggest, out of a sense of opposition to everything the Jews, Christians, and other communities did, said, taught, or practiced. But that is another subject. Anyway, the important thing to note here is that there may well have been circumstances which prompted this particular prohibition. And the Islamic legal principle which may then be applied is that a ruling made under certain circumstances may be changed if the circumstances themselves change. So, in regard to a Muslim's wearing braided hair during *salah* (prayer), the prohibition may have been made under circumstances requiring the Muslims to refute any identity but their own. Where these circumstances do not apply, the prohibition will not apply. Certainly, there is nothing in the manuals of fiqh that describe the performance of salah, often in painstaking detail, about such a prohibition being anything more than *makruh* (discouraged). Nowhere is it described as being among the things that invalidate salah. So, in the modern North American context, where the fashion is so widespread, there is probably no reason to suppose it even makruh. This is one opinion. And Allah knows best.

The last question you asked was how the wearing of braids could be a barometer of one's faith. The answer to this question is that only Allah knows the state of one's faith. As Muslims, we are to deal with one another purely on the basis of our confessed faith, the *shahadah*. Even the Prophet of Allah, upon him be peace, when he undoubtedly knew of the duplicity of the *munafiqin* (hypocrites) in Madinah, dealt with them as he dealt with all Muslims, in the sense that he married them in accordance with the Shariah, buried them in the Muslim graveyard, distributed their estates, and so on. The well-known teaching on the subject is that all those who say the shahadah and turn toward the *qiblah* (direction of prayer) in salah are Muslims . . . so long as they do not come out and deny something that it is an essential part of faith, like the finality of prophethood, the eternal nature of the Qur'an, the oneness of Allah, and so on. Generally speaking, those who concern themselves with trying to read the "barometers" of another's faith, had better look to their own faith first, because the Prophet taught: "A Muslim is his brother's mirror."

Moreover, the notion of community is a very important one to Muslims. As a Muslim living under some very real constraints, it is all the more important for you to be a member of the Muslim community where you live.

In order to grow spiritually it is important that you contribute in a positive way to the welfare of others, and you should begin with those closest to you, the Muslims around you. Think about this. The Prophet, upon him be peace, taught a lot about this subject. He warned Muslims about straying off on their own by giving the example of how a wolf will prey on strays, while those who keep together as a flock will be safe.

And Allah knows best.

IV. Haircuts as a Point of Dispute

The Prophet of Allah, upon him be peace, taught that of all lawful things the one most hated by Allah is divorce. As the family unit is the foundation of all Muslim society, it is the duty of Muslim spouses to strive and sacrifice for the sake of their family. If they find themselves unable to do so on their own, they should take help from their families in sorting out their problems; and if there is no family nearby, then from respected members of the Muslim community. We mention this to you, even though it is evident from your letter that the divorce between you is irrevocable (*talaq ba'in*), because you need to consider how far your situation has degenerated; and to what extent you want each of your five young children to be affected by it. The picture of your situation that emerges from between the lines of your letter is one of a broken marriage and of children caught in between two warring parents. In such a situation, you must remember that the best interests of the children must be given priority. Undoubtedly, this is a point on which both of you agree. Where you differ, however, is in how you interpret what the best interests of your children may be.

It is clear from your letter that you are a serious and committed Muslim for whom the moral and ethical teachings of Islam are of great importance. You also mention that your wife comes from a Muslim family. And, while you describe her as rebellious and threatening, you do not mention any danger of her turning away from Islam. This being the case, let me caution you here that you must not allow Islam to become an issue between you, as this can impact in a very negative way with your children. There is certainly a danger in your situation of the haircut issue being blown out of proportion, and of its becoming a means to involve the children in the conflict between their parents. While you may feel that a proper haircut may be more in keeping with the teachings of Islam, there are many different ways that you may convey this to your boys. To force them to recut their hair, against the wishes of their mother, and then by means of your action to make yourself the target of a child-abuse charge was certainly not the best way of teaching the boys, or the girls, about Islam!

Please consider the following, before thinking to yourself, "But I was right to do so because this is what Islam teaches." In forcing your will on your boys in the name of Islam they might very well (especially when we take their tender and impressionable ages into account) come to a number of faulty conclusions about Islam (conclusions which a secular and oftentimes hostile—toward Islam especially—society will confirm for them time after time, in school, on the street, on the playground, in the homes of friends and neighbors, and, most powerfully, in the media):

A. that Islam is cruel, unfeeling, and puritanical
B. that Islam is authoritarian
C. that Islam empowers men to ignore the wishes of their wives
D. that Islam is somehow in conflict with the law of the land.

Now, in purely legalistic (*fiqh*) terms, when we consider which of the two is less offensive in the eyes of the Shariah (*akhaff al-darrarayn*), it is clear that to allow the hair of two (out of five) children to remain in a questionable, or even in an objectionable state (which is a simple matter of practice) is far to be preferred over matters which may negatively affect the beliefs of all five children. Unfortunately, in our zeal to carry out the letter of the law, we often lose sight of the spirit. This becomes all the more unfortunate when we attempt to see that others carry out the letter of the law. In the case of parents, the issue is often fogged by emotions and the legitimate desire on their part to see that their children grow up as "good Muslims." Sometimes the reason that parents miss the point is that they are overwhelmed by the awesomeness of the responsibility Islam charges them with in regard to bringing up children properly. Instead, the focus of Muslim parents should always be on the children themselves, and not so much on their own parental responsibilities toward the children. Furthermore, the goal of that focussing should be that the children learn to love Allah and His Prophet, upon him be peace, and that they have a full rather than a partial (such as a literal or a merely legalistic) understanding of Islam and its spiritual richness.

In regard to the issue about which you specifically asked. The Prophet's prohibition of the practice called *al-qaza'* should be understood as falling under the general category of prohibitions related to the imitation of the practices of other religious communities. In another version of the same hadith, Abu Dawheyd included that the Prophet, upon him be peace, had added, ". . . because it is the custom of the Jews." While the traditional commentators on hadith may have debated this point, the Hassidic Jews do just this, they leave locks of hair (sidelocks, or *pe'oth*) to grow out, one on each side of the head. The idea behind the prohibition was that Muslims should not suppose themselves more pious by aping what others thought to be piety. In any case, the commentators tell us that al-qaza' was considered, by *ijma'* or consensus, to be an objectionable (*makruh*) practice. Therefore, your objection to your sons' haircuts on the grounds that those haircuts represented al-qaza' was, strictly speaking, incorrect. Your concern, however, that such haircuts represented some sort of an affinity for the styles and ways of street gangs was a very real and legitimate one. It should not, however, have become what it became, as explained above.

We hope that you do not feel offended at what is written here, but that you attempt to understand it for what it really is: advice and counsel from one concerned Muslim parent to another. Our wives and our children are a trust from Allah, and we must do all that is in our power to protect and maintain that trust. In your particular case, it might be wiser, especially in view of your wife's obvious intransigence, to refrain from agitating her, and certainly from involving the children (regardless of how good your intention is) in the dispute you have with her.

V. Muslim Dress

We have read Mr. _____'s letter to you concerning the Immigration and Naturalization Service (INS) regulation for the naturalization photograph. Evidently, Mr. _____ is under the impression that only certain sects or "religious orders" have directions concerning *hijab*. Clearly, this is not the case. The likelihood is that the particular INS regulation was originally drafted in order to accommodate Catholic nuns. Thus, it would seem that grounds and guidelines must be established by means of which both parties may be able to proceed. This, essentially, would entail explaining that Islam, while related to Christianity (and Judaism), is quite different in its particulars (even if it is similar in its general principles and beliefs), and must therefore be considered as such. To equate hijab with a nun's habit is to ridicule the whole Islamic social system.

To move from the general to the specific, the way that we read Mr. _____'s letter is that he has observed some Muslim women who object to "removing their headdresses for purposes of the naturalization photograph" and some who do not. Then, by analogy with what he knows of religion, he has supposed that those who have objected must have done so on the basis of their membership in a religious order, much as the Catholic nuns would object on the basis of their vows.

What needs to be explained, therefore, is that his observations were not of Islam, per se, but of Muslims. Some of the Muslims he encountered may have been "practicing" Muslims, and others may not have been. It is likely that non-practicing Muslims would not have objected to photographs; but it is unlikely that they would have "removed their headdresses," as they would not have been wearing "headdresses" in the first place. However, among the "practicing" Muslims, there may have been those who objected and those who did not. Those who did not object may have had a number of reasons for not doing so. Firstly, it is possible that their personal understanding of the injunctions of the Qur'an and the Sunnah in relation to the subject of hijab is that these teach modesty in dress, and that is the true meaning of hijab. For some, this is a cultural norm. Others, however, may believe in a more literal or traditional reading of the texts, but may nonetheless have removed their "headdresses" on the basis of the Islamic teachings in regard to permitting the forbidden on the basis of need, or by choosing the lesser of two evils.

Whatever the case, the point that needs to be made is that Islam is both culture and religion; and that Islam in America is very much a multi-cultural mix. For that reason, the INS interviewers may observe many different manifestations of what it means to be a Muslim.

But certainly there is no "religious order" that dictates hijab as a condition for membership. Even so, the laws that have made accommodations for members of such "orders" should definitely be extended to cover those Muslim women who object to "removing their headdresses," because the same religious devotion and sincerity apply equally in both cases; and in both cases there is ample scriptural authority for the practice.

This is what we make of the situation, and Allah knows best as to what is correct.

VI. Using Donations from Sinners

Donations for mosques from non-Muslims or from Muslim sinners may be accepted, though it is better if these are used for the construction of conveniences or facilities needed by the mosque (i.e. bathrooms, sidewalks, parking lots, gardens, etc.), or kept in trust (*waqf*), or used to purchase furniture or equipment not used in salah or the places where salah is performed.

VII. Using the Proceeds from the Sale of Sacrificial Animals

The sale of the hide of a sacrificial animal is lawful, and the proceeds of that sale may be used for charitable purposes, such as the mosque fund you described. The sale of the animal's meat, however, is unlawful, as this meat is the right firstly of the relatives and friends of the one in whose name the slaughter is performed, and thereafter of the poor and the needy, Muslims first, and non-Muslims thereafter.

VIII. Questions about Christmas

Question 1: I am a new Muslim. My family is Christian. Is it OK for me to spend Christmas with my family? It is the only time our whole family is together.

Reply: To quote from the minutes of the Fiqh Council's meeting in Kansas City, Mo., on the sixth of Rabi al-Awwal, 1413 (9/3/92):

Item 9. The Council considered questions put to it by certain converts to Islam on the subject of their participating in the ceremonies occasioned by the joys and sorrows of their non-Muslim families and relations, like marriages and funerals and the like. The Council explained that one's maintaining the best of relations with one's family, in addition to being a part of a Muslim's duty to treat all people in the very best manner, may be considered a subtle form of da'wah as well. Therefore, there is nothing wrong with one's maintaining good relations with one's non-Muslim relations, especially one's parents. Indeed, a Muslim should exemplify for his/her family all the characteristics of goodness, kindness, and decency.

The answer to this question, therefore, may be prefaced by alluding to the Islamic principle which says that "Islam means to maintain, not to break up, relationships" (al-Islam yasil wa al-yaqta'). It is therefore a Muslim convert's duty to remain close to his family. If the Christmas holiday affords such an opportunity, there is nothing wrong with a Muslim's meeting with his family at that time and partaking in the family's activities. Obviously, however, as a Muslim, he or she would not participate in Christian religious services (except, where necessary, as an observer).

Question 2: Can I attend work-related Christmas parties where alcohol will be served? These functions are important for business contacts.

Reply: In the absence of a strong reason to attend, it will be better not to attend such gatherings. If necessary, however (and the success of one's business or career may be considered necessary), one may attend so long as one maintains one's dignity and composure, and feels in one's heart a sense of aversion to whatever munkarat (actions not condoned by Islamic law) may be taking place.

Question 3: Can a Muslim accept Christmas gifts from Christian friends and family? What about giving them a gift?

Reply: There is nothing wrong with your accepting a gift from a Christian friend or family member. We might add that the exchange of gifts may become an important bridge of understanding between Muslims and their Christian friends and relatives. For, through your accepting gifts on Christmas, you obligate them, at least morally, to accept your gifts and greetings on the two 'Ids, and thereby lead them to participate, even if at a distance, in our Muslim celebrations. If you have children, and their grandparents or cousins are Christians, this arrangement has further significance. We would also recommend that Muslim parents who are joined with their Christian families and friends for the Christmas holidays should give their own children gifts. But the gifts they give their children for 'Id should always be made to seem more special. And Allah knows best.

Question 4: What should I respond when people wish me a Merry Christmas?

Reply: One may respond by saying, "Thank you," or anything to indicate your appreciation of the sentiment. Or your response might be to acknowledge their greeting with a smile, and then to reply, "Salam! Peace on earth!" This is both sincere and thought-provoking. A lot of your friends and relatives may stop and think about that reply and what it says about Islam and Muslims.

We hope that these replies will be found to be of use to you and to all the brothers and sisters in your community. And it is Allah who guides to the truth.

Notes

1. Yvonne Yazbeck Haddad and Adair Lummis, *Islamic Values in the United States: A Comparative Study* (New York: Oxford University Press, 1987), pp. 59–60. It might be noted here that very few of the figures called upon for such counseling are formally qualified to do so. Even in the schools for the training of imams in the Muslim world, little or no attention is paid to training for "pastoral" responsibilities.

2. While most works on *usul al-fiqh* contain at least passing mention of the mufti, in the chapters devoted to ijtihad, there are several works from the classical period which deal with the subject of the mufti in detail. These include Ibn al Qayyim's, *I'lam al-Muwaqqi'in 'an Rabb al-'Alamin*, Ibn Hamdan al-Hanbali's, *Sifat al-Fatwa wa al-Mufti wa al-Mustafti*, al-Khatib al-Baghdadi's, *al-Faqih wa al-Mutafiqqih*, and al-Qarafi's, *al-Ihkam fi Tamyiz al-Fatawa wa al-Ahkam*, to name a few.

3. While the mufti may engage in legal consultation, as a jurisconsult his concern is with elaborating points of law and not necessarily with solving actual problems. The qadi, however, is a facilitator.

4. Being well informed about American society is one of the characteristics most desired in an imam by the Muslims interviewed in the survey undertaken by Haddad and Lummis. It may readily be assumed that this characteristic is deemed even more important in a mufti (Haddad and Lumis, *Islamic Values*, p. 60).

5. The nature of contemporary American society is very different from anything experienced by Muslims in the past. Take, for example, poverty. In the United States, 91 percent of those regarded as "poor" own color televisions, and their greatest single health problem is obesity. Obviously, every society is different, and only those who are familiar with the circumstances of a society can be trusted to give reasonable replies to the sort of questions generated by those circumstances.

6. Consider, for example, the irreparable havoc raised by fatwas regarding the beginnings of the lunar months, marking the beginning and end of fasting, when the criteria for crescent visibility are subject to local weather conditions.

7. See T. J. al-Alwani, "Missing Dimensions in Contemporary Islamic Movements," *American Journal of Islamic Social Science* 12:2 (Summer 1995): "Muslim intellectuals and scholars seem to have forgotten that Imam Shafi`i initially produced his jurisprudence in Baghdad, where he wrote his book *al-Hujja* and read it to such scholars as Ahmad ibn Hanbal, Abu Thaur and Karabisi. However, when Shafi`i left Baghdad for Cairo, he reconsidered his jurisprudence in toto and revised all but thirteen questions in the corpus of his work. In other words, Shafi`i, in his lifetime, produced two different versions of comprehen-

sive jurisprudential thought. This was the experience of a man who lived for only fifty years! Although the differences between the Baghdadi and the Cairene societies at the time were not very pronounced, certainly not as significant as the differences between Japanese society today and that of the Najd or America, contemporary Muslim scholars insist on making the Muslim of today conform to a societal order that is completely different, and based on the jurisprudence of schools founded in the Hijaz, or Kufa in the second century of the hijra. They try to put the camel through the eye of a needle simply because they do not realize that the concept of universality in Islam means the capacity to encompass different societal orders within the framework of absolute value, and not within the framework of perceptual variables of belief that are influenced by innumerable factors."

8. In particular, a number of American Muslim students (though, probably not more than 40–50) have studied at the Islamic University at Medina. Very few of these, however, have actually graduated. The factors in the high rate of attrition deserve research, but language and culture seem to figure quite prominently among them. Far fewer have studied at other universities in the Arab and Islamic world, like al-Azhar in Cairo. Recently, the International Islamic University in Malaysia has attracted some American Muslim students. Even fewer have managed to complete the programs of study offered by the traditional *madaris* in India and Pakistan, or those in North Africa, especially in Mauritania. In addition, there are a few instances of students studying informally with teachers in mosques at various places in the Muslim world.

9. The advantages and disadvantages, as well as the variety of experiences, in pursuing the study of fiqh by such alternative methods will make up the topic of another study. In the final analysis, however, there is a clear need for the development of institutions in North America for understanding Islam, or fiqh, in the broadest sense of the term and the discipline.

10. For a summarized discussion of traditional opinion on this issue, see Yusuf al-Qaradawi, *al-Fatwa Bayn al-Indibat wa al-Tasayyub* (Cairo: Dar al-Sahwa, 1988), pp. 20–41.

11. Bernard Weiss, *The Search for God's Law* (Salt Lake City: University of Utah Press, 1992), p. 688.

12. Fiqh scholars working with Islamic banks have had to develop specializations in, for example, certain aspects of *mu'amalat* and finance if they are to advise on the day-to-day transactions that take place in the bank. If they are to advise on investment banking, they will have to specialize in certain other aspects of mu'amalat and economics, and so on.

13. The acknowledged mujtahid and imam Abu Hanifa worked on a regular basis with about forty scholars; see Zahid al-Kawthari's introduction to al-Zayla'i's, *Nasb al-Raya*, 2nd ed. (Beirut: Dar Ihya' al-Turath al-'Arabi, 1973), pp. 37–38.

14. This quotation is taken from a document in the files of the Fiqh Council of America. It is incomplete and its authorship is unknown.

15. The significance of the plural, "ways," rather than the singular, "way," cannot be overemphasized. While this may seem a trivial and insignificant point, it is one that is often overlooked by Muslims with interests in maintaining the exclusivity of the claims of their particular agendas, be these spiritual, legal,

political, cultural, or otherwise. In fact, plurality and tolerance are important, though little understood, elements of the Shari'a, *al-shari'a al-samha'*.

16. The council has recently commissioned the first in what it hopes will become a series of publications on contemporary issues of practical interest to Muslims in North America. This work, entitled *Prohibited and Unclean Substances in Food and Medicine: Between Theory and Application*, is by Dr. Nazih Hammad, and deals with the topic from the perspective of legal theory, *usul al-fiqh*.

17. Thus, for example, a request to consider the legality of consuming pork or alcohol would not be considered. The council might, however, deal with a question about investing in a company in which a small portion of its business is based on the sale of these products, or with a question regarding the use of these substances for medical purposes, particularly in surgical procedures.

18. The efforts of this committee culminated in the council's decision to advocate a lunar calendar based on calculations, and to reject the traditional practice of listening to reports of supposed naked-eye sightings of the crescent moon as the basis for establishing the beginnings of the lunar months.

19. Where the Shari'a stipulation is that one possess the means to travel; see Qur'an 3:97 and its commentaries.

20. Owing to the importance of the *maqasid al-shari'a*, the International Institute of Islamic Thought has published three major works on the subject in the past three years; Ahmad Raysuni's, *Nazariyat al-Maqasid 'inda al-Imam al-Shatibi* (1993); Yusuf al-'Alam's, *al-Maqasid al-'Ammah li al-Shari'a al-Islamiya* (1994); and Isma'il al-Hasani, *Nazariyat al-Maqasid 'inda al-Imam Muhammad al-Tahir ibn al-'Ashur* (1995).

21. This is the Institute of Muslim Minority Affairs. Its English language journal, *Journal of the Institute of Muslim Minority Affairs*, has been published in London since 1980. For an engaging study of how Muslim majority jurists in the classical period viewed Muslim minority affairs, see Khaled Abou El Fadl, "Islamic Law and Muslim Minorities: The Juristic Discourse on Muslim Minorities From the Second/Eighth to the Eleventh/Seventeenth Centuries," *Islamic Law and Society* 1, no. 2 (August 1994): 141–87. See also the proceedings of a seminar held in London in 1978 to discuss problems of Muslim minorities, *Muslim Communities in Non-Muslim States* (London: Islamic Council of Europe, 1980).

22. My own take on this issue is that the "minority" fiqh produced in Sri Lanka, for example, would differ in significant ways from minority fiqh in India, though the two countries are separated by only a few miles of ocean. Owing to the wealth and political influence of the small Muslim community in Sri Lanka, their minority position is quite other than that of the huge, but oppressed, Muslim minority in India.

23. B. A. Roberson, "Islam and Europe: An Enigma or a Myth?" *Middle East Journal* 48, no. 2 (Spring 1994): 292–93.

24. See my comments in review of Bernard Weiss, "The Search for God's Law," *American Journal of Islamic Social Science* 11, no. 4 (Winter 1994): 579–82.

25. Termination will generally take place by means of *talaq, khul'a,* or *faskh*. In the instance you have described, the pronouncement was of talaq.

26. When a husband divorces his wife by saying to her, "You are divorced, divorced, divorced."

27. Generally speaking, if the divorce occurs before intercourse, the wife retains only half her dower, unless she agrees to forgo it (Quran 2:237). But in a very few instances, such as the one outlined here, the entire dower is forfeit. In the example given, if dissolution takes place after intercourse, the husband will be required to pay half the sadaq.

28. Dr. Muhammad Ra'fat 'Uthman, *Mahr al Zauja* (Cairo: Matba'at al- Sa'adah, 1982), p. 202.

4

Muslims and Identity Politics in America

MOHOMMED A. MUQTEDAR KHAN

Identity may be an imaginary property of humans, but its effects on society are real, both on the individual level and collectively in the form of communities, nations, ethnicities, and civilizations. Identity connects the individual to the collective; it establishes relations whose nature is political and which is known as "identity politics." Through the shaping and reshaping of the "I" and the "we" the individual and the community shape and reshape each other.

Both the individual and the collective are repositories of identity. Through various symbolic activities, like performing the *salah* (prayer) on Fridays, fasting, celebrating festivals, wearing traditional garb, and frequenting community places such as the mosque, the restaurant, and the parochial school, the Muslim individual reproduces the community, and these distinct practices give the community its meaning or identity. In seeking to reproduce a particular community, however, the individual allows collective practices to shape his or her own personality to some extent. In other words the process of reproducing collective identity involves the constitution of the individual self. In reproducing an Islamic community, the individual also produces the Muslim personality.

Construction or crystallization of identity involves two processes: drawing boundaries and investing meaning in the spaces inside and outside the boundaries.[1] The Muslim community, for example, draws boundaries to differentiate between who belongs to a Muslim community and who does not. It also defines what makes a Muslim community Muslim, and what does not, by identifying the characteristics of the collective and contrasting them with others and then giving meaning and relevance to these characteristics.

Community construction thus involves the identification of symbols and boundaries and their interpretation.

The process of inclusion and exclusion is integral to the process of drawing boundaries to define communities. Who is included as a member of the group and who is excluded, while contingent on religious symbols and their meanings, is clearly a political issue. Whether the drawing of boundaries provides material benefits, or power, or simply comfort through association, emphasizing difference is often a consequence of political calculation. This emphasis on difference over commonality is considered identity politics.[2]

Identity has been much studied by social psychologists and sociologists. The first concentrate on the constitution of the self, the "I," the second on the formation of collective selves, the "we." As a consequence of globalization, we have seen the emergence of new multicultural societies, mass migrations of peoples, and the proliferation of ethnic identities. In this postmodern society the emphasis on difference has become a driving force in politics.[3] The post-modern society with its technologies of mass communication and transport has both reduced and enhanced the distance between peoples. The Muslim society has not escaped the effects of post-modernity, and it too now manifests identity politics.[4]

In the past, Muslim society relied on two competing sources of identity—Islamic ideals and *asabiya* (ethnicity).[5] With the evolution of the science of jurisprudence, the *usul al-fiqh*, new sources of difference based on the *madhahib* (schools of jurisprudence) emerged leading to a uniquely Islamic form of pluralism.[6] Political differences leading to conflicting interpretations of Islamic principles had already created new identities such as the Kharijites and the Alids. The advent of the nation-state in the modern era added a newer dimension to difference in the Muslim world in the form of nationalism.[7] Thus, over a period of 1400 years Muslims have been developing sources of identity and difference which have systematically chipped away at the monolithic conception of the Muslim *umma*.

The sources of meaning that influence the process of identity formation in the Muslim society of North America are subjective, intersubjective, ideal, structural, and historical. Subjective sources are essentially dependent on the self-narrative of the individual and contingent primarily on how a person interprets past experiences. This subjective identity emerges through an autobiographical discourse that is politically self-conscious.[8] Isma'il Raji al-Faruqi[9] and Seyyed Hossein Nasr[10] are good examples of individuals who have sought to define themselves through self-narratives.

Intersubjective sources are essentially an amalgam of shared understandings and collective memories of groups which, when dominant, become sources of identification. Members of the Muslim Student Association (MSA) of the early 1970s provide a good example of intersubjective identification. Their shared understanding of the Muslim mission in America, the proclamation of Islam, and the common struggle to establish Islamic institutions, such as the Islamic Society of North America (ISNA), and the Association of Muslim Social Scientists (AMSS) in the United States, have given them a distinct identity that is a consequence of commonly shared values and experiences. Wahhabism, the strict, puritanical form of Islam preached by Muhammad Ibn 'Abd al-Wahhab, an eighteenth-century *mujaddid* from Arabia, is another example of intersubjectively formed identities based upon a shared interpretation of Islam and on the exclusion of other, specifically identified, interpretations.[11]

Ideal sources are those beliefs and practices which in every Muslim mind define the Islamic identity, based solely upon an individual's Islamic beliefs and practices.[12] This notion of Islamic identity is ideal in its construction: it is both acontextual and ahistorical. It presupposes the supreme domination of Islamic values to the extent that the believer is immune to the material and political contingencies of any particular time or location. Needless to say, this remains an ideal that all Muslims, at an individual and collective level, aspire to achieve.[13]

Structural sources of identity are primarily political in nature and are based on the distribution of power and resources in society. The most prominent manifestation of this form of identity formation is nationalism. While national identities are often based on ethnic, racial, and historically shared values, in the Muslim world they are constructed by the nation-state system.[14] The Kuwaitis, the Iraqis, and the Saudis have more shared values than differences, yet they are maintained as different nationalities.[15] These differences can only be explained through the institutionalization of the externally endowed (by the British) distribution of power and resources. Structural sources can also be understood as contemporary context. The emergence of distinct identities among Indian and Pakistani Muslims, in spite of many cultural, linguistic, and ethnic commonalities, is indicative of the role of the contemporary sociopolitical context in shaping identity.

Finally, the historical sources of Muslim identity are the differences that have emerged in the historical construction of the meanings and significance of Islamic values, symbols, and events.[16] The best example of this historically emerging difference is the gradual divergence in Sunni and Shi'i theology and jurisprudence. Groups, sects, and schools of jurisprudence have gained legitimacy and identity through meanings which are historically constructed by invoking symbols or authoritative figures from the past and romanticizing them.[17] Similarly, many other historically constituted Muslim identities have proliferated in Islam's 1400-year history.

While these five sources of Muslim identity are analytically distinct, in reality they overlap in every individual and every community. Nobody is only Hanafi, or only Shi'i. Muslims today can show a complex amalgamation of identities, with some exaggerated and others muted. This muting of some sources of identity and emphasis on others involves a political process of drawing boundaries.

Understanding identity and its formation is important. Many social theorists argue that action and identity are so closely related that suggesting that

"I act because of who I am" explains individual action.[18] If what we do is contingent on who we are, then who we are gains great significance, and if what we do politically is a consequence of who we are, then who we are is also determined by political considerations. Thus, politics and identity are intertwined and mutually dependent.

Through their discourse and their practices, American Muslims are drawing circles of identities and producing meanings for the spaces inside and outside these circles. But the decisions and practices of who is included or excluded from these circles has generated politics of identity which appear to be determined primarily by the political context of the Muslim world. Groups like the American Muslim Council (AMC) are trying to draw wide and inclusive circles to generate power based on numbers by creating the identity of American Muslims. Groups like the Qur'an and Sunnah Society (QSS), on the other hand, are drawing smaller circles based upon their interpretation of what is Islam and driven by concerns of "perceived purity," not political power. One can see similar drawing and redrawing of boundaries as Muslims struggle to define and redefine their identity based upon competing and sometimes conflicting purposes, even as Islam begins to adjust to the new context of American society.

Identity politics in the Muslim world involve the separation of self and the other at two levels, one within the Muslim community and one without. When Muslims draw the big circle that differentiates between Muslim and non-Muslim they are basically giving meaning to self in opposition to the "external other," the unbeliever. The external other could be an individual, another religious community (in India Hinduism, in Nigeria Christianity, and in Palestine Judaism), a state (for Pakistan it is India and for Arabs it is Israel) and even a group of states like the West (for Iran).

Within the community, Muslims draw other circles of identity and difference based on ethnicity, interpretation of Islamic law, interpretation of Islamic history, and nationalistic fervor. These inner circles draw boundaries between the self and the "internal other." The Sunni-Shi'i divisions are an example of the longest lasting "self-internal other" dichotomy within the Muslim umma. Among African-American Muslims the difference between the followers of Imam Warith Din Muhammad and Minister Louis Farrakhan can be seen as the self–internal other dichotomy. These two forms of identity politics—between a broadly defined self and the external other and between the narrowly defined selves and the internal others—which are proliferating in the Muslim world, are now being reproduced in the United States.

Identity Politics of Selves vs. Internal Others

The Muslim world is concerned both with the assertion of Islamic unity and with the maintenance of difference, trends that are manifest in its international organizations and social movements. Institutions such as the Organization of Islamic Conferences (OIC),[19] the Arab League, and the Gulf Cooperation Council (GCC) demonstrate the privileging of particularism.[20] The OIC represents over fifty nation-states, most of which have a Muslim majority.[21] The Arab League is an international institution that includes Muslim states with Arab nationality. The GCC represents a particular type of Arab state, essentially one that is willing to accept Saudi Arabia's hegemony in return for security and protection from the domination of Iran or Iraq.

The existence and nature of these institutions suggest that Muslim states seem not to be able to resolve the tensions between interests and identity. When Islamic sentiments matter they turn to the OIC and its slogans of Islamic identity and solidarity; when material interests matter they fall back on parochial and particularist organizations such as the GCC. Relations between Muslim states are far from peaceful. Iran and Saudi Arabia are at odds over many issues including the role of America in the Persian Gulf. Iran and Iraq have yet to resolve their differences after having fought a decade-long war. Relations between Afghanistan and Iran are tense over the ambitions of the Taliban. Sudan and Egypt are at odds over Sudan's support of Islamists. Turkey and Syria argue over Turkey's military projects with Israel.

The differences between Muslims are not confined to nationalist politics alone. The feud between the Shi'a and Sunni continues unabated. In India, Pakistan, Afghanistan, and Saudi Arabia it erupts frequently in the form of riots or discriminatory practices, just as in other parts of the Muslim world ethnic differences lead to riots between Sindhis and Punjabis in Pakistan, Pashtuns and Uzbeks in Afghanistan, Arabs and non-Arabs in Sudan, Berbers and Arabs in Algeria.

Beyond these ethnic and nationalistic differences Muslims are beginning to discriminate and indulge in the politics of exclusion based on the interpretation of religious texts. For example, the exclusion of the Ahmadiyyas has created a new "internal other" in Pakistan. Tensions between the Wahhabis and the Sufis has taken on a global character. More and more groups are ready to use the dreaded "K" word—*kafir* (unbeliever)—for other Muslims over disagreements in interpretation of religious texts. Based on various sources of identity, Muslims in the traditional Muslim world are drawing boundaries within the community and generating more and more "internal others."

The impact of identity politics in the Muslim world can be seen in the United States as well.[22] Because American Muslims have so far failed to articulate a cohesive domestic political agenda, they concentrate instead on the politics of their native countries,[23] which then becomes the source for drawing narrower boundaries and creating internal others. Far from being united as an American Muslim community that seeks to establish itself, American Muslims are allowing the identity politics of the Muslim world to fragment them into various sectarian groups.[24] Muslims from India and Pakistan cooperate on Islamic issues, but efforts by Indian Muslim groups, such as the Indian Muslim Relief Committee (IMRC), to help victims of riots in India get little cooperation from their ethnic brethren from Pakistan or fellow Muslims from other parts of the Muslim world. Pakistani Muslims are suspicious of Indian Muslims because they disagree with their agenda on Kashmir. For them Pakistani nationalism is Islamic, but Indian nationalism is definitely not. Pakistanis assume that Indian Muslims have been assimilated into Hindu culture, and their derision alienates Indian Muslims.[25] Indian Muslims are equally dismayed when they come in contact with Pakistanis who neglect Islamic practices or contemplate Pakistan's corruption and moral decline which they regard as a betrayal of Islam.

Differences in national origins, still strong because of involvement in politics back home, have hindered unity among American Muslims. Even on college campuses, discussions on issues of Islamic identity can generate bitterness between Pakistani and Bangladeshi immigrants. Some of them have been American nationals for over three decades, but their obsession with the politics of their native countries impedes their capacity to understand and relate to issues of identity and interests in the American context.

Tensions between Saudi Arabia and Iran are replayed in competition, criticism, and non-cooperation among Muslim groups supported by Saudi Arabia or with majority Arab populations and immigrants from Iran.[26] Muslim organizations are funded by foreign nationals and foundations and are under pressure to respect the international interests of the donating states. In rare cases they are even expected to pursue the interests of the donating nations in their activities as American Muslims.[27] The Arab-Israeli conflict casts a particularly long shadow: groups break up or even undermine each other's efforts depending on the foreign policy of their native country toward Israel.[28]

The growing tensions between Iran and Saudi Arabia are reflected in the relations between Iranian and other Shi'i immigrants and Arab and other Sunni Muslims.[29] Organizations funded by Saudi Arabia no longer attract Iranians or other Shi'i living in America. Perhaps as the community grew the old hostility between Shi'i and Sunni would in any case have reemerged, but the Iran–Saudi Arabia tension has certainly exacerbated it.

The Center for Islamic Studies at Florida International University (FIU) in Miami, with which I was affiliated, organizes book-review sessions and seminars relating to Islam and politics. It has a loyal following among Arab, Indo-Pakistani, and African-American Muslims, who told us how "useful," "informative" and "necessary" our programs were for Muslims in Miami. In the spring of 1995 we invited Professor Abdul Aziz Sachedina of the University of Virginia to speak there. The auditorium was packed, as 110 people had crowded into a room designed for 80. I was surprised to note, however, that only four of them were our loyal "regulars"; the rest were new. It was later explained to me that because Sachedina was a Shi'a who wrote about Iran, the regulars stayed away because of their Sunni beliefs and their antipathy towards Shi'ism.[30]

The experience was repeated when Professor Sachedina visited Georgetown University to give a talk on "Jihad in Islam" in the spring of 1997. The talk was organized by the campus Muslim Student Association (MSA) and the Center for Muslim-Christian Understanding. The audience was made up predominantly of Iranian Shi'i students who do not attend regular Friday prayers and other activities organized on campus by the MSA. The Georgetown MSA, like most others, draws its members from the Muslims of Indian, Pakistani, and Arab origin; again the Arab and most other Sunni members stayed away. Only the academically inclined Sunnis and American-born members, whether of Arab or South Asian origin, came to the talk. Clearly "identity issues" are still preventing American Muslims from cooperating on issues common to all. These patterns of behavior are indicative of the preference for symbolism over rationalization of interests. In his talk at FIU, Sachedina categorically denounced the differences between Shi'i and Sunni and condemned the use of these doctrinal differences to fragment Muslims in America and the rest of the world as an un-Islamic practice.

The assumption that Sachedina's Shi'i identity would necessarily affect his talk, motivated as it would be by sectarian interests, appears to be a continuation of political practices imported from the Muslim world. Muslims in America are reacting to individuals and events as they would in the societies whence they came. The presence at the talk of Sunni Muslims born and brought up in the United States suggests that when Muslims are not brought up with the prejudices of old-world politics, they tend to be less sectarian and are not so apt to reproduce the identity politics of the Muslim world. The production of internal others is by and large confined to the activities and discourses of immigrant Muslims.

Identity Politics of Self vs. the External Other

While various issues of identity and diversity converge in the relations between Muslim groups and Muslim states, Islamic identity is more important than Muslim diversity when Muslims interact with non-Muslims. Before the colonial period, Muslims considered themselves to belong to a single political unit,[31] at least de jure. Even though there were many sultans, amirs, and kings ruling the Muslim states, most of them deferred to the authority of the caliph.[32] Though the caliphate, in later centuries, had degenerated into a defunct institution, it carried a sense of legitimacy with Muslim rulers, who deferred to the institution for purely symbolic reasons. Muslim states interacted with each other and Muslim states interacted with the non-Muslim world.[33]

The norms that guide international politics today are the principles of international relations articulated by jurists between 750 and 1100 in the interests of the Islamic empires.[34] In keeping with the legitimizing discourse and religio-cultural context of their time, they outlined these principles in

Islamic terms. The earliest of them is called *siyar*,[35] and many scholars today continue to refer to siyar as the Islamic theory of international relations. However, it is more a combination of ontological classification and normative injunctions than it is a theory.

The Islamic paradigm for international relations basically divides the world into the Dar al-Islam and non-Islamic polities. It then divides the non-Islamic polities into two categories; those that have peace treaties with the Islamic polity (Dar al-'Ahd, house of alliance) and those at war with the Islamic polity (Dar al-Harb, house of war).[36] The paradigm suggests the appropriate posture that an Islamic entity should adopt toward each:[37] wage jihad against the Dar al-Harb until it is conquered, converted, or joins the Dar al-'Ahd[38] and maintain peace with the Dar al-'Ahd.[39] An Islamic polity is not expected to violate the principles of the treaty.[40] The Qur'an is strict about keeping one's word (9:4; 4:90): *Pacta sund servanda* (promises made must be kept) is one of the most important principles of international law. Needless to say, this paradigm, though outdated, still often guides Muslim attitudes and policies vis-à-vis the non-Muslim world.

It is impossible to conceive of the world today merely in terms of the Dar al-Islam and the Dar al-'Ahd. With international institutions like the United Nations and multilateral treaties that outlaw aggression, one can argue that the Dar al-Harb has ceased to exist, since there is no state or coalition which has explicitly declared war against Islam. The emergence of the nation-state system and the fragmentation of the Islamic world system notwithstanding, however, many Muslims continue to look at world politics in those terms.[41] Such politics can be described as "identity-realism" and world politics as an arena where entities of different identities are involved in a struggle for power. Some contemporary scholars, however, have attempted to advance a more idealist understanding of Islamic sources.[42]

Identity politics undermines the role of "material and rational interests" in determining group behavior; when Muslims are caught up in this "us vs. them" mind set, they become identity groups whose politics are determined by their perception of "who they are," and "what they want and must do." This type of politics characterizes the identity politics of self vs. "external other," and this dynamic is now reproduced in Muslim politics in America, manifesting itself in the dichotomy of America vs. Islam.

Many Muslims are critical of American foreign policy towards Muslim countries. They see the United States as supporting Israel against the Arabs[43] and Russia in its invasion of Muslim Chechnya; they see it delaying the rescue of Muslims in Bosnia and permitting the ethnic cleansing of Muslims by not intervening early, by preventing Muslims states from intervening, and by preventing the arming of Bosnians.[44] The enthusiastic willingness of the United States to impose and execute U.N. sanctions against Muslim countries while doing exactly the opposite in the case of Israel has convinced many Muslims that the United States, influenced by Zionist and anti-Muslim Christian groups, is determined to "destroy Islam."[45]

The constant vilification of any call to Islam as "fundamentalism" and its repeated portrayal as the "world's enemy number one" by many officials and Western scholars, combined with repeated calls to fight Islamism, places the United States on a collision course with Islam.[46] This particular interpretation of American foreign policy convinces Muslims that the American government does not wish to see Islam thrive and will not allow Muslims to live as Muslims. This interpretation is in varying degrees shared by many Christian and Jewish scholars as well.[47] Muslims believe that this American attitude toward Islam is directed against Muslims at home as well as abroad.[48] Ilyas Bayunus, a sociologist, cites Congress's new anti-terrorism bill as an effort to punish the entire American Muslim community under the pretext of providing security.[49]

This attitude that Islam is a major threat to the West[50] in the post-communist era alienates many American Muslims, putting them on the defensive and creating barriers that discourage their assimilation. Many American experts and scholars often fail to distinguish between accepting Muslims and accepting Islam. America will continue to alienate its Muslim population as long as it continues to demonize Islam each time it faces resistance to foreign objectives in Muslim states or from Muslim movements.

Judaism was not vilified when Baruch Goldstein massacred scores of praying Palestinians and when an extremist assassinated Rabin; Muslims expect the same deference to Islam when Iran kills its dissidents in Europe, or when Hezbollah resists Israeli occupation in southern Lebanon. The media usually label such events as "Islamic" terrorism, while similar acts by Jews or Christians (Goldstein in Palestine, Tim McVeigh, and scores of abortion-related terrorist activities in the United States and IRA terrorists in Britain) are handled with great delicacy and sensitivity towards the followers of those faiths. Indeed Judaism and Christianity are rarely held responsible for the acts of their believers.[51] These media tactics not only set public opinion against Islam and American Muslims but lead to hate crimes against them,[52] and encourage the belief among American Muslims that America is antagonistic to Islam.

Thus, in a way the demonization of Islam by the American media compels Muslims to indulge in identity politics. They concentrate on defending their faith from a perceived American assault rather than on their role as American residents seeking liberty, equality, and prosperity. The negative image of America, a consequence of its foreign policy in the Middle East, inspires a paradoxical response from Muslims. Its prosperity and freedom attracts them, but once they are here, its policies and its attitudes towards Muslims and Islam alienates them. The result is a dilemma for American Muslims: they like living here but they love to hate America.

I asked Dr. Yunus, a physician practicing internal medicine on the west coast of Florida and the current president of the ICNA (Islamic Circle of North America) to spell out the obligations of naturalized Muslim citizens to their new country, keeping in mind the Qur'anic injunction (9:4) that promises made must be kept. He said that in the opinion of many scholars whom he had consulted, becoming a citizen should be understood as a treaty between the Muslim individual and the United States. All Muslims who agree to this compact are required to fulfill their obligations as proper citizens, obey the law, pay taxes, and so on. If for some reason Muslims do not like American society, their only alternative is to terminate their agreement and leave. However, he also said that "of course, Muslims are not obliged to obey laws and policies which are specifically against Islamic belief," and he pointed to the options for bringing about change that the Constitution provided its citizens, recommending that Muslims avail themselves of them.

While this answer seemed rational, sensible, and even enlightened to most Muslims in the audience, it failed to address some problems. When Muslims become naturalized citizens, they do not inform the government that their acceptance of citizenship is conditional. They do not make it explicit that they will remain good citizens as long as no law or policy that appears to them to be anti-Islamic is legislated or implemented. If they did, the government would no doubt not agree to any such conditions since, after all, it was the Muslim's choice to apply for citizenship in the first place. Many Muslims who see Islam and the United States in conflict have enormous problems thinking of themselves as American Muslims. They want the prosperity and the freedom but not the foreign policy, and Muslim leaders who oppose assimilation without opposing naturalization inadvertently place Muslims in a moral dilemma.

The termination of the caliphate in 1924, the emergence of many Muslims states identified as Islamic (Saudi Arabia, Iran, Pakistan) or as secular democracies (Turkey, Egypt), and the rapid globalization of the nation-state as a result of decolonization have expanded the vocabulary for Muslim discourse on international relations. Terms like Dar al-Aman (house of order) and Dar al-Kufr (house of unbelief)[53] first emerged in the context of Muslim politics in India. India is a secular democracy and allows Muslims complete freedom to practice their religion and live by the Shari'a. It therefore cannot belong to the Dar al-Harb because it is not hostile to Islam; it also does not qualify as Dar al-Sulh or Dar al-'Ahd because it has no specific treaties with obligations to Muslims. For that reason Muslims began to refer to India as Dar al-Aman, a place where there is peace and tolerance and freedom of religion. But this term is restricted to India in its use, perhaps because of its subcontinental origins.

Dar al-Kufr is a state or territory which is predominantly non-Muslim but which neither has a treaty with Muslims nor is at war with them. The West has often been referred to as Dar al-Sulh and by some as Dar al-Kufr depending on whether someone wants to emphasize conflict between Islam and the West or peaceful and cooperative relations.

Many American Muslims, particularly African-American Muslims, are proud to be American citizens. They are native to America, and Islam has given them the dignity and self-esteem to make their lives meaningful even as they struggle against racial discrimination.[54] Immigrant Muslims share their sentiments to the extent that they are grateful for the opportunity that America has given them to prosper and practice their faith. They believe that America is Dar al-Sulh and in many of its practices much more Islamic than are many contemporary Muslim states. A minority of both native and immigrant Muslims, however, are of the opinion that since this is a country where Islamic Shari'a is not applied, it is Dar al-Kufr, the abode of disbelief. Because this minority is active in Muslim politics, however, it has a disproportionate impact on the American Muslim discourse, although it is an attitude of people very poorly informed about the American political system and its liberal philosophical underpinnings and with a very limited understanding of the spirit of democracy and the essence of Islamic governance. Driven purely by terminological difference some Muslims, such as the members of Hizb-ul-Tahrir (the movement associated with the journal *Khalifornia*), reject American political ideas as "unbelief" and place Islam and America in the dichotomy of belief vs. unbelief.

One of the reasons why Islam has fared better than Judaism and Christianity against the assaults of modernity and secularism is that it is more rational than the other Abrahamic traditions.[55] If modernity is a rationalization of Judeo-Christian ethics, then it should be much closer to Islam than the two religious traditions that have enriched it. Many American Muslims, who differ from the "America as Dar al-Kufr" group, have either well reasoned or an intuitive sense of the shared values of modernity and Islam and are more comfortable with democracy and pluralism.[56]

Thus, the identity politics of self and the "external other" manifests itself in America as a struggle over whether to define political space in America as one of order or of unbelief. If the consensus were to emerge that America is in a state of unbelief, it would lead to escalation of conflict between Muslims and America because Muslims would then understand that assertion of Islamic identity entailed the rejection of America as a *kafir* system. On the other hand, if a consensus emerged that America was either Dar al-Sulh or Dar al-Aman, then assertion of Islamic identity would not conflict with American identity and an American Muslim identity could emerge among both native-born and immigrant Muslims. This is clearly contingent on two developments. One is the victory of those who see more similarities than dissimilarities between Islamic principles and American values over those who emphasize their differences. The other is a shift in the coverage of Islam by the mainstream American media towards more acceptance and less demonization of Islam.

Muslims in America are by now sufficiently numerous to begin showing their distinct brand of politics in finding enemies inside as well as outside the community.[57] American Muslims are today at a delicate point in their development as a community. They are in the process of assessing their community as having a legitimate claim to a distinct identity, interests, and a place in American society. To achieve this, the community is trying to answer questions about the future identity of the "self" and initiating a dialogue with American society to ascertain its place on the American horizon.

The effort among Muslims to define the self, to give meaning to their new identity as American Muslims, has manifested itself primarily in differentiating the good Muslim from the bad or the "true" Muslim from the pretender. These struggles are apparent in the tensions between the Shi'i and the Sunni, the native-born and the immigrant, the Arab and the non-Arab. It is basically the politics of difference.

Muslim politics in America also manifests itself in the identity politics of the self and the external other, i.e., the Muslim and the non-Muslim, to realize the political obligations of Muslims purely by virtue of their identity as Muslim. It seeks to establish the terms of existence and recognition between the self and the external other.

The simultaneous existence of nationalist and Islamic sentiments prevails in most of the contemporary Muslim world. Pakistani, Kuwaiti, Iraqi, Bangladeshi, Egyptian, Tunisian, and other Muslims seem to have no problem in nurturing dual loyalties to Islam and to their "lands." The wars between Arab states, between the Yemens before unification, between Afghan groups, and between various ethnic groups in Pakistan indicate that Islamic identity has not prevented Muslims from being loyal to "other sources of identity" to the point of going to war.

There is no reason to believe, given the history of Muslim politics in America, that Muslims in America will be different from Muslims in other states. It is possible that the next generation of American Muslims will simultaneously subscribe to the Islamic as well as the American identity, very much as African-American Muslims do now. The emergence of the American Muslim identity, I believe, will reconcile many of the tensions between Muslims and America. As future generations of Muslims are raised in the United States. such a mutually beneficial relationship between American Muslims and the American society becomes more likely.

Notes

Author's note: I would like to thank John Esposito and Yvonne Haddad for their useful criticisms; their suggestions helped enhance the quality of this essay. I alone am responsible for its flaws. I would also like to recognize the support of the Center for Muslim-Christian Understanding at Georgetown University. Finally, without Reshma's constant support this project, like many others, would not have been possible.

1. See Joane Nagel, "Constructing Ethnicity: Creating and Recreating Ethnic Identity and Culture," *Social Problems* 41, no. 1 (February 1994): 152–76.

2. See Eli Zaretsky, "Identity Theory, Identity Politics: Psychoanalysis, Marxism, Poststructuralism" in *Social Theory and the Politics of Identity*, ed. Craig Calhoun (Oxford: B. H. Blackwell, 1994), p. 198.

3. See William E. Connoly, *Identity/Difference: Democratic Negotiations of*

Political Paradox (Ithaca: Cornell University Press, 1991), pp. 64–68. See also Craig Calhoun, "Social Theory and the Politics of Identity" in C. Calhoun, ed., *Social Theory and the Politics of Identity*, pp. 20–26.

4. See Akbar Ahmad, *Postmodernism and Islam: Predicament and Promise* (London: Routledge, 1992).

5. See Abraham Marcus, *The Middle East on the Eve of Modernity* (New York: Columbia University Press, 1989), pp. 18–21. See also Dale Eickelman and James Piscatori, *Muslim Politics* (Princeton, N.J.: Princeton University Press, 1996), pp. 102–3.

6. See Abu Ameenah Bilal Philips, *The Evolution of Fiqh* (Riyadh: International Islamic Publishing House, 1996), pp. 63–90.

7. See James Piscatori, *Islam in a World of Nation-States* (Cambridge: Cambridge University Press, 1986).

8. See Marya Schechtman, *The Constitution of Selves* (Ithaca: Cornell University Press, 1996), pp. 93–135.

9. See John L. Esposito, "Ismael R. Al-Faruqi: Muslim Scholar-Activist" in Yvonne Haddad, ed., *The Muslims of America* (Oxford: Oxford University Press, 1991), pp. 65–79.

10. See Jane I. Smith, "Seyyed Hossein Nasr: Defender of the Sacred and Islamic Traditionalism" in Haddad, ed., *Muslims of America*, pp. 80–95.

11. See Qutbi M. Ahmad, "Muslim Organizations in the United States," Haddad, ed., *Muslims of America*, pp. 11–25.

12. See Marcus, *Middle East on the Eve of Modernity*, pp. 39–48.

13. See Sulayman S. Nyang, "Convergence and Divergence in an Emergent Community: A Study of Challenges Facing U.S. Muslims," in Haddad, ed., *Muslims of America*, pp. 237–38.

14. See Dale Eickelman, "Ethnicity" in John L. Esposito, ed., *Oxford Encyclopedia of the Modern Islamic World* (New York: Oxford University Press, 1995), 1:447–51.

15. See A. Uner Turgay, "Nation" in Esposito, ed., *Oxford Encyclopedia of the Modern Islamic World*, 3:234.

16. See Aziz Al-Azmeh, *Islams and Modernities* (London: Verso, 1993), pp. 18–19.

17. See Philips, *Evolution of Fiqh*, pp. 52–56.

18. See Margaret R. Somers and Gloria D. Gibson, "Reclaiming the Epistemological 'Other': Narrative and the Social Constitution of Identity" in Calhoun, ed., *Social Theory and the Politics of Identity*, p. 53.

19. See Abdullah al Ahsan, *OIC: The Organization of The Islamic Conference* (Herndon, Va.: International Institute of Islamic Thought, 1988).

20. See *The Middle East* (Washington, D.C.: Congressional Quarterly, 1994).

21. See J. P. Bannerman, "OIC: Structure and Activities" in Esposito, ed., *Oxford Encyclopedia of the Modern Islamic World*, 3:262.

22. See M. A. Muqtedar Khan, "Tribalism the Historical Nemesis of Islam," *The Message*, March, 1996.

23. The recent annual convention of the American Muslim Council, April 26, 1997, Washington D.C., highlighted this aspect of Muslim political activism. Several speakers, including Jim Zoghby, M. A. Muqtedar Khan, and Mamoun Fandy, pointed to the need to develop a domestic political agenda for American Muslim activism.

24. See Yvonne Haddad and Jane Smith, *Mission to America: Five Islamic Sectarian Communities in North America* (Miami: University Press of Florida, 1993).

25. See Athar, *Reflections of an American Muslim*, p. 87.

26. See Steve A. Johnson, "Political Activity of Muslims in America," in Haddad, ed., *Muslims of America*, p. 119.

27. See ibid., pp. 118–19.

28. Sentiments of this nature were expressed by the executives and members of the American Muslim Council at the their first annual convention in Washington D.C., 25–27 April 1997.

29. See Johnson, "Political Activity of Muslims in America," pp. 118–19.

30. For Sunni-Shi'i differences in America, see Athar, *Reflections of an American Muslim*, p. 211.

31. In an interesting article, John Voll argues that the Islamic world is a separate system; see John Voll, "Islam as a Special World-System," *Journal of World History* 5, no. 2 (Fall 1994): 213–26.

32. See Glen E. Perry, "Caliph," in Esposito, ed., *Oxford Encyclopedia of the Modern Islamic World*, 1:240.

33. To understand how the problem of sovereignty was tackled, see M. A. Muqtedar Khan, "Sovereignty in Modernity and Islam," *East West Review*, Summer 1995, pp. 43–57.

34. See A. A. Abu Sulayman, *Towards an Islamic Theory of International Relations* (Herndon, VA: International Institute of Islamic Thought, 1993), p. 55.

35. Ibid., pp. 17–33.

36. See James Piscatori, "International Relations and Diplomacy" in Esposito, ed., *Oxford Encyclopedia of the Modern Islamic World*, 2:216–20.

37. See Abu Sulayman, *Towards an Islamic Theory of International Relations*, pp. 17–33, 51–55.

38. See the chapter on "War and Peace," in Bernard Lewis, *The Political Language of Islam* (Chicago: University of Chicago Press, 1988), pp. 71–90.

39. See M. A. Muqtedar Khan, "Islam as an Ethical Tradition of International Relations," *Islam and Christian-Muslim Relations*, Summer 1997.

40. See Majid Khadduri, *War and Peace in the Law of Islam* (Baltimore: The Johns Hopkins University Press, 1955).

41. For a more detailed argument against the Dar al-Harb and Dar al-Islam construction of world politics, see Muqtedar Khan "Islam as an Ethical Tradition of International Relations."

42. See Sohail Hashmi, "Is There an Islamic Ethic of Humanitarian Intervention?" *Ethics and International Affairs*, 1993; also Muqtedar Khan, "Islam as an Ethical Tradition of International Relations."

43. See Bernard Lewis, "The Roots of Muslim Rage," *Atlantic Monthly*, September, 1990, p. 52.

44. See Graham Fuller and Ian Lesser, *A Sense of Siege: The Geopolitics of Islam and the West* (Boulder: Westview Press, 1995), pp. 27–46, 81–98.

45. See Lewis, "Roots of Muslim Rage," pp. 52–53.

46. See John L. Esposito, *The Islamic Threat: Myth or Reality?* (New York: Oxford University Press, 1995).

47. See Arthur Lowrie, "The Campaign against Islam and American Foreign Policy," *Middle East Policy* 4, nos. 1–2 (September, 1995): 210–19; Esposito,

Islamic Threat: Myth or Reality; Yvonne Haddad, "American Foreign Policy in the Middle East and Its Impact on the Identity of Arab Muslims in the United States" in Haddad, ed., *Muslims of America*, pp. 217–35; Jochen Hippler, "The Islamic Threat and Western Foreign Policy" in Jochen Hippler and Andrea Leug, ed., *The Next Threat: Western Perceptions of Islam* (London: Pluto Press, 1995), pp. 117–53; finally Leon Hadar, "What Green Peril," *Foreign Affairs* 72, no. 2 (Spring 1993).

48. See Lowrie, "The Campaign against Islam and American Foreign Policy," pp. 210–19.

49. See Ilyas Bayunus, "On Terrorism and the Bandwagons," *The Message*, June 1995, p. 25.

50. See John L. Esposito, "American Perceptions of Islam and Arabs," *The Diplomat*, October 1996, pp. 10–11.

51. See Fred R. von der Mehden, "American Perceptions of Islam" in John L. Esposito, ed., *Voices of Resurgent Islam* (New York: Oxford University Press, 1983), pp. 18–32.

52. See Mary H. Cooper, "Muslims in America," *Congressional Quarterly Researcher*, April 30, 1993, pp. 365–66.

53. See Dale Eickelman and James Piscatori, *Muslim Politics* (Princeton, NJ: Princeton University Press, 1996), p. 144.

54. See Steven Barboza, *American Jihad: Islam after Malcolm X* (New York: Doubleday, 1993), pp. 19–24.

55. Western philosophers such as Hume and Nietzsche held the same view; see Bryan S. Turner, *Religion and Social Theory* (London: Sage Publications, 1991), pp. 35–37.

56. See M. A. Muqtedar Khan, "Dialogue of Civilizations?" *The Diplomat*, June 1997, pp. 45–49.

57. See Eickelman and Piscatori, *Muslim Politics*.

PART II

NORTH AMERICAN PLURALISM AND THE CHALLENGE OF THE VEIL

5

The *Hijab* and Religious Liberty

Anti-Discriminion Law and Muslim Women in the United States

KATHLEEN MOORE

Scholars have argued that developments since the 1960s in the judicial interpretations of the religion clauses[1] of the First Amendment to the Constitution have produced a "more generous and accepting spirit" toward the religious practices of minority religions in the United States.[2] It has further been said that certain statutes enacted by the federal government have gone beyond simply allowing free exercise (up to a point) to intervening in social and economic life to ensure that Americans are not deprived of certain rights because of the religious prejudices of their fellow citizens.[3] Civil-rights and hate-crimes legislation have specifically targeted discrimination based on racial, ethnic, and national origins, and sexual, as well as religious, differences. The prescribed solution to discrimination of all types, according to these laws, is the creation of a uniform civil code of protection for all persons regardless of their ascribed characteristics (e.g., skin color) or religious beliefs. The liberal guarantee of nondiscrimination and equal protection of the law, so fundamental to the U.S. Constitution and the Enlightenment ideal of an Archimedean point—in other words, a point of view from nowhere[4]—are present in the formulation of such uniform codes. For instance, rules and regulations promulgated in compliance with the federal Civil Rights Act of 1964, prohibiting discrimination in the workplace, reflect the normative claim for equal or "color blind" treatment.[5]

Yet recent appellate court decisions tell a different story. They belie the espoused commitment to neutrality and suggest that earlier research indicating a "more generous and accepting spirit" toward minority religions needs to be reconsidered in light of a conservative shift of late in the judiciary.[6] In 1986 the U.S. Supreme Court told Orthodox Jews that they may not wear yarmulkes while on duty in uniform when this violates a military dress code.[7] In a 1994 decision the Court denied public funding for a public school district, created exclusively for a community of Satmar Hasidic Jews, to run special needs educational programs for handicapped children of the Jewish sect.[8] Native Americans who lost their jobs and subsequently were denied unemployment benefits because they used peyote in religious rituals sought relief through the courts, but were told that the state had acted rationally in firing them.[9] Sikhs and Muslims have suffered a similar fate, losing their livelihood and unemployment compensation when their religiously prescribed clothing conflicted with workplace regulations.[10]

From these recent court cases we can gain some important insights about the current state of the "Americanization" process. First, it is clear that there are competing claims about rights and duties. The two claims models can be understood in the following terms. We have, on the one hand, the so-called universalistic claims of classical liberal democratic thought which embrace the principles of nondiscrimination and equal treatment and form the basis of current anti-discrimination statutes and, on the other, the putatively particularistic claims of minority religions whose members engage in "rights talk"[11] for the purpose of demanding at a minimum the recognition (if not the enforcement) by the state of the personal laws of each respective religious minority community. In the first instance, the argument is for the state to apply the same rules to all in the so-called public sphere (presuming the public/private distinction can easily be made), where theoretically, according to the equality principle, difference does not matter. In the second instance, the argument is for the state to refrain from interfering in certain so-called private or nonpolitical social spheres[12] where individuals are free to make choices about religious beliefs and practices, cultural preferences, and conceptions of the good, thereby developing group identities that manifest significant social differences.

Problems arise because the first claims model, based on an individualistic framework, denies the public relevance of the collective or communitarian identities of particularistic groups, such as faith communities, when they make political choices and engage in identity-based politics.[13] The dichotomy between these two orientations fails to capture adequately the claims and demands presented by each side, and contains the seeds for conflict between the values of individual liberty and group rights.[14]

The second insight is that these cases indicate that there are judicially defined limits within which cultural and legal pluralism is allowed to develop in society. Law presents one view on the legal subject—the objective or "universalistic" view in which the specifics of the individual's makeup and position in the world matter little. It is limited in its ability to foster cultural dialogue. But if we were to take a hermeneutic approach, and try to take into account the way participants in the legal system perceive their situation, we would have to move beyond the conceptual separation between the objective and the particular.

Third, because we are dealing with matters of education, employment, and workplace regulations in each of these cases, the impact of judicial outcomes is of material consequence. As political theorist Will Kymlicka suggests, their impact is material because it goes beyond mere lifestyle choices (which can be socially marginalized) to affect the life chances of the litigant, including employment opportunities.[15] Thus, the seemingly irreducible social differences between an observant Muslim woman who believes her religion requires her to wear certain clothing and the secular state create genuine problems of accommodation at considerable cost to the individual. The significance of this fact is not communicated in the language of the law, and the failure to communicate it reveals the shortcomings of the law, namely, its inability to construct a cultural dialogue.

Here I will examine the degree to which the concept of equality before the law has been honored and expanded in the law to include fair treatment for Muslims, granting legitimacy to religious practices as well as beliefs for a significant minority religion that is, more often than not, publicly represented as illiberal, anti-Enlightenment, misogynistic, and violent. The general point is to see whether and to what degree Muslims are allowed to act in accordance with particular religious convictions without its undermining their success in the economic and political institutions of the dominant society.[16] This will entail a look at how Muslims have been treated in employment, an important area of law where the government has taken upon itself the task of eradicating discrimination. Specifically, I shall look at the status of Title VII[17] anti-discrimination case law with regard to religious discrimination suits brought by Muslim women in the United States who have been fired or reprimanded at work for wearing Islamic attire. In some instances women have been prohibited from wearing the *hijab* or Muslim head scarf because of employers' dress regulations which forbid the wearing of clothing which attracts attention.[18] Instituted in the 1960s, originally to prevent female employees from wearing miniskirts or other revealing attire, ironically this regulation has been enforced recently to hinder women who choose to conceal parts of their bodies for religious reasons.[19] Under other circumstances women have been told not to wear the head scarf and other modest attire while at work because these articles of clothing clearly indicated their religious affiliation, which their employers did not wish to appear to endorse. For instance, in *EEOC v. Presbyterian Ministries, Inc.* (1992), a Presbyterian-operated retirement home forbade a receptionist from wearing the Muslim headscarf while at work because by doing so she was asserting non-Christian religious belief in a manner deemed inappropriate by her employer.[20] In *EEOC v. Reads, Inc.* (1991), a public school district in Philadelphia refused to hire Cynthia Moore, a Muslim woman, as a third-grade counselor in two parochial schools (the school district provides parochial schools with auxiliary services such as counseling) because she would not agree to remove her headscarf during the work day. In these cases what seems to be crucial is the religious significance of wearing the headscarf and not the article of clothing itself; if a woman had chosen to wear a scarf as an expression of taste or fashion the problem of endorsement of a particular viewpoint would not have arisen.[21]

Legal challenges to such workplace rules ask the courts to decide whether the rules violate the statutory prohibitions against discrimination contained in Title VII of the 1964 Civil Rights Act in particular and, more generally, the religion clauses of the First Amendment.[22] Instances where the hijab and modest dress are at issue demand a difficult standard of justice from the courts. The courts, on the one hand, are guided by precedent to rule according to the principle of nondiscrimination on the basis of sex and religion in these cases and must strike down regulations which violate this principle without proof that some overriding concern exists—e.g., the nonestablishment of religion in schools.[23] The problem with this standard of justice is that in recent years the courts have recognized some overriding concerns, articulated by the state, which have prevailed over the interests of the less powerful individual identified with the minority religion. Such concerns include preserving the neutrality of the state.[24]

A second problem is that this standard of justice would ignore completely the perspectives of the Muslim women who are the legal claimants in these cases. This standard of justice does not allow for the emergence of "narratives," or for making more explicit the minority female experience in the general field of anti-discrimination law. How can the law and legal claimants' perspectives each be developed in order to take the other into account? How do they, in conjunction, govern the thoughts, beliefs, and actions of the individual? Perhaps the tension created by holding them in opposition, without suppressing either element, may generate something new. Demands advanced by proponents of cultural diversity for culturally informed methods of policymaking and, in judicial proceedings, the "cultural defense,"[25] require of the courts an accommodation of the personal laws and internal requirements of the minority religion. However, the courts to date have given little attention to the latter in their administration of justice. To do so would require the courts to engage in a subjective analysis, reflecting on "what kind of subject a particular person or legal claimant appears to be, what kind of influences have shaped her, and what kinds of groups can lay claim to her loyalties or affiliations"[26]—something which the courts are reluctant to do. It would also require the courts to consider the locus of subjective perception, that is, "the perceptual framework through which she [the legal claimant] views the world."[27]

This last point is at the core of the critique made by legal scholars of the postmodern feminist and critical race theory positions. They argue that the judiciary's current conceptions of rights, remedies, and human agency are too narrow and reductionist to resolve conflicts involving people at the margins of society, such as women of color, who are located "within at least two subordinated groups that frequently pursue conflicting political agendas."[28] For instance, religious discrimination complaints presented by Muslim women who wear the head scarf and other Islamic attire in the workplace are particularly complex because they can claim "intersectional forms" of discrimination,[29] that is, identities which fall into more than one of the existing statutory categories under Title VII—religion (Muslim), sex (female), and in many of the court cases, race (African-American). Accordingly, Kathryn Abrams suggests, for example, that to understand these claims, "complex narratives are, first and foremost, a promising vehicle for introducing legal decision-makers to a more complex, ambiguous legal subject."[30]

In terms of Islamically prescribed attire, then, the experiences of Muslim women in the United States are frequently the product of their intersectionality, as Muslim women usually of color, and the current status of anti-discrimination law is incapable of providing remedies for the specific harms suffered by these victims of workplace discrimination. What is at stake here as well are matters of intragroup differences (e.g., differences of perspective among women, or among Muslims, about the significance of the head scarf) which, due to their location in the interstices of conventional legal categories, resist telling in judicial proceedings. What this requires, according to postmodern feminists and critical race theorists, is a new jurisprudence which would allow the subjective perceptual framework to be employed in the judicial decisionmaking process.[31]

At this point I should offer the following caveat: the prescription of a new jurisprudence, while powerful, is not in my view adequate to deal with the problem of accommodation of religious practices in the workplace. These problems can be resolved politically and historically and, although they are matters of law, they are not exclusively in the domain of judicial decision makers.[32] Jurisprudence can represent only a part of what shapes the experiences and life chances of Muslim women in the United States. Certainly, it needs to be comprehended as a contributing factor, but only one of many to be taken into account when seeking to understand the grounds of identity constituting the social world of women in general and Muslim women in particular. My point is that an expanded judicial role, as a new jurisprudence would imply, would not be sufficient to resolve the problems of workplace discrimination presented by religious expression. Conceivably, an option might be to create the space within the law for the telling women's stories,[33] as the emerging sociolegal literature on narratives suggests.[34] However, my focus here is on the need to account for the limitations of the law for the development of a cultural dialogue when considering how Muslim women—both immigrant and native-born—cope with the pressures to conform to the American mainstream.

To examine how an appeals court has analyzed the issue of the Muslim headscarf (considered to be religious garb) under provisions of Title VII, I will consider in detail one case, *United States v. Board of Education of the School District of Philadelphia*,[35] decided on appeal by a federal circuit court in 1990. Like the Muslim headscarf controversy in France beginning in 1989,[36] this case involves the public education system, where religious symbols are banned because "the school is an instrument of the secular state for the public education of the future citizens . . . [and the] prohibition to wear the headscarf is the reaffirmation of the boundaries of the secularized public sphere against any religious interference."[37]

Religious Attire as Protected Religious Practice

Title VII of the Civil Rights Act of 1964 was designed to protect employees in both the public and private sectors from discrimination in the workplace on the basis of race, sex, color, religion, or national origin. This piece of legislation radically changed our conceptions of discrimination as well as the larger civil rights movement that produced it. A heightened consciousness about racial equality and equal treatment of the sexes, as well as expectations about the utility and protection of the law, have influenced the debates about civil liberties, tolerance, and the law in a manner that suggests certain types of behavior and inhibits others. However, the critical issue of religious discrimination has received far less attention than race or sex discrimination in civil rights practice and scholarship. While a small but increasing number of complaints of religious discrimination have been filed with the Equal Employment Opportunity Commission (EEOC), and with state and county human relations or fair employment commissions, relatively few cases have been brought to the courts.[38] Until recently, Muslims, who constitute a significant religious minority in the United States estimated to number over four million,[39] have not been much heard from in equal employment opportunity debates and concerns over discriminatory treatment in the workplace.

The legal mobilization of Muslim claimants has accelerated of late, mainly in the form of women complaining of anti-hijab discrimination in a number of professions and occupations, including medicine, education, the hospitality industries (such as hotels and restaurants), retail sales, and secretarial work. The Council of American-Islamic Relations (CAIR) and the American Muslim Council (AMC), two advocacy groups, have documented several instances in which Muslim women were not allowed to wear the hijab at work, usually because it violated an employer's dress code, or were discriminated against because of their attire. Using press conferences, letter-writing campaigns, and the Internet to publicize offenses, these groups have brought pressure to bear upon employers in a bid to get them to accommodate the hijab. For instance, women who were not hired, or were fired, because they wore the hijab while on the job in hotels (e.g., at the reception desk or the hotel telephone switchboard) became the object of press conferences and letter-writing campaigns in 1996.[40] At universities women have complained of ostracism and lost opportunities for advancement, which they attribute to anti-Muslim bias.[41]

The following EEO religious discrimination case illustrates the changing conceptions of discrimination and the federal government's attempt to accommodate minority religious practices and what protections Title VII provides and what Title VII requires of employers.

The Facts of the Case.   In 1984 Alima Dolores Reardon, a Muslim who holds the religious conviction that Muslim women are required by their faith to wear a concealing headscarf and long, loose dress in public,[42] was fired from her job as a substitute teacher in Philadelphia's public schools pursuant to Pennsylvania's "religious garb" statute.[43] Originally enacted in 1895 at the peak of nativist anti-Catholic sentiments in the United States, the state law prohibits a public school teacher from wearing anything indicating adherence to any religious denomination.

This statute is not unique to Pennsylvania; it is one of four states with a religious-garb statute which proscribes the wearing of religious attire by public school teachers.[44] While these statutes have been enforced very infrequently, their importance is more than symbolic. As a practical matter they have been used recently (seemingly in a disparate manner) by school boards to prohibit the practice of wearing religiously inspired or mandated clothing by a Sikh[45] and, in the case considered in this section, by a Muslim school teacher.[46]

The History of Pennsylvania's Religious Garb Statute.   In 1895 the Pennsylvania legislature enacted a religious garb statute on the heels of the unpopular Pennsylvania Supreme Court ruling in *Hysong v. Gallitzin Borough School District.*[47] In this case the state supreme court held that "the wearing of traditional religious habits by Catholic nuns teaching in public schools did not constitute sectarian teaching unless the nuns conveyed religious instruction during school hours."[48]

In an effort to keep Catholic nuns and priests out of the public schools, the newly enacted religious-garb statute prohibited any public school teacher from wearing "any dress, mark, emblem, or insignia indicating . . . that such teacher is a member or adherent of any religious order, sect, or denomination."[49] The statute also provided a criminal penalty for any public school administrator, such as a school principal, who failed to suspend or fire the offending teacher. According to the provisions of the 1895 statute, a principal may be fined up to $100 and may lose his or her job for failure to remove the teacher who is in violation of the statute.

The religious-garb statute was challenged in court fifteen years after its enactment, but the Pennsylvania Supreme Court held that the statute did not offend the liberty and freedom-of-conscience provisions of the state constitution because the statute did not interfere with religious beliefs, but only with religious practices of public school teachers wile acting in their capacity as teachers.[50] Although the state constitution guarantees individuals a right to worship according to their own conscience and that no persons shall be disqualified from holding any public office because of their belief in a God,[51] the state supreme court held that the proscription of a practice, such as wearing religious attire, was not inconsistent. Sixteen years after the *Hysong* ruling, the Pennsylvania Supreme Court reversed itself with regard to its position on the wearing of religious attire and whether it conveyed a sectarian message to school children.

In the intervening eighty-five years since the *Commonwealth v. Herr* decision, much has changed in the social and political climate in the United States—the civil rights movement and enactment of civil rights legislation, the advent of the welfare state, and greater involvement of government at all levels in the lives of its citizens. Concomitant with these changes, First Amendment jurisprudence regarding both the free exercise and establishment clauses has also evolved. Dolores Reardon's case of religious discrimination in the workplace presents a question for the first time in federal courts: is Pennsylvania's religious-garb statute consistent with Title VII's prohibition of religious discrimination in employment? A case comment in the *Georgetown Law Journal* points out that "religious garb statutes have been challenged on various grounds in the past but *United States v. Bd. of Education* marks the first time a [federal appellate] court has had occasion to examine the religious garb statute in the context of Title VII, which prohibits religious discrimination in employment."[52] In addition, there is a corollary question: would compliance with Title VII mean that the school district was violating the establishment clause of the First Amendment to the U.S. Constitution? Title VII, especially the "reasonable accommodation" provision, exists on uneasy terms with the establishment clause.

Title VII's Religious Discrimination Clause. Section 703(a) of Title VII provides in its relevant part:

> (a) It shall be an unlawful employment practice for an employer 1) to fail or refuse to hire or to discharge any individual with respect to his compensation, terms, conditions, or privileges of employment, because of such individual's race, color, religion, sex, or national origin. . . .

Two approaches to prove employer liability have evolved in Title VII case law and are present in religious discrimination cases. Discrimination may result from (1) disparate treatment or (2) disparate impact. Either approach may be taken singly in a case, or both may be applied to a set of facts. Claims of disparate treatment are based on intentional discrimination: the argument applies when the employer is alleged to have favored some people over others, and to have had as motive for such disparate treatment some reason based on race, color, sex, religion, or national origin. With respect to religion there are circumstances under which an exception to the prohibition of Title VII may be granted. In instances where religion is a "bona fide occupational qualification" (BFOQ), the employer may successfully defend disparate treatment of employees. In other words, Title VII allows an employer to employ a person "on the basis of religion . . . in those cases where religion . . . is a bona fide occupational qualification reasonably necessary to the normal operation of that particular business or enterprise. . . ."[53] Thus a business necessity may permit an exception to the provisions of the Title VII religious discrimination clause. But it is difficult to defend disparate treatment because the employment policy at issue overtly discriminates on the basis of religion. In order to pass scrutiny under Title VII the employer has the heavy burden of showing that religion is a BFOQ "reasonably necessary to the normal operation of [the] particular business or enterprise." The few cases where this has been allowed include *Kern v. Dynaelectron Co.*[54] In *Kern* the plaintiff challenged Dynalectron Company's policy that all helicopter pilots flying over Mecca in Saudi Arabia convert to Islam. The federal district court held that the policy did not violate Title VII because religion was a BFOQ, given that Saudi law prohibits entry by non-Muslims into the holy city of Mecca under penalty of death.[55]

In contrast to disparate treatment, the disparate-impact approach argues that an otherwise valid, facially neutral employment policy leads to unequal results. For instance, a requirement that all male employees be clean-shaven does not, on its face, specifically address religion. However, such a policy has a disproportionate impact on employees practicing a religion which forbids the shaving of facial hair. To raise a disparate impact challenge, it must be shown that a given policy has a harsher effect, however unintentionally, on members of certain religious groups than on the entire category of individuals affected by the policy. An employer's defense may be based on the showing that (1) reasonable efforts were made to accommodate the employer's religious beliefs, or (2) accommodation of those beliefs would result in an undue hardship on the employer.

The disparate treatment and disparate impact conceptions of discrimination each require a slightly different remedy. When a person raises a disparate treatment challenge to an employment policy, he or she is in effect demanding to be treated equally. The vision of a remedy is uniform treatment of all employees regardless of race, color, religion, sex, or national origin. The concept of "equality under the law" is central to this type of remedy. An examination of the legislative history shows that when Title VII was enacted in 1964, legislators had in mind the disparate treatment conception of discrimination and equal treatment as the desired remedy. However, within a few years of enactment it became clear that disparate treatment was not the only problematic form of discrimination which Title VII needed to address. Complaints of disparate impact began to appear, which alleged discrimination on the part of employment policies that were applied in an equal manner but, because they were uniformly applied, resulted in a particular harm to a minority group. The remedy envisioned by the disparate impact approach is not equal treatment, but accommodation of difference. Plaintiffs alleging disparate impact seek religious exemption from otherwise valid policies, and ask to be treated as exceptional cases who want to be treated differently with respect to specific religious practices. This type of remedy was not adequately provided for in the original version of Title VII and required amendment to the law.

Reasonable Accommodation. When Title VII was originally enacted in 1964, it prohibited employment discrimination based on religion, but it contained no provision to define the extent of the protection or the lengths the employer must go in order to accommodate an employee's religious beliefs and practices. So, in 1972, Title VII was amended to add the following "reasonable accommodation" provision (sec. 703[j]):

> The term "religion" includes all aspects of religious observance and practice, as well as belief, unless an employer demonstrates that he [or she] is unable to reasonably accommodate to an employee's or prospective employee's religious observance or practice without undue hardship on the conduct of the employer's business.[56]

The reasonable-accommodation provision was added in order to strengthen the provisions for religious protection contained in the 1964 version of Title VII and to resolve ambiguities in the original legislative language. The original language guards against intentional discrimination (disparate treatment) on the basis of religion and the purpose of the 1972 reasonable accommodation provision is to mitigate the second conception of discrimination, the disparate impact of facially neutral employment policies that affect the religious practices of some employees. It stiffens the requirements of Title VII by requiring an employer to "reasonably accommodate" religious observances and practices of current and prospective employees unless to do so would result in an "undue hardship" for the employer's business.[57] More than half of all religious discrimination complaints since the 1972 amendment have been based on an alleged failure on the part of the employer to "reasonably accommodate" a religious observance or practice.[58]

Now it would appear that the extent of an employer's obligation to accommodate an employee's religious practice is limited only by the definition of the meaning of the term "undue hardship." In Title VII jurisprudence the meaning of the term "undue hardship" has evolved to include anything that would involve more than a "de minimus cost" to the employer.[59] This would mean that if, in order to accommodate the religious practices of the individual, the employer would have to violate the seniority provision of a collective bargaining agreement, or pay overtime wages to substitute workers on Saturdays so that a Sabbatarian would not have to work on Saturdays for religious reasons, the accommodation would constitute an "undue hardship." As case law now stands, accommodations resulting in the violation of a valid collective bargaining agreement, overtime wages, or lost efficiency constitute undue hardship.

However, an employer's hypothetical argument that he or she may suffer undue hardship in the future as a result of hiring a Sabbatarian, for instance, have not been accepted in the courts.[60] In no case prior to *United States v. Bd. of Education*, in which Reardon's religious discrimination charge was reviewed, "has a hypothetical or theoretical burden been deemed sufficient" to prove an undue hardship.[61]

United States v. Board of Education of School District of Philadelphia, 911 F.2d 882 (3d Cir. 1990).[62] Reardon had been working in the Philadelphia school district for twelve years when she decided in 1982 to adopt the religious attire she believes her religion requires. She continued teaching after 1982 wearing a headscarf and long dress, and she received no complaints about this practice either "from the community or the school administration" for two years.[63] At the end of 1984 Reardon was told, on three separate occasions by three different school principals, that she could not teach while wearing her religious attire. She was not allowed to teach as a substitute and was sent home on all three occasions because she arrived at the schools wearing her headscarf and concealing dress.

In November 1984 Reardon filed a Title VII complaint with the EEOC against the school district of Philadelphia charging discrimination on the basis of religion. The EEOC investigated the complaint and, finding Reardon's complaint to be valid, attempted reconciliation meetings with the school board. Reardon was reinstated as a substitute teacher in November 1985 and was permitted to teach full time in the Philadelphia school district while dressed in her religiously inspired clothing.[64] However, she was not awarded back pay, nor did the school district concede that the religious garb statute was applied in a discriminatory fashion, nor did it promise not to continue to enforce the statute in like manner.

The EEOC transferred Reardon's complaint to the U.S. Department of Justice in order to sue the school board of Philadelphia in the federal district court in the Eastern District of Pennsylvania. The complaint in court included two theories of employer's liability: "(1) Failing or refusing to employ as public school teachers individuals who wear or who seek to wear garb or dress that is an aspect of their religious observance, and (2) failing or refusing reasonably to accommodate individuals who wear or who seek to wear garb or dress . . . that is an aspect of their religious observance or practice."[65]

Initially Reardon's case was successful. The district court held that Title VII prohibited the enforcement of the Pennsylvania religious garb statute. Reardon received back pay for the period of time she was denied employment, and the school board was enjoined from continuing to enforce the religious garb statute. The district court noted that the school board's application of the religious garb statute to Reardon was selective and disparate treatment because "several others in the Philadelphia public school system wore religious garb or symbols without complaint or incident, [and] there was no evidence that any student perceived such attire as an endorsement of a particular religion."[66]

However, on appeal the Court of Appeals for the Third Circuit overturned the district court ruling. The circuit court opinion interpreted the reasonable accommodation provision of Title VII in such a way as to exonerate the employer, the school board.

With respect to the reasonable accommodation provision of Title VII, the district court found that Reardon's employer must reasonably accommodate Reardon's religious practice unless the school board could show that such an accommodation would present an "undue hardship" to the schools. The school board had done nothing to accommodate Reardon and so had the burden of proving that it was unable to accommodate her religious practice without suffering undue hardship. The school board claimed that accommodation of Reardon's religious practices would hypothetically expose its administrators to the possibility of criminal penalties—convictions, fines, and expulsion from their profession—under Pennsylvania's religious garb statute. However, the district court rejected this argument, noting that no action had ever been taken to enforce the religious garb statute. The court concluded that "the specter of a penal sanction did not constitute undue hardship."[67]

The district court also rejected the school board's argument that it would suffer undue hardship because an accommodation of Reardon's religious practice would force the school board to violate the establishment clause of the First Amendment to the U.S. Constitution.[68] The establishment clause would be violated, the school board argued, by its acquiescence in Reardon's wearing of religious attire, which might lead schoolchildren to form the (mistaken) impression that the school board endorsed Reardon's religious viewpoint. The district court concluded that by allowing Reardon to wear religious attire the school board would not necessarily be communicating its endorsement of her convictions.[69]

On appeal, however, the U.S. Court of Appeals accepted the school board's argument that accommodating Reardon's religious practices would constitute an undue hardship for the employer. The appeals court concluded that accommodation would work an undue hardship in two ways: (1) it would put the school board and the individual school principals in the position of violating a valid statute, thereby exposing administrators to the risk of criminal prosecution, fines, and the loss of their jobs pursuant to the religious garb statute; and (2) it would require the Commonwealth of Pennsylvania to sacrifice a compelling state interest in preserving the secular appearance of its public school system.[70] While the courts have not accepted hypothetical undue hardship allegations in the past, this decision represents a departure from previous case law in the Third Circuit in this respect. The appellate court found that the prospect of criminal prosecution, no matter how remote, when combined with an interest in preserving the secular appearance of the schools, was sufficient to rule in favor of the employer. The appellate decision held that Title VII does not prevent the school board from denying Reardon the opportunity to teach while wearing the clothing she believes is mandated by her religious faith. In fact, the appellate court decision implies, but never explicitly holds, that Title VII's requirement of reasonable accommodation may place the public official in danger of violating the establishment clause by creating the impression that he or she endorses particular religious convictions.

Part of the Muslim community that was attentive to these court proceedings responded with dismay at the appellate court ruling. The *Muslim Media Watch* (published and distributed from Orange County, California), noted with considerable irony of the circuit court's decision to overturn the lower court ruling, "Free country, isn't it?"

Title VII doctrine attempts to accommodate diversity in the workplace; it does not simply mandate uniformity, allowing for reasonable accommodation of practices unless they present a substantial cost or, as in the case presented by Reardon, the non-economic risk (of criminal prosecution) to the employer. Whether this will fail to meet the standards of the establishment clause remains a question that has yet to be addressed by the U.S. Supreme Court.

Muslims Under Title VII: The Impact of Anti-Discrimination Law

The Muslim headscarf case is only one example of changing conceptions of discrimination, equal treatment, and reasonable accommodation of religious practices in the workplace. The outcome in this case is that the headscarf—"a strong, loud, perhaps provocative expression of individual religious choice"[71]—is not tolerated within the limits of nondiscrimination and religious liberty, but instead rejected as perhaps a threat of proselytism in public space and definitely as something which interferes with the secular nature of public education. This not only stigmatizes the headscarf, but also raises certain normative questions about the creation of a third position as an alternative to both liberalism and particularism, where reciprocal respect and recognition are exchanged and accommodation is allowed, and the adequacy of law to consider these claims and demands. The contextual analysis of the headscarf case indicates that the current status of Title VII law falls short of these tasks and presents observant Muslims in some instances with the necessity of choosing between breaking religious law and keeping a job.

Now the question is, what follows on the heels of litigation in terms of public action? In general, perhaps the most interesting effect has been the adaptation of legal norms and resources on the part of Muslims to change their environment, which has in turn contributed to an overall transformation of their self-identification.[72] The result of a moderate record of success in litigation is that the plaintiffs become more attentive to the courts as an institution that legitimately defines and protects individual rights. However, the courts generally have not been very sympathetic to claims for reasonable accommodation of religious practices. EEOC plaintiffs claiming religious discrimination, over half of which seek accommodation on the part of their employers, lose an estimated 64 percent of their cases, which is a higher proportion of losses than in race and sex discrimination cases.[73]

In the Muslim communities in the United States there has been an underlying effort to resist the "lure of litigation"[74] and to temper an increasing attentiveness to American legal institutions by strengthening a sense of cultural and religious autonomy. An investigation of the writings of various Muslims on this topic shows evidence of a continuing effort to put forward options for maintaining Muslim life within the framework of pluralism and diversity.[75] Yet much of what has been written is from the viewpoint of the "majoritarian" Muslim living in a predominantly Muslim society, and relatively little has been written from the perspective of the Muslim living as a minority in a non-Islamic society. As legal scholar Khaled Abou al-Fadl suggests, "Most of the available resources are written from the perspective of [male] Muslim jurists,"[76] and this can be problematic for Muslims who live permanently in Western societies, because "the traditional criteria worked out by earlier generations of Muslim jurists pose difficult questions for the modern age, when the application of Muslim personal or family law in a secular state has become a difficult matter."[77]

What is lost in the American legal setting is the qualitative aspect of the stories Muslim women have to tell. The court records provide only a partial picture of the social realities encountered by Muslim women in the United States. The absence of narrative[78] points to a loss for these women and for society at large, because they are treated as though they had no voice. Something is lost for pluralism even in those cases where the judicial outcome is favorable to Muslim women to the extent that the judicial proceedings have forced the issue of the headscarf into a problem that had to be managed and litigated, rather than leaving it as something that does not require separate attention and legal protection because it is simply part of social life. The "hegemonic" story—in other words, the court's interpretation of anti-discrimination law in a manner which allows school boards to prohibit the headscarf on the basis of a church/state separation claim, without hearing from the affected women what the headscarf means for identity—"reproduce[s] existing relations of power and inequity, [and] fails to make visible and explicit the connections between particular lives and social organization."[79]

Interest in the conditions of Muslims living as minority communities in the West has been growing during the last two decades. Recently a Fiqh Council has begun to operate in the United States, offering an alternative dispute resolution mechanism for those in the community who consent to bring their conflicts to experts in Islamic legal jurisprudence rather than the American legal system. The secretary of the Fiqh Council of North America has noted that as the North American Muslim community continues to grow and become more ethnically and culturally diverse, "the phenomenon of the 'imported' mufti becomes more problematic." Immigrant and indigenous Muslims in the United States have "often been disappointed by the lack of appreciation for local conditions and circumstances on the part of such 'imported' muftis" and community leaders have come to realize that "the legal *responsum* and *fatawa* obtained, so to speak, through the mail from muftis in Muslim majority countries often fail to address the crux of the issues presented to them for consideration."[80] These features have led to the development of local experts on Islamic law and to the somewhat better organization of Islamic legal resources. But this still leaves the matter of relations between the majority society, with its formal political and legal institutions, and the minority religious community to be mediated and adjudicated within the framework offered by the dominant legal order.

Scholars of law and religion in pluralist societies need to be attentive to the ways in which Muslims in the United States may build on and at the same time remain relatively independent from the formal legal order.[81] In the American context this raises interesting questions. Can a Muslim minority live as an integrated part of a pluralistic society, or must it insist on exclusivity? Can the community maintain its difference while at the same time demanding that it be treated equally and be given equal access to resources? What about sharp differences within groups as well as the tensions between communities? The larger questions that drive my interest in this research concern the identity formation of Muslims who choose to challenge regulations that interfere with their religious practices. What happens to Muslims who file formal complaints through a federal administrative agency such as the Equal Employment Opportunity Commission (EEOC) or in the courts? What happens to the collective Muslim communities as they develop the institutional bases they need to define and defend their identity in a non-Islamic society? Answers to these questions raise issues of self-representation and lifestyle for Muslims in the United States and provide and refine various models for Muslim minority life. The issue of accommodation of Muslim practices in the workforce and, specifically, the degree of success Muslims achieve in asserting claims for accommodation have a transformative effect on Muslim life in the United States.

The intention in this essay and ongoing research is to bring the human factor into sharper focus by looking at the activity and divergent views of a significant religious minority which has utilized legal structures in the United States to assert and protect its claims for equal protection. When we take into account the activity and views of Muslims as they interpret and act on law, we may apprehend the ways in which they, as a religious minority, signal and strengthen their relations with the larger society. As Harvard law professor Martha Minow explains, "Those claiming rights implicitly invest themselves in a larger community, even in the act of seeking to change it."[82]

Rights claims, however, may challenge the exclusion from the workplace of some people who are "different," but fail to indicate how the workplace can be remade to accommodate difference. The unstated norms against which we define difference remain powerful.[83] It is under these conditions that Muslims who file complaints of religious discrimination in employment have forged two paths: one toward equal treatment (seeking the right to be treated equally), and the other toward equal respect (seeking greater accommodation of their differences). Both of these paths imply slightly differing visions of pluralism. Historically, the path toward equal treatment has led to the right to receive uniform treatment—"to be treated the same way as the majority."[84]

This outcome has failed to satisfy some members of subject groups, such as Muslims, who seek a broader conception of equality, one that includes a public recognition of collective identities and allows groups to maintain their distinctive ways of life. These would instead seek to follow the second path toward workplace policies that make accommodation of difference possible.

These features are increasingly important to comprehend as various societies worldwide face the growing pressures of the contemporary global migration. By focusing attention on the place of Islam in identity formation and negotiation with society at large and on the particular challenge this presents to the (re)constitution of the secular society, this inquiry provides a basis from which to theorize about the constitutive role of law in migration and acculturation.

Solving the problems of religious communal relations in multi-ethnic nation-states will become in the next century just as important in sustaining stable pluralistic societies as race relations have been in this century. The move toward greater accommodation of religious difference, articulated in the "reasonable accommodation" provision of Title VII, indicates an acknowledgment of American society as increasingly pluralistic. The intent here has been to lay the foundation for a continuing examination of the role of law in mediating relations between a significant religious minority and the institutions of the state. While it would be incorrect to suppose that a heterogeneous population, such as the Muslims of the United States are, forms a single, unitary group, it ought not to be forgotten that Muslims constitute an important presence in a richly textured and complex society.

Notes

Author's note: I am grateful to Professor Richard Hiskes for his helpful comments on an earlier version of this essay.

1. The religion clauses are the "establishment" and "free exercise" clauses.

2. See Frank Way and Barbara J. Burt, "Religious Marginality and the Free Exercise Clause," *American Political Science Review* 77 (1983): 652–65. See also Kent Grenawalt, *Religious Convictions and Political Choices* (Oxford: Oxford University Press, 1988).

3. See Gloria T. Beckley and Paul Burstein, "Religious Pluralism, Equal Opportunity, and the State," *Western Political Science Quarterly* 44 (1991): 185–

208, esp. 186. The federal laws to which I refer include the Civil Rights Acts of 1964 and 1991, the Hate Crimes Act of 1988, and the Hate Crimes Statistics Act of 1990, and the Religious Freedom Restoration Act of 1992.

4. See H. L. A. Hart, *The Concept of Law* (Oxford: Clarendon Press, 1961). For a discussion of universalism in rights theory, see Martha Minow, *Making All the Difference: Inclusion, Exclusion, and American Law* (Ithaca: Cornell University Press, 1990), esp. pp. 60–61; and Valerie Kerruish, *Jurisprudence as Ideology* (London: Routledge Press, 1991). For an assessment of the validity and limits of objectivity, see Thomas Nagel, *The View from Nowhere* (New York: Oxford University Press, 1986).

5. The history of "color blindness" in American jurisprudence dates back to the nineteenth century. In *Plessy v. Ferguson* (1896), establishing the "separate but equal" doctrine, Justice Harlan (dissenting) posited that "our Constitution is color-blind, and neither knows nor tolerates classes among citizens . . ." (163 U.S. 537, 559). See also Jerome McCristal Culp, Jr., "Neutrality, the Race Question, and the 1991 Civil Rights Act: The 'Impossibility' of Permanent Reform," *Rutgers Law Review* 45 (1993): 965–1010.

6. Another line of argumentation suggests that the neutrality principle of liberal democratic thought has never in fact been truly neutral. Instead it is tailored to include only those conceptions of the good which already appear to be compatible with the liberal polity, while "filtering out those produced by alien cultures" (Anna Elizabetta Galeotti, "Citizenship and Equality: The Place for Toleration," *Political Theory* 21 [1993]: 589). Moreover, the ostensibly value-neutral modern state cannot help but promote specific, if unacknowledged values, such as toleration, because all social practices are derived from and reinforce a particular cultural ethos. Thus, the purported universalism of the liberal tradition is really only another form of particularism (see ibid.; and Bruce Ackerman, "What is Neutral About Neutrality," *Ethics* 93 [1983]: 372–90; and Charles Taylor, *Human Agency and Language*, Philosophical Papers I [Cambridge: Cambridge University Press, 1989], and *Multiculturalism and "The Politics of Recognition"* [Princeton: Princeton University Press, 1992).

7. *Goldman v. Weinberger*, 475 U.S. 503 (1986).

8. *Board of Education of Kiryas Joel Village School District v. Grumet*, 114 S.Ct. 2481 (1994).

9. *Employment Division of Oregon v. Smith*, 494 U.S. 872 (1990).

10. With regard to Sikhs, see *Cooper v. Eugene School District*, 301 Or. 358, 723 P.2d 298 (1986), appeal dismissed, 480 U.S. 942 (1987). With respect to Muslims see *United States v. Board of Education of School District of Pennsylvania*, 911 F.2d 822 (3rd Cir. 1990).

11. Mary Ann Glendon, *Rights Talk: The Impoverishment of Political Discourse* (New York: Free Press, 1991).

12. Galeotti, *Citizenship and Equality*, p. 588.

13. Ibid., p. 590.

14. Another significant problem, of course, is that the "normal" views of important social differences, commonly held by the liberal Enlightenment position, are inadequate to grasp what is at stake (Galeotti, *Citizenship and Equality*, pp. 586, 590). According to the liberal model, differences are conceived as simply a matter of choice rather than in some cases as ascriptive differences. Thus, tolerance is difficult to achieve in a democratic polity because the posi-

tions held by the majority are considered to be inherently superior to positions held by a minority (which are regarded to be a matter of choice). This is considered to be true because of the premise that in a democracy we have a "free marketplace of ideas" where the "best" ideas will thrive and inferior ideas will fail. Thus, in the Americanization process the unpopular views or conceptions of the good of "alien cultures," such as Islam, given time, will succumb to the hegemonic views of the majority culture on a number of issues, including women's equality and the importance of secular conduct and appearance in the public space. For discussion of this, see Galeotti, *Citizenship and Equality*.

15. Will Kymlicka, *Multicultural Citizenship* (New York: Oxford University Press, 1995), p. 202, n. 26.

16. Ibid., p. 31.

17. Title VII of the Civil Rights Act of 1964, Pub. L. 88–352, tit. VII, 78 Stat. 241, 253–66, (codified as amended principally at 42 U.S.C. 2000e-17 (1988 & Supp. III 1992).

18. In EEOC Decisions No. 71–2620 (1971) CCH EEOC Decisions P-6283, the employer's dress regulations discouraging attention-attracting clothing were the basis for firing a female Muslim employee because she wore an ankle-length dress. In this case the EEOC held that the employer's policy amounted to unlawful religious discrimination in violation of Title VII of the 1964 Civil Rights Act.

19. Political theorist Anna Elizabetta Galeotti makes an interesting point when she writes that in the French context, "a woman with her head covered by a scarf in a room is...as visible as the first who wore a miniskirt in the early 1960s" (*Citizenship and Equality*, p. 593).

20. *EEOC v. Presbyterian Ministries, Inc.*, 50 Fair Empl. Prac. Cas. (BNA) 579 (1992).

21. For observations of the fashion/religiously prescribed scarf dichotomy, see Homa Hoodfar, "The Veil in Their Minds and on Our Heads: The Persistence of Colonial Images of Muslim Women," in *Review of Feminist Research* 22 (1994): 5–18.

22. Cases involving Muslim complainants comprised about 11 percent of all religious discrimination lawsuits (243) examined in one study through early 1987 (Beckley and Burstein, "Religious Pluralism"). Examples not discussed here are *EEOC v. Rollins* (DC Ga 1974), in which a Muslim woman alleges she was fired for wearing certain clothing required by her religious beliefs in the Nation of Islam, and EEOC Decisions No. 71–2620 (1971) and P 6283—in which a Muslim female employee's religion and dress did not conform to the employer's standards of conduct and appearance.

23. Presumably, allowing women to wear religious attire survives the establishment-clause barrier, i.e., is permissible, provided it does not create a union between religion and state, or have the principal effect of advancing religion or endorsing any religious viewpoint. These standards are derived from the *Lemon v. Kurtzman* 403 U.S. 602 (1971) test.

24. The concept of state neutrality is problematic, however, and defies a single explanation. As Galeotti suggests, neutrality "is a relational concept and, by its very logic, cannot ever be absolute but must be always contextually defined." Further, the problem of state neutrality is its "fundamental insensitivity" to differences (*Citizenship and Equality*, p. 589).

25. Note "The Cultural Defense in Criminal Law," *Harvard Law Review*,

vol. 99(6) pp. 1293–7 (1986), and Alison Dundes Renteln, *International Human Rights: Universalism vs. Cultural Relativism* (Newbury Park: Sage Publications, 1990).

26. Kathryn Abrams, "Title VII and the Complex Female Subject," in *Michigan Law Review* 92 (1994): 2481.

27. Ibid. As Patricia Ewick and Susan Silbey point out, the narrative form has been spurned in sociolegal analysis and judicial decision-making since the 1930s and 1940s as "an ambiguous, particularistic, idiosyncratic and imprecise way of representing the world" (Patricia Ewick and Susan S. Silbey, "Subversive Stories and Hegemonic Tales: Toward a Sociology of Narrative," *Law and Society Review* 29 [1995]: 198). However, this convention has been reembraced lately in order to "incorporate subjective, contextualized, and specific accounts of social life" once again (ibid.).

28. Kimberle Williams Crenshaw, "Mapping the Margins: Intersectionality, Identity Politics, and Violence against Women of Color," *After Identity: A Reader in Law and Culture*, ed. Dan Danielsen and Karen Engle (New York: Routledge, 1995), p. 337.

29. Abrams, "Title VII and the Complex Female Subject," p. 2481.

30. Kathryn Abrams, "Unity, Narrative, and the Law," *Studies in Law, Politics, and Society*, vol. 3, ed. Austin Sarat and Susan Silbey (Greenwich, Conn.: JAI Press, 1993), p. 30.

31. Kimberle Williams Crenshaw, "Beyond Racism and Misogyny: Black Feminism and 2 Live Crew" in *Words That Wound: Critical Race Theory, Assaultive Speech and the First Amendment*, ed. Mari Matsuda et al. (Boulder, CO: Westview Press, 1993), and "Mapping the Margins."

32. Law matters in the sense that it sets constraints in which women's lives evolve. See *After Identity*, ed. Danielsen and Engle, generally.

33. Especially the stories of women who are the least able to take advantage of the law, who are socially and economically the most marginal.

34. See especially Mary Joe Frug, "A Postmodern Feminist Legal Manifesto" in *After Identity*, ed. Danielsen and Engle, pp. 7–23; and Ewick and Silbey, "Subversive Stories and Hegemonic Tales," pp. 197–226.

35. 911 F.2d 882 (3rd Cir. 1990); heard at the District Court level as 50 Fair Emp. Prac. Cas. (BNA) 71 (E.D. Pa. May 17, 1989).

36. In October 1989, local school authorities in Creil, France, expelled three French girls from school for wearing the Muslim headscarf. In another French school district in November 1993 several more girls received school suspensions because they insisted on wearing the Muslim headscarf, and in 1994 the coalition centrist-rightist government in France banned the wearing of Muslim headscarves in public schools. For details on the debates over the French headscarf affair, see Norma Claire Moruzzi, "A Problem with Headscarves: Contemporary Complexities of Political and Social Identity," *Political Theory* 22 (1994): 653–72.

37. Galeotti, *Citizenship and Equality*, p. 592.

38. According to political scientists Gloria Beckley and Paul Burstein, the number of religious discrimination complaints filed with the EEOC amounts to about 2.4 percent of the total number of complaints based on Title VII protections, and "the 243 federal court decisions in EEO religious discrimination cases published through early 1987 is even a slightly lower percentage" ("Religious

Pluralism," p. 188). Yet each year the actual number of complaints of religious discrimination has increased fairly steadily, "from 169 in fiscal year 1967 to 1,176 in 1972 and 3,417 in 1984" (ibid.).

39. Carol Stone, "Estimates of Muslims Living in America," in Yvonne Yazbeck Haddad (ed.) *The Muslims of America* (New York: Oxford University Press, 1991), p. 34. Further, Stone states that "relative to the total number of immigrants entering the United States, the number of Muslim immigrants has more than doubled over the last two decades, increasing from 4% of all immigrants in 1968 to 10.5% in 1986" (ibid., p. 31).

40. See Council on American-Islamic Relations, "The Status of Muslim Civil Rights in the United States, 1997" (Washington, D.C.).

41. See *The Capital Times* (Wisconsin), 29 June 1996.

42. Whether it is obligatory for women to cover remains a contentious issue, and is being debated among Muslims. For example, a verse often cited from the Qur'an to support the mandate to wear *hijab* is the following: "Say to the believing women to cast down their glance and guard their private parts and reveal not their adornment except such as is outward and let them cast their veils over their bosoms and reveal not their adornments except to their husbands, their fathers, or their husbands' fathers . . ." (24:31).

43. PA. STAT. ANN. tit. 24, 11–1112 (1982), provides: "a) that no teacher in any public school shall wear in said school or while engaged in the performance of his [or her] duty as such teacher any dress, mark, emblem or insignia indicating the fact that such teacher is a member or adherent of any religious order, sect, or denomination.

"b) Any teacher . . . who violated the provisions of this section shall be suspended from employment in such school for the term of one year, and in case of a second offense by the same teacher he [or she] shall be permanently disqualified from teaching in said school. Any public school director who after notice of any such violation fails to comply with the provisions of this section shall be guilty of a misdemeanor, and upon conviction of this first offense, shall be sentenced to pay a fine not exceeding one hundred dollars ($100), and on conviction of a second offense, the offending school director shall be sentenced to pay a fine not exceeding one hundred dollars and shall be deprived of his [or her] office as a public school director.

44. Nebraska, North Dakota, and Oregon also have state laws prohibiting teachers in public schools from wearing religious attire. See NEB. REV. STAT. 79–1294 (1987); N.D. CENT. CODE 15–47–29 to -30 (1981); and OR. REV. STAT. 342.650, .655 (1989).

45. *Cooper v. Eugene School District*, 301 Or. 358, 723 P.2d 298 (1986), *appeal dismissed*, 480 U.S. 942 (1987). In *Cooper*, the plaintiff, a Sikh denied employment as a public school teacher pursuant to the Oregon religious garb statute, alleged that the Eugene school board's actions violated Title VII and her free exercise right under the First Amendment. However, the Oregon Supreme Court did not consider the Title VII issue, and the U.S. Supreme Court dismissed the petition for review for lack of a substantial federal question (see Holly M. Bastian, "Case Comment: Religious Garb Statutes and Title VII: An Uneasy Coexistence," *Georgetown Law Journal* 80 (1991), p. 219.

46. I have briefly examined this case elsewhere; see Kathleen M. Moore, "Mus-

lim Commitment in North America: Assimilating Transformation?" *American Journal of Islamic Social Sciences* 11, 232–244. Bastian, "Case Comment," 1991.

47. 30 A. 482 (PA 1894).

48. Bastian, "Case Comment," 1991: 213; see also 30 A. 483.

49. PA. STAT. ANN. tit. 14, 11–1112; see also Bastian, "Case Comment," p. 213.

50. *Commonwealth v. Herr*, 78 A. 68 (PA 1910) at 70–71.

51. Ibid., 70.

52. Bastian, "Case Comment," p. 211. Cases that have reviewed religious garb statutes include *O'Connor v. Hendrick*, 77 N.E. 612 (N.Y. 1906); *Cooper v. Eugene Sch. Dist.*, 301 Or. 358, 723 P.2d 298 (1986), appeal dismissed, 480 U.S. 942 (1987); and *Commonwealth v. Herr*, 78 A. 68 (PA 1910).

53. 42 U.S.C. 2000e-2(e)(1) (1988).

54. 577 F. Supp. 1196 (N.D. Tex. 1983), aff'd. 746 F.2d 810 (5th Cir. 1984).

55. *Kern v. Dynalectron Co.*, 577 F. Supp. 1196 (N.D. Tex. 1983), aff'd. 746 F.2d 810 (5th Cir. 1984) at 1200.

56. 42 U.S.C. 2000e(j) (1988).

57. For legislative history, see 118 CONG. REC. 705 (1972).

58. Beckley and Burstein, "Religious Pluralism," p. 193.

59. *Trans World Airlines v. Hardison*, 432 U.S. 63 (1977).

60. See, for instance, *Brown v. General Motors Company*, 601 F.2d 956 (8th Cir. 1979). (GM already hired extra workers to replace absentee workers on Saturday shifts, but argued that if GM were required to accommodate a Sabbatarian, absenteeism on Friday evenings would escalate to a point where GM would have to hire additional replacement workers); *Anderson v. General Dynamics Convair Aerospace Division*, 589 F.2d 397 (9th Cir. 1978), cert. denied, 442 U.S. 921 (1979) (court noted that "undue hardship cannot be proved by assumptions nor by opinions based on hypothetical facts"); and *Smith v. Pyro Mining Co.*, 827 F.2d 1081 (6th Cir. 1987), cert. denied, 485 U.S. 989 (1988).

61. Bastian, "Case Comment," p. 223.

62. Heard at the district court level as 50 Fair Emp. Prac. Cas. (BNA) 71 (E.D. Pa. May 17, 1989).

63. Bastian, "Case Comment," 1991: 215.

64. 50 Fair Empl. Prac. Cas. (BNA) at 73.

65. Cited in Bastian, "Case Comment," 1991: p. 215.

66. 50 Fair Empl. Prac. Cas. (BNA) at 84.

67. Id. at 81; Bastian, "Case Comment," 1991: 217.

68. U.S. Const. amend. 1: "Congress shall make no law respecting an establishment of religion. . . ."

69. The district court applied the *Lemon v. Kurtzman* (403 U.S. 602 [1972]) test which has been prominent in establishment-clause jurisprudence, and found that the proposed accommodation of Reardon's attire satisfied the three-part *Lemon* test. To pass the *Lemon* test a statute must : (1) have a secular purpose; (2) have the primary effect of neither advancing or inhibiting religion; and (3) not foster excessive governmental entanglement. Allowing Reardon's religious practice: (1) would serve a secular purpose by complying with the reasonable accommodation provision of Title VII; (2) would not have the principal effect of advancing or inhibiting religion, nor endorsing a particular religious view-

point; and (3) there was no governmental entanglement with religion (see Fair Empl. Prac. Cas. [BNA] at 82, and Bastian, "Case Comment," 1991: p. 217). However, recent U.S. Supreme Court decisions under the establishment clause indicate that the *Lemon* test may not govern decisions regarding church-state relations much longer. For instance, Justice Scalia in Lamb's Chapel v. Center Moriches, 124 L. Ed. 2d 352 (1993), made colorful reference to the *Lemon* test: "Like some ghoul in a late night horror movie that repeatedly sits up in its grave and shuffles abroad, after being repeatedly killed and buried, *Lemon* stalks our Establishment Clause jurisprudence" (ibid., at 365). Six of the current justices, said Scalia, had "personally driven pencils through the creature's heart" (id.) but still the *Lemon* test lingers. Court watchers expect that the *Lemon* test may be repudiated by the Court in the case before it at this writing, *Rosenberger v. Rector*, No. 94–329 (1995), which involves the guidelines of the student council at the University of Virginia, where a Christian student group was denied funding for a religious publication on the ground that the publication contained religious content.

70. Bastian notes, "In reaching this conclusion, the [appellate] court ignored the fact that there was no record of any actual or attempted enforcement of the provisions of the garb statute in the nearly one hundred years that the statute has been in existence" ("Case Comments," 1991: 225).

71. Galeotti, *Citizenship and Equality*, p. 596.

72. I have examined the court record of the First Amendment cases launched by Muslims in prison and the impact of their use of law to challenge prison regulations that interfered with religious observances and practices elsewhere (see Kathleen M. Moore, "Muslims in Prison: Claims to Constitutional Protection of Religious Liberty" in Yvonne Y. Haddad, *Muslims of America* [Oxford: Oxford University Press, 1991], pp. 136–156; and *Al-Mughtari Burl: American Law and the Transformation of Muslim Life in the United States* [Albany, NY: State University of New York Press, 1995]).

73. Beckley and Burstein, "Religious Pluralism," p. 197.

74. Gerald Rosenberg, *The Hollow Hope: Can Courts Bring About Social Change?* (Chicago: University of Chicago Press, 1991), p. 341.

75. For articles on this topic, see in particular *The American Journal of Islamic Social Sciences, Journal of the Institute of Muslim Minority Affairs* (London), and *Islamic Law and Society*. For an excellent analysis of the contradictory pressures on Muslim women, see Shahnaz Khan, "Race, Gender and Orientalism: Muta and the Canadian Legal System," *Canadian Journal of Women and the Law* 8 (1995).

76. Khaled Abou al-Fadl, "Islamic Law and Muslim Minorities: The Journalistic Discourse on Muslim Minorities from the Second/Eighth to the Eleventh/Seventeenth Centuries," *Islamic Law and Society* (1994): 182.

77. Ibid., p. 186.

78. Ewick and Silbey, "Subversive Stories."

79. Ibid., p. 197.

80. Yusuf Talal De Lorenzo, "Islamic Law, American Civil Law and the Role of the *Fiqh* Councilor," paper presented at the Southwest Asian and North African Program, Annual Meeting, Binghamton University, NY, Oct. 30–31, 1994.

81. Political scientist Michael McCann makes a similar point about the study of social movements and the law in his work on the pay equity movement. See Michael W. McCann, *Rights at Work: Pay Equity Reform and the Politics of Legal Mobilization* (Chicago: University of Chicago Press, 1994).

82. Minow, *Making All the Difference*, p. 377.

83. Ibid.

84. Beckley and Burstein, "Religious Pluralism," p. 203.

6

Muslim Women in Canada

Their Role and Status as Revealed
in the *Hijab* Controversy

ESMAIL SHAKERI

In Canada, both within the Muslim community and between Muslims and
the rest of society, the role and status of Muslim women is being debated.
The growth of the Muslim population in the last two decades and continued immigration have brought a heightened sense of their "minority status"
among Muslims, and raised many questions concerning religious values and
expression. Muslims, particularly women, want to keep their religious
identity, while adopting the other aspects of the host culture such as language, educational system, employment patterns, and civic life. For them
integration means acceptance by the larger Canadian society of their separate identity, including their distinctive religious practices, patterns of family
relationship, and mother tongues.

In Canada, however, ideas of assimilation, absorption, and integration
are part of the ideology of the dominant group. Any community which remains unabsorbed, or unassimilated, is usually considered to be upsetting
the equation of social relations in the society. The phenomenon itself is not
novel, but what interests us here is the response of Muslims, especially of
Muslim women, to this attitude. This lies at the center of the debate.

Muslim Women and Canadian Public Opinion

Women of color in general, but especially those who are at the same time
Muslim, have faced difficulties with the attitude of the majority population.
The religious expressions and values of Muslim women due to differences
in outlook and behavior are seen by the majority community to be alien.
Problems with the female dress code, the hijab, have arisen all across Canada.

The majority norm is considered right, and any behavior that deviates from it is regarded as inferior, and by some even deviant. Sometimes the problem is simply ignorance about the cultural background of Muslims and Islam, but most often it is prejudice and discrimination against Muslim women and other minority groups.

An example: In the fall of 1994 in Montreal Muslim students Emilie Ouimet and Dania Baali enrolled in schools under the jurisdiction of two different school boards, were sent home by school officials for wearing hijab. School officials declared that religious headgear did not conform to the school dress code, and hence unless until students removed their hijab they could not attend school. The incident sparked protests from Montreal Muslim community groups as they charged the school boards with intolerant and racist attitudes.[1]

In the wake of this incident, a stream of other anti-Muslim activities occurred in Montreal,[2] adding a particular Quebec flavor to the intolerant debate on the hijab. For some Quebecers hijab seemed like a political statement, reflecting the religious fervor, violence, and intolerance associated with Islamic fundamentalism as portrayed in Western television and film.[3] To others, particularly Francophone Quebecers, the linkage between the hijab controversy in Quebec and events in France (where the government banned "ostentatious religious symbols" including hijab from publicly supported schools in September 1994 and expelled at least 17 students) was inevitable. They view acceptance of hijab, under the guise of accommodation or multiculturalism, as divisive and a betraying French identity in Quebec.[4] The situation in Algeria is a sensitive subject for many Quebecers, since Algerians have increasingly made this province their home in recent years. Many draw a negative connection between the insistence of the Islamic Salvation Front of Algeria that Muslim women should be forced to wear the hijab and the controversy in Quebec.[5]

Quebec's policy on immigration and integration (issued in 1990 and known as "interculturalism") emphasizes French identity, which may also have contributed to the attitude of Quebec society toward Muslims. This policy has been described as an integration project (comparable to the melting pot in the United States), which asks newcomers to become part of Quebec society based on a "moral contract."[6] Despite this government policy, the Quebec Council on the Status of Women, responding to the strong reaction by some to the expulsion of Muslim students from public schools, released in May 1995 a report supporting the right of Muslim women to wear hijab in schools.[7] Only days later, however, the largest teacher's union in the province, the Central de l'Enseignment du Quebec (CEQ), voted to ban hijab in school even though the CEQ's executive had voted in favor of it.[8]

The hijab controversy in Quebec appears to be unique. No similar cases have been reported elsewhere in Canada, and officials at school boards outside Quebec had trouble believing that hijab had been banned by the teachers' union in that province.

The Debate in the Muslim Community Over Hijab

In the wake of the hijab controversy in Quebec, Muslims in the Islamic communities of Canada have been debating the requirement of hijab in Islam. While no consensus has been achieved on what is the ideal model to be followed in the North American context, there is at least tacit agreement that it should be left up to the individual Muslim woman to decide on whether or not to wear it. Many believe that modest dress is sufficient; a small minority of Muslims are, however, more observant than others and a few, to the strong objection of the majority, even wear the face veil despite the hostility they encounter in Canadian society. As is true of any other religion, the Muslim community continually seeks a satisfactory solution among the options for maintaining the Islamic way of life within the framework of diversity.

The controversy over hijab and the division it has caused within the Canadian Muslim community are only part of a larger problem this community is facing in defining its identity and role as well as its future prospects in an area far from the rest of the Islamic world. According to Professor Yvonne Haddad, the question in the United States is whether a minority group, such as the Muslim community, should insist on maintaining its exclusivity and distinction, while at the same time demanding equal treatment and equal access to resources.[9] The debate in Canada is moving in much the same direction and is, as in the United States, divided between what Haddad identifies as accommodationists (those who seek religious equality and equal access to society's resources) and isolationists (those who stress the distinctiveness of Islam and strive to preserve Islamic cultural modes of representation). Many Muslims, especially those born in Canada, feel that exclusivity and isolation set the Muslim community on a confrontational course with the host culture that results in discrimination. On the other hand, isolationists advocate maintaining a distinct, insular entity in the midst of the Canadian society, favoring Islamic over Western norms. Advocates of this view, as Professor Haddad points out, insist that, "while there is no stipulation as to what kind of style Muslim women must use in covering their hair, there is one that requires them to do so. Local or individual variations are acceptable as long as they remain faithful to the basic requirements."[10]

The tension between these two interpretations characterizes the debate. The majority of Muslims in Canada clearly favor the accommodationist model, since isolationism encourages hostility to the community. The Muslim experience in Canada and an increase in Islamic consciousness are slowly providing the Muslim community with ideas on how best to adapt to North America without depending on guidance from Muslim authorities in the Islamic world.

The debate over hijab has generated a stream of interpretations and arguments about the role and status of Muslim women in a non-Islamic environment. The views expressed by feminists and women's right activists and the responses of Muslim women to these views have generated lively discussion in opinion pieces and editorials in newspapers and magazines across Canada, particularly over the role Muslim women have taken in defining themselves and their reactions to others defining them.

Sociologists consider role behavior to be a structural component of every human society, as societal norms prescribe behavioral sanctions for interactions between the sexes. Role behavior may vary according to different situations or may remain the same irrespective of the context. Applying this to our study, Muslim women living in the West can be placed on a continuum, at one end of which is the ideal and at the other the realities. When the two are confused it leads to contradictions in Muslim women's role and status in a non-Islamic society.

The ideal is structured by Islamic norms from which are derived the Islamic role expectations for female behavior. At the same time, contextual reality provides other models for the role performance of females as determined by the surrounding cultures and structures of societies within which they live out their lives.[11] Role expectations give the incumbent an idea of what role performance should be. These expectations are derived from norms which may be prescribed in secular or religious codes. Islam, if defined as a way of life, expects Muslim women to perform certain roles irrespective of circumstance. Muslim women adhering to this traditional brand of Islam argue that feminist definitions of women's role are incompatible with the expectations of Islam. The two camps are also divided over the definition of gender interests, the nature of social arrangements, and visions of a better society. Therefore, the behavior of teenage Muslim students in reclaiming hijab, resisting assimilation, and signaling adherence to traditional Islamic concepts of the role of women are perceived by Canadians in general and women's rights activists in particular as representing a contradiction among young Muslim women who are living and studying in the West, but representing regressive trends in the Muslim community.

The argument of Canadian feminists against hijab and the responses of Muslim women to their logic runs as follows. Canadian feminists see an association between hijab and the subordination of Muslim women; it is considered a visible manifestation of segregation between the sexes, and segregation is assumed to associate men with public space and women with domestic roles, thereby making them dependent on men. Michele Lemon who has a Master's degree from the Institute of Islamic Studies at McGill University, in an article entitled "Understanding Does Not Always Lead to Tolerance" and published in the *Globe and Mail*, describes a Muslim woman with face veil in the Canadian streets:

> This woman is a walking billboard that proclaims public space is reserved for men. Her outfit proclaims a woman's place is indoors.
>
> It is not the woman I despise, but her compliance in a charade that can in no way be defended on religious grounds, that handy refuge of the desperate authoritarian.[12]

The same perspective is expressed by Canadian journalist Agnes Gruda in *La Presse*, following Emilie Ouimet's expulsion: "Islamic veil is more than a religious garb. It is one of the most powerful symbols of servitude."[13]

Muslim women, on the other hand, see hijab as having a totally different purpose. The point of view expressed by Western feminists—that Islam limits women's activities to the home—they find to be a prejudicial perception prevalent in the West; in many Muslim as well as non-Muslim societies Muslim women are engaged in a wide variety of social and economic activities regardless of hijab. They believe that the power women have in Muslim societies is simply more private and indirect than that of Western women and, therefore, much less accessible to Western analysts. The very form of public clothing that outsiders see as the ultimate symbol of weakness, for them is representative of a more complex reality.[14]

Second, feminists interpret veiling as an admission on the part of Muslim women that they are the source of evil in society: to protect society from sin and anarchy they must hide themselves from the public eye. Muslim women, they say, should work instead on civilizing and restraining the handful of men who cannot be trusted to control themselves. Catherine Meckes, a student of journalism in Toronto in an article entitled "Uniform of Oppression," wrote in the *Globe and Mail*:

> Choosing to wear hijab is a form of hiding, of crying uncle, of saying to men who leer and gape, "you win"; it is my fault you are staring, assaulting, raping. You guys cannot control your sexual urges, so it is up to me to make sure there is not even a suggestion of a body under my clothes to tempt you. My fault, sorry.[15]

The response of Muslim women, particularly the feminists among them, to this point of view is very interesting. Rahat Kurd, a freelance writer, believes that "female responsibility for the control of male desire in the public sphere might be a popular concept, but it's not an Islamic one."

> Quran commands men to lower their gaze and to dress and behave modestly in front of women ... [T]hese injunctions clearly indicate Islam's support and approval not only for women's access to public space but also their active presence in a multireligious, multicultural society.

She continues:

> I don't cover to please any men, and I'm not going to uncover to please any women. The minute either group [Muslim fundamentalists and Western feminists] begins calling for the law to impose or ban any kind of religious dress, I'll fight it, since my right to believe and practice what I choose is at stake.[16]

Hijab in Canada is widely interpreted by women's rights activists as a blanket endorsement of oppression. According to this interpretation, Muslim women are forced to cover themselves under threat of penalties imposed by men. These activists criticize Muslim women for enduring the kind of behavior meted out to them by Muslim men in the name of Islamic tradition. Moreover, wearing hijab is seen to be degrading to all women, Muslims and non-Muslims alike, and a violation of their rights. Michele Lemon explains:

> I feel I've been punched in the stomach. Her oppression, for oppression it is, becomes a symbol of the difficulty all women once faced and a startling reminder that the struggle for equality has not ended. ... How could anyone defend the outfit as preserving anything but the low regard and true unimportance of women, all protestations of respect to the contrary?[17]

In this regard, another author seeing few hijabi women in her neighborhood writes:

> I found the sight of these women with their hidden faces disturbing. It's one thing to see covered faces as the exotic and mysterious product of another culture you can leave behind when you return home. But finding them on my home turf, I have to confront my fears about what this kind of dress represents for me, and for all women: backwardness, submissiveness, degradation.[18]

From the point of view of Muslim activists, it is a familiar stereotype in the West that Muslim women are oppressed, have no dignity, and are properties of their men. They argue that contrary to modern-day popular opinion in the West, hijab does not represent oppression to Muslim women, but, on the contrary, freedom and liberation. Naheed Mustafa, an activist in Toronto's Muslim community, writes in an article entitled "My Body Is My Own Business":

> Wearing the hijab has given me the freedom from constant attention to my physical self. Because my appearance is not subjected to scrutiny, my beauty, or perhaps lack of it, has been removed from the realm of what can legitimately be discussed.[19]

An interesting point common to all Muslim women who are young, Canadian-born and raised, university-educated, and yet observing hijab, is that they have spent all their teenage years trying to meet the Western standards of beauty and to live according to Western norms and conventions. Finding this difficult and often humiliating, they have rejected the Western norms and mores which dominated their lives, returned to their roots, and created in the process a new identity for themselves. Now they are fighting a culture that is not consistent with Islamic ideals, and are asking that they be judged by their abilities, rather than physical attributes. For them hijab is simply a woman's assertion that judgment of her physical person is to play no role whatsoever in social interaction.

Another point often brought up by hijab-observing Muslim women in Canada is that they are oppressed, not by their religion or their men, but by other women who claim to be their "saviors." They argue that they are wearing hijab out of their own free will. They are content with it and feel liberated. As women, they feel they are true to themselves, a key concept in feminist ideology. To their surprise, however, Western feminists use the same argument Muslim fundamentalists use in the Islamic world, viz., these women should be stopped for their own good.[20]

The Islamic veil, according to some women activists and some government officials in Quebec, is more than a religious garb. It is loaded with other associations, an aggressive symbol of a political agenda, reflecting Islamic fundamentalism which they associate with religious fervor, violence, and intolerance. When they see women in North America dressed as women in Muslim countries, it reminds them that Islam in North America is merely an extension of Islam as practiced in Muslim countries.[21]

Hijab-observing women in Canada deny these accusations. Rahat Kurd, for example, says:

As long as the Muslim identity is portrayed as alien, linked to turbulence in Muslim countries, Islamic dress will seem shocking, foreign, and rootless in Canadian soil. The Islam you see being practiced on the streets of Canadian cities grew up here.[22]

Sajidah Kutty, another Muslim activist in Toronto, attributes the increased interest in Islam and subsequent observance of hijab to the war in the Persian Gulf. She believes young secular Muslims were shaken into self-examination by the backlash against Muslims whose beliefs were equated with terrorism. In looking at the source of discrimination, "we discovered we were different, but it made us stronger. So we banded together."[23]

Zuhair Kashmeri, a journalist, author, and reporter for the *Globe and Mail*, in his book, *The Gulf Within: Canadian Arabs, Racism and the Gulf War*, writes that when the Canadian government went to war against Iraq, many Canadians of Arab or Muslim background found that they were being identified with the enemy. A constant stream of complaints of physical and racist attacks issued from the Arab community as the war coverage on television became an evening spectacle. On the streets, in the workplace, in schools, and in the media particularly Arabs became the targets of ignorance, hostility, and paranoia. In a few cases, as Kashmeri points out, Muslim women wearing hijab were beaten and their hijabs were ripped. There were reports that even school administrators failed to take measures against instances of racism triggered by the war.[24]

Some people in Quebec see the hijab as an aggressive sign that the person wearing it refuses to integrate into society and have even suggested that those who wear hijab are being intolerant of others. Jocelyn Berthelot of the Centre de l'Enseignement du Quebec, for example, says, "There must be an ongoing dialogue with the immigrant community in the form of cultural education." She believes what is missing in Quebec is an intercultural policy. Bernard Landry, Quebec's Cultural Community minister, said that "religious freedom, like all the others, has its limits. [The government's] role is not simply to allow the exercise of these freedoms but also to establish limits."[25]

Muslim activists think that those who insist on the integration of minorities really seem to be talking about assimilation, not integration. Samira Qureshi, the vice president of the Islamic Cultural Network in Montreal, says: "What they are saying is you can assimilate only. You can have a different colour but you have to possess a Western psyche." Some academics support this point of view. For example, John Moisset, professor of education planning at Université Laval, points out that "Quebec's society today is far from homogeneous. The government cannot force immigrants to assimilate to a particular idea of culture."[26]

Marginalizing women who wear the hijab by banning them from public schools would hardly promote integration. To integrate immigrants successfully, one must allow them some degree of freedom of expression.

Hijab has also been recognized by some as a political statement on the part of Muslim women. A hijabi woman is making a radical statement about her political ideas which is considered to violate other women's rights. For feminists, having such women in the North American landscape is frightening.

Hijab from the Muslim women's point of view is fundamentally part of worship, but also has become a political statement symbolizing a rejection of the West. Muslim women think, however, that fear of the "veiled woman" is unfounded since wearing hijab has nothing to do with anyone else; it has only to do with a woman's commitment to Allah.

Muslim women do not find the hostility of Western feminists difficult to understand. A woman who covers herself, they say, is not just stating something about what she accepts, but is also saying something about what she rejects. In a world that tends to judge women by their appearance and reduce them to sex objects, wearing hijab, as they put it, means rejecting that role and forcing other people to focus on their personality and intellect. Nahid Mustafa writes:

> Women have always been expected to play some kind of role in every society. In North America, a great part of this role revolves around sex and the aura of sexuality. Any relationship involving man and woman has some kind of sexual undertone. When a woman covers herself she is rejecting that role, she is saying sex will have nothing to do with the public's life [sic]. It is the fact that she has taken out of the discussion her physical self that people find so upsetting.[27]

From this argument one can only conclude that Muslim women in North America reject not only gender roles but also the associated politics of gender. They see a paradox and confusion among feminists in North America. While feminists loathe the fact that the female body is used for selling everything from cosmetics to clothing to cars, when Muslim women cover themselves and protest the very same thing, they are seen as oppressed.[28]

What may be the most interesting point in this debate is the discussion over "real choice." In opinion pieces and editorials in Quebec publications, Muslim women are told repeatedly that "wearing hijab might not be a real choice." For example, in an article in the *Montreal Gazette*, Eve McBride writes:

> We see a society that honors all religions but we are also a society that values choice. That's why some of us are concerned about the hijab. We do not see it as equivalent to the wearing of a crucifix or a yarmulke. We see it as a covering up, a containing of a segment of the population by controlling other segments, to whom the edict does not apply. That's why in our classrooms where we're struggling to reinforce and expand women's choices, enforced physical covering up, which must surely extend to the voice, distresses us.[29]

Dr. Sheema Khan, a Harvard educated chemist working at McGill University, in a response published in The *Muslim Voice*, writes:

> As many of us have realized, so long as our choice agrees with the prevailing western feminist paradigm, it is valid but if our choice is contrary to what "intellectuals" are comfortable with, then it is not a real choice. It is acquiescence which is valued. Similarly, it is not the hijab which is worrisome, instead it is the rejection of western feminism by women who have been raised and educated in North America.[30]

Furthermore, it is argued that Western feminists in Canada are practicing cultural imperialism in insisting that Muslim women should adopt their values. Samia Costandi, a lecturer in the philosophy of education at McGill University, told a conference of Arab-Canadian women in June 1995:

> We refuse the homogenizing discourse of western feminism proclaiming that women of Arab countries should emulate western feminists in order to be liberated.
>
> Western women cannot continue to inflict standards on us. . . . They must listen to us. Perhaps we can offer better ways to see the world.

Opposing hijab in public schools by Quebec feminists is also interpreted as practicing a form of imperialism. "We have our own feminists and liberating experiences. We have to speak with our voices, and our differences must be recognized and celebrated, not accepted and tolerated."[31]

The point raised both by Sheema Khan and Samia Costandi is supported, at least on the surface, by Muslim women academics who are against the hijab. Homa Hoodfar, an Iranian-born anthropology professor at Concordia

University, who had spoken out against the attempts by Iran to enforce hijab, emphasizes just as strongly her opposition to any attempt to prohibit its use in Canada. She says: "It is not the veil I object to. It is the notion that somebody should think they can tell women what to wear and what not to wear."[32] According to her, most Muslim women who have taken the veil in Canada are highly educated and are not the passive victims of Muslim misogyny that some ill-informed critics might like to imagine.

Shahrzad Mojob, professor in social sciences at Concordia University, who fled Iran in 1983 after getting into trouble for her feminist views, believes that Canadians wrongly see hijab as a symbol of oppression in their midst. It is true that in some Middle Eastern countries such as Iran, Saudi Arabia, and Kuwait women fight against wearing the hijab. "But we are not living in a society where social and political pressure imposes it on a woman. In Canada, we are talking freedom of choice. Women make the decision."[33]

The hijab controversy in Quebec and the debate between proponents and opponents seem to have had some positive impact in Canadian society. In opinion pieces and editorials published in Quebec and the rest of Canada, one can see viewpoints expressing support for the right of Muslim women to wear hijab in schools and in public. One editorial in the *Montreal Gazette*, for example, remarked, "Given the intolerant tone of some of the public debate on this issue, it seems that there is a need for more education about respect for religious freedoms."[34] Ed Broadbent, the former leader of the Federal New Democratic Party and the director of the Montreal-based International Centre for Human Rights and Democratic Development, in a letter to newspaper editors states: "The hijab is a powerful and controversial symbol: we must respect the rights of both those who choose to wear it and those who choose not to. . . . How can we possibly deny the right to wear the hijab here, and turn around and defend the right of women not to wear the hijab in Muslim countries?"[35]

The Quebec Human Rights Commission also produced a sensible report supporting the right of Muslim women to wear the hijab as a way of expressing their religious convictions. The authors stress the need for mutual tolerance. They say that society has a duty to make reasonable accommodations for those who choose to wear it as a matter of personal conscience. However, just as the rights of hijab wearer should be respected, the freedom not to wear it should be respected. The report acknowledges arguments made by opponents that it is a sign of social inequality, and in some countries women who refuse to wear it have been attacked. But it says that in Quebec one should presume that hijab wearers are expressing their religious convictions, and that the hijab should be banned only when it is demonstrated—and not just presumed—that public order or sexual equality is in danger.[36]

The Quebec Council on the Status of Women came to the same conclusion as the Human Rights Commission. In a 54-page document issued in May 1995, it attacked Western women who think the hijab is too sexist to tolerate, arguing that "they live within a sexist system and around symbols they are not comfortable with." The council's study will be incorporated into an advisory report on women's rights and diversity to be presented to the provincial government next year.[37]

Muslim Women's Organizations, Their Goals and Activities

Probably no country in the world is more hospitable to immigrants than Canada, but its value system and outlook on life are totally different from those with which immigrant Muslims are familiar. As a result they are confronted by customs, beliefs, and notions of honor and shame absolutely contrary to their own value system and their attitudes toward life. This is perhaps especially true where Muslim women are concerned. The problems are more pronounced for women than for men because their dress makes them conspicuous. The lack of preparation for facing the situation also causes problems. Muslim women in most parts of the Islamic world have traditionally been passive and have not participated in social or religious activities. In North America, in contrast, immigrants are expected to be responsible for the total and efficient management of their families. One of their responsibilities is to preserve their religious and cultural heritage. Compared to the past, some Muslim women are taking great interest in religious activities in mosques, Islamic centers, and other types of Muslim associations.

In terms of active participation, Muslim women can be loosely divided into four groups. The first usually belong to the first generation and have followed their husbands in search of work and better living conditions; they have limited contact with Canadian society. The cultural bonds of these women to their traditional Muslim role remain intact throughout the years, despite the fact that they are not always well versed in Islamic religious teachings and devotional practices. At least at first, they often gather in small groups but mainly for social and ethnic reasons and not for religious education.

A second group consists of the daughters and granddaughters of the first-generation women, either brought to the country as children or born in Canada. They have had a markedly different and somewhat better start than the older generation. Nonetheless, as the first generation of teenage Muslims, these women often face problems that are more acute than those faced by the previous generation, including conflicts between parents with very traditional conservative values and daughters who have grown up exposed to a totally different set of norms. They also encounter difficulties in maintaining self-identity as Muslims and experience rejection and hostility as part of a minority group in an unsympathetic environment. These problems and pressures, along with the worldwide Islamic resurgence and the growth in the size of the Muslim community, have led these young women to participate more and more actively in religious activities in mosques, Islamic centers, and other types of Muslim associations.

A third group consists of native Canadian (and sometimes American or European) women who have converted to Islam after marrying Muslim men now living in Canada. These women are among the most active and energetic Muslims in Canada and often go beyond their Muslim-born peers in observing hijab and Islamic teachings. Because of their familiarity with the environment, these women have also played an active role in the establishment of Islamic centers, Islamic foundations, and other religious organizations.

The fourth group consist of wives of Muslim students who have come to Canada on a temporary (five- to eight-year) basis. These women remain relatively isolated within a small kin or ethnic-based subculture. The wives of both Iranian students (receiving stipends from the Iranian government) and Saudi students fall into this category. Iran has sent almost 2,000 students with their wives and children to Canadian universities, mostly in Ontario and Quebec. With the help of the Iranian government, these students have set up both temporary and permanent religious establishments. The Iranian embassy in Canada, for example, has established a few full-time elementary schools in Montreal, Ottawa, and Toronto for the children of Iranian students; its teachers are supplied by the Iranian government. During the months of Moharram and Ramadan, religious figures are also sent to Canada to give sermons to these students and their wives. There are reports that businessmen close to the Iranian government have inquired about establishing mosques and Islamic centers in Canada as well.[38]

The focus of this study has been on the second and third groups; these are the most active among Muslim women in Canada. They use the mosque for worship, lectures, dinners, weddings, and religious discussions. With a burgeoning number of young hijabis who choose to attend Friday night and Sunday study sessions, mosques in Canada have become very active centers in educating Muslims. These young Muslim women have begun to analyze the Qur'an and to attend religious discussions, which were once the monopoly of Muslim men. Moreover, they exchange ideas on matters that turn out not to be Islamic. Some women, for example, have discovered that many of their parents' habits, which they thought were prompted by religious observance, are actually cultural in origin. A good example is the size of dower popular among some Muslim communities: while these young hijabis accept *mahr* or dower as Islamic and for the bride's exclusive use in case of her husband's death or if there is a divorce or an emergency, they reject the idea that it must be a very large amount, particularly if it is beyond the financial resources of a potential spouse and apt to become a source of friction between their newly related families. They also reject the concept of a traditionally arranged marriage and firmly believe that God will find them partners if that is their destiny.[39]

Women have also played, and continue to play, an active role in organizing social events for the community and raising funds for religious purposes. They also teach in elementary and Sunday schools, helping parents to raise their children with Islamic identity. Participation in these activities has resulted in their acquiring a good deal of influence in mosques and other Islamic organizations.

Whenever women gather in mosques or Islamic centers in which a variety of opinions are represented, hijab is still probably the topic that receives the most attention. An important recent development is the inclusion of non-*hijabi* women, who have attended mosques in the past and on special occasions, to these discussions. According to one non-hijabi Muslim girl from the University of Toronto attending these gatherings:

> It used to be that most of the Muslim teenagers with whom I was acquainted were either Muslim by name only, or what I will term "part-time" Muslims. Suddenly, I have found myself surrounded by many devout young Muslims, Alhamdulillah. . . . I, like many Muslim women, do not yet wear hijab. I feel like there is something missing from my *deen* [religion] without it and I intend to wear it. Insha-Allah. It does not help me to be told that I am wrong because I will never deny that. I have many apprehensions about wearing hijab, and, of course they are all very trivial compared with pleasing Allah. . . .⁴⁰

Young hijabi women are also now put in charge of training camps and recreational activities which are organized through mosques and Islamic centers. It is often in such places that hesitant Muslim girls overcome their doubt over hijab. One high-school student living in Toronto explains her problem in an article, "My Struggle and Decision With the Hijab":

> I had just come back from the 1993 MYNA camp. Before that I did not wear hijab; I could not wear one. It was just one of those things. I would only wear it if I went to gatherings where everyone would be wearing one or if I attended halaqas. . . .
>
> After that I started wearing my hijab full time. Not only to my school, but to all gatherings, shopping . . . everywhere. I even wore it to my relatives' houses. They were shocked and said I was becoming a "very good girl." Like I wasn't before?⁴¹

Given these activities by young hijabis, one can see some changes in the make up and direction of women's associations. There are umbrella organizations such as the Canadian Council of Muslim Women and the Islamic Society of North America (Canada Office), as well as local Muslim women's centers (established in almost every major Canadian city) whose members are drawn from different Muslim countries and language groups. Muslim women's associations, however, have to rely financially on their members to carry out their activities or even to survive.

Unlike associations which are established on the basis of culture and the country of origin, Islamic associations are not eligible for government grants. Under the policy of multiculturalism, both local and federal governments in Canada have recognized and funded national rather than Islamic associations. Therefore, while such organizations as the Canadian Federation of Arab women and the Canadian Organization of Iranian Women receive grants and subsidies to pursue cultural activities and grow, Muslim women's associations have remained small in each city. From the point of view of the Muslim community as a whole, the policy of the Canadian government creates the danger of fostering divisiveness. This is most visible when Muslims come together in large cities to pray, but break up into ethnic groups for other cultural activities, where Islam is less a factor in group identity and language becomes more important.

The hijab controversy in Montreal, then, serves as a point of focus for some of the most pressing issues facing the Muslim community in North America today. It provides a forum for discussion and opinion on issues of identity, religious commitment, political affirmation, and positioning vis-à-vis Western feminism. It brings into sharp relief the differences between the Muslim and non-Muslim perspective, as well as differences within the Islamic community. Finally, it calls into question whether or not Western society can be sufficiently flexible and open to allow Muslims to determine their own forms of self-definition.

Notes

1. The author is grateful to Dr. Sheema Khan of McGill University for sharing he newspaper reports published in Montreal concerning the hijab controversy in the province of Quebec. Amber Nasrulla, "Educators Outside Quebec Mystified by Hijab Ban," *The Globe and Mail*, 13 December 1994, pp. A1–4.

2. According to the Centre d' Études de Development du Maghreb, Canada, on 25 May a student at Lucien Pagé High School in Montreal and her mother were physically attacked on a nearby street. Both women had their hijab pulled off during the incident. According to the same center's report, in April a similar incident occurred in a Montreal subway, where a Muslim woman was attacked on the platform by a man who pulled off her hijab. See Chris Cheridan, "Islamophobia," *Mirror* 10, no. 52 (1 June 1, 1995): 11–12.

3. According to Muslim activists, Muslims have become targets, fueled in part by the image of the crazed fundamentalist launching a jihad on the world popularized in films such as *Not Without My Daughter* and *True Lies* (see *Mirror*, ibid., p. 11).

4. Amber Nasrulla, *Globe and Mail*, 13 December 1994.

5. See *Mirror*, p. 12. Algerian-born radio journalist Mohammed Nekili who works for station CFMB in Montreal, says he was harassed in Quebec City by a woman who told him, "I know what you are doing to women in Algeria." According to his female harasser, Nekili was no different from an FIS member. Like other Muslims, he was guilty by association.

6. Nasrullah, *Globe and Mail*, 13 December 1994.

7. See Chris Sheridan, "Islamophobia," *Mirror*, 1 June 1995, p. 12.

8. Ibid.

9. Yvonne Y. Haddad. "The Challenge of Muslim 'Minorityness'" in *The Integration of Islam and Hinduism in Western Europe*, ed. W. A. R. Shahid and P.S. van Koningsveld (Kampen, Netherlands: Kok Pharos Publishing House, 1991), pp. 134–51.

10. Ibid.

11. Freda Hussain, ed., Introduction to *Muslim Women* (London: Croom Helm, 1984).

12. Michele Lemon, "Understanding Does Not Always Lead to Tolerance," *Globe and Mail*, 31 January 1995, p. A2.

13. Cited in ibid.

14. Marilyn Robinson Waldman, "Reflections on Islamic Traditions, Woman and Family" in *Muslim Families in North America*, ed. Earl H. Waugh et al. (Edmonton: University of Alberta Press, 1991), pp. 317–18.

15. Catherine Meckes, "Wearing a Uniform of Oppression," *Globe and Mail*, 5 July 1993, p. A12.

16. Rahat Kurd, "My Hijab Is an Act of Worship—and None of Your Business," *Globe and Mail*, 15 February 1995, p. A20.

17. Lemon in *Globe and Mail*, cited above, n. 12.

18. Catherine Meckes in *Globe and Mail*, cited above, n. 15.

19. Naheed Mustafa, "My Body Is My Own Business," *Globe and Mail*, 29 June 1993, p. A26.

20. Interview with some of Muslim activists in Toronto and Montreal and female students in London, Ontario, Summer 1995.

21. See "Hijabophobia in Quebec?" editorial in the *Montreal Gazette* attacking government officials on the issue of hijab, 24 November 1994.

22. Rahat Kurd, *Globe and Mail*, cited above, n. 16.

23. Amber Nasrulla, "Their Canada Includes Hijab," *Globe and Mail*, 22 August 1994, p. A1–2.

24. Zuhair Kashmeri, *The Gulf Within: Canadian Arabs, Racism and the Gulf War* (Toronto: James Lorimer & Company, 1991), pp. 22–23 and 42–43.

25. Richard Venturi, "Integration or Assimilation in Montreal's Schools," *McGill Tribune*, 15 November 1994, p. 10.

26. Ibid.

27. Nahid Mustafa, "The Fear of Hijab," *Message Canada*, January 1995, p. 15.

28. Ibid.

29. Eve McBride, "The Hijab's Contradictions: A Form of Freedom without Choice," *Gazette*, 6 October 1994, p. A2.

30. Sheema Khan, "The Root of the Hijab Controversy in Quebec," *Muslim Voice*, 2, no. 2, November 1, 1994, p. 4.

31. Irwin Block "Feminists at Odds," *Gazette*, 3 June 1995.

32. Alexander Norris, "Lemieux Blasted for Remarks Attacking Hijab," *Montreal Gazette*, 24 November 1994, p. A1.

33. Ann McIlroy, "Hijab: Politically Charged Piece of Cloth," *Ottawa Citizen*, 2 November 1994, p. B2.

34. "Hijab Report Is Right on the Mark," *Gazette*, editorial, 16 February 1995.

35. Irwin Block, "Banning Hijab Infringes on Basic Rights: Broadbent," *Gazette*, 15 January 1995.

36. *"Hijab* Report is Right on the Mark," 16 February 1995.

37. Lynn Moore, "Don't Bar Girls Wearing Hijabs from Schools: Women's Council," *Gazette,* 14 May 1995.

38. Interviews with Iranian community leaders in Toronto.

39. Raneem Azam, "Helping Each Other in Righteousness," *Muslim Voice,* 2, no. 5 (February, 1995).

40. Nasrulla, "Their Canada Includes Hijab."

41. Hina Syed, "My Struggle and Decision with the Hijab," *Muslim Voice,* 2, no. 7 (April 1995).

7

American Women Choosing Islam

CAROL L. ANWAY

A small but growing number of American-born women are choosing to become Muslim, helping the process of making Islam the fastest growing religion in the United States. This growth can be attributed not only to immigration and increase in births, but to the success of *da'wa* (witnessing by Muslims to the non-Muslims) in America.[1] A growing number of families are finding themselves with daughters or sons who have chosen to leave the Christian tradition to become a follower of Islam.

From September 1993 through July 1994, I conducted a study of American-born women who had converted to Islam in the United States and Canada.[2] Questionnaires were distributed to women converts at Muslim conferences, mailed to those responding to notices in *Islamic Sisters International*, and sent to converts who were identified by those completing the questionnaire for the study. Of the 350 questionnaires given out, fifty-three American Muslim women returned the completed form. The respondents were from sixteen states and one Canadian province, all eager to share stories of their choice to be Muslim. The response rate of 15 percent is fairly low and may be affected by many factors, including the length of time required to answer the ten parts of the questionnaire, the many such questionnaires already floating around asking for the stories of Muslim women converts, and perhaps an unwillingness to share information with a non-Muslim conducting the survey. The letter with the questionnaire stressed that the study was only for Muslim women converts wearing *hijab*, which also eliminated some converts.

The group of women who did answer is self-selected in that they chose to respond to the survey and therefore is not representative of all women who convert to Islam, for their experience tends to be more positive than the norm. However, information yielded from the survey does at least provide a basis on which to frame questions for future study of a segment of people so far rarely targeted for study. The respondants talked about their religious backgrounds (mainly Christian); explained how they became Muslim and how they learned Islamic practices; described their relationships with their families as a result of their conversion and their roles as wives, mothers, students, and/or employees; and shared the feelings of strength they found in their adopted religion.

Profile of the Participants

The educational background of the respondents (53) ranged from high school graduates to women with doctoral degrees. Fifty-three percent had a bachelor's degree or above: 35 percent of these had a bachelor's degree (B.A. or B.S.) only; 12 percent a Master's (M.A. or M.S.), and 6 percent had an M.D. or Ph.D. degree. At the time they responded, seven of the women were college students working toward higher degrees.

The respondents ranged in age from twenty-one to forty-seven years. The duration of their commitment to Islam ranged from six months to twenty-two years. While the age of conversion varied, it occurred most frequently at the young-adult stage from ages 18 to 30: 27 of the 53 women (51 percent) converted between 18 and 23; 18 (34 percent) between 25 and 30; six between 33 and 44 years of age (11 percent); two of the women did not provide their ages.

Approximately 40 percent of the women reported that they worked outside the home either part time or full time, two women have their own in-home businesses, and 12 percent were working toward college degrees. Half were full-time homemakers, with a fourth of those choosing to teach their school-age children at home.

All but two of the women indicated that they observe Islamic practice by wearing the hijab all the time. For the most part, all observed daily prayers, fasted during the month of Ramadan, and participated in other religious duties. They reported that they were finding fulfillment and happiness in their decision to live as Muslims. As one convert put it, "I am more grounded, more relaxed, more focused. You can't stray too far when the next prayer pulls you back. It has certainly had a positive effect on our marriage and family life, and helped me to be a better and calmer mate and mother." She wrote that spiritual work and spiritual development were most meaningful for her.

Non-Muslims often assume that women who choose Islam do so because of pressure put on them by Muslim husbands. In this sample, however, 20 of the 53 women (38 percent) converted while still single. Half of these were introduced to Islam by Muslim friends they met at college or by Muslim neighbors. Two were attracted to the faith while traveling in Muslim countries. Two had been divorced from Muslim husbands, and after the divorce began to search and read about Islam. Others found their interest piqued as they read about Islam or had a college course which introduced them to the religion. Most of the women later married Muslim men. Only five were still single at the time of the questionnaire, and two of those have since written to say they have married Muslims.

Single women in the sample (divorced, widowed, or never married) indicated that they were sometimes uncomfortable at Muslim gatherings and thought that marriage would improve their position in the Muslim community. They felt some loss of power after conversion since being married is considered "the natural state" in the Islamic community, and their connection and role in decision making at the mosque was through the husband. Two of the single women, recent converts in their forties, indicated a dissatisfaction with the level of acceptance extended to them by the Muslim community. One felt mistreated and alienated as a woman. The other felt that other women did not trust her because she was single.

Thirty-three of the women reported that they had converted at the time of marriage or within one year thereafter. Where pressure to convert was applied, it was before the fact, with the prospective husband indicating that he would not marry the woman if she did not become Muslim. In some cases, it was agreed ahead of time that the children would be raised as Muslims. "[My husband] would not marry me without my committing to raise any children we might have as Muslims. I felt he had a sound value system and my initial exposure to the Qur'an did not convince me one way or the other. I saw nothing [in Islam] that I felt adverse about teaching [our] children."

At the time of the survey, 90 percent of the women were married and reported successful and happy marriages. They indicated considerable satisfaction at the position they felt was theirs in the Islamic setting. A woman who was unmarried at the time of the questionnaire later married and wrote:

> You are probably wondering why I am telling you all of this. I just want you to understand that in Islam the institution of marriage is what has helped me to practice my religion to the fullest amount possible. As an American convert, I found it very hard at first to be a good Muslim and follow all the changes I had to make in my life, even though I did do it gradually. Now with my husband, I feel even more fulfilled. In my heart I know that I have made the right decision. I am most lucky because Allah has guided me to the right path. I am not saying I have no problems, but all I do now is look into my heart and read Qur'an and I feel that all is better.

The Families of Origin

The converts reported a variety of responses from their families to their conversion. Nine women indicated that their parents heard them out and accepted the change after they had become convinced that it was their daughter's free choice. One woman reported that "there was no need to work anything out with my family because they were supportive." According to another, "After my conversion, I presented myself wearing *hijab*. I explained myself to them. I never worried much about my family. I knew they would accept what I was happy with. I explained and answered questions freely." A third one said, "When I came to Islam, I told my parents. My father was understanding and supportive. My mother was apprehensive . . . [and] voiced her concerns, which is just what I was looking for when I told my parents—questions, concerns and comments."

Twenty-two of the women indicated that their decision to convert caused stress in the family, but that after the initial shock there was a certain degree of acceptance and a willingness to work on the relationship. One said that telling her parents she "was a Muslim was like a slap in the face to them. It was as if I had rejected everything they had taught me as a child. . . . My mother realized [my husband] was not going to leave me and slowly began to accept my conversion to Islam." Another said that "it has been three years and a lot has changed. My family recognizes that I didn't destroy my life. They see that Islam has brought me happiness, not pain and sorrow. . . . Our relationship is back to normal."

The women who participated in this survey do not seem to have chosen Islam out of any feelings of rebellion against their parents or the religion in which they were raised. They generally acknowledged that relationships with families that were strained or fractured because of their becoming Muslim needed to be worked on carefully so that the family could accept changes in dress, food, celebrations, thought, and worship. Often appreciation was expressed for what the parents had given them, but with the acknowledgment that they were now choosing to live out their lives in a different way from that of the parents.

Ten of the women indicated that, although they still had a relationship with their families, the family had made very little effort to understand and accept the decision. Four reported their parents have turned their backs on them and were no longer in contact. Two of the respondents expressed the opinion that whatever they chose to do as adults was their own business, and two indicated they had no family. The remainder gave no indication of the family relationship. With sadness two of the women told of broken relationships. "I have not worked it out with my parents. It has been almost three years . . . since they have seen us, and they still want nothing to do with us." Another said, "I was adopted. The parents who adopted me do not see me any more. They do not even allow me at their house now that I am Muslim. I have no hope for improvement with them because they will not even let me come over."

While many of the women indicated that their families were improving in their attitude, the conversion had brought stress in most family relationships. Some families blamed the husband for their daughter's conversion.

Problems such as where and how to spend holidays, what foods could and could not be eaten, and the proper environment for the grandchildren continued to require attention. The hijab was apparently often a point of conflict. "My parents disowned me, and I have not spoken to them in four years. They are atheists and do not believe God exists and they do not approve of, as they say, 'wearing the rag on your head.'"

Interviews with seven of the parents revealed that their feelings toward the conversion of their daughter had changed over time. In every case, there was movement toward acceptance from the way they had felt at the beginning. One mother said:

> She was our daughter. We loved her and wanted to continue being a part of her life. Plus I believe everyone has a right to their own relationship with God and has the right to live their own life in their own way. We argued, fussed, cried, wrote letters until we were basically satisfied. It was a very trying time for me.

Religious Backgrounds of the Respondents

The women in the survey grew up in homes that reflected a variety of religious commitments. Even when a denomination was not named, there was some indication that a majority of parents were Christians. Only seven of the women indicated that the family was not involved actively in some religion.[3] Six of the women appear to have been on a religious quest and had experimented with other faiths.[4]

Some of the interviewees seemed to have a need for the religious experience whether or not their parents were involved. One woman changed denominations at age 18. She had read about all the world's religions and was active in both denominations to the point of receiving medals, certificates, and other awards. She considered herself very religious and wanted to become a nun, even inquiring about life in a convent.

Seventeen of the women reported parents who were devout and active in religious organizations. Some said they were turned off from Christianity by the strict attitudes and requirements of their parents.

> I did not subscribe to any kind of organized religion even though I did believe in God. I grew up going to church and that is why I was not interested. My parents . . . were very strict about going to church and church activities and religion. But it wasn't really a thing that I wanted to do—it was just one of those things you do because you have to. When I turned 18 and got out of the house, I wanted to get far away from it.

Of the fifty-three respondents, thirty-one (58 percent) described themselves as very devout religiously or as coming from families with strong a Christian commitment which they felt influenced their own religious interests. Six came from families which, while claiming to be Christian, went to church only occasionally. Seven indicated that their families had minimal association with a church and hardly claimed to be Christian at all. Five of the families represented had no commitment to organized religion.

Three of the women, prior to converting to Islam, were hoping to convert their husband to Christianity by agreeing to study Islam if the husband would consider Christianity. One woman started asking questions of ministers and theologians to help her prove the superiority of Christianity to her husband. She said, "I wanted it so badly; I cried to several of them to help me and most of them said, 'I'm sorry—I don't know' or 'I'll write you,' but I never heard from them."

Concerns with Christianity

Nine of the women expressed problems with the belief in Jesus as God, Jesus as the Son of God, or the concept of the Trinity. Five others said they had major questions about Christianity that no one had satisfactorily answered. Four more felt the Bible has been corrupted. One invited a Muslim friend she had met to attend Mass with her. He said he could not go with her because he was Muslim. In the conversation that followed about Islam, she found herself agreeing with many of his beliefs. She said, "It was just the 'Jesus thing' that kept us at opposite ends of the spectrum." In her search for answers in the following week, she went to a nun and poured out her heart. No help was forthcoming. Then she went to a religion teacher, a lay person, where she grew even more confused. "'Look, I just want you to tell me that, undoubtedly and with full conviction, Jesus Christ is the Son of God.' He didn't look at me when he said, 'I can't tell you that.'"

Part of the strength some of these women saw in Islam was that questions were always answered, albeit from an Islamic perspective. The women often said that what was offered from the Islamic viewpoint seemed more logical, though whether or not they could have expressed these concerns before studying Islam is questionable. These are issues that Muslims stress in their basic reasoning and teaching, and as these questions were raised, the women understood their own confusion regarding these points and were unable to find from Christianity the kinds of specific answers that they could use to dispute these Islamic views.

Three of the women expressed fear of going to hell for accepting the new concepts regarding Jesus. They felt guilty of blasphemy, and it took some time for them to work through these fearful feelings. One described it this way:

> My hardest hurdle was getting over the fiery images from my Sunday school books and training of what we would look like burning up in hell. I had been told so many times that if I did not believe that Jesus had died for my sins and was my personal savior, I would go to hell forever.

Others were assured by the logic of Islam which seemed to respond to the doubts they had regarding Christianity. Many were intrigued by the practice of daily prayer and the peace and commitment that those they observed the Islamic way seemed to enjoy. Several of the women spoke of the feeling of personal enlightenment and that they were being directed by God. One experienced her conversion out of anguish of heart and life.

> Our first son was 18 months old. Our marriage was in deep trouble for a variety of reasons. I turned to the Qur'an to find ways I could use it to manipulate my husband into counseling. Our conflict reached a zenith . . . and I asked him for a separation. I felt I had no options, even though I still loved him. I was calm driving to work. Out of my soul came an intense pain. I cried out aloud for God to help me. At that moment I recognized my desire to be Muslim and it did not matter if my marriage broke up or not. I wanted to be Muslim for me.

The Islamic Way Connects with American Ideals

It is clear that the values these women cherished in Islam had much in common with traditional American ideals including family, dedication to God, good works, commitment to a religious community, education, religious freedom, and discipline. They nevertheless were reluctant to espouse feelings of nationalism and patriotism and instead express bitterness over some of the current foreign-policy decisions of the American government and about much of what is happening in American society today that seems to be in direct conflict with the ideals and values of the past.

The heritage of religious freedom in the United States and Canada allows new converts to appropriate Islamic practices and to integrate them into the routines of daily life. However, they found that these practices often come into conflict with American ways. It is apparent that at the time of conversion, these women were not aware of how marginalized they could feel, or how persistent the discrimination they would encounter would be, especially if they covered their hair. As Haddad writes, "Muslims feel they are living in a country that is hostile, not only to their ethnic origin, but increasingly to Islam and Muslims in general. Their situation has been likened to being on a roller coaster on which they are forced to experience new heights of distortion and vilification."[5] Despite this experience, they continue to hope that the American ideal of religious freedom will mean that they can eventually gain acceptance, respect, and peace.

Converting to Islam inevitably meant rejecting many aspects of the religion and culture in which they had been raised. More important, many also soon found out that the choice by implication appeared to their parents as a rejection of the values they had tried to impart.

The study revealed that although many immigrant Muslims have a prescribed interpretation of what Muslim life involves, the converts found themselves faced with a range of possibilities. They varied in their assessment of how much they could accept or reject of Western culture, often depending on where they were in their own learning and practice. All of them were continually negotiating their relations to the world around them from an Islamic perspective. One woman reflecting on Islam and Westernization wrote:

> Islam does not reject the West's positive values or progress. Believing in God and the Qur'an doesn't mean being old-fashioned or authoritarian. Quite the opposite! We are not rejecting "your" culture! We affirm whatever is good in every culture and religion; we believe Islam has come to provide the "finishing touches" to benefit all mankind, not eradicate what they have done.[6]

The women in this survey were practicing Muslims who had accepted what they felt to be Islamically required of them. This does not mean that they all agreed on how to live out their lives, but there were numerous similarities among them. Many of the customs they were adopting were commonplace in countries that are predominantly Muslim, but very different from the conventional American way of doing things.

Putting Islam into Practice in America

With the declaration of faith begins the journey on the path to being Muslim, thereby changing one's life, relationships, beliefs, and religious practice as one selectively rejects the past American culture or combines it with what is Islamic.

One of the first things the converts learn to do is perform the five daily prayers (*salat*) in the Arabic language with the proper positions and ablutions or cleansing. For those working outside the home, it is difficult to get in all the required prayers because there is usually no area at the place of employment where it is appropriate to prepare for and perform them.

After conversion women usually begin to wear more modest clothing, including in many cases the hijab. Fifty-one of the fifty-three respondents in this study cover their hair. Some took to it easily; others found it a daily sacrifice and a test of endurance. As one woman declared: "My biggest battle is the head covering, the scarf. Nobody knows this though, since I accept and submit to the covering for modesty reasons." The hijab also caused particular tension with many parents. One father twisted his daughter's arm in anger and said, "Take that thing off because I don't want to be seen with you in public." Another family that was able to accept the conversion balked when the daughter started wearing for "they worried that I was cutting myself off from society, that I would be discriminated against, that it would discourage me from reaching my goals, and they were embarrassed to be seen with me. They thought this was too radical." One woman expressed how most of the women felt at heart about dressing hijab: "My husband didn't make me dress this way, and I'm not oppressed. I'm set free—free from the bondage of fashion, clothes, hair, shoes, and the like." Another added, "The American Muslim woman is not oppressed and our cover (hijab) is our right, not a punishment."

Taking of a new first name and even last name with Islamic meaning may happen very quickly in the Muslim convert's life. Some keep their original name for use by the family of origin and as the legal name, and use the new name only in the Muslim environment. Others change their name legally and ask the members of her family of origin to call them by that name as well. Only one mentioned in the survey that she had her name changed legally. Of the 53 respondents, 20 gave first names that seem specifically Islamic, while five others adopted an Islamic name as a middle name or put it in parenthesis. For instance, the author's daughter is called Tahireh by Muslim friends and her husband, but she uses her given name, Jodi, in her profession, business dealings, and with family and non-Muslim friends. One convert who had a preschool-age daughter changed the daughter's name as well. A Muslim woman at marriage may take on the last name of her husband or keep her maiden name.

Diet changed as they no longer ate the forbidden (*haram*) pork and pork products and had to avoid alcoholic drinks and drugs. Many Muslims also choose to eat only *halal*, or approved meats which have been killed in an Islamically prescribed manner. These dietary changes make it very difficult to eat in the homes of relatives or at restaurants and in many cases limit the social interaction with friends and family who are non-Muslim.

Some found the dietary restrictions so cumbersome that they tried to avoid eating in their parents' home or leaving their children with the family. One woman wrote,

> I do not leave my children with my family. We have never visited for more than a couple of hours at a time since I became Muslim. In doing this, I avoid another potential problem—that of halal food. My parents do not understand or accept the concept with halal/haram food. We simply avoid the issue—I don't eat at their house.

Other women are more flexible, taking halal meat with them to a family dinner or eating what they can of the meal. Some of the families plan their menus around foods which the visiting Muslim family can eat, or keep halal meat on hand in the freezer. The author's grandson, who attends public school, usually takes his lunch, but he also eats at school, having been trained even by first grade not to eat the meat. One day he told me he gave his teacher the turkey sandwich in the lunch he bought but he ate the rest of the meal.

Converting to Islam involves acceptance of a totally new system of relations between the sexes. Dating and flirting or even friendly relationships with men are no longer appropriate, and the women must think through how best to relate to co-workers, to male acquaintances, and to Muslim men other than husband or relatives. The patriarchal system and separation of sexes in the mosque and Muslim meetings and activities are seen as a rejection of the way males and females relate in America. One woman described her apprehension when she is

> around Muslim males who won't make eye contact or speak to me when I'm around them. I don't bother to ask why. I just tell myself that they don't know English. I don't feel restricted at all as a woman, although I am still trying to get used to the division of the sexes at social functions and at my daughter's school.

Another woman expressed her sense of being

> empowered wearing hijab and loose clothing. I feel like no man has the right to undress me anymore with his eyes. Sure they can use their imagination, but my body is protected. I am not a sex object, and to be the "American Dream Girl" is a nice skin to shed. I feel empowered by prayer and the security of Allah's promise directly to me.

Still another woman finds the separation of the sexes a little more difficult, especially at the mosque:

> Sometimes I feel the Muslim women aren't given a change to speak out about their opinions or views on things within the Muslim community. They are put in the back and hidden away. If I go to a lecture [that is not in the masjid], I like to sit near the front, so I can see and hear the speaker. I am dressed Islamically, so why should I sit in the back just because someone thinks men cannot control themselves? Men need to take the responsibility for their own actions. Women cannot always be hidden so that men won't think bad thoughts. We should dress and act so as not to promote that, but I still will not live my life locked up in a cage or in the back row at a university lecture. I can live my life with respect and dignity, and live as a Muslim woman at the same time.

Television, movies, magazines, and popular music are all areas of potential concern for Muslim women. Dating, flirting, love scenes, rock music, dancing, bad language, and disrespect to parents are just some of the scenes and images to be avoided, leaving little the American media offer that is acceptable. As one mother described it:

> I don't like them [the children] to watch commercials or dancing, rap music, dating situations, looseness on TV—anything which you can see by turning it on for two minutes or less. Also I don't want them to get used to musical instruments or music which has adult rock and roll rhythm even if it has children's lyrics.

Appropriate education for children is a major consideration. Home training, private education including Islamic schools, and public schools may all be options. Of the women surveyed, 75 percent had children, although not all were of school age. Forty-seven percent sent their children to public schools, 11 percent had children enrolled in non-Muslim private schools, 26 percent had children in Islamic schools, and 26 percent taught them at home. (This adds up to more than 100 percent because families with more than one child often have them in different kinds of schools.) They want the children to have the opportunity to be with Muslim peers and to avoid the Western values that other children in the schools represent. Many parents want their children to have the opportunity to learn Arabic so they will be able to read the Qur'an. Often children go to a special Arabic class on Saturday mornings or other scheduled times.

Christian and national holidays often pose stressful situations insofar as the renunciation of these holidays may be perceived by relatives as a rebuff of the family itself and can become a source of conflict and pain for both the family and the Muslim daughter. Some of the converts have worked it out; others still struggle with the problem:

> I think that for my family, the main point of stress was probably Christmas, whether it's okay to give us gifts, include us for dinner, etc. It took a lot of time and talk to come to terms with Christmas because I cannot turn my back on my family. My husband and I join my family for dinner and receive gifts from them with the understanding that this is a celebration in which we do not participate and that we wouldn't reciprocate the gift exchange. We will, however, reciprocate by including my family in our Islamic celebrations. Everyone was in agreement and this idea and the spirit of the "season" was not dampened.

It becomes more complicated when there are children:

> I try to avoid talking about the holidays. My brother and sister understand that I don't celebrate them and respect me for it. But my parents don't understand and keep asking every year if I am coming over for the holidays and what to do with the presents they got for me and my husband and the kids.

Some families are more open in dealing with holidays and celebrations:

> My sisters and parents are sensitive to the fact that we don't celebrate Christian holidays. They always ask before giving or doing anything which could be construed to be related to such holidays. They respect our holidays. It helps that we have a varied family encompassing many types of Christian, Jewish, Buddhist, and Muslims. It is an unspoken family rule to respect others' beliefs so long as they aren't harming themselves or others.

Muslims, of course, have their own holidays to celebrate. A particular unifying bond is Ramadan. Several of the women stated that they were sad when that special period of fasting and worship was over, even though at first they may have been concerned that they would not be successful.

These Muslim women, having rejected their former American life and adopted the Islamic way, are engaged in a process of acculturation which

Marcia Hermansen[7] defines as confronting a new cultural context and worldview and having to choose where to adapt to aspects of the context or worldview in one's own life. She describes the three stages of a major life transition as (1) separation—moving from the original personal status and social structure to (2) liminality—a transitional anxiety-ridden state between detachment from the old to attachment to the new, and then to (3) reintegration—moving into the community with reenergized and reinvested commitment. These women take on these new roles not only for themselves but, if married, for their husband and children.

Concern for the Husband's Homeland

Some of the women in the survey indicated that they meant to try to live according to Islam in America as free as possible from the cultural influences either of America or of the husband's country of origin. They believe that if they were to move to the husband's homeland, it would be harder to practice Islam free of the culture of that country. Others understand that they must accept a blending of cultures, trying to let the Islamic emerge as much as possible. Some of them said that they tried to cook the foods their husbands liked, but that their main concern was to try to look at things Islamically:

> The only culture is Islam. I even try not to follow the American culture. I try to put Islam first in everything I do. My husband's family is very stuck in traditions from their Indian culture. This gave us many problems on our visit.

Another said:

> Our daily life not cultural or traditional—just normal everyday living. What is different about our family is that we look at life from an Islamic point of view, and we explain Islam to our children using events that happen in our daily lives.

Some women reported the family had plans to go to the husband's homeland when finances or situations were more stable. This tends to give them the sense that life in America is temporary. Years may pass in this "temporary" mode, before they finally decide either to make the move or admit they will be staying in the United States or Canada. This situation can cause the woman to feel like a stranger in both countries. One woman expressed this as a feeling of being alienated here—a foreigner in her own land living the Muslim lifestyle and waiting for the time when she will go to her husband's country. But she also admitted that making a visit overseas to his family in a Muslim country made her feel foreign there because of her American ways even though she was Muslim. She had a feeling of always being "a stranger in a strange land." For her, moving overseas in order to feel more comfortable about her beliefs and dress and manner is not the answer, for that would require even more adapting. This woman concluded:

> I realize that how Islam affects my life is what I do with it. I can follow a culture and old traditions; go with the basics and try to ignore the rest; or study and understand Islam as it affects me in whatever surrounding I am living in. The Muslims of America have a unique opportunity to understand Islam and how to live and practice in a non-Islamic society just as in the early days of Prophet Muhammad (peace be upon him).[8]

Embracing the Ideals of Family Values

A primary role for Muslim women is the care of children, home, and husband, and work outside the home should not interfere with that role. What this means is interpreted in a variety of ways according to the situation in which the woman finds herself, by expectations of herself and of her husband, their school of Islamic thought, and her educational background.

In an unpublished research paper, Zahra Buttar[9] divided American Muslim women in two major categories. Into the first she placed American Muslim women in orthodox settings whose activities were described in the following way:

- Majority of time spent on child-rearing, cooking, husband
- Low level of decision making over income and household matters
- Not working out of the home (some not allowed to drive cars)
- Male head of family with final decision-making authority
- Women may lack daily "network" of friends, religious study or social group
- Sex-segregated activities
- Often wearing special type of clothing
- Encouraged to pray alone and always sexually segregated

Women in orthodox settings seem to have little choice as to whether to reject or accept Westernization, for they are under the control of the husband's interpretation of how they are to behave and operate. This category might be considered at one end of a continuum where isolation of the woman and control by the male is extreme.

At the other end of the continuum is the category of Muslim women who see themselves as tending toward a feminist view. The term "feminist" is used here to designate women who understand that they have rights under Islam and some power in expressing those rights. Nevertheless, they still have some characteristics in common with those classified as orthodox. They may wear hijab, at certain stages in life they may spend most of their time in child and husband care, or be sex-segregated in activities. Women in this category tend to be well educated and active in society. Many of them "felt they 'had it all' . . . family, career, social community with like values, a spiritual peace and a strong sense of self-identity and self-worth. The most important element was a strong self-identity/self-worth concept, and the spiritual peace achieved through Islam."[10]

Buttar also identified another trend among the American Muslim women who appear to reject traditional Islam while espousing theoretical or Qur'anic Islam.

> They realize that traditional Islam as practiced by immigrant males is cultural, patriarchal and oppressive to women and other social groups that are perceived as threatening, to the cultural norms of Islam these male immigrants have brought to America. The true problem is that male immigrants do not know what is Islamic and what is cultural. The two have been so intertwined through the centuries.[11]

The women who have more choice about how they relate to, or reject, Western values are generally either single or in marriages that are more egalitarian, allowing the wife to determine her own actions.

When they used the word "feminist" it is synonymous with the Western understanding of feminist only in that they both favor women's rights. They part company insofar as Muslim feminists do not ask for the same rights that Western women demand. Buttar says they ask for "complete spiritual, political and social equality as prescribed by God."[12]

The fifty-three women in my survey[13] tended to describe themselves in ways that would place them in Buttar's Muslim feminist category. The husbands were described as cooperative and helpful in child care; many of the women had careers or worked part-time; and the women described a sense of partnership in the marriage, though one well within the framework of their practice and beliefs of Islam.

The women have great hopes that they can raise their children to be practicing Muslims, extending themselves in trying to create an environment in which that training takes place on a day-to-day basis. By doing so they find it easier to protect themselves from those things in American society which would draw them away from the Muslim path. Care is taken in the selection of playmates, schools, entertainment, caretakers, recreation, always trying to avoid situations that would interfere with the values they want for their children. "American Muslims cherish the hope that their children will not so identify with Western culture that they abandon their faith and that they will continue to espouse and live by the sacred values of their Islamic heritage."[14]

Being in the World But Not of the World

The women in my survey reflected a very positive view of the life of American women who choose to be Muslim. While they regret the strain on their relationships with their family and are not too keen about adjusting to the lack of power in the *umma* or masjid, they are adapting to their new lives, accommodating to the expectations of their husband's culture, while holding on to some of their own American upbringing and interpreting Islamic practices in the American setting. What they have taken on demands strength, commitment, and discipline, and the courage to deal with the pressures that American society places upon them.

It is clear that they are eager to assume leadership in exercising the rights that they believe are guaranteed to them in Islam. Those who return to their husband's country of origin may well exercise a special kind of influence there as they bring new interpretations of what it means to be a woman in a more truly Islamic manner, less encumbered by the many cultural traditions and expectations that have kept women from attaining their fundamental rights as set forth in the Qur'an.

Notes

1. Larry Poston, *Islamic Da'wah in the West* (New York: Oxford University Press, 1992). Mr. Poston gives an overview of the Muslim missionary strategy in North America and the dynamics of conversion to Islam.

2. Carol L. Anway, *Daughters of Another Path* (Lee's Summit, MO: Yawna Publications, 1996). This survey of 53 American Muslim women comprised a collection of stories elicited from ten areas of questioning.

3. The women indicated their denominational backgrounds as follows: Catholic, 12; "holy roller," 1; Nazarene, 1; Reorganized Church of Jesus Christ of Latter Day Saints, 2; Southern Baptist, 5; Christian, 2; Episcopal, 2; Methodist, 2; Lutheran, 1; Quaker, 1; Presbyterian, 1; World Wide Church of God, 2; Greek Orthodox, 2; Seventh Day Adventist, 1; Jehovah's Witness, 2: generally Christian, 4; no denomination given, 10; indication of atheist or no religious background, 2.

4. Some had changed denominations before the conversion to Islam: Catholic to Jehovah's Witness (1), Methodist to Catholic (1), Presbyterian to Catholic (1), Church of God to Episcopal (1), Catholic to "born-again" Christian (1), general Christian to Hindu (1).

5. Yvonne Yazbeck Haddad, "American Foreign Policy in the Middle East and Its Impact on the Identity of Arab Muslims in the United States" in *Muslims of America*, ed. Yvonne Yazbeck Haddad (New York: Oxford University Press, 1991), p. 230.

6. Portion of a letter to Carol L. Anway written August 1995, by Noor Grant, editor of *Islamic Canada Reflections*, after her review of *Daughters of Another Path*.

7. Marcia K. Hermansen, "Two-Way Acculturation" in *Muslims of America*, cited above.

8. Personal observation written by Jodi Mohammadzadeh, July 1995, on file with Carol L. Anway.

9. Zahra Buttar, "American Female Muslim Conversion Survey," an unpublished paper presented 3 September 1993, to the University of Nevada Las

Vegas, Sociology Department. It was a preliminary study of American female Muslims.

10. Ibid., p. 14.

11. Ibid., p. 15.

12. Ibid., p. 15.

13. Anway, *Daughters of Another Path*.

14. Yvonne Yazbeck Haddad, "American Foreign Policy in the Middle East," p. 230.

PART III

AMERICANS ON THE ISLAMIZATION PATH?
The African-American Experience

8

Identity and Destiny

The Formative Views of the Moorish Science Temple and the Nation of Islam

ERNEST ALLEN, JR.

Since whiteness is a mark of degeneracy in many
animals near the pole, the negro has as much
right to term his savage robbers albinos and
white devils, degenerated through the weakness
of nature, as we have to deem him the emblem
of evil, and a descendant of Ham, branded by
his father's curse. I, might he say, I, the black,
am the original man. I have taken the deepest
draughts from the source of life, the Sun: on me,
and on everything around me, it has acted with
the greatest energy and vivacity.
                    —Johann Gottfried Herder, 1784

The original man, Allah has declared, is none
other than the black man. The black man is the
first and last, maker and owner of the universe.
From him came brown, yellow, red and white
people. By using a special method of birth
control law the black man was able to produce
the white race. . . . The white race is not, and
never will be, the chosen people of Allah (God).
They are the chosen people of their father
Yakub, the devil.
                    —Elijah Muhammad, 1965[1]

The embrace of Islam by African Americans in the twentieth century is a phenomenon perhaps as understandable as it is mystifying. Understandable, to a certain extent anyway, in that a not insignificant number of enslaved Africans carried to the Americas in chains were already practicing Muslims when they arrived. In this way contemporary African-American Islam may be viewed—but with great difficulty, one might add—as a historical revival or recovery of practices thought to be long-buried. Somewhat mystifying, on the other hand, in that by the early nineteenth century African Americans had overwhelmingly converted to Christianity, and for over a century and a half had held fast to their adopted religion as if it were a mighty rock in a weary land.

That devotion was breached in the 1970s by a widespread African-American conversion to Islam. Ultimately, what we wish to understand is the historical process underlying this phenomenon. The final stage of that process— the transition from an African-American syncretic or "proto" version of the Islamic faith to a more traditional Sunni Islam—is more than a twice-told tale, and will not be replicated here.[2] The initial African-American passage from Christianity to syncretic Islam in the 1920s and 1930s, on the other hand, is a story which, up until now, has been largely confined to sociological description or to folklore.

The present chapter approaches this unruly task by means of a comparative study of the world views of the Moorish Science Temple of America (MSTA) and the Nation of Islam (NOI)—sometimes referred to in the early years as the Lost Found Nation of Islam.[3] More precisely, we shall find ourselves intensely concerned with the ways in which these two organizations, themselves purveyors of syncretic versions of Islam, addressed issues of African-American identity and a corresponding, predetermined destiny, one either foretold by the scriptures or prescribed in self-ordained myths. Although the elaboration of such identities and prophetic destinies do not wholeheartedly coincide with the overall world views of either organization, they come close to doing so, and in any case promise an engaging perspective from which to view the phenomenon of African-American Islam as a whole.

Towards the end of the nineteenth century the most significant, sacred identities appropriated by African-American Christians in the service of their own national identity were those of the Hamitic, Ethiopian, and Hebrew class. By the mid-1920s the Moorish Science Temple (reportedly founded in Newark, New Jersey, in 1913) established headquarters in Chicago, declaring Islam to be the true religion of Asiatic (blacks and other "peoples of color") in North America, while at the same time claiming descent from biblical Moabites. An amalgam of theosophically-inspired Christian writings, this sacred Moorish text bore the name of *Holy Koran*. In 1930 a competing proto-Islamic world view issued forth from a similar group based in Detroit and known as the Nation of Islam, an organization which eschewed biblical identity pretty much altogether, but drew support for its views from biblical scripture as readily as from the passages of the Qur'an.

The syncretic tendencies of both organizations, it turns out, had much in common with African-American syncretic Judaism which, beginning in the 1880s, eventually wound its way from the upper South to urban areas of the Midwest and Northeast before World War I. A separate, less heterodox stream of syncretic Black Hebrewism arrived via West Indian and African immigrants to the United States, probably around the turn of the century.[4] Taken together, however, these disparate Hebraic influences were hardly sufficient to explain all the vital elements of proto-Islamic beliefs and practices which coalesced in the 1920s and 1930s. Freemasonry and its attendant creeds, the fallout from an internal crisis besetting late nineteenth-century American Protestantism, and African-American reactions to the rise of political and cultural pan-Asianism at century's end also would contribute their share to the eclectic and dynamic doctrines of Moors and Lost-Founds alike.

The Core Narratives of Syncretic Islam

Stripped down to their basic details, the Moorish Science and Nation of Islam world views shared partially similar narrative structures bearing on the origins of, and solutions to, the miseries of African Americans as a people. While containing within themselves an outline of almost all the essential features of both theologies, what these scripts revealed in particular was an affirmation of close linkages between the prophetic destiny and identity (or identities) of black folk considered as a whole. In response to the plaint, "Why Do Black People Suffer?" MSTA and NOI narratives at first diverged, with the Moorish Science Temple placing the initial blame for black affliction on the blacks themselves and the Nation of Islam laying it squarely at the door of white America. As for the follow-up inquiry, "How Can This Suffering Be Brought to an End?" MSTA and NOI commentaries tended towards broad-scale agreement, with both groups casting primary responsibility upon black people themselves to improve their condition. Here the shadow of the Apocalypse encouraged not only righteous behavior, but also an ultimate sense of futility regarding human initiative.

Black people suffered, according to the MSTA's Noble Drew Ali, more or less in the following way. Having once led an implied, idyllic existence, blacks fell into a state of material and existential deprivation hundreds of years ago because they turned away from God. Forcibly snatched from their ancestral home and cast into slavery as a consequence, they adopted a counterfeit identity, a false religion and culture, and a God which was not their own. NOI leader W. D. Fard, on the other hand, departed from familiar African-American theodicies, ascribing black suffering to the work of the devil incarnate, the white man, whom God had capriciously allowed to reign on earth for a prescribed number of years. Tricked into slavery, blacks subsequently adopted a counterfeit identity, a false religion and culture, and a God which was not their own.

With regard to bringing black suffering to an end, however, Prophets Ali and Fard were basically in accord—at least regarding the broad contours of their respective outlooks. In order to place themselves once more in harmony with their Creator, African Americans first had to recover their true faith and authentic sense of self. Second, while black peoples' reclaiming of their original identity would transport them from the periphery to the very center of spiritual existence, such a step remained insufficient. Although God provides for those who believe in Him, African Americans had to take the initiative in attending to their material condition—such as, for example, maintaining orderly families and proper eating habits, adopting frugal practices, observing appropriate behavior in public, and engaging in gainful employment. Sacrifices thus made bore a two-fold character: not only would they lead practitioners to a state of spiritual and material fulfillment in the here and now, but they would also serve as preparation for the final call.

To facilitate the process, God had sent a prophet, a Messiah, to direct African Americans along the true and only path to redemption. Salvation's goals, moreover, could best be accomplished by a turning inward socially as well as economically, thereby maintaining a social existence apart from that of Euro-Americans. And, ultimately, inevitably, the Apocalypse: if the attractions of a marvelously uplifted way of life proved insufficient to black folk, the promise of an imminent judgment visited upon them by God would provide additional impetus to turn them from their dissolute ways. The principal difference between the two groups in this regard was that the NOI actually named a date for the final battle between Good and Evil, whereas the MSTA timeline remained open-ended.

The core narratives of MSTA and NOI world views partly overlapped, but even in their congruencies God often appeared radically dissimilar in the details. Both accounts claimed the existence of a plethora of secular/sacred group identities among blacks prior to the arrival of the slave trade. For the MSTA, for example, African Americans were primordially identified as Asiatics, as Muslims, as biblical Moabites, and as Moors. An affirmation of semi-deific status added yet another element to the constellation of Moorish self-naming practices. And in accord with their claim to American citizenship, Moors also wished to be known as Moorish Americans. The NOI world view, on the other hand, fully endorsed the MSTA notion that the primeval identities of blacks were both Muslim and Asiatic. But appearing to shun biblical identities altogether, it additionally offered up the Lost Tribe of Shabazz and the Original People as ostensible substitutes, drawing upon a cosmogony all its own. The term, "Lost Found Nation," was used collectively to describe converts to NOI teachings. And the NOI, for its part, claimed full deific status for black people, with the proviso that all such mortals were subordinate to the supreme God, Allah, who was also mortal.

Both groups were also certain as to what they were not. According to Moorish Americans, the fall from grace had resulted in "marks"—the designations Negro, Black, Colored and Ethiopian—being placed upon uprooted Moroccans. But these marks, or ascribed identities, had been imposed not by the Creator, but by Europeans, and were vigorously contested by the Moors. The Lost-Founds, for their part, repudiated the label "African" applied by whites to the black American population. And where the MSTA denied the existence of the "colored" man altogether, for the NOI said "colored" man was the Caucasian.

The Permanent Struggle for Recentering and Restoring

One way black Americans have responded to their psycho-social marginalization in American society has been to exert a countervailing movement toward demarginalization. Marginalization rests upon the ability of the powerful successfully to turn the perceived differences of the weak into a sense of "otherness." Paradoxically, the enduring struggle for African-American existential recentering often proceeds down the opposite path or sometimes both at the same time. One route has tended to stress sameness, or the indistinguishability of African Americans from the whole—for example, Christians as a group or, say, humanity writ large. In itself, this trend would seem to suggest assimilationist tendencies of one sort or another.

An opposing tendency is for African Americans to emphasize their differences relative to other ethno-racial groups, but with the category of difference treated not as otherness, but as a special dispensation. This reaction would seem to suggest a nationalist option. Both in addition and in contrast to the broad-based Christian identity historically embraced by black Americans are the frequent connections made to particular biblical peoples such as Hamites, Ethiopians, or Hebrews.[5] Thus, beneath an overarching, universal Christian identity which denies difference flourishes a handful of singular identities that extol it. But whether by eradicating perceived distinctions altogether, or, conversely, by consecrating and transforming distinctions into a special status, or "chosen-ness," the aim is to eliminate the pejorative or marginalized status of black folk. In the example of particularity within universality, both tasks are fulfilled simultaneously, with African Americans sharing in a universal Christianity while celebrating distinctive group characteristics of their own.

Treading the path where difference is treated as a special dispensation, the process of recentering has occasionally taken the form of a quest for the restoration of, or return to, origins. (This individual/collective restoration is not to be confused with a "restoration" of the African continent to its former glory, a related but separate matter.) One factor tending to strengthen the sense of group identity among African Americans has been the collective sense of loss associated with their uprooting from the African continent.

Fortified by the perdurably marginalized status of black people in American society, this feeling of deracination evokes a desire for the physical or existential restoration of their original condition, whether in the form of an actual physical return to Africa or in the ostensive reclaiming of their lost heritage: original names, languages, cultures, and religions. Invariably, such longings became intertwined with complementary notions of religious redemption, with their attendant, overlapping emphasis on rebirth; of a return to a primordial, blessed state; of salvation through intervention of a divine power; and of millenarianism as well.

Historically, the theme of restoration has been most strongly associated with the idea of emigration. An early example is the petition of 73 black Freemasons to the Massachusetts legislature in 1787, in which they expressed a "desire to return to Africa, our native country . . . for which the God of nature has formed us."[6] The same desire was expressed most dramatically, of course, by Marcus Garvey's Back to Africa movement of the 1920s. The pursuit of spiritual and cultural redemption lay at the heart of African-American Hebrew sects that began to appear in the 1880s and reach its peak in the African-American cultural nationalism of the 1960s. This restorative theme, in its existential aspects, is central to the world views of the MSTA and NOI as well.

Christian Identity, Universal and Particular

There was, of course, no text more centrally regarded by nineteenth-century African Americans than the Bible. While there were many reasons why African Americans both free and slave were attracted to Christianity's fold, a not insignificant one was the leveling effect offered by Christian universality: no matter what one's station in life, all human beings were equal in the sight of the Lord. But equally attractive to African Americans were some of the more narrowly conceived particular identities and, less unanimously, corresponding destinies found in the powerful Old Testament books of Genesis, Psalms, and Exodus. "That blacks had a divinely appointed destiny," Raboteau notes, "no black Christian in the nineteenth century denied. But what was it? Since its fulfillment was yet to come, who could be certain of its features?"[7] These destinies, African Americans believed, were inscribed in the scriptures, with several in particular having been located in favored scriptural identities.[8]

The ninth chapter of Genesis, for example, contains the "Table of Nations," a detailed description of Noah's progeny following the Deluge and their subsequent peopling of specific regions of the earth. Instructed by Euro-American men of the cloth in the Bible's revelations, African Americans soon discovered that they were really Hamites, descendants of the second son of Noah, who were eventually to fill the African continent with the strength of their numbers after migrating from western Asia.[9] Due to the disrespect shown by Ham to his father, God in his infinite wisdom determined that Ham's fourth son, Canaan, should bear a curse. He and his heirs were to be as servants—"hewers of wood, and drawers of water"—unto the extended families of Shem and Japhet, the brothers of Ham (Gen. 9:22–27). However, the popular Antebellum interpretation of the fable, having dispensed with the subtleties concerning which of Ham's sons actually received the imprecation, concluded simply that all blacks had been cursed by God to serve as slaves in the New World.[10]

Ambivalence thus beclouded the black folks' embrace of their accursed Hamitic identity. On the one hand, they tended to accept the Hamite (and, by extension, Cushite and Canaanite) designations for a very good number of reasons. Affirming black membership in the universal tribe of humanity, these scriptural identities not only confirmed black people's existence on earth immediately following the Flood, but also established them—by way of Mizraim and Cush, the sons of Ham—as the progenitors of the ancient civilizations of Ethiopia and Egypt.[11] Hamitic destiny was severely flawed in its social implications, however, and in assenting to the Hamite designation, African Americans at the same time tended to reject the notion that God had intended their fate to be that of slaves. Indeed, the Book of Exodus, as we know, was seen to provide exculpatory evidence to that effect. Some black preachers declared the curse of Ham to have been invalidated due to Noah's state of inebriation. Others optimistically viewed the imprecation as the sign of a more positive role that the race was eventually destined to play. But there were still others, such as the irreverent Sierra Leone preacher who, turning the Hamitic tables, argued that the mark bestowed by God upon Cain (Gen. 4:15) was none other than "white" skin coloring:

> My brethren you see white man bad too much, ugly too much, no good. You want sabby how man like dat come to lib in de world? Well, I tell you. Adam and Eve, dey colored people, berry handsum, lib in one beautiful garden. Dere dey hab all things dat be good. Plaintains, yams, sweet potatoes, foo foo[,] palm wine, he-igh, too much! Den dey hab two childrum, Cain and Abel. Cain no like Abel's palaver; one day he kill'm. Den God angry and he say, *Cain!* Cain go hide himself: he tink him berry clebber. Heigh-heigh! God say again, Cain, you tink I no see you, you bush-nigger—eh? Den Cain come out, and he say yes massa, I lib here,—what de matter massa? Den God say in one big voice, like de tunder in de sky, *"Where'm broder Abel?"* Den Cain turn white all ober wid fear—dat de first white man, breddren![12]

An equivalent African-American version of God's confrontation with Cain gained currency in the United States as early as the 1820s.[13] Having been subjected to racial tinkering by Euro-Americans, the Book of Genesis now faced a corrective which would not be the last. In the process the African origin of God's first human creatures, Adam and Eve, was clearly affirmed as well.

Ethiopia, too, was mentioned in the Bible, most frequently in Isaiah. But far more important in this regard was a single, prophetic verse in the Book of Psalms: "Princes shall come out of Egypt, and Ethiopia shall soon stretch forth her hands unto God" (Ps. 68:31). "Ethiopianism" is a term frequently used to describe African as well as African-American religious and political responses to this ambiguous biblical passage, and it would be difficult to improve on Shepperson's transcontinental overview of the phenomenon:

> In 1611 the Authorized or King James Version of the Bible was first issued. Its translation from the Hebrew and Greek Scriptures frequently employed one of the sixteenth- and early seventeenth-century English words for a black man: Ethiopian. Indeed, the word "Ethiopia" was given a much wider significance than modern Ethiopia and was often used for sub-Saharan Africa as a whole. In this way, as the Bible was read, openly or surreptitiously, to the slave populations of the British North American and Caribbean colonies, which were established in the seventeenth century, persons of African descent learned to recognize their lost country and heritage in the references to Ethiopia and Ethiopians. They began to cherish all Ethiopian references in the Bible which had a liberatory promise and which, when contrasted with the indignities of plantation bondage, showed the black man in a dignified and humane light. With the growth of the abolitionist movement and the development of independent Negro Churches in the New World in the last quarter of the eighteenth century, one of these references, the thirty-first verse of the sixty-eighth Psalm, became a standard slogan for Negro aspirations wherever the King James Version was understood. The spread of Christian missionary activity in West Africa in the nineteenth century, particularly in areas such as Sierra Leone and Liberia where Negro evangelists from the United States and the British West Indies were at work, extended the process. "Ethiopia" had begun to stretch out her hands unto God in both the New World and the Old by the middle of the nineteenth century in the form of independent Churches, schools, and States: uprooted black men had begun to get ideas above the humble and humiliating stations in life to which white men had assigned them. The term "Ethiopianism" was not, at this time, applied to this process; but the years in which it was first extensively employed, from the 1870s to the 1920s, drew heavily on these pre-1871 experiences of Negro liberation.[14]

Psalm 68:31 was open to diverse interpretation, but following Raboteau, three major clusterings of African-American expressions of Ethiopianism (a term which he does not employ) may be identified. There once was a time, according to one of these accounts, when the African race enjoyed a glorious past in both Egypt and Ethiopia, and presently the moment was nigh for African peoples to be restored to their rightful dignity among the nations.[15] Ironically, the identification with ancient Africa was accompanied by an extreme aversion to contemporary African life. This negative ranking achieved even more prominence in a second theme, which held that Africa's redemption could be accomplished only through knowledge of Christ, and that the prophetic task of African-American Christian missionaries was to raise the inhabitants of the Dark Continent to a more enlightened spiritual state. Finally, in the coming new age it would be "the destiny of those who were oppressed but did not oppress, those who were enslaved but did not enslave, those who were hated, but did not hate, to realize the gospel on earth."[16] Several of these themes at least continued well into the era of African decolonization in the late 1950s and early 60s.[17]

In African-American eyes, the Book of Exodus emerged as one of most attractive accounts of the Bible, since it registered God's assistance to an enslaved people.[18] Central tropes included the positing of divine leadership in the person of Moses, deliverance through migration, and the divine punishment of one's oppressors. From the late eighteenth century onward, most African-American Christians tended to embrace Hebrew identity in a metaphorical, not literal, way. One of the earliest recorded manifestations of millenarian sentiment among African Americans is found in Gabriel's 1800 slave conspiracy in Virginia, where would-be insurrectionists closely identified themselves with the Israelites of the Old Testament.[19] Denmark Vesey's attempted rebellion in 1822 was similarly tinged with Hebrew identification on the part of slave conspirators.[20] Towards the latter part of the nineteenth century, however (but possibly much earlier), a small number of believers—primarily of rural and urban working-class background—managed to cross the slender divide separating identification *with* from identification *as*.[21] Moving beyond a self-comparison with the ancient Hebrews, some African Americans began to think of themselves as the Hebrews of the nineteenth century; for others, the full transformation into the people of the Pentateuch would not be far behind.[22] As will soon become apparent, this discussion of Black Hebrew identity is especially important in that it provides valuable insight into the structure of African-American Islamic identity as well.

Origins of Black Hebrew Identity and Syncretic Judaism

It was apparently left to the Church of the Living God, Pillar Ground of Truth for All Nations, to provide the first documented instance of an African-American house of worship based on a literal identification of its members as the scriptural Hebrews.[23] Founded in Chattanooga, Tennessee, by Prophet F. C. Cherry in 1886, the church later moved to Philadelphia where it flourished well into the World War II era and beyond.[24] The Church of the Living God was the forerunner of numerous Black Hebrew sects ranging from Christian churches espousing little more than a formal Jewish identity to groups embracing the Torah and following Jewish Law. In 1896 another Black Hebrew congregation, the Church of God and Saints of Christ, was initiated by Father William Saunders Crowdy in Lawrence, Kansas.[25] It moved to Philadelphia four years later, and eventually to a previously established colony at Belleville, Virginia, near Portsmouth. By 1909 a South African branch was in existence as well.[26]

Somewhat closer to orthodox Jewish religious practices were the observances of a number of New York City congregations. In Brooklyn an organization known as the Moorish Zion[ist?] Temple was founded by Leon Richlieu in 1899. The Moorish Zionist Temple begun by Mordecai Herman in 1921, and which soon established additional temples in Harlem, Philadelphia, and Newark, was either a reorganization of Richlieu's group, or a new organization altogether.[27] By the 1920s a host of other Black Hebrew-identified houses of worship had surfaced in Harlem, including Warren Robinson's infamous and decidedly heterodox Temple of the Gospel of the Kingdom (1917), with branches in Atlantic City, Philadelphia, Detroit, Chicago, and Abescon, New Jersey;[28] Wentworth Arthur Matthew's well-known Commandment Keepers of the Living God (1919);[29] and Arnold J. Ford's Beth B'nai Abraham (House of the Sons of Abraham, 1924),[30] which maintained ambivalent ties to the Garvey movement. The membership of a number of the more or less orthodox New York sects sometimes included immigrant Jews from North Africa, Ethiopia, and India as well.[31] Chicago, too, had its Hebrew-identified groups, including one known as the International Peace and Brotherly Love Movement (1913).[32] And sometime in the mid-twenties or slightly later, the Spiritual Israel Church was formed in Kansas City, Missouri.[33]

In many cases the actual or anticipated migration experiences of African Americans fortified their embrace of Hebraic literalism. That the Church of God and Saints of Christ should have originated in Kansas at the time that it did, for example, seems entirely appropriate. The recipient of some 6,000 migrants from Texas, Mississippi, and Louisiana in the late 1870s, Kansas was viewed by dusky migrant sharecroppers—"Exodusters," in their own parlance—as a prairie Canaan for those oppressed by white supremacist pharaohs of the Deep "Egyptian" South.[34] Several decades later a member of an Arkansas-based group of Black Cherokees seeking emigration to Africa sermonized: "We is de Lord's chillen of Israel of de nineteenth centery; dere ain't no doubt at all about dat. . . . If we can't get to Liberia any oder way, de Lord he'll just open up a parf through the 'Lantic ocean jes' as he did for dem oder chillen through the Red Sea."[35] An analogous situation prevailed during the Great Migration of World War I:

> Thus it was, for example, that the movement was called the "exodus" from its suggestive resemblance to the flight of the Israelites from Egypt, *The Promised Land, Crossing over Jordan* (the Ohio River), and *Beulah Land*. At times demonstrations took on a rather spectacular aspect, as when a party of 147 from Hattiesburg, Mississippi, while crossing the Ohio River, held solemn ceremonies. These migrants knelt down and prayed; the men stopped their watches and, amid tears of joy, sang the familiar songs of deliverance, "I done come out of the Land of Egypt with the good news." The songs following in order were "Beulah Land"

and "Dwelling in Beulah Land." One woman of the party declared that she could detect an actual difference in the atmosphere beyond the Ohio River, explaining that it was much lighter and that she could get her breath more easily.[36]

From Syncretic Judaism to Syncretic Islam

The often contradictory and incomplete information available for the majority of syncretic congregations noted above makes for tortuous, if not impossible, comparisons. Nonetheless, for most Black Hebrews it appears that Ethiopia (broadly or strictly considered), but not Palestine, was considered the original homeland. For Beth B'nai Abraham in particular, the Arabic and Hebrew taught to its members were considered the original languages as well.[37] Most communicants claimed parentage from several or more of the original Twelve Tribes of the House of Israel; some insisted that those tribes were African in origin, and that European Jews originated in intermarriages across the color line. Members of both the Commandment Keepers and the Moorish Zionist Temple claimed to be the descendants of either two or three Jewish tribes driven into Africa as a result of strife among Hebrews.[38] But Moorish Jews also supported the creation of a Palestinian homeland which would be open to all of Jewish descent.[39] One of Beth B'nai Abraham's several legends claimed that Black Jews originated in Carthage (the northernmost strip of present-day Morocco, Libya, Algeria, and Tunisia). Yet another affirmed that the original Hebrews were the ancestors of the Hausa peoples, and "that the ancient path of Jewish migration" was from Ile Ife in southwest Nigeria "eastward to Egypt and thence north to Palestine."[40]

The syncretic practices of Black Hebrews all drew upon Christian and Jewish traditions in differing measures, but Beth B'nai Abraham appears to have been unique in its observance of Ramadan.[41] Views ranged from the avowedly Christian, such as the Church of God and Saints of Christ, to fiercely anti-Christian, such as the Commandment Keepers, though the Commandment Keepers embraced Christ as the Savior, which the Beth B'nai Abraham and Moorish Zionist Temple congregations did not. Among the more Judaic-oriented Black Hebrew groups a pairing of Hebrew and Ethiopian identities appears to have been the rule. Like the later Rastafarians, Beth B'nai Abraham, the Moorish Zionists, and the Commandment Keepers invoked Ethiopian as well as Hebrew lineage, enjoined identities resulting from the physical union of Solomon and Sheba (1 Kings 10; 2 Chron. 9). In combining their Hebrew and Ethiopian loyalties, congregants thus experienced a kind of "double chosen-ness": two divine prophecies dwelling in one.[42]

Whether oriented more towards Judaism or Christianity, a number of Black Hebrew congregations were in accord regarding the need for economic self-sufficiency. As Rabbi Arnold J. Ford put the question, "The Negro must turn his thoughts and energies to his own miserable condition on this earth."[43] Long before the genesis of the Universal Negro Improvement Association (UNIA), the Church of God and Saints of Christ had established a colony at Belleville, Virginia, where a company of several hundred black folk owned and cultivated a thousand acres of land and operated "several small industries, a commissary, school, and homes for orphans and the aged."[44] The Commandment Keepers, too, established "a home for the aged," and operated "several cigar and stationery stores, a laundry, and some other business enterprises in co-operation with white Jewish merchants in Harlem."[45] Rabbi Ford, for his part, formed the short-lived Beth B'nai Abraham Corporation, a joint-stock company devoted to the promotion of industry and commerce relative to West Africa.[46] In this case, especially, one can see the overarching influence of the UNIA, for which Ford once served as choir director.

Black Hebrew identity thus flowed from two apparently independent sources. On the one hand, by virtue of a Hebrew identity gleaned from the Bible, a relatively small band of native-born Black Americans executed selective breaks with the Christianity of their birth while at the same time embracing an eclectic range of Judaic religious practices. On the other could be counted a smaller number of West Indian and African immigrants to the United States, some claiming actual Jewish spiritual heritage, but embracing similarly eclectic religious practices. Together they discovered a passageway that would soon be filled by practitioners of a nominal Islam. The actual historical link between syncretic Judaism and syncretic Islam may yet be found in influences transmitted in one way or another by the Moorish Zionist Temple to its probable namesake, the Moorish Science Temple. But aside from similarity in name, the appeal to Moorish heritage, and the fact that both conducted religious affairs at one time or another in Newark, New Jersey, there is little else at the moment to render the argument conclusive.

Without benefit of latent fingerprints or DNA samples it would seem, nonetheless, that Black Hebrewism contributed at least four essential characteristics to the emerging African-American syncretic Islam of the 1920s and 1930s. First of all, the enjoining of Christian and Judaic elements in Black Hebrewism provided a rough paradigm for the merging of Christianity and Islam in the world views of both the Moorish Science Temple of America and the Nation of Islam. Second, in naming Judaism as the original religion to which people of African descent had purportedly turned their backs, Black Hebrews of more orthodox mien for the first time brought a sense of the "concrete"—if that is the appropriate term—to the African-American incorporation of Hebrew destiny invoked by Deuteronomy 28.[47] Third, Black Hebrews broadened the field of possibilities regarding the territorial origins of African Americans from a historically grounded West and Central Africa to a mythical North Africa and Palestine. And last, while the notion of black economic self-sufficiency hardly originated with Black Hebrews, their particular embrace of the doctrine of economic uplift, in combination with the previously noted characteristics, may certainly have inspired the MSTA and the NOI along similar lines. Apart from these congruencies, however, there remain significant differences between African-American syncretic Judaism and syncretic Islam to be accounted for.

The Crisis of Late Nineteenth-Century Protestantism

Migrations of southern blacks to the upper South, and ultimately to destinations further north, began building slowly in the wake of Reconstruction's collapse. That these population movements prepared the ground for many to accept the truly novel world views and new identities which burst upon the scene in the years spanning World War I and the Great Depression constitutes only one side of a complicated story. But that the content of some of these views was largely rooted in the well-known doctrinal and organizational crises of late nineteenth-century American Protestantism, on the one side, and in influences occasioned by the rise of Asian cultural and political resistance to European colonial intrusions, on the other, may come as something of a surprise. After all, rural black churches of the fire-and-brimstone variety—to which the majority of black Christians of the late nineteenth century overwhelmingly belonged—manifested few signs of having been affected by evolutionist teachings, higher criticism, secularist yearnings, or mysterious influences from the East[48] (although among the Prince Hall Masonic lodges of the South which, along with other fraternal organizations, came to rival the popularity of the Black Church toward the end of the century, expressions of Eastern metaphysics may have found a certain resonance).[49] By the time African Americans had settled in northern cities in large numbers, these scientific and ideological challenges, as well as responses to them from within the white church establishment, had been underway for well over a generation. Yet the delayed impact of this crisis within Protestant Christianity would be felt by African Americans nonetheless, but in ways so unique and so complex as to obscure knowledge of the relations between cause and effect even into our own era.

The significance of the political and cultural influences of robust Asian nationalism and religions on African-American life from the turn of the century onward are also just beginning to be contemplated.[50] While we are becoming more aware of the political effects of Japanese and Indian nationalism on African-American aspirations for social justice and the religious influence of Ahmadi Islam from India's former Punjab region, the impact on Black Americans of other forms of Eastern religious and cultural importations to the United States remains uncharted territory.[51]

The challenges leading to the crisis of American Protestantism in the late nineteenth century were basically of two kinds: to Christianity as a system of thought and to Protestant Christianity as an institution.[52] Within Christian thought a family of dichotomies neatly bisected the universe into the grand realms of the natural and supernatural, where visible matter was counterposed to invisible spirit, the human to the divine, the here to the hereafter, reason to revelation, rational to metaphysical knowledge, and belief in human efficacy to an opposing faith in divine determination. Soon such dualisms would be challenged in everyday experience and on the terrain of science as well. On the experiential side, from 1860 to 1890 widespread urbanization emerged as one of the multifaceted results of rapid American industrial growth. Urban existence posed a fundamental problem for organized religion in that it seemed to render irrelevant the relationship between everyday life, itself characterized by intense human activity leading to material progress, and the realm of the supernatural as taught by the church.[53]

The experiential confrontations with late nineteenth-century Christian orthodoxy were in many ways linked to the doctrinal challenges posed by science. Darwin's theory of evolution, of course, flew squarely in the face of the Creation as recounted in the Book of Genesis. Archbishop James Ussher had argued two hundred years earlier that the earth had come into being in 4004 B.C. Although many continued to accept his "proof-text" calculations as infallible wisdom, the contemporary findings of paleontologists, archeologists, and geologists had effectively relegated such biblical timelines to the dustbin.[54] Finally, the ever mounting "higher criticism" of Christian texts, a trend "which began to arouse popular interest in the 1880s, was akin to Darwinism both in principle and effect. For it represented the application in biblical studies of the same evolutionary principle that Darwinism had applied so convincingly in biology."[55] Resulting pressures led to a greater concern on the part of Christian theologians with making spiritual life more immediate, on the one hand, and coming to some form of accommodation with science, on the other.[56] In response to this spiritual upheaval an abundance of religious doctrines imported from the "mysterious East" began to turn up as well.

Held in conjunction with the 1893 Columbia Exposition in Chicago, the Parliament of Religions was apparently the first ecumenical world religious gathering of its kind.[57] The Parliament's convening attracted Indian, Japanese, and other Asian missionaries to the United States, to a gathering that eventually included Hindus, Sikhs, Babists, Baha'is, Buddhists, Sufis, Jainists, and Ahmadi Muslims as well. An American interest in Buddhism could be traced backed to the Transcendentalists, of course, and the Theosophical Society, founded a generation later, in 1875, had done much to popularize—if not obfuscate—Buddhist and Hindu ideals.[58] But here were actual foreign missions on American soil, spreading word of the superiority of Eastern spiritual teachings. Among the very first was the Vedanta Society, initiated in New York City by Swami Vivekananda in 1894. His goal of propagating knowledge of Hinduism throughout the United States was fortified by the presence, over the next three and a half decades, of sixteen additional Ramakrishna swamis.[59] Five years later the Japan-based Jodo Shinshu mission, which subsequently became a separate organization known as the Buddhist Churches of America, was established in California.[60] But the most far-reaching spiritual event for Black Americans was the arrival in Detroit of the Ahmadi Muslim missionary Mufti Mohammed Sadiq in 1920. As fate would have it, of the Ahmadiyya movement's thousand plus converts over the next five years, many, if not most, would turn out to be of African-American descent.[61]

Identity and Destiny in Syncretic Islam

As with Christianity, one of the principal attractions of Islam for African Americans had to do with its professed racial egalitarianism: all human creatures were equal in the sight of God.[62] In contrast to their life-long encounters with American Christians, however, scores of black folk soon learned from their interaction with Ahmadis that Islam could rightfully claim a better record when it came to relations between practitioners of the same faith. It is hardly surprising, then, that some African Americans would begin to regard Islam as the "opposite" of Christianity. "Go to the East and you will find the fairest people of Syria and Turkestan eating at the same table with darkest Africans and treating each other as brothers and friends," counseled the journal *Moslem Sunrise*.[63] Echoing the African-American nationalist theme of "restoration" on another occasion, the journal extended a special embrace to black Americans in a way that radical organizations like the Socialist Party, in their own language, had proved incapable of doing:

> My Dear American Negro—Assalaam-o-Alaikum. Peace be with you and the mercy of Allah. The Christian profiteers brought you out of your native lands of Africa and in Christianizing you made you forget the religion and language of your forefathers—which were Islam and Arabic. You have experienced Christianity for so many years and it has proved to be no good. It is a failure. Christianity cannot bring real brotherhood to the nations. So, now leave it alone. And join Islam, the real faith of Universal Brotherhood.[64]

Ahmadiyya Islam also promised to fill the void between everyday life and the world of the spirit, a gap that had recently thrown American Protestantism into a state of urgent reflection and reform: "It is Islam alone which teaches its followers that the door of Divine revelation can never be closed," wrote the head of the Ahmadiyya movement in 1923, "and that it is impossible that God, who at one time used to hold converse with men, now has ceased to guide His people and discontinued speaking to them."[65]

Some of the enduring qualities of Moorish Science and Nation of Islam cosmologies were connected with their religious esotericism: the union of God and humanity; the notion that thought transcends both time and space; the supposition that heaven and hell were lived experiences on earth, rather than actual locations to which one's spirit would be dispatched following physical death; the MSTA's belief in metempsychosis; the denial of spiritual existence on the part of the NOI; and the divergence of both regarding traditional Christian and Islamic concepts of Satan (the devil as the "lower self," in the case of the MSTA; and as "the white man," according to the NOI).[66] Finally, in common with the Black Hebrews, an essential distinguishing feature of both organizations was their shared belief that the existential and physical fate of black Americans was inextricably tied to their claiming their pre-slave, "original" identities—a line of reasoning that seemed to harbor Gnostic overtones.[67]

Reincarnation and the notion of upper and lower spiritual selves were the provinces of Hinduism by way of Theosophy. Among mystical Islamic sects such as Isma'ilis and Druzes one could find ample references to numerology, gnosticism, and, within the views of the latter group, the presence of God in human form. The Druze, for example,

> recognized one God, without seeking to discover the nature of his being or his attributes; asserted that he can neither be apprehended by the senses nor defined by discourse; believed that Divinity is revealed to men of different epochs in a human form, but without the weaknesses and imperfections of humanity; that he became visible, finally, in the person of al-Hakim bi-Amr Allah at the beginning of the fifth century of the *hijra;* that this was his final manifestation, after which no other could be anticipated; that al-Hakim had disappeared in the year 411 of the *hijra* in order to test the faith of his followers and to allow reign to the apostasy of hypocrites as well as to those who had embraced the true religion only in anticipation of worldly and immediate gain; and that shortly he would appear, filled with glory and majesty, in order to vanquish his enemies, extend his empire over the entire earth, and bring eternal happiness to the faithful. . . .[68]

Here one may recall some rather intriguing parallels to Nation of Islam dogma surrounding the disappearance of NOI founder W. D. Fard in 1934! But these Eastern elements need not be accounted for, necessarily, by the legendary sojourn of Noble Drew Ali in Egypt or even the professed Meccan origins of Prophet W. D. Fard, for many such ideas could readily be found within the borders of the United States by the first quarter of the twentieth century.[69]

For the MSTA as well as the NOI, both of which appear to have been significantly influenced by Ahmadiyya thought, Muslim identity became a new universal supplanting the former Christian one, enjoining their members to millions of co-religionists worldwide. But for black folk with a penchant towards nationalism the Holy Qur'an contained no reference to any tribe or group that might serve as a suitable *point d'appui* for a sense of African-American peoplehood. If particular identities (in the manner of Hamites, Ethiopians, or Israelites in the Christian tradition) were going to find expression under these circumstances, they would be forced to do so outside existing Islamic conventions. Accordingly, compared to Black Hebrews the proponents of the new Islamic heterodoxies would have even greater recourse to syncretic borrowings, mythopoeic license, and the creation of multiple fictive identities.

Sacred Identity: Relationship to God and the Scriptures

We shall now examine in some detail those plural identities articulated by the NOI and MSTA, and the related subject of prophetic destiny. To compare them these identities have been given the descriptive rubrics of Sacred, Territorial, Civic, and Personal.[70]

Islamic.   As has frequently been noted, the Moorish *Holy Koran* was derived largely from apocryphal, Christian-based scriptures: *The Aquarian Gospel of Jesus the Christ* (1907) and *Infinite Wisdom* (1923).[71] But the fact that the *Aquarian Gospel* was based in part on a similarly inauthentic work by Nicholai Notovich, *The Unknown Life of Jesus Christ* (1894), provided the *Holy Koran* with an unanticipated link to Ahmadiyya Islam as well.[72] However that might be, a number of Prophet Ali's remarks indicate that he was not totally unfamiliar with traditional Islamic precepts: "The cardinal doctrine of Islam is the unity of the Father—ALLAH," he maintained. "We believe in one God, Allah who is all God, All mercy, and All Power. He is perfect and holy, All Wisdom, All Knowledge, and All Truth. . . . This unity of Allah is the first and foremost pillar of Islam and every other belief hangs upon it."[73] On at least one occasion Ali admitted that his version of Islam departed from that of the Prophet Muhammad. In announcing a forthcoming, new edition of the Moorish *Holy Koran* in late 1928, he wrote, intriguingly, that "to Americanize the Oriental idea of Islam involves many changes that are more or less negative to the main purpose of the Islamic Religion. . . ." Without volunteering any hints as to what that "main purpose" might have been, he continued:

> The philosophy of the ancient Prophets is the main initiative in the compilation of the [Moorish] Koran. No thoughts of propaganda enter this work, as has been the case of many former religious works, such as the Bible and other books of creed. . . .
> All of the secrets of the ages known to man are put into this work. The secrets, known only to the Magi, are here revealed: the reading of the stars, the interpretation of marriage relationships, the understanding of the span of life and other[s] such as has been kept from the occidental world are in this book boldly brought out.[74]

No such admission seems to have slipped from the pen of W. D. Fard, who never claimed to be teaching anything other than a traditional form of Islam.[75] Beynon noted that the Qur'an itself "was soon introduced as the most authoritative of all texts for the study of the new faith. The prophet, however, used only the Arabic text which he translated and explained to the believers. Here too they were completely dependent upon his interpretation." But the extent to which Fard's teachings were actually informed by Islamic scripture remains an open question. True, Elijah Muhammad reported that he first received copies of the Ahmadiyya English translation of the Holy Qur'an from Prophet Fard several months before Fard left in 1934. But when apprehended by the Detroit police in late 1932, Fard was reported to have had a "Bible of Islamism" in his possession: "On page 354 of the 'Bible,'" reported the Detroit *Free Press*, "is the following quotation, which was underlined, and which Farad [*sic*] claimed he used as part of his teachings—'God is liar. Ignore Him and do away with those who advocate His cause.' He stated that this was a favorite passage of his and that he used it often in his teachings."[76]

In an apparent melding of organization and religion itself, and with a depiction more appropriate to the Vedas, say, than to Islamic scripture, Fard declared Islam and the Nation of Islam to be timeless:

9. Q: What is the birth record of the said Nation of Islam?
   A: The said Nation of Islam has no birth record. It has no begin
      ning nor ending.
10. Q: What is the birth record of said others than Islam?
    A: Buddhism—35,000 years old
       Christianity—551 years old.[77]

Freemasonry and Islam. A Masonic legacy equating Freemasonry with Islam also contributed to the syncretic character of MSTA and NOI religions. One of the enduring threads of that legacy was constituted by the self-identification of the Bektashi Sufis of Anatolian Turkey with Freemasons.[78] As Zarcone recently observed,

> The resemblance between Freemasonry and the Islamic brotherhoods coalesced around two principal points: in terms of structure, the ceremonial practices—perhaps even pagan ones in the case of the Bektashis—inherited from an ancient cultural source; and, from a socio-religious perspective, the Sufist philosophical tradition in Islam and the hermetic-alchemic and corporative one in Christianity.[79]

Seizing upon these Sufist-Masonic affinities, the American Masonic Order known as the Ancient Arabic Order of the Nobles of the Mystic Shrine elevated them to mythical status. The "Bektasheeyeh's representative at Mecca," one of its manuals claimed, was "the chief officer of the Alee Temple of Nobles, and in 1877 was the Chief of the Order in Arabia."[80] Initiates into the Order of Nobles were greeted with the phrase, "By the existence of Allah and the creed of Mohammed; by the legendary sanctity of our Tabernacle at Mecca."[81] Via the Black Shriners (Ancient Egyptian Arabic Order of the Nobles of the Mystic Shrine), whose autonomous organization, provocatively enough, was founded in Chicago at the time of the 1893 Columbia Exposition, such ideas filtered into the ranks of African-American Freemasons as well.

Freemasonry's role in African-American syncretic Islam seems to have been as a provider of symbols and rituals—in the case of the MSTA, especially—as well as a carrier of metaphysical creeds (e.g., numerology and astrology, and perhaps even gnosticism and alchemy) whereby the mysteries of the universe might be more readily contemplated and manipulated in concert with God's grand designs. Its practitioners became bearers of a secret knowledge available only to the elect. In the solemn struggle between prophetic destiny and human efficacy, Freemasonry and its attendant doctrines weighed in on the side of organizational and individual initiative.

Father Hurley's Universal Hagar's Spiritual Church provided a colorful model for the blending of Christian and Masonic rituals.[82] But if his was a Christian house of worship that appropriated Masonry into its daily life, then Noble Drew Ali's Moorish Science Temple of America might be characterized as a Masonically tinged fraternal organization transformed into an Islamic house of worship. Nor were such combinations particularly unusual: the Royal Order of Ethiopian Hebrews (fraternal arm of the Commandment Keepers), formed in 1936, was also said to have Masonic affinities, and during the Great Depression as well a nationalist-emigrationist group known as the Pacific Movement of the Eastern World incorporated Masonic rituals into its operating structure.[83]

Neither the MSTA nor NOI imported degree structures or their corresponding rituals into their respective organizations, but Prophet Drew Ali's "Noble" title does seem to have been appropriated from the Nobles of the Mystic Shrine. The representation of a Masonic "grip" (graced by the underlying caption, "Unity") graced the pages of the weekly *Moorish Guide* as well as other MSTA publica tions. Gardell has noted a reference to Masonic symbolism in the Moorish *Holy Koran* describing Jesus as "climbing up a twelve step ladder" and carrying "in His hands a compass, square and ax."[84] How many of the Moors considered themselves to be Masons, though, is anyone's guess. Save for Elijah Muhammad, the number of Masons, former or active, who joined the Nation of Islam in its earliest years is also unknown. However, in the late 1940s some 145 of the NOI's 172 male converts to Islam claimed membership in the order.[85] Prophet Fard, too, acknowledged an affinity between Freemasonry and Islam that would be elaborated upon later by his favored lieutenant.[86] Whether he believed black Shriners to be authentically Muslim is not clear from extant documents, but that he considered their white counterparts to be "Moslem sons," there is no doubt:

Q: Why does Mohammed make the devil study from 35 to 50 years before he can call himself a Moslem son and wear the greatest and only flag of the universe? And why must he add a sword to the upper part of the holy and greatest universal flag of Islam?
A: So that he could clean himself up. A Moslem does not love the devil regardless to how long he studies.[87]

All Shriners were Freemasons, but the reverse was not necessarily the case. For the later twentieth century one writer has estimated that three-fourths of all eligible Masons (i.e., of the highest degree) were members of the Shrine.[88]

Divinity and Humanity. The interpenetration of the human and the divine was a feature common to both MSTA and NOI teachings. For Moorish Science, God and humanity were one, but not identical: "Man himself is not the body, nor the soul; he is a spirit and a part of Allah." Conversely, "spirit-man as seed of Allah held deep within himself the attributes of every part of Allah." As in traditional Islam and Christianity, God was a spirit: "Who is ALLAH? ALLAH is the Father of the Universe. Can we see him? No." And God as spirit, according to Moorish Science teachings, constituted one's "upper self." Conversely, the devil, too, as spirit, inhabited one's "lower self."[89] For the Nation, on the other hand, the mutual permeation was complete, if not dualistic: the original people were God, and God was also a specifically designated man. "The Holy Qur'an or Bible is made by the original people who is Allah, the Supreme Being or (Black man) of Asia," proclaimed Master Fard in one of his *Lost Found Lessons.*[90] He decried, on the other hand, false teachings which claimed "that the almighty true and living god is a spook and cannot be seen with the physical eye."[91] The only god was the Son of Man, and the Son of Man was known by the name of none other than Prophet W. D. Fard.[92] In the same way that God was a man, according to Nation of Islam theology, so, too, was Satan "the white man."

There were many sources which W. D. Fard might have been drawn upon to support the concept of God as a human being. The esoteric tradition in Islam endorsed such a notion, but home-grown variations of this theme were also available. An early nineteenth-century Mormon document, for example, posed the question: "What is God? He is a material intelligence, possessing both body and parts. He is in the form of man, and is in fact of the same species. . . ."[93] Father Divine, whose ministry covered the period under discussion, was considered by his followers to be the personification of God, of course.[94] But also let us not overlook the possible influence of the mainstream Christian tradition that held Jesus to be the manifestation of God in the flesh.

Scriptural. For purposes of self-identification, the Moorish Science Temple selected two biblical tribes: the Canaanites (linked to their Hamitic progenitors) and the Moabites (a case of mistaken identity). By way of contrast, Nation of Islam doctrine declined to employ scriptural identities in any direct way. Bypassing Genesis altogether, the NOI introduced its own, unique cosmogony and corresponding sacred identities to African-American religious life.

"The inhabitants of Africa," averred the Moorish *Holy Koran,* "are the descendants of the ancient Canaanites from the land of Canaan" (ancient Palestine, presumably located in West Asia). The eventual founders of the Moroccan empire, the Moabites from the land of Moab, in turn "received permission from the Pharaohs of Egypt to settle and inhabit North-West Africa, and were joined by "their Canaanite, Hittite and Amorite brethren seeking new homes." Hence, claimed the *Koran Questions for Moorish Americans*, "Moroccans" was the modern name for the ancient Moabites.[95]

But how had biblical Moabites, who inhabited what is now the nation-state of Jordan, become modern-day Moroccans occupying the northwest corner of the African continent? Noble Drew Ali's intention, it seems, was to lay claim to the grandeur of the former Moorish empire while at the same time grounding Moorish American identity in biblical antiquity. From the scriptures Prophet Ali extracted a Moabite identity for African Americans, but his real goal, or so it appears, was to appropriate the more recently arrived and decidedly non-biblical Morabites, or Almoravids—an error no doubt attributable to post-vocalic -r deletion in African-American speech patterns (Ebonics be praised!). The term Morabite was derived from the Arabic word *murabti*, meaning "bound," as in a religious order.[96] *Murabti* was the name assumed by North African Muslims who submitted to a purified Islamic doctrine during the period spanning the mid-eleventh to the mid-twelfth centuries. After conquering North Africa, the Murabtin (Almoravids) traversed the Straits of Magellan (Gibraltar?) and gave renewed impetus to the Moorish empire in Spain. Hence Morabites were indeed Moors who inhabited the northwestern shores of Africa and beyond. And were it actually possible for Moorish Americans to trace their ancestry directly to the Moors of Morocco, Morabite—but not Moabite—ancestors likely would be found among them.[97]

Lost Tribe of Shabazz.   Although the Nation of Islam as a rule shunned biblical identities long favored by black Christians, at least one of its own innovations appears to have been biblically inspired. A less-developed aspect of NOI identity, the Lost Tribe of Shabazz—a generic name assigned to African Americans—was a riff on the theme of the "mysterious" disappearance of the Lost Tribes of Israel[98] (the notion of the Lost Found Nation of Islam undoubtedly derives from this theme as well). The term Lost Tribes, of course, refers to ten of the twelve tribes which constituted the Northern Kingdom of Israel in ancient times, and which were carried away by the King of Assyria in 722–721 B.C.E., never to be seen again (2 Kings 17:6).[99] Old Testament prophets kept alive the hope that the Lost Tribes would one day be reunited with their brethren: "I will take the people of Israel from among the nations," proclaimed Ezekiel, "and gather them on every side, and bring them into their own land" (Ezek. 37:21).[100] The meaning of the "Lost Tribe of Shabazz" thus carried with it a sense of African Americans as a "lost people" who, prophetically, would eventually be reunited with their own kind on their own soil.

The name Shabazz was pure NOI invention, however, and one is tempted to see in its pronunciation a corruption of the Arabic word *al-Hijaz*, the Kingdom of Hijaz, wherein are located the holy cities of Mecca and Medina. The Hijaz came into prominence in the years 1916–1924, when it secured and successfully defended its independence from Ottoman rule. In 1932 it became a province of the newly formed Kingdom of Saudi Arabia. Since Master Fard considered the Asiatic black man to have been carried away from his original home in Mecca—not unlike the fate of the Lost Tribes of Israel—it is conceivable that he also may have viewed African Americans as belonging to a mythical "Lost Tribe of Hijaz," with Hijaz subsequently transformed into an unrecognizable signifier.

Original People. The "Lost Tribe" nomenclature was also tied to the NOI's notion of blacks as the "Original People" of the planet, thereby calling into question traditional Muslim and Christian teachings regarding the origins of humanity. At issue were three imponderables: who was the first human being; when and where did the first humans originate; and what was the genetic relationship between peoples with widely varying physical characteristics? For the Bible, in any case, Adam was the original man, created in the Garden of Eden some 4,000 years before the birth of Christ, following Archbishop Ussher's timeline. The Qur'an (49:13) and the Bible (Acts 17:26) had declared all of humanity to be descended from a single genetic pair. Finally, the biblical conundrum denoting Ham, Shem, and Japhet, the sons of Noah and his wife, as the forebears of Africans, Asians, and Europeans respectively was simply a truth that had to be accepted on faith.

Not everyone was prepared to do that. The discovery of the New World by Christopher Columbus raised questions in Europe as to whether or not the people he found there were descended from the biblical Adam. Following a series of related debates, in the mid-seventeenth century the French writer Isaac de La Peyrère advanced the thesis that there existed, in biblical times,

> other men beside the family of Adam, which then consisted of only three persons; and that these other men, or this other race, must have been previously created. They were, he thought, the ancestors of the Gentiles, while Adam was the ancestor of the Jewish race, with whose creation and history the Bible is mainly occupied.[101]

The concept of *Prae-adamitae*, as one of La Peyrère's works was entitled, was soon to take a racial turn in the justification of New World slavery. Long before Darwinist influences allowed racists to contemplate black people as the "missing biological link" between humans and beasts, the Pre-Adamite construct would serve a similar purpose.[102]

The more general question of Pre-Adamism was revived two centuries later when the excavations of ethnologists and paleontologists brought an indirect challenge to Ussher's chronology. If Adam had been created some 6,000 years earlier, how might one explain the discovery of human remains whose age could be calculated at tens of thousands, if not hundreds of thousands, of years? In the defense of biblical integrity it could be conceded there were, indeed, documented human beings who preceded Adam, and that these were none other than angels or devils present in the scriptures who had assumed corporal form. Others, however, were prepared in the name of science to jettison what they deemed to be insupportable, biblical conjecture. "There are . . . very learned ethnologists," complained James Gall in *Primeval Man Unveiled* (1871), "who assert that the existing varieties of the human race can only be accounted for by the creation of several Adams—a white Adam and a black Adam, a red Adam and a yellow Adam, as the case may be; each deriving his existence from his Maker independently of the others."[103]

In his *Pre-Adamite Man* (1863), the spiritualist Paschal Beverly Randolph, a self-identified African American until late adulthood, opined that Adam "was the Hebraic, and, possibly, the Caucasian protoplast," but that he was not "the originator of either the Negro, Egyptian, Assyrian, Chinese or American Indian races of men."[104]

Alexander Winchell's *Preadamites* (1901) held that blacks were the first peoples on earth, predating the biblical Adam, whom he considered to be white. But while not exactly holding to a strict polygenetic argument, Winchell's results were the same: Adam the white, having been divinely created, was superior to his dark human predecessors.[105] Arguing outside the Pre-Adamic framework in his *Origin and Evolution of the Human Race* (1921), the prolific writer of Masonic tracts, Albert Churchward, went against the grain of perceived wisdom by arguing that "man originated in Africa." But the triumph was short-lived. Considering Africans to be on a lower scale of evolution, Churchward argued that the "True Negroes" of West Africa, who remained in a state of arrested development, "never left Africa except as Slaves."[106]

Here lay the immediate background to W. D. Fard's ruminations concerning the biological origins of whites and blacks. Master Fard may have learned of "Rousseau's belief in the superior virtues of Original Man" from Van Loon's *Story of Mankind* (1921), a work which he reportedly recommended to his followers.[107] In any event, claiming that blacks were indeed God's Original People, Fard postulated that whites were grafted into existence by Yakub, an evil black scientist, around 6,000 years ago.[108] The theme of black people as originators of civilization had an African-American pedigree dating back to the 1830s.[109] Ironically, however, in combining the notions of black people as the "original people" and as "originators of civilization," Prophet Fard also separated "civilized blacks" from the continent of Africa.

Territorial Identity: Primordial Homeland

African. The Hamitic and Ethiopian scriptural identities of African Americans were also African identities, to be sure. But at the turn of the century, even for Black Christians who viewed the continent in a positive light, Africa's glory tended to repose in the ancient past, not the present. Moorish

Science Temple and Nation of Islam communicants alike considered themselves to be Muslims and Asiatics, above all, but MSTA members also freely acknowledged their African heritage: "We, as a pure and clean nation descended from the inhabitants of Africa," averred the Moorish *Holy Koran*, "do not desire to amalgamate or marry into the families of the pale skin nations of Europe."[110] The NOI was not so generous. As one of Master Fard's *Lost Found Moslem Lessons* formulated the issue:

> Q: Why does the devil call our people Africans?
>
> A: Answer: To make the people of North America believe that the people on that continent are the only people they have and are all savage. . . . The original people live on this continent and they are the ones who strayed away from civilization and are living a jungle life. The original people call this continent Asia, but the devils call it Africa to try to divide them. He wants us to think that we all are different.[111]

Although whites were charged with being the source of a taxonomic distinction between civilized and uncivilized Asiatics, the more important schism was the one lodged between African Americans and Africans by W. D. Fard's Asiatic schema itself, a division compounded by an apparent ignorance of, and consequent antipathy toward, the African continent both past and present.[112] But Fard's aversion to contemporary Africa, one should not forget, was shared by his Black Christian peers.

Asiatic. One of the hallmarks of both Moorish Science and Nation of Islam world views was the claim that people of African descent were of Asiatic stock.[113] The notion originated with the MSTA, and was given fullest expression in its *Holy Koran*. Asiatic identity was universal in the sense that it appeared to incorporate the overwhelming majority of humankind. Moreover, the consequent subordination or eradication of African identity, secular as well as scriptural, relieved both organizations of having to concern themselves with the fulfillment of prophetic destiny relative to the continent of Africa.

According to Prophet Drew Ali, the key of civilization was in the hands of the Asiatic nations, comprised of a motley assemblage of Moors, Egyptians, Arabians, Japanese, Chinese, Hindus, Moorish Americans, Mexicans, Brazilians, Argentineans, Chileans, Colombians, and San Salvadorans, not to mention Turks.[114] All were descended from the Moabites, "the founders and true possessors of the present Moroccan Empire" whose dominion—prior to "the great earthquake, which caused the Atlantic Ocean"—extended from Africa to North, Central, and South America, as well as the Atlantis Islands.[115]

An acquaintance with the Atlantis legend, as it turned out, was indispensable to comprehending Ali's curious collection of Asiatic peoples. One of the late nineteenth-century popularizers of this and a great many other imaginative accounts was Madame Blavatsky, who affirmed that the "perfect identity of the rites, ceremonies, traditions, and even the names of the deities, among the Mexicans and ancient Babylonians and Egyptians, are a sufficient proof of South America being peopled by a colony which mysteriously found its way across the Atlantic."[116] However, for a "handful of thoughtful and solitary students," the mystery was resolved. The cataclysm that separated the continents and doomed Atlantis to the bottom of the sea also scattered a once-unified culture to many different sectors of the globe.

Noble Drew Ali, for his part, was able to contribute an Asiatic gloss to one of the more ingenious models of imaginary cultural diffusion of his time. Documents from the NOI's earliest years seem to indicate that Prophet W. D. Fard made no attempt to deduce an Asiatic identity for African Americans using biblical sources, as had Noble Drew Ali, but simply affirmed that Asia was the original and true name of the African continent.[117]

In the absence of documentation, one can only speculate as to how Black American identification with Asia was ultimately transformed into a relative handful of black folk claiming identification as Asiatics. Although by the first quarter of the twentieth century a number of African Americans continued either to extract a sense of dignity and pride from the glories of ancient Ethiopia and Egypt or to seek Africa's redemption through missionary activity, others had begun to look to contemporary Asia for salvation. Several factors account for the shift. Most important, by the turn of the century Asian reactions to European colonial expansion had taken a dramatic turn on the political as well as cultural plane.[118] Politically speaking, the Japanese naval defeat of the Russians in 1905–1906 had a tremendous impact not only on Asians but African Americans.[119] As John Edward Bruce noted in 1913, "Around the Japanese question the hopes and aspirations of the darker races of the world are centered. Whatever its solution is to be no man living can now tell. But there is a strong conviction that the disillusionment of the 'superior' race is an event scheduled to take place on this earth in the next few years."[120] Japan's rapid economic development proved attractive to African American would-be entrepreneurs. "Speaking for the masses of my own race in this country," wrote Booker T. Washington the previous year,

> I think I am safe in saying that there is no other race living outside of America whose fortunes the Negro people of this country have followed with greater interest or admiration. The wonderful progress of the Japanese people and their sudden rise to the position of one of the great nations of the world has nowhere been studied with greater interest or enthusiasm than by the Negroes of America.[121]

With the success of the Turkish revolution in 1908, Western colonialism in Asia was now menaced by an independent and modernizing Turkish nation on the western border and a Japanese nation of similar description in the Far East. (On the other hand, despite Ethiopia's military victory over

Italy at Aduwa in 1896, and the determined but ultimately ill-fated rebellion of the Rif people of Morocco led by Abd El-Krim against Spanish colonizers in 1920,[122] neither event seems to have registered with African Americans now looking to Asia for deliverance.) Japan's rise to global prominence especially had unleashed a spate of books in the West—for example, Bertram Lenox Simpson, *The Conflict of Colour: The Threatened Upheaval Throughout the World* (1910); Lothrop Stoddard, *The Rising Tide of Color Against White World-Supremacy* (1920); Maurice Muret, *The Twilight of the White Races* (1926); and Upton Close, *The Revolt of Asia: The End of the White Man's World Dominance* (1927)—analyzing (and in some cases lamenting) what appeared to be the imminent fall of global white supremacy. The alarms were premature, to say the least, but the underlying realities were not entirely clear in the 1920s and 1930s.

Religious Offerings from the East. Meanwhile, African Americans—especially those residing in northern urban centers—began to be apprised of the existence of spiritual offerings from Southeast Asia. Small but determined bands of proselytizers representing a select number of Eastern religions— Islam included—had begun entering the United States in the 1890s. The transmission of Orientalist notions from West to East had convinced many Asians that their ideals stood in some sort of diametrical opposition to those of the Western world, but with a reversal of the valuations traditionally assigned the two hemispheres by Westerners.[123] In the face of the growing industrial and military might of Europe and the United States, East Indians and Japanese especially were prepared to claim the superiority of Eastern spirituality over the materialist preoccupation of the West, not to mention the parity of Japan's developing military-industrial machine. All these events were connected to the rise of cultural and political pan-Asianism in India, China, and Japan at the turn of the century. Counterbalancing the imposed racial categories of the West, pan-Asianism frequently couched itself in terms of racial solidarity, pointing the way to a unified resistance to Euro-American colonialism. Nicolaevsky noted that the Japanese

> tried to combine their pan-Asiatic ideals with efforts towards a new social order. All of them had in common an aversion for the "capitalistic," "plutocratic," "imperialistic" political and social order of Western Europe and America. Even greater was their hostility toward the socialist ideals of the Western world. European culture itself was repugnant to them and aroused their deep antipathy. They aimed at eliminating the domination and hegemony of the "white race" not only in the economic field but also in that of ideas. The desperate tirades of the pan-Asiatics on the subject of the "white danger" were directed against the economic and political order and against the whole culture of the European-American world.[124]

Such formulations were made to order for African Americans conditioned by a society where obsession with race permeated every aspect of daily life.

They also tended to reinforce the notion of the inherent superiority of an Eastern Islam over a Western Christianity.

Secular and Sacred Histories: The Asiatic Connection.   Contrasting sharply with the highly negative depiction of Africa and African peoples in Western texts, Euro-American historiography and ethnography at times accorded an immense respect to Asia and its peoples. This was true even in the handful of works which conceded that the origins of humanity were to be found in Africa. Among a number of "world histories" published during the late nineteenth and early twentieth centuries was Van Loon's *Story of Mankind,* a work which, as noted earlier, was reportedly recommended by W. D. Fard. Van Loon viewed the history of civilization as an ongoing conflict between "Asia, the ancient teacher, and Europe, the young and eager pupil," a struggle which continued into the twentieth century. Preparing to discuss the historical contributions of ancient Egypt, he affirmed that the Nile Valley "had developed a high stage of civilization thousands of years before the people of the west had dreamed of the possibilities of a fork or a wheel or a house. And we shall therefore leave our great-great grandfathers in their caves," Van Loon sighed, "while we visit the southern and eastern shores of the Mediterranean." The southern shore, it turned out, defined the northern rim of the African continent. Excluded from "universal history," Africa was accorded no mention until his discussion of the European colonial era.[125]

Many biblical scholars continued to support the notion that Asia had given birth to civilization some 6,000 years earlier. Bolstering scriptural claims as well, readers in ancient history were not unmindful of the distinction between Asiatic and African blacks made by Herodotus in the mid-fifth century B.C. Higgins's *Anacalypsis* (1836), too, had posited the existence of an ancient, "great black nation" in Asia.[126] With such a preponderance of secular and scriptural evidence, the African American embrace of an Asiatic self-reference would not be far behind.

Morocco and Mecca.   For Moorish scientists the ancestral home was Morocco, located in the northwest quadrant of the African continent: "Why are we Moorish-Americans? Because we are descendants of Moroccans and born in America," explained the *Koran Questions for Moorish Americans*[127] (a variant of this theme specified Africa's southwest shore as well, but without mentioning any country by name).[128] For the NOI, however, the original homeland was Mecca: "The root of civilization is in Arabia at the Holy City Mecca, which means where wisdom and knowledge of the original man first started when the planet was found," Master Fard proclaimed.[129] In general, the NOI world view completely disassociated itself from Africa, whereas that of the MSTA favored the northern section of the continent. The MSTA does not seem to have spoken of any physical return to Morocco, but at least one early NOI document affirmed that "the Lost Found Nation of Islam will not return to their original Land [presumably Mecca] unless they first have a thorough Knowledge of their own."[130] Unlike the Garvey movement, the NOI under Fard's leadership revealed no plans for emigration anywhere. The Back to Africa theme nonetheless remained a subtext of the NOI's outlook until it blossomed publicly in the late 1950s—still without conviction and in response to the theme of "integrationism" then prevalent among many, if not most African Americans.[131]

Civic Identity: Relationship to the State

The nationalisms of both the MSTA and NOI were also reflected in their national flags. The idea of a national flag itself was probably sparked by the UNIA, whose red, black, and green banner foretold the political independence of the African continent. The Moorish flag, for its part, was based on the Moroccan national emblem, while the NOI's "national," or universal flag of Islam, was derived from that of the Turks. (The Moors also used the Turkish star and crescent as a product symbol on its commercially vended soaps, oils, and elixirs.) The stance of each group regarding American civic identity flowed in opposing directions, however.

Vigorously linked to American citizenship, Moorish-American national identity had to be openly declared in order to be acknowledged by government: "All men now must proclaim their free national name to be recognized by the government in which they live and the nations of the earth . . . ," declared Act 6 of the Moorish *Divine Constitution*. The *Constitution*, moreover, placed considerable emphasis on obedience to law:

> ACT 4. All members must preserve these Holy and Divine laws, and all members must obey the laws of the government, because by being a Moorish American, you are a part and partial of the government, and must live the life accordingly.

> ACT 5. This organization of the Moorish Science Temple of America is not to cause any confusion or to overthrow the laws and constitution of the said government but to obey hereby.

Prophet W. D. Fard, on the other hand, repudiated the existence of any ties between his followers and American governmental institutions. As "citizens of the Holy City of Mecca . . . their only allegiance was to the Moslem flag."[132] This stance led to considerable persecution of NOI members by the Justice Department during World War II.

Identity and Naming Patterns

Both organizations held that blacks had to reclaim their individual as well as group names. For the individual renaming practices that constituted such a return, Moors attached the suffix El (pronounced Eel) or Bey to their

American names (e.g. Henry Louis Bey), whereas in the early years of the NOI the "slave" surnames of recent converts were replaced with a transitional X (e.g. Cornell X) until Prophet W. D. Fard was able to assign them their "righteous" Muslim names (e.g., Mohammed Shah). Following Prophet Fard's departure in 1934, and in anticipation of his return, the X's assigned to proselytes—or multiple X's to avoid duplication—became their permanent last names by default.[133]

The emphasis on name conversions for members of either organization could have had its inspiration in any number of sources. Although Rabbi Arnold J. Ford referred derogatorily to the African-American Christian name as the "name in slavery,"[134] name changes among Black Hebrews seem to have occurred mostly among the leadership, and even then rather inconsistently. Conversions to Ahmadiyya Islam, on the other hand, appear always to have been accompanied by name changes: Loucille Frazier became Fatima; Lee Hutchinson bore the new name Muhammad Ali; Carolina Bush took the name Hameeda; and Moses Johnson assumed the mantle of Moosa, to cite a few examples.[135] Yet another model of rebirth through renaming could be found beneath the wing of Father Divine's Peace Mission, where George Baker, Jr., became Father Divine, Leila Slaughter was known as Buncha Sweetness, Viola Wilson went by the appellation of Faithful Mary, and other devotees assumed sobriquets like Equality Smart, Wisdom Smiling, Sincere Satisfying, and Victory Dove.[136]

Prophetic Destiny and Human Intervention

Islam and Christianity alike posit the existence of an omniscient and omnipotent God, raising complications in the way of attempts to explain not only the existence of evil in the universe but also the role that human beings might be permitted to exercise in determining their own destiny on earth. Marcus Garvey had dealt with both issues by concluding that God's purview ended with the creation of life on earth, and that, for better or for worse, the course of human affairs was fully in the hands of human beings. However, in Psalms 68:31 Garveyism did recognize at least one exception to God's isolation from human affairs in the matter of Ethiopia's destiny.

The theological views of the Moorish Science Temple and the Nation of Islam, however, were more complex in at least one respect. While both groups naturally viewed the apocalypse as preordained, they reacted to the approaching end of time not only by preparing for the gloriously inevitable, but by directing their efforts towards the material improvement of the conditions of the race—or at least the conditions of their respective followers—in the here and now. Such interventions could not simply proceed on their own initiative, of course, but were given sanction via God's raising of a prophet who would not only redeem the fallen, but also lead them to a higher stage of material existence before the final sounding of the trumpets. From the perspectives of both organizations, these mundane concerns acquired even greater propriety because one's heaven and one's hell were judged to be on this earth.

The reason for the fall from grace of the original Asiatics was ascribed to different causes by Moorish Scientists and Lost-Founds. Invoking an explanation that could be traced back to Deuteronomy 28 and the Israelite connection, the Moorish *Holy Koran* held that the descent occurred because black people had renounced their true God for the "Gods of Europe":

16. Through sin and disobedience every nation has suffered slavery, due to the fact that they honored not the creed and principles of their forefathers.

17. That is why the nationality of the Moors was taken away from them in 1774 and the word negro, black and colored, was given to the Asiatics of America who were of Moorish descent, because they honored not the principles of their mother and father, and strayed after the Gods of Europe of whom they knew nothing.[137]

Prophet W. D. Fard's theodicy offered quite another explanation as to why the original or Asiatic black man fell into a state of domination that began with slavery. Demonstrating that the march of science did not always lead to positive social ends, Fard exposed the machinations of one Dr. Yakub, a black scientist gone astray. After grafting white people—otherwise known as "devils"—from the biological stock of the Original People some six thousand years ago, Yakub, in his wisdom, then taught them how to rule blacks through the use of "tricknollogy."[138] But the question remained as to why God allowed such a fate to befall the original Asiatics:

Q: Then why did God make a devil?
A: To show forth his power, that he is all wise and righteous, that he could make a devil which is weak and wicked and give the devil power to rule the earth for six thousand years and then destroy the devil in one day without falling a victim to the devil's civilization; otherwise to show and prove that Allah is the God; always has been and always will be.[139]

Tricknollogy, compounded by gullibility (and possibly cupidity) on the part of Asiatic black laborers, was the reason why a trader (presumably slave trader) was able to carry them away from their original homeland:

25. Can the devil fool a Moslem?
26. Not nowadays.
27. Do you mean to say that the devil fooled them three hundred and seventy-nine years ago?
28. Yes, the trader made an interpretation that they would receive gold for their labor; more than they were earning in their own country.
29. Did they receive gold?
30. No! The trader disappeared and there was no one that could speak their language.

31. Then what happened?

32. Well, they wanted to go back to their own country, but they could not swim 9,000 miles.[140]

Whether the loss of the original Asiatics was due to their straying away from God, or to God's inexplicable capriciousness, the goal of both Moors and Lost-Founds was to recover their original identity and religion, improve their material well-being, and prepare for the millennium. To that end God had raised a prophet to guide the lost sheep to the promised land. Within Moorish Science theology, however, the very notion of prophethood introduced a fatal flaw. In a chapter appropriated from the *Aquarian Gospel*, the Moorish *Holy Koran* heralded the fact that believers required no intermediary between themselves and God: "When man sees Allah as one with him, as Father Allah he needs no middle man, no priest to intercede."[141] Yet in another section presumably written by Prophet Ali himself, the Moorish holy book declared the need for such an interceder: "The last Prophet in these days is Noble Drew Ali, who was prepared divinely in due time by Allah to redeem men from their sinful ways; and to warn them of the great wrath which is sure to come upon the earth."[142]

Master Fard based his claim to prophethood largely on a New Testament foundation. In the Gospels Jesus is often quoted as using the curious term, Son of Man (also present in earlier scriptures), in a self-referential way. But by referring to himself in the third person, certain passages, especially in the apocalyptic context of Matthew, have often been interpreted as Jesus foretelling a Messiah who would come after him. Certainly this is the way in which W. D. Fard construed such verses: "The only god is the Son of Man . . . ," claimed the NOI founder, and "no relief came to us until the Son of Man came to our aid, by the name of our prophet, W. D. Fard."[143]

Until the post-World War II era, at least, the notion of economic self-sufficiency was most fully developed by the MSTA. According to Noble Drew Ali, spiritual fulfillment could not be forthcoming without economic security:

In connection with our religious aims and beliefs, we must promote economic security. . . . No other one thing is more needed among us at this time than greater economic power. Better positions for our men and women, more business employment for our boys and girls[,] and bigger incomes will follow our economic security. We shall be secure in nothing until we have economic power. A beggar people cannot develop the highest in them, nor can they attain to a genuine enjoyment of the spiritualities of life.

Our men, women and children should be taught to believe in the capacity of our group to succeed in business, in spite of the trials of some of them. . . . Except in cases of actual dishonesty, discourtesy, lack of service and actual unreliability, our business enterprises in every field of endeavor should have the fullest of confidence, cooperation and patronage whenever and wherever they can be given.[144]

The MSTA developed its own product line of lubricants and nostrums, including a Moorish Body Builder and Blood Purifier, Moorish Mineral and Healing Oil, and Moorish Antiseptic Bath Compound. This last product claimed to be "beneficial for dandruff, rheumatism, stiff joints, tired and sore feet [and] also skin troubles, when used as a face wash."[145]

Despite his reputation as a purveyor of silks and other exotic items in Detroit's "Paradise Valley," W. D. Fard seems to have shunned entrepreneurialism as an organizational aim. However, he remained quite vigorous in fostering the notion of individual self-reliance. "Would you sit up at home and wait for a mystery god to bring you food?" inquired one of the *Lost Found Moslem Lessons*. "Emphatically no," was the response.[146] Rather, the key to one's deliverance lay in harnessing divine mathematics to material goals:

> After learning Mathematics, which is Islam, and Islam is Mathematics, [it] stands true, you can always prove it at no limit of time. Then you must learn to use it and secure some benefit while you are living—that is, luxury, money, good home, friendship, in all walks of life. Sit yourself in Heaven at once! That is the greatest desire of your Brother and Teachers. Now you must speak the Language, so you can use your mathematical Theology in the proper term, otherwise you will not be successful, unless you do speak well. . . .[147]

Along with economic security, both organizations promoted the idea of individual duties and responsibilities. Declared the Moorish *Constitution*:

> Husband, you must support your wife and children; wife you must obey your husband and take care of your children and look after the duties of your household. Sons and daughters must obey father and mother and be industrious and become a part of the uplifting of fallen humanity. All Moorish Americans must keep their hearts and minds pure with love, and their bodies clean with water.[148]

While men underwent military training in the Nation, women had to learn "how to keep house, how to rear their children, how to take care of their husbands, sew, cook and in general, how to act at home and abroad."[149] Whites had taught blacks "to eat the wrong food," and as a result they had become "poison animal eaters." The flesh of all such beasts—"hogs, ducks, geese, 'possums and catfish"—was to be religiously avoided, but that of the noble barnyard chicken was permitted.[150] Although outside the time frame of this essay, it is worth noting that in 1939 the MSTA established an old folks home in Prince George County, Virginia, near Petersburg, some 40 miles from the colony established much earlier by the Church of God. The group also held land in the Berkshires of western Massachusetts; Long Island, New York; and Woodstock, Connecticut. In 1945 the NOI established its own farm on some 140 acres of land in southwest Michigan.[151]

Last Days and Times

And I saw an angel come down from heaven, having the key of the bottomless pit and a great chain in his hand. And he laid hold on the dragon, that old serpent, which is the Devil, and Satan, and bound him a thousand years, And cast him into the bottomless pit, and shut him up, and set a seal upon him, that he should deceive the nations no more, till the thousand years should be fulfilled: and after that he must be loosed a little season. (Rev. 20:1–3)

Entitled "The End of Time and the Fulfilling of Prophecies," chapter 48 of the Moorish *Holy Koran* does not refer directly to the Book of Revelation, but the connection is clear. "In these modern days," declared the Moorish *Holy Koran*,

there came a forerunner, who was divinely prepared by the great God-Allah and his name is Marcus Garvey, who did teach and warn the nations of the earth to prepare to meet the coming Prophet; who was to bring the true and divine Creed of Islam, and his name is Noble Drew Ali: who was prepared and sent to this earth by Allah, to teach the old time religion and the everlasting gospel to the sons of men. That every nation shall and must worship under their own vine and fig tree, and return to their own and be one with their Father God-Allah.[152]

The year 1914, designated by the Nation of Islam as the time when the white man's rule was judged to be up, seems to have been directly appropriated from the Jehovah's Witnesses.[153] Witnesses referred to the "Time of the End,"

a period of one hundred and fifteen years, from A.D. 1799 to A.D. 1914, [which] is particularly marked in the Scriptures . . . discoveries, inventions, etc., pave the way to the coming millennium of favor, making ready the mechanical devices which will economize labor, and provide the world in general with time and conveniences . . . the increase of knowledge among the masses [will give] to all a taste of liberty and luxury, before Christ's rule is established . . . class-power . . . will result in the uprising of the masses and the overthrow of corporative trusts, etc., with which will fall also all the present dominions of earth, civil, and ecclesiastical. . . . All the discoveries, inventions and advantages which make our day the superior of every other day are but so many elements working together in this day of preparation for the incoming millennial age, when true and healthful reform, and actual progress in every direction, will be the order, to all and for all.[154]

But whereas the pre-millennial apocalypse foreseen by the witnesses was synonymous with late nineteenth-century class warfare, the post-millennial, twentieth-century version divulged by the NOI assumed a decidedly racial form.[155]

Finally, a brief closing remark. The African-American path to Islamization has been as ambiguous as it has been paradoxical, lending weight to

Wilson's observation that without the appearance of "heresies" during what might be viewed (but only after the fact) as a transitional stage from Christianity to Sunni Islam, the journey most likely would not have reached its fulfillment.[156] The passage from Christianity to Islam was obviously not a one-step process, but appears to have wended its way in the late nineteenth century from the Hebrew identity of the Old Testament to the subsequent embrace of a syncretic Judaism; then, under the influence of a heterodox Ahmadiyya Islam, as well as other diverse attractions, from syncretic Judaism to an equally syncretic Islam; and finally, by the 1970s, from Islamic syncretism to the Sunni tradition. This provisional (and, in this summary form, oversimplified) paradigm, like so many others before it, may yet bend or break beneath the weight of further, revealed evidence. But if, in the meantime, it serves to elucidate in whatever way the early development of a significant and growing branch of African-American religious life, or to stimulate further research in that vein, then it will have more than served its purpose.

Notes

Author's Note: I wish to offer my profound thanks, first of all, to the staff of the Interlibrary Loan Office at the University of Massachusetts at Amherst, as well as to Rowland Abiodun, Akbar Muhammad Ahmed, Muhammad al-Ahari, John H. Bracey, Jr., Prince A. Cuba, John Higginson, Akbar Muhammad, Robert W. Paynter, Vernis Wellmon, and Robert Paul Wolff, who directed me toward materials critical to the present study. Finally, Robert Chrisman and William Eric Perkins offered critical appraisals for which I am truly grateful.

1. *Message to the Blackman in America* (Chicago: Muhammad's Temple No. 2, 1965), pp. 53, 134.

2. See, for example, C. Eric Lincoln, "The American Muslim Mission in the Context of American Social History " in *The Muslim Community in North America*, ed. Earle H. Waugh, Baha Abu-Laban, and Regula B. Qureshi (Edmonton: University of Alberta Press, 1983), pp. 215–33; Lawrence H. Mamiya, "Minister Louis Farrakhan and the Final Call: Schism in the Muslim Movement" in ibid., pp. 234–55; Zafar Ishaq Ansari, "W. D. Muhammad: The Making of a 'Black Muslim' Leader (1933–1961)," *American Journal of Islamic Social Sciences* 2,2 (1985): 245–62. The Islam of the MSTA and NOI clearly have to be distinguished from the teachings of the Prophet Muhammad, but I am not altogether comfortable with existing nomenclature. For the moment I shall be more or less content to employ the term "syncretic" to denote the African-American forms in question. On the other hand, since syncretism essentially entails a selection of ideological elements across established religious demarcations, one wonders, really, how this process differs in function from the selections and borrowings which tend to demarcate denominations, sects, and cults from one another within established religions.

3. This chapter assumes a basic acquaintance with Moorish Science and Nation of Islam views. For studies of the NOI and its eschatology, see E. U. Essien-

Udom, *Black Nationalism: A Search for an Identity in America* (Chicago: University of Chicago Press, 1962); C. Eric Lincoln, *The Black Muslims in America*, 2nd ed. (Boston: Beacon Press, 1973); Martha F. Lee, *The Nation of Islam: An American Millenarian Movement* (Syracuse: Syracuse University Press, 1996); Mattias Gardell, *In the Name of Elijah Muhammad: Louis Farrakhan and the Nation of Islam* (Durham: Duke University Press, 1996); Claude A. Clegg, III, *An Original Man: The Life and Times of Elijah Muhammad* (New York: St. Martin's Press, 1997). For similar inquiries concerning the MSTA, see Arthur Huff Fauset, *Black Gods of the Metropolis: Negro Religious Cults in the Urban North* (Philadelphia: University of Pennsylvania Press, 1944), pp. 41–51; Arna Bontemps and Jack Conroy, *Anyplace But Here* (New York: Hill and Wang, 1966), pp. 205–8; Yvonne Yazbeck Haddad and Jane Idleman Smith, *Mission to America: Five Islamic Sectarian Communities in North America* (Gainesville: University Press of Florida, 1993), pp. 79–104; Peter Lamborn Wilson, *Sacred Drift: Essays on the Margins of Islam* (San Francisco: City Lights Books, 1993), pp. 13–50.

4. Early on, Howard Brotz signaled the existence of parallels between Islamic and Hebrew groups after World War I, but later scholarship devoted to studies of the MSTA and NOI totally ignored his sightings. Like most researchers at the time, Brotz assumed that Judaic and Islamic syncretisms emerged just after the Great Migration of World War I. Recent studies of Black Hebrew congregations, however, show that these expressions developed long before the rekindling of interest of Islam among African Americans in the 1920s. See Howard M. Brotz, *The Black Jews of Harlem: Negro Nationalism and the Dilemmas of Negro Leadership* (New York: Schocken, 1970), p. 9; Merrill Singer, "The Southern Origin of Black Judaism" in *African Americans in the South: Issues of Race, Class, and Gender*, ed. Hans A. Baer and Yvonne Jones (Athens: University of Georgia Press, 1992), pp. 123–38.

5. For a discussion of these identities within a wider American context, see Theophus H. Smith, *Conjuring Culture: Biblical Formations of Black America* (New York: Oxford University Press, 1994); Werner Sollors, *Beyond Ethnicity: Consent and Descent in American Culture* (New York: Oxford University Press, 1986).

6. Cited in Sidney Kaplan, "Blacks in Massachusetts and the Shays Rebellion," *Contributions in Black Studies* 8 (1986–87): 9.

7. Albert J. Raboteau, *A Fire in the Bones: Reflections on African-American Religious History* (Boston: Beacon Press, 1995), p. 41.

8. For a trenchant critique of black suffering and black theology, see William R. Jones, *Is God a White Racist? A Preamble to Black Theology* (Garden City, NY: Doubleday, 1973).

9. See, for example, Martin R. Delany, *The Origin of Races and Color* (1879; rpt. Baltimore: Black Classic Press, 1991), pp. 19, 37–38, 41–42. Denys Hay, *Europe: The Emergence of an Idea* (1957; rpt. New York: Harper & Row, 1966), p. 9, notes that the first adaptation of the Table of Nations in Genesis to Hellenistic geography was made by the Jewish scholar Josephus around 93 C.E.

10. See St. Clair Drake, *Black Folk Here and There*, 2 vols. (Los Angeles: Center for Afro-American Studies and the University of California, Los Angeles, 1990), 2:1–30; Thomas Virgil Peterson, *Ham and Japhet: The Mythic World of Whites in the Antebellum South* (Metuchen, NJ: Scarecrow Press, 1978).

11. See Wilmore, *Black Religion and Black Radicalism*, pp. 120–22; George Wilson Brent, "The Ancient Glory of the Hamitic Race," *A.M.E. Church Review* 12 (October 1895): 272–75; Rufus L. Perry, *The Cushite, or The Children of Ham (The Negro Race), as Seen by the Ancient Historians and Poets* (Brooklyn: Literary Union, 1887). Self-affirmed Hamitic identity among African Americans as reflected in George Wells Parker's Hamitic League of the World, for example, continued into the early twentieth century. See *Crusader* (December 1918): 3; Adelaide Cromwell Hill and Martin Kilson, comps. and eds., *Apropos of Africa: Sentiments of Negro American Leaders on Africa from the 1800s to the 1950s* (London: Cass, 1969), pp. 172–73.

12. W. Winwood Reade, *Savage Africa* (New York: Harper, 1864), p. 31.

13. See Lawrence W. Levine, *Black Culture and Black Consciousness: Afro-American Folk Thought from Slavery to Freedom* (Oxford and New York: Oxford University Press, 1977), p. 85. Cain's mark, however, was not a curse but rather a sign that he was under the protection of God. On the other hand, African Americans also sometimes associated whiteness with the curse of Miriam, whom God smote with leprosy after she and Aaron spoke out against the marriage of their brother Moses to an Ethiopian woman: "Behold, Miriam became leprous, white as snow" (Num. 12:10). The association of whiteness with leprosy has remained popular in some strains of Black Hebrew thought. For example, Prophet F. S. Cherry of Philadelphia's Church of the Living God taught that "the first white man was Gehazi, who received his white color as the result of a curse which was placed upon him for sin (2 Kings 5:27)." Fauset, *Black Gods of the Metropolis*, p. 34. See also Clarke Jenkins, *The Black Hebrews of the Seed of Abraham—Isaac and Jacob of the Tribe of Judah-Benjamin and Levi after 430 Years in America* (Detroit, 1969).

14. George Shepperson, "Ethiopianism Past and Present," in *Christianity in Tropical Africa*, ed. C. G. Baëta (London: Oxford University Press, 1968), pp. 249–50.

15. John H. Bracey, Jr., and August Meier, "Black Ideologies, Black Utopias: Afrocentricity in Historical Perspective," *Contributions in Black Studies* 12 (1993–94): 111–16, have recently compared the late nineteenth-century fascination with ancient Ethiopia (and Egypt) on the part of a handful of African American intellectuals to the current fascination of their twentieth-century counterparts with ancient Egypt.

16. Raboteau, *A Fire in the Bones*, pp. 37–56, citation p. 56. The earliest known reference to this verse by a black churchman was by Richard Allen in 1793. See Randall K. Burkett, *Garveyism as a Religious Movement: The Institutionalization of a Black Civil Religion* (Metuchen, NJ: Scarecrow Press and American Theological Library Association, 1978), p. 34. For a discussion of African-American missionary interest in Africa, see St. Clair Drake, *The Redemption of Africa and Black Religion* (Chicago: Third World Press, 1970); St. Clair Drake, "Negro Americans and the African Interest" in *The American Negro Reference Book*, ed. John P. Davis (Englewood Cliffs, NJ: Prentice-Hall, 1966), pp. 632–35; Sylvia M. Jacobs, ed., *Black Americans and the Missionary Movement in Africa* (Westport, CN: Greenwood Press, 1982); Walter L. Williams, *Black Americans and the Evangelization of Africa* (Madison: University of Wisconsin Press, 1982); J. Mutero Chirenje, *Ethiopianism and Afro-Americans in Southern Africa, 1883–1916* (Baton Rouge: Louisiana State University Press, 1987).

17. Embracing the first message while rejecting the second, for example, the Garvey movement nonetheless viewed Christianity in the 1920s as a vehicle of racial uplift no less fervently than did Black Christian missionaries. But the UNIA's "Universal Negro Catechism" also interpreted Psalms 68:31 in a more secular vein: "That Negroes will set up their own government in Africa, with rulers of their own race." In terms of projected destiny, Marcus Garvey's Ethiopianism, as it turned out, bore a close resemblance to Theodor Herzl's Zionism (see Burkett, *Garveyism as a Religious Movement*, p. 34).

18. See Raboteau, *Fire in the Bones*, pp. 17–36; see also Albert J. Raboteau, *Slave Religion: The "Invisible Institution" in the Antebellum South* (New York: Oxford University Press, 1978), pp. 311–12.

19. Based on an analysis of newspaper clippings conducted some sixty years after the aborted insurrection, Thomas Wentworth Higginson reported that, during the planning of the insurrection, "a man named Martin, Gabriel's brother, proposed religious services, caused the company to be duly seated, and began an impassioned exposition of Scripture, bearing upon the perilous theme [of insurrection]. The Israelites were glowingly portrayed as a type of successful resistance to tyranny; and it was argued, that now as then, God would stretch forth His arm to save, and would strengthen a hundred to overthrow a thousand." Thomas Wentworth Higginson, *Black Rebellion* (1889; rpt. New York: Arno Press, 1969), p. 77. In enlisting combatants, however, Gabriel was also said to have been desirous of including "partially the *Outlandish* [native-born African] people, because they were supposed to deal with witches and wizards, and of course useful in armies to tell when any calamity was about to befall them." H. W. Flournoy, ed., *Calendar of Virginia State Papers and Other Manuscripts from January 1, 1799, to December 31, 1807; Preserved in the Capitol, at Richmond*, 11 vols. (Richmond, VA, 1890), 9:153.

20. Like Gabriel, Vesey relied on magical practices to guide his followers. Higginson, *Black Rebellion*, pp. 112, 114, 119–20.

21. Regarding the ambivalent feelings of African American towards Jews, see James Baldwin, *The Price of the Ticket: Collected Nonfiction, 1948–1985* (New York: St. Martin's/Marek, 1985), pp. 7–8.

22. A detailed exploration of the class bases underlying these biblical identifications cannot be dealt with here. Raboteau notes, however, that the theme of Exodus dominant during slavery gave way to that of Ethiopianism thereafter. Nineteenth-century Ethiopianism, however, whether in the form of a Christian redemption of Africa or a veneration of ancient Egypt and Ethiopia, was largely the province of churchmen and other members of the black educated elite. From Reconstruction through World War I the concern with migrationist or emigrationist movements seems to have once again thrust the theme of Exodus and Hebrew identification to the forefront at the grassroots level. Nonetheless, during World War I and after, Ethiopianism also assumed popular expression in the mass-based UNIA, above all, as well as in sects such as the Star Order of Ethiopia and Ethiopian Missionaries to Abyssinia (the Abyssinian Movement). An intense mass identification with modern Ethiopia, reflected in organizations such as the Ethiopian World Federation, followed the Italian invasion of that country in 1935. See Raboteau, *Fire in the Bones*, p. 41; Burkett, *Garveyism as a Religious Movement*, p. 34; Joseph E. Harris, *African-American Reactions to War in Ethiopia, 1936–1941* (Baton Rouge: Louisiana State Univer-

sity Press, 1994), pp. 127–41; Chicago Commission on Race Relations, *The Negro in Chicago: A Study of Race Relations and a Race Riot in 1919* (1922; rpt. New York: Arno Press and the New York Times, 1968), pp. 59–64; Bernard Makhosezwe Magubane, *The Ties That Bind: African-American Consciousness of Africa* (Trenton, NJ: Africa World Press, 1987), pp. 159–78.

23. For general background on the Black Hebrew tradition, see Hans A. Baer and Merrill Singer, *African-American Religion in the Twentieth Century: Varieties of Protest and Accommodation* (Knoxville: University of Tennessee Press, 1992), pp. 115–17; Graenum Berger, *Black Jews in America: A Documentary with Commentary* (New York: Commission on Synagogue Relations, Federation of Jewish Philanthropies of New York, 1978); Deanne Shapiro, "Factors in the Development of Black Judaism," in *The Black Experience in Religion*, ed. C. Eric Lincoln (Garden City, NY: Anchor Press/Doubleday, 1974), pp. 254–72; Albert Ehrman, "Black Judaism in New York," *Journal of Ecumenical Studies* 8 (Winter, 1971): 103–14; Elias Fanayeye Jones, "Black Hebrews: The Quest for Authentic Identity," *Journal of Religious Thought* 44 (Winter–Spring 1988): 35–49. Two Black Hebrew sects, the International Reassemble of the Church of Freedom League (New Orleans and Chicago) and the House of Israel (Newark), were among a number of African American organizations whose leadership was charged with sedition or draft evasion during World War II.

24. Singer, "The Southern Origin of Black Judaism," pp. 128–29; Fauset, *Black Gods of the Metropolis*, pp. 31–40; Joseph R. Washington, Jr., *Black Sects and Cults* (1972; rpt. Lanham, MD: University Press of America, 1984), pp. 133–35.

25. See Elmer T. Clark, *The Small Sects in America*, rev. ed. (New York: Abingdon, 1949), 151–53; Washington, *Black Sects and Cults*, pp. 132–33; J. Gordon Melton, ed., *The Encyclopedia of American Religions*, 3 vols. (1989; rpt. Tarrytown, NY: Triumph Books, 1991), item 1286; Baer and Singer, *African-American Religion*, pp. 114–15; Raymond J. Jones, "A Comparative Study of Religious Cult Behavior Among Negroes with Special Reference to Emotional Group Conditioning Factors," *Howard University Studies in the Social Sciences* 2, no. 2 (1939). The Bureau of the Census, *Religious Bodies: 1936* (Washington, D.C.: U.S. Government Printing Office, 1941), 1:900–1, reported 1,823, 3,311, 6,741, and 37,084 members for the Church of God and Saints of Christ in 1906, 1916, 1926, and 1936 respectively.

26. Around 1909 a dismissed South African Wesleyan Methodist preacher named John Msikinya visited the United States and returned to South Africa as a bishop of the Church of God. Another South African by the name of Enoch Mgijima joined the movement and, when Halley's Comet appeared the following year, announced that it was a sign that "Jehovah was angry, and that unless men turned to their ancient religion there would be a disaster." The New Testament, he warned, "was a fiction of the white man's and they must worship on the model of the Israelite patriarchs who in their day had been liberated from the yoke of oppressive rulers." After Msikinya died, the South African branch split, with half the parishioners following Mgijima until in 1918 he was "discommunicated" from the Church of God parent organization for allegedly claiming to have received visions indicating that South African whites should be crushed by blacks. Three years later his group of "Israelites," facing an ultimatum after failing to disperse following the observance of their Passover, charged at police and soldiers with swords and spears; 163 Israel-

ites were killed, 125 wounded. Monica Hunter, *Reaction to Conquest: Effects of Contact With Europeans on the Pondo of South Africa*, 2nd ed. (London: Oxford University Press, 1961), pp. 563–65; George Shepperson, "Nyasaland and the Millennium" in *Millennial Dreams in Action: Studies in Revolutionary Religious Movements*, ed. Sylvia L. Thrupp (New York: Schocken, 1970), p. 152; Edward Roux, *Time Longer Than Rope: A History of the Black Man's Struggle for Freedom in South Africa*, 2nd ed. (Madison: University of Wisconsin Press, 1964), pp. 135–39.

27. Jacob S. Raisin, *Gentile Reactions to Jewish Ideals, with Special Reference to Proselytes* (New York: Philosophical Library, 1953), p. 792; Arthur Dobrin, "A History of the Negro Jews in America," unpublished ms. [1965?], p. 40 [Schomburg Center for Research in Black Culture]; Berger, *Black Jews in America*, pp. 70–71. It was reported in 1928 that Rabbi Modeki [Mordecai Herman?], "a member of the tribe of Juda [*sic*] and connected with the Moorish Zionist faith would establish a synagogue in Baltimore." Monroe Work, ed., *Negro Year Book, 1931–1932* (Tuskegee, AL: Negro Year Book Publishing, 1932), p. 258. A banner prominently displayed in photos taken of the Harlem congregation by James Van Der Zee in 1929 bore the name "Moorish Zionst [*sic*] Temple of the Moorish Jews," with an address at 127 W. 137th Street. See Liliane De Cock and Reginald McGhee, eds., *James Van Der Zee* (Dobbs Ferry, NY: Morgan & Morgan, 1973), pp. 62–63. For an additional Van Der Zee photograph apparently taken at the same session, see Godbey, *Lost Tribes a Myth*, unpaginated photo insert.

28. Baer and Singer, *African-American Religion*, p. 115; Ira De A. Reid, "Let Us Prey!" *Opportunity* September 1926: 277; Ruth Landes, "Negro Jews in Harlem," *Jewish Journal of Sociology* 9 (December 1967): 178–79. Landes notes that (like Prophet Cherry) Robinson's religious work also began in the South.

29. Brotz, *Black Jews of Harlem*; Howard Brotz, "Negro 'Jews' in the United States," *Phylon* 13 (December 1952): 324–37; Howard Waitzkin, "Black Judaism in New York," *Harvard Journal of Negro Affairs* 1, no. 3 (1967): 12–44: Carl Helm, "Negro Sect in Harlem Mixes Jewish and Christian Religions," *New York Sun* (29 January 1929): 6; "4,000 Black Jews Hail Advent of Year 5698," *Baltimore Afro-American*, 11 September 1937: 8. For the years 1919–31, Brotz identified eight Black Hebrew congregations in the New York City region, only a handful of which enjoyed a significant following.

30. Sydney S. Kobre, "Rabbi Ford," *Reflex* 4 (January 1929): 25–29; Landes, "Negro Jews in Harlem," pp. 175–89; K. J. King, "Some Notes on Arnold J. Ford and New World Black Attitudes to Ethiopia," *Journal of Ethiopian Studies* 10 (January 1972): 81–87; William R. Scott, "Rabbi Arnold Ford's Back-to-Ethiopia Movement: A Study of Black Emigration, 1930–1935," *Pan-African Journal* 8 (Summer 1975): 191–202; William R. Scott, *The Sons of Sheba's Race: African-Americans and the Italo-Ethiopian War, 1935–1941* (Bloomington: Indiana University Press, 1993), pp. 181–84; Helm, "Negro Sect in Harlem," p. 6. For short biographies of Rabbi Ford, see Robert A. Hill, ed., *The Marcus Garvey and Universal Negro Improvement Association Papers* (Berkeley: University of California Press, 1983), 2:398 n.1; and J. Gordon Melton, *Biographical Dictionary of American Cult and Sect Leaders* (New York: Garland, 1986), 90–92.

31. Brotz, "Negro Jews," pp.326–27.

32. Allan H. Spear, *Black Chicago: The Making of a Negro Ghetto, 1890–1920*

(Chicago: University of Chicago Press, 1967), p. 193. In 1925 it was reported that a congregation of 300 blacks had planned to erect a synagogue in Chicago; Work, *Negro Year Book, 1931–1932*, p. 258. Baer and Singer, *African-American Religion*, p. 113, mistakenly identify the "Abyssinian Movement" (Star Order of Ethiopia and Ethiopian Missionaries to Abyssinia) as a Black Hebrew sect.

33. Hans A. Baer, *The Black Spiritual Movement: A Religious Response to Racism* (Knoxville: University of Tennessee Press, 1984), pp. 26–29.

34. See Nell Irvin Painter, *Exodusters: Black Migration to Kansas after Reconstruction* (New York: Alfred Knopf, 1977); Robert G. Athearn, *In Search of Canaan: Black Migration to Kansas 1879–80* (Lawrence: Regents Press of Kansas, 1978).

35. Cited in Edwin S. Redkey, *Black Exodus; Black Nationalist and Back-to-Africa Movements, 1890–1910* (New Haven: Yale University Press, 1969), p. 106.

36. Emmett Scott, *Negro Migration during the War* (1920; rpt. New York: Arno Press, 1969), pp. 45–46.

37. Kobre, "Rabbi Ford," p. 28; Reid, "Let Us Prey!" p. 277.

38. "4,000 Black Jews Hail Advent of Year 5698," p. 8; Godbey, "The Lost Tribes a Myth," caption accompanying photo of Moorish Zionist Temple members, unpaginated photo insert.

39. Dobrin, "History of the Negro Jews," p. 40. Although Arnold J. Ford eventually emigrated to Ethiopia, he also supported the Palestine Fund in 1925 (Kobre, "Rabbi Ford," p. 28).

40. Shapiro, "Factors in the Development of Black Judaism," p. 269; Landes, "Negro Jews in Harlem," p. 182. This particular legend is compatible with an "extreme" strand of Yoruba tradition which, according to Biobaku, "regards Ile Ife as the spot where God created man, white and black, and from where mankind dispersed all over the world" (S. O. Biobaku, *The Origin of the Yoruba* [Lagos: University of Lagos, 1971], p. 11. I am indebted to Rowland Abiodun for this citation).

41. Landes, "Negro Jews in Harlem," p. 184. References to Allah also occurred in the songs of Arnold J. Ford's *Universal Ethiopian Hymnal*; see King, "Some Notes on Arnold J. Ford," p. 83.

42. The fusing of Hebrew and Ethiopian identities remains a fundamental characteristic of Rastafarianism, with its ideological roots in Christianity, Garveyism, and perhaps Freemasonry as well; see M. G. Smith, Roy Augier, and Rex Nettleford, *The Rastafari Movement in Kingston, Jamaica* (Mona, Jamaica: Dept. of Extra-Mural Studies, University of the West Indies, Mona, Jamaica, 1978); Ken Post, *Arise Ye Starvelings: The Jamaican Labour Rebellion of 1938 and Its Aftermath* (The Hague: Nijhoff, 1978), pp. 159–201; Leonard E. Barrett, Sr., *The Rastafarians: Sounds of Cultural Dissonance*, rev. ed. (Boston: Beacon Press, 1988).

43. Cited in Kobre, "Rabbi Ford," p. 27.

44. Clark, *Small Sects in America*, p. 151.

45. In 1945 the group announced plans "to establish a co-operative agricultural project on Long Island" for five hundred families, which would include "a temple, a theological school, a recreation center and a convalescent home for returning service men." Following the group's purchase of land, the project ran into immediate racial and religious opposition from white residents, and had

to be scrapped. Clark, *Small Sects in America*, p. 164; Berger, *Black Jews in America*, p. 97.

46. Landes, "Negro Jews in Harlem," pp. 184–85.

47. "But it shall come to pass, if thou wilt not hearken unto the voice of the LORD thy God, to observe to do all his commandments and his statutes which I command thee this day; that all these curses shall come upon thee, and overtake thee...." (Deut. 28:15). George Washington Williams and other articulate black observers of the nineteenth century associated the decline of African civilization with moral degradation, with a "turning away from God." Unlike the Black Hebrews, however, they failed to designate the specific religion from which Africans purportedly turned away. Given a choice, no doubt, they would have preferred to specify Christianity as that religion, but such divergences from the historical record were better left to leaders of grassroots religious sects and cults; see Raboteau, *A Fire in the Bones*, p. 44.

48. See, for example, Benjamin Elijah Mays and Joseph William Nicholson, *The Negro's Church* (New York: Institute of Social and Religious Research, 1933), pp. 58–93.

49. See Howard W. Odum, *Social and Mental Traits of the Negro* (New York: Columbia University, 1910), p. 98.

50. See, for example, Sudarshan Kapur, *Raising Up: The African-American Encounter With Gandhi* (Boston: Beacon, 1992); Reginald Kearney, "Afro-American Views of Japanese, 1900–1945," Ph.D. diss., Kent State University, 1991; revised version forthcoming from SUNY Press; Reginald Kearney, "Japan: Ally in the Struggle Against Racism, 1919–1927," *Contributions in Black Studies* 12 (1993–94): 117–28; Richard Brent Turner, "The Ahmadiyya Mission to Blacks in the United States in the 1920s," *Journal of Religious Thought* 44 (Winter-Spring 1988): 50–66; Richard Brent Turner, *Islam in the African-American Experience* (Bloomington: Indiana University Press, 1997); Ernest Allen, Jr., "When Japan Was 'Champion of the Darker Races': Satokata Takahashi and the Flowering of Black Messianic Nationalism," *The Black Scholar* 24 (Winter 1994): 23–46; Ernest Allen, Jr., "Waiting for Tojo: The Pro-Japan Vigil of Black Missourians, 1932–1943," *Gateway Heritage* 16 (Fall 1995): 38–55.

51. A case in point is the proliferation of pseudo-Eastern prophets, seers, mystics, and corresponding sects in African-American urban communities beginning around World War I. From the 1890s onward, the Vedanta Society's conversions of European immigrants residing in the United States raised additional assistants for the Hindu cause. The English-born Margaret Noble, for example, became Sister Nivedita; Herr Leon Landsberg changed his name to Swami Kripananda; and Mme. Marie Louise received the title of Swami Abhayananda. However, the ability of the non-Hindu-born to rise to a position of Hindu spiritual leadership (a phenomenon unknown in India itself), not to mention a newfound opportunity for the Negro to "pass" as Hindu, provided unanticipated openings: "We must remember," wrote a sympathetic observer of Hinduism in the United States, "that certain Americans, by virtue of their complexion, are naturally equipped to play the role of a popular Hindu teacher. ... The astute Joe Dowling," for example, "of coal-black visage and some small town in Illinois appeared on Keith's vaudeville circuit under the name of 'Joveddah de Raja,' an opulent nomenclature smacking of Roman divinity, French nobility and Hindu

royalty all in one. . . . In 1926 the princely Joveddah, now a profound 'philosopher and psychologist,' began broadcasting words of Oriental comfort and wisdom from radio stations in New York and environs. . . ." De Raja ran a thriving correspondence-course business until his operation was finally shut down by "de police." Wendell Thomas, *Hinduism Invades America* (New York: Beacon, 1930), pp. 79, 81, 218–19.

52. Arthur M. Schlesinger, "A Critical Period in American Religion, 1875–1900," *Proceedings of the Massachusetts Historical Society* 64 (October 1930–June 1932): 524. The challenge to the Protestant church as an institution came in several forms: an increased estrangement from working-class urban dwellers and, even for those parishioners who attended church regularly, an indifference masked by the persistence of religion as social convention. Unlike working-class Catholic immigrants who found the Roman Catholic Church to be "the one familiar landmark in a strange and alien land, many native-born, urban white wage earners continued to profess a belief in Christianity while remaining opposed to Protestant "churchianity." The conspicuous materialism of many urban churches—their imposing stone edifices, lavish interiors, expensive pipe organs, and like accouterments—appeared to the working-class poor to be totally divorced from the spirit of Christian ideals. Moreover, the impersonal character of large urban congregations stood in marked contrast to the intimate quality of their small rural counterparts. Further eroding the Church's ties to labor was the initial public support given industrialists by prominent ministerial leadership during the tumultuous labor strikes of the later 1800s, as well as the church's determination to shut down legitimate businesses devoted to leisure activities on Sunday. See Stephen Gottschalk, *The Emergence of Christian Science in American Religious Life* (Berkeley: University of California Press, 1973), p. 18; Winthrop S. Hudson, *Religion in America* (New York: Scribner's, 1965), p. 295; Aaron Ignatius Abell, *The Urban Impact on American Protestantism, 1865–1900* (Cambridge, MA: Harvard University Press, 1943), p. 64; H. F. Perry, "The Workingman's Alienation from the Church," *American Journal of Sociology* 4 (March 1899): 622.

53. The phenomenon was hardly restricted to the United States; a devitalization of Christian doctrines and symbols had been taking place throughout industrialized Europe as well; see Gottschalk, *Emergence of Christian Science*, p. 3.

54. Carter, *Spiritual Crisis*, p. 33; R. Buick Knox, *James Ussher: Archbishop of Armagh* (Cardiff: University of Wales Press, 1967), p. 105.

55. Gottschalk, *Emergence of Christian Science*, p. 7; for one of the earliest examples of the "higher criticism," see David Friedrich Strauss, *The Life of Jesus, Critically Examined*, trans. from 4th German ed. (1860; rpt. St. Clair Shores, Mich: Scholarly Press, 1970).

56. I have addressed some of the implications of these developments for Nation of Islam ideology in my "Religious Heterodoxy and Nationalist Tradition: The Continuing Evolution of the Nation of Islam," *Black Scholar* 26 (Fall–Winter 1996): 8–11.

57. See Richard Hughes Seager, *The World's Parliament of Religions: The East/West Encounter, Chicago, 1893* (Bloomington: Indiana University Press, 1995); Richard Hughes Seager, ed., *The Dawn of Religious Pluralism: Voices from the World's Parliament of Religions, 1893* (La Salle, IL: Open Court, 1993). One

of many speakers to address the Parliament was Mohammed (Alexander Russell) Webb, formerly thought to have been the first American convert to Islam.

58. See Carl T. Jackson, *The Oriental Religions and American Thought: Nineteenth-Century Explorations* (Westport, CN: Greenwood, 1981); Thomas, *Hinduism Invades America*; Thomas A. Tweed, *The American Encounter with Buddhism, 1844–1912: Victorian Culture and the Limits of Dissent* (Bloomington: Indiana University Press, 1996); Emma McCloy Layman, *Buddhism in America* (Chicago: Nelson-Hall, 1976); Turner, "The Ahmadiyya Mission," pp. 50–66; Stoyan Krstoff Vatralsky, "Mohammedan Gnosticism in America: The Origin, History, Character, and Esoteric Doctrines of the Truth-Knowers," *American Journal of Theology* 6 (January 1902): 57–78; E. Allen Richardson, *East Comes West: Asian Religions and Cultures in North America* (New York: Pilgrim Press, 1985); Bruce F. Campbell, *Ancient Wisdom Revived: A History of the Theosophical Movement* (Berkeley: University of California Press, 1980); Peter Washington, *Madame Blavatsky's Baboon: A History of the Mystics, Mediums, and Misfits Who Brought Spiritualism to America* (New York: Schocken Books, 1995).

59. Only eight representatives were present at any one time, however. Thomas, *Hinduism Invades America*, p. 105; remarking upon the spread of Hinduism to Western countries, Coomaraswamy concluded, "The East has indeed revealed a new world to the West, which will be the inspiration of a 'Renaissance' more profound and far-reaching than that which resulted from the re-discovery of the classic world of the West" (Ananda K. Coomaraswamy, *The Message of the East* [Madras: Ganesh, n.d. (after 1909)], p. 4.

60. Layman, *Buddhism in America*, p. 28.

61. Turner, "The Ahmadiyya Mission," pp. 50–66; A. T. Hoffert, "Moslem Propaganda: The Hand of Islam Stretches Out to Aframerica," *Messenger* 9 (May 1927): 141, 160. See also James Thayer Addison, "The Ahmadiya Movement and Its Western Propaganda," *Harvard Theological Review* 22 (January 1929): 1–32; Yohanan Friedmann, *Prophecy Continuous: Aspects of Ahmadi Religious Thought and Its Medieval Background* (Berkeley: University of California Press, 1989).

62. A specific attraction of Ahmadi Islam to Moorish Science Temple and Nation of Islam leaders would seem to have been its championing of an Islamic prophethood succeeding that of Prophet Muhammad—a heresy in the eyes of traditional Muslims, to be sure, but a unique spiritual opportunity for one properly qualified to mediate between God and humanity.

63. "The Only Solution of Color Prejudice," *Moslem Sunrise* 1 (October 1921): 42. See also Bernard Lewis, *Race and Color in Islam* (New York: Harper & Row, 1971); Drake, *Black Folk Here and There*, 2:77–184.

64. "True Salvation of the American Negroes," *Moslem Sunrise* 2 (April–July 1923): 184.

65. Mirza Bashir-ud-din Mahmud Ahmad, "Sign of a Living Religion," *Moslem Sunrise* 2 (January 1923): 159.

66. A comparative analysis of some of these themes can be found in Abbie Whyte, "Christian Elements in Negro American Muslim Religious Beliefs," *Phylon* 25 (Winter 1964): 382–88.

67. As Valentinus noted, "What liberates us is the knowledge of who we were, what we became; where we were; wherinto we have been thrown; whereto we speed, wherefrom we are redeemed; what birth is, and what rebirth. Such knowl-

edge is not only the instrument of salvation but also the form in which the goal of salvation—perfection is realized. But self-knowledge in this case is not to be understood as a self-reflecting upon the quality of one's individual strengths and weaknesses, nor a fulfillment of the task, as suggested by Gramsci, of compiling a trace-inventory of the historical processes that have shaped one's being. Rather, the maxim, 'Know thyself,' is to be viewed strictly as an unfolding process of spiritual revelation." Hans Jonas, *The Gnostic Religion: The Message of the Alien God and the Beginnings of Christianity*, 2nd ed. (Boston: Beacon Press, 1963), pp. 35, 45; Antonio Gramsci, *Il materialismo storico e la filosofia di Benedetto Croce* (Turin: Giulio Einaudi, 1944), p. 4.

68. Antoine-Isaac Silvestre de Sacy, *Exposé de la religion des Druzes*, 2 vols. (Paris: L'Imprimerie royale, 1838), 1:i–ii [my trans.]. See also Robert Brenton Betts, *The Druze* (New Haven: Yale University Press, 1988); Farhad Daftary, *The Ismailis: Their History and Doctrines* (Cambridge: Cambridge University Press, 1990); Julian Baldick, *Mystical Islam: An Introduction to Sufism* (New York: New York University Press, 1989).

69. A particular combination of esoteric features within the NOI world view led Morroe Berger ("The Black Muslims," *Horizon* 6 [Winter 1964]: 61) to surmise that W. D. Fard might be of Druze or Ismai'li origin. But Prophet Fard's equivocal atheism would seem to preclude such an argument. In any case, all such features could be found in religious views imported to the United States by others. Although perhaps more appropriate to a discussion of the Farrakhan years, a case in point is the Babi religion, a Persian descendant of Shi'ism and immediate predecessor of the Baha'i faith. Babism, which doted on the mythical wonders of the number 19, found expression in a Wisconsin/Illinois-based group known as the Truth-Knowers at the turn of the century. See Vatralsky, "Mohammedan Gnosticism in America," pp. 57–78; Arthur de Gobineau, *Les religions et les philosophies dans l'Asie centrale*, 2 vols. (1865; rpt. Paris: G. Crès, 1923), 2:57–58; Abbas Amanat, *Resurrection and Renewal: The Making of the Babi Movement in Iran, 1844–1850* (Ithaca: Cornell University Press, 1989). See also Yvonne Yazbeck Haddad and Jane Idleman Smith, *Mission to America: Five Islamic Sectarian Communities in North America* (Gainesville: University Press of Florida, 1993), pp. 137–72, for a discussion of more recent purveyors of the number 19, the United Submitters International.

70. The absence here of a specific discussion of gender identity does not constitute an oversight. Unlike the 1950s and later (with respect to the NOI in particular), documents from the years 1920–30 to which I have had access reveal almost nothing in the way of discussions relative to the subject of gender. In general, however, it can be said that the NOI was much more a rigidly patriarchal organization than was the MSTA. For an additional brief remark on this subject, see my "Religious Heterodoxy and Nationalist Tradition," p. 8.

71. See G. H. Bousquet, "Moslem Religious Influences in the United States," *Moslem World* 25 (January 1935): 40–44; Frank T. Simpson, "The Moorish Science Temple and Its 'Koran'," *Moslem World* 37 (January 1947): 56–61; Edwin E. Calverley, "Negro Muslims in Hartford," *Moslem World* 55 (October 1965): 340–45. Both *The Aquarian Gospel of Jesus the Christ* (1907; rpt. Marina Del Rey, CA: DeVorss & Co., 1991) and *Infinite Wisdom* (Chicago: deLaurence, 1923; distributed by the Rosicrucian Order under the title *Unto Thee I Grant* [1925; rpt. San Jose, CA: Supreme Grand Lodge of AMORC, 1968]) bear unsubstanti-

ated claims of having been discovered in Tibetan monasteries. For a critique of the *Aquarian Gospel*, see Edgar J. Goodspeed, *Famous "Biblical" Hoaxes* (Grand Rapids, MI: Baker Book House, 1956), pp. 15–19.

72. Also purportedly based on materials found in a Tibetan monestary, Notovich's work postulated that the eighteen undocumented years in the life of Jesus were spent in India, a theme given further embellishment in the *Aquarian Gospel*. Ahmadis, on the other hand, claimed that Jesus, while sojourning in India, subsequently died and was buried in a tomb in Srinagar, Kashmir. See Peter Lamborn Wilson, "Shoot-Out at the Circle Seven Koran: Noble Drew Ali and the Moorish Science Temple," *Gnosis* 12 (Summer 1989): 45; Nikolai Notovich, *The Unknown Life of Jesus Christ* (Chicago: V. R. Gandhi, 1894); Ghulam Ahmad, *Jesus in India; Being an Account of Jesus' Escape from Death on the Cross and His Journey to India* (1899; rpt. Rabwah [West Pakistan]: Ahmadiyya Muslim Foreign Missions Dept., 1962?). A photo of Jesus' alleged Kashmir tomb was reproduced in *Moslem Sunrise* 2 (January 1923): 168. For critiques of Notovich, see Max Müller, "The Alleged Sojourn of Christ in India," *Nineteenth Century* 36 (October 1894): 515–22; J. Archibald Douglas, "The Chief Lama of Himis on the Alleged 'Unknown Life of Christ,'" *Nineteenth Century* 39 (April 1896): 667–78.

73. Noble Drew Ali, "What Is Islam?" in *Moorish Literature*, (n. p., n.d.), 10.

74. "Masterpiece of Religious Literature; Secrets of Other Creeds Revealed," *Moorish Guide* (December 15, 1928). The first edition of the Moorish *Holy Koran* was published in 1927, and it is unclear whether a revised version ever saw the light of day. Ali's idiosyncratic version of the Holy Qur'an was hardly the first. In Morocco in the 740s, for example, Salih ibn Tarif declared himself to be the awaited Mahdi, and introduced his own Qur'an to his followers. Budgett Meakin, *The Moorish Empire: A Historical Epitome* (New York: Macmillan, 1899), p. 46.

75. NOI departures from traditional Islam have been duly noted in Zafar Ishaq Ansari, "Aspects of Black Muslim Theology," *Studia Islamica* 53 (1981): 137–76. While steadfastly asserting the authenticity of his Muslim beliefs, Elijah Muhammad nonetheless seemed ill at ease with a version of Islam cobbled together from disparate sources. For several decades he argued that the Torah had been given to Moses as a guide for Israel, the Holy Qur'an to the Prophet Muhammad for the Arab world, and the Gospels to Jesus as a guide and warning to Christians. Hence, he reasoned, African Americans needed a holy book of their own, one tailored specifically to their needs. The argument came close to denying the universality of Islam. Such a book was never forthcoming, however (Muhammad, *Message to the Black Man*, p. 87).

76. Erdmann Doane Beynon, "The Voodoo Cult among Negro Migrants in Detroit," *American Journal of Sociology* 43 (May 1938): 900; Hatim A. Sahib, "The Nation of Islam," M.A. thesis, University of Chicago, 1951, p. 71; *Detroit Free Press*, November 26, 1932, p. 2.

77. *Student Enrollment*, Q & A 9, 10. Compare to Swami Vivekenanda's discourse on Hinduism in *Dawn of Religious Pluralism*, p. 421.

78. John P. Brown, *The Dervishes; or, Oriental Spiritualism* (Philadelphia: Lippincott, 1868), pp. 59–60; Henry R. Coleman, *Light from the East: Travels and Researches in Bible Lands in Pursuit of More Light in Freemasonry* (Louisville, KY: The author, 1881), p. 264.

79. Thierry Zarcone, *Mystiques, philosophes et francs-maçons en Islam: Riza Tevfik, penseur ottoman (1868–1949)* (Istanbul: Institut français d'études anatoliennes; Paris: J. Maisonneuve, 1993), p. 302 [my trans.].

80. George Livingston Root, *Ancient Arabic Order of the Nobles of the Mystic Shrine for North America*, rev. ed. (San Antonio, TX: 1916), p. 11; Allen, "Religious Heterodoxy and Nationalist Tradition," pp. 6–7.

81. *The Mystic Shrine: An Illustrated Ritual of the Ancient Arabic Order, Nobles of the Mystic Shrine*, rev. ed. (n.d.; rpt. Chicago: Ezra A. Cook, 1975), p. 11.

82. Baer, *The Black Spiritual Movement*, pp. 82–109.

83. Roi Ottley, *New World A-Coming* (1943; rpt. New York: Arno Press, 1968), p. 148; Berger, *Black Jews in America*, p. 102; Allen, "Waiting for Tojo," p. 48. Parallels can also be found among the early Mormons; see John L. Brooke, *The Refiner's Fire: The Making of Mormon Cosmology, 1644–1844* (Cambridge: Cambridge University Press, 1994), passim.

84. The compass and the square seem to have developed separately as Masonic symbols and appeared in their familiar, interlaced form beginning in the mid-eighteenth century. The axe as symbol is not prominent in Freemasonry, however, but does appear in an earlier version of the 22nd (Knight of the Royal Axe) degree in the Scottish Rite. The Masonic ladder has only three steps, representing the values faith, hope, and charity. Although the ladder mentioned in the *Holy Koran* consisted of twelve unnamed steps, it also contained a "trinity of steps, faith, hope, and love." Moorish *Holy Koran*, 5:20, 6:11; Gardell, *In the Name of Elijah Muhammad*, pp. 41–42; Kenneth Mackenzie, *The Royal Masonic Cyclopaedia* (New York, 1877), s.v. "Royal Axe"; Henry Wilson Coil, *Coil's Masonic Encyclopedia* (Richmond, VA: Macoy Publishing and Masonic Supply Co., 1996), s.v. "Ladder."

85. Sahib, "Nation of Islam," pp. 90, 105, 108.

86. See, for example, Elijah Muhammad, *The Secrets of Freemasonry* (Cleveland: Secretarius Publications, 1994); Elijah Muhammad, *The Theology of Time* (Hampton, VA: U.B. & U.S. Communications Systems, 1992), pp. 282–86.

87. *Lost Found Moslem Lesson No. 1*, Q & A 9 (Beynon cites the *Lost Found Moslem Lessons* as *Secret Ritual of the Nation of Islam*, Parts I and II). Fard's sword reference here was to the Shriner symbol: a scimitar placed above the "universal flag of Islam" (in this case, a downward facing star and crescent). The star and crescent were joined as a symbol of both the Ottoman Empire and Islam under the rule of Sultan Selim III in 1793. For a pictorial representation of the Shriner symbol, see Wilson, *Sacred Drift*, p. 27.

88. William J. Whalen, *Christianity and American Freemasonry*, rev. ed. (Huntington, IN: Bruce Publishing, 1987), p. 112.

89. Moorish *Holy Koran*, 1; *Koran Questions for Moorish Americans* (Chicago: 1928), Q & A 2, 3, pp. 65–76; Moorish *Holy Koran*, 3:5–12. The reference to upper and lower selves in the *Aquarian Gospel*, whence this particular section of the Moorish *Koran* was extracted, likely came from Theosophy. Theosophists, in turn, derived the concept from the sevenfold nature of human existence as taught by certain Buddhist doctrines, according to which one's upper, or spiritual being was comprised of three principles, and one's lower, or carnal-sensuous being of four (see Campbell, *Ancient Wisdom Revived*, pp. 66–68).

90. *Lost Found Moslem Lesson No. 2*, Q & A 1.

91. *Lost Found Moslem Lesson No. 2*, Q & A 15.

92. *Lost Found Moslem Lesson No. 2*, Q & A 10, 11. Elijah Muhammad later clarified this dualistic notion by affirming that the black man was God, but that the supreme God was Allah in the person of Master Fard.

93. Rpt. in B. H. Roberts, *The Mormon Doctrine of Deity: The Roberts-Van der Donckt Discussion* (1903; rpt. Bountiful, Ut.: Horizon Publishers, 1976), p. 255.

94. See Jill Watts, *God, Harlem U.S.A.: The Father Divine Story* (Berkeley: University of California Press, 1992).

95. Moorish *Holy Koran*, 47:1, 6; *Koran Questions*, Q & A 31.

96. The Western-language terms *marabout* (Fr.) and *morabit* (Eng.) derive from the original Arabic, as does the Spanish word *morabito*. See John G. Jackson, "The Empire of the Moors," in *Golden Age of the Moor*, ed. Ivan Van Sertima (New Brunswick, NJ: Transaction, 1992), p. 87; Stanley Lane-Poole, *The Story of the Moors in Spain* (1886; rpt. Baltimore: Black Classic Press, 1990), p. 178; Meakin, *The Moorish Empire*, pp. 49–50n.

97. The biblical Moabites inhabited the uplands east of the Dead Sea in present-day Jordan, and not "the North Western and South Western shores of Africa" which Drew Ali claimed for them. Ali also claimed that African Americans were enslaved because "they honored not the creed and principles of their forefathers" and had "strayed after the gods of Europe." The offspring of an incestuous relationship between Lot and one of his daughters (Gen. 19:37), Moab, however, had not turned to another god, but was punished along with his people because he had become too prideful, had magnified himself against the Lord (Isa. 16:6–7, Jer. 48:42). See also Moorish *Holy Koran*, 47:6; Moorish Science Temple of America, *The Divine Constitution and By-Laws*, Act 6.

98. See Allen H. Godbey, *The Lost Tribes A Myth: Suggestions Towards Rewriting Hebrew History* (1930; rpt. New York: KTAV Publishing House, 1974), for an exhaustive treatment of the subject. In his own writings, Elijah Muhammad also sometimes invoked the parable of the lost sheep in Luke 15:4.

99. Interestingly enough, one version of the story held that the Ten Tribes were deported to Africa; see Raisin, *Gentile Reactions to Jewish Ideals*, p. 424.

100. Similar hopes were voiced in Isa. 11:11 and Jer. 31:7.

101. Ebenezer Burgess, *What Is Truth? An Inquiry Concerning the Antiquity and Unity of the Human Race; with an Examination of Recent Scientific Speculations on Those Subjects* (Boston: I. P. Warren, 1871), p. 171. See also Isabella Duncan, *Pre-Adamite Man; or, The Story of our Old Planet and Its Inhabitants Told by Scripture and Science* (London: Saunders, Otley, and Co., 1860), p. ix; Richard H. Popkin, *Isaac La Peyrère (1596–1676): His Life, Work and Influence* (Leiden: E. J. Brill, 1987).

102. For an illuminating study of the differences between European and North American views of Pre-Adamites, see Giuliano Gliozzi, *Adamo e il nuovo mondo; la nascita dell'antropologia come ideologia coloniale: dalle genealogie bibliche alle teorie razziali (1500–1700)* (Florence: La nuova Italia, 1977), pp. 514–621.

103. James Gall, *Primeval Man Unveiled: or, the Anthropology of the Bible* (London: Hamilton, Adams, & Co., 1871), p. 195.

104. Griffin Lee [Paschal Beverly Randolph], *Pre-Adamite Man: The Story of the Human Race, from 35,000 to 100,000 Years Ago* (New York: Sinclair

Tousey, 1863), p. 61. See also John Patrick Deveney, *Paschal Beverly Randolph: A Nineteenth-Century Black American Spiritualist, Rosicrucian, and Sex Magician* (Albany, NY: State University of New York Press, 1997).

105. Alexander Winchell, *Preadamites: or a Demonstration of the Existence of Men Before Adam*, 5th ed. (Chicago: Scott, Foresman, 1901).

106. Albert Churchward, *Origin and Evolution of the Human Race* (London: G. Allen & Unwin, 1921), pp. 3–7. See also Albert Churchward, *The Origin and Evolution of Freemasonry Connected with the Origin and Evolution of the Human Race* (London: G. Allen & Unwin, 1920), p. 87.

107. Hendrik Willem van Loon, *The Story of Mankind* (1921; rpt. New York: Liveright, 1984), p. 382; Beynon, "The Voodoo Cult," p. 900. Since original man (*l'homme originel, l'homme sauvage, l'homme naturel*), according to Rousseau, "desired only the things that he knew, and knew only those things in his possession or easy to acquire, there was nothing more peaceful than his soul or more circumscribed than his spirit" (Jean-Jacques Rousseau, *Du Contrat social: ou, Principes du droit politique* [Paris: Garnier Frères, n.d.], p. 113) [my trans.] Special thanks to Robert Paul Wolff for assistance in locating this passage.

108. *Lost Found Moslem Lesson No. 2*, Q & A 21–28. Rooted in Prophet Fard's original concept, Elijah Muhammad later elaborated a cosmogony that essentially served as replacement for the Book of Genesis. See Elijah Muhammad, "Know Thyself," *Pittsburgh Courier Magazine*, November 24, 1956, p. 2; rpt. in *Message to the Blackman*, pp. 31–32. For a more recent view in the same vein, see Prince A. Cuba, *Before Adam: The Original Man*, revised ed. (Hampton, VA: United Brothers Communications Systems, 1992).

109. See, for example, Hosea Easton, *A Treatise on the Intellectual Character, and Civil and Political Condition of the Colored People of the U. States . . .* (Boston: I. Knapp, 1837); Robert Benjamin Lewis, Light and Truth: Collected from the Bible and Ancient and Modern History . . . (Boston: A Committee of Colored Gentlemen, 1844); Joseph Elias Hayne, *The Negro in Sacred History: or, Ham and His Immediate Descendants* (Charleston, SC: Walker, Evans & Cogswell Co., 1887); Rufus Perry, *The Cushite, or the Descendants of Ham* (Springfield, MA: Willey, 1893); Joseph E. Hayne, *The Black Man; or, The Natural History of the Hametic Race* (Spartanburg, SC: W. Du Pre, printer, 1893); James Morris Webb, *The Black Man, the Father of Civilization* (Seattle: Acme Press, 1910); George Wells Parker, *Children of the Sun* (1918; rpt. Baltimore: Black Classic Press, 1978); as well as the infinitely more scholarly Drusilla Dunjee Houston, *Wonderful Ethiopians of the Ancient Empire* (1926; rpt. Baltimore, MD: Black Classic Press, 1985). For an overview of the literature, see August Meier, "The Emergence of Negro Nationalism: A Study in Ideologies" in *Along the Color Line, Explorations in the Black Experience*, ed. August Meier and Elliott Rudwick (Urbana: University of Illinois Press, 1976), esp. pp. 198–207.

110. Moorish *Holy Koran*, 48:6; see also *Koran Questions*, Q & A 31–33.

111. Lost Found Moslem Lesson No. 1, Q & A 7.

112. Beynon, "The Voodoo Cult," p. 900, has indicated that Breasted's *Conquest of Civilization* was one of the books recommended by the Prophet to his followers. If so, it is not difficult to imagine where Fard may have derived some of his unenlightened views. That which a handful of other Western writers of the period were prepared to grant to peoples of Asian descent (as well as deny to those of African heritage), Breasted claimed for Europe alone. Civilization,

according to the noted Egyptologist, was the province of the Great White Race, sired in a triangular region known as the Great Northwest Quadrant. This "vast triangle" included "all Europe, southwestern Asia and northern Africa," and had been, "until recently the scene of the highest development of life on our planet." Although Mongoloids now inhabited the quadrant, they did not arrive there "until long after civilization was already highly developed." Isolated from the Great White race by an impassable Sahara Desert, on the other hand, "and at the same time unfitted by ages of tropical life for any effective intrusion among the White Race, the negro and negroid peoples remained without any influence on the development of early civilization." William Breasted, *The Conquest of Civilization* (New York: Harper, 1926), pp. 112–13.

113. Fascinating in this regard are certain origin—myths of the Yoruba, who variously consider themselves to have emanated from Egypt or Arabia. One version even claimed that "the Yoruba sprang from Lamurudu, . . . one of the kings of Mecca" (Biobaku, *The Origin of the Yoruba*, p. 11). Again, I am indebted to Rowland Abiodun for this citation.

114. Moorish *Holy Koran*, 45:2–7. Noble Drew Ali no doubt would have appreciated the following remarks of Dr. Tsunekichi Komaki of Kyoto Imperial University, delivered in a series of radio broadcasts during World War II: "America originally belonged to Asia and the Indians in America belong to the Asiatic race. Europe, which is a peninsula of Asia, embraces the Mediterranean Sea . . . India, Burma . . . belong to Asia, as well as Australia. . . . The people of 'Japanese race' advanced along the shore of Alaska and North America as far as the coast line of Peru. . . . Traces we find in the Andes districts in Peru give clear evidence of a cultural connection with sun worship which is characteristic of Japan. . . . Africa is also a part of Asia. In ancient Greece, it was considered a part of the Asiatic continent. . . . In northern Europe there is Asiatic blood running thick in the veins of the inhabitants. In southern Europe, in France, we find many ancient tools formerly used by the people of Asia" (cited in Saul K. Padover, "Japanese Race Propaganda," *Public Opinion Quarterly* 7 [Summer 1943]: 194–95).

115. Moorish *Holy Koran*, 47:6–7.

116. H. P. Blavatsky, *Isis Unveiled: A Master-Key to the Mysteries of Ancient and Modern Science and Theology*, 2 vols. (1877; rpt. Pasadena, CA: Theosophical University Press, 1988), 1:557–58. The role of Atlantis as a non-Jewish substitute for the "chosen people" myth is fascinatingly recounted by Pierre Vidal-Naquet, "Atlantis and the Nations" in *Questions of Evidence: Proof, Practice, and Persuasion Across the Disciplines*, ed. James Chandler, Arnold I. Davidson, and Harry Harootunian (Chicago: University of Chicago Press, 1994), pp. 325–57. I am beholden to Robert W. Paynter for this citation.

117. *Lost Found Moslem Lesson No. 1*, Q & A 7.

118. François Godement, *The New Asian Renaissance: From Colonialism to the Post-Cold War* (London: Routledge, 1997), pp. 1–61.

119. Kearney, "Afro-American Views of Japanese, 1900–1945." For studies of pro-Japan movements among African Americans during the Great Depression, see Allen, "When Japan Was Champion of the Darker Races," pp. 23–46; and Allen, "Waiting for Tojo," pp. 38–55.

120. "Blessings in Disguise" in *The Selected Writings of John Edward Bruce: Militant Black Journalist*, comp. and ed. Peter Gilbert (New York: Arno Press and The New York Times, 1971), 104–5.

121. Booker T. Washington to Naoichi Masaoka, December 5, 1912, in *The Booker T. Washington Papers*, ed. Louis R. Harlan and Raymond W. Smock, 14 vols. (Urbana, IL: University of Illinois Press, 1982), 12:84. Ironically, Washington's biographer notes that "Japanese who had read *Up from Slavery* in translation saw in Tuskegee methods one of the means of overcoming their nation's technological lag behind the West" (Louis R. Harlan, *Booker T. Washington: The Wizard of Tuskegee, 1901–1915* [New York: Oxford University Press, 1983], p. 277).

122. David S. Woolman, *Rebels in the Rif: Abd El-Krim and the Rif Rebellion* (Stanford, CA: Stanford University Press, 1968).

123. See Edward W. Said, *Orientalism* (New York: Random House, 1978); Stephen N. Hay, *Asian Ideas of East and West; Tagore and His Critics in Japan, China, and India* (Cambridge: Harvard University Press, 1970), p. 4.

124. B. Nicolaevsky, "Russia, Japan, and the Pan-Asiatic Movement to 1925," *Far Eastern Quarterly*, 8, no. 3 (May 1949): 286–87.

125. Van Loon, *Story of Mankind* pp. 17, 47, 451.

126. Frank M. Snowden, Jr., *Blacks in Antiquity: Ethiopians in the Greco-Roman Experience* (Cambridge, MA: Belknap Press, 1970), pp. vi–vii, 104–7. The existence of "Asiatic blacks" and "African blacks" was also a theme subsequently taken up by Godfrey Higgins, *Anacalypsis: An Attempt to Draw Aside the Veil of the Saitic Isis or An Inquiry Into the Origin of Languages, Nations and Religions*, 2 vols. (1836; rpt. Brooklyn: A & B Books, 1992), 1:51–59.

127. *Koran Questions for Moorish Americans* (Chicago: 1928), Q & A 14; rpt. as "A Moorish Temple Catechism," *Moslem World* 32 (January 1942): 55–59.

128. "The Moorish Americans are the descendants of the ancient Moabites who inhabited the North Western and South Western shores of Africa," *Divine Constitution and By-Laws*, Act 6.

129. *Lost Found Moslem Lesson No. 1*, Q & A 4. Actually, MSTA and NOI versions may not have been as far apart as they appeared, for the Moorish *Holy Koran* averred, "The key of civilization was and is in the hands of the Asiatic nations. The Moorish, who were the ancient Moabites, and the founders of the Holy City of Mecca" (Moorish *Holy Koran*, 45:2).

130. Prophet W. D. Fard, *This Book Teaches the Lost Found Nation of Islam. A Thorough Knowledge of our Miserable State of Condition in a Mathematical Way, When We Were Found by Our Saviour W. D. Fard* (n.p., n.d., c. 1934), Problem No. 32. (Beynon cites this work as *Teaching for the Lost Found Nation of Islam in a Mathematical Way*.) One of Master Fard's lessons cautioned that "All Moslems will murder the devil because they know he is a snake and also if he be allowed to live, he would sting someone else. Each Moslem is required to bring four devils, and by bringing and presenting four at a time, his reward is a button to wear on the lapel of his coat, also free transportation to the holy city of Mecca to see Brother Mohammed" (*Lost Found Moslem Lesson No. 1*, Q & A 10).

131. Sahib, "Nation of Islam," pp. 83, 85, 105, 229, 233; Louis E. Lomax, *When the Word Is Given* (Westport, CN: Greenwood, 1963), p. 79.

132. Beynon, "The Voodoo Cult," p. 903.

133. Sister Mary Bey, head of a local Georgia branch of the Moorish Science Temple, explained that "Bey" was the "international name" appended to the Christian name of temple officers, whereas "El" was the suffix assigned regular followers. Monroe Work, ed., *Negro Year Book, 1937–1938* (Tuskegee, AL: Negro Year Book Publishing, 1938), p. 219. Bey is a Turkish title originally used

by Ottoman administrators. For the NOI, on the other hand, "X" signified "ex-slave" as well as the traditional symbol assigned unknown algebraic quantities.

134. Landes, "Negro Jews in Harlem, " p. 185.

135. "One Year's Moslem Missionary Work in America," *Moslem Sunrise* I (July 1921): 13. Each issue of the *Moslem Sunrise* carried a list of the former and converted names of new proselytes to Ahmadi Islam.

136. Sara Harris, *Father Divine* (1953; rpt. New York: Collier Books, 1971), passim.

137. Moorish *Holy Koran,* 47:16–17.

138. *Lost Found Moslem Lesson No. 2, Q & A* 21–28. The Yakub myth may have been created out of whole cloth by Prophet Fard, but an actual historical incident perhaps related to this invention in some obscure way is worth recounting. In 1194 the army of the Almohad Caliph Ya'qub al-Mansur routed the Franks at the Battle of El Arcos (or Alarcos). Following their defeat, some 40,000 European prisoners of war were taken to Morocco to work on Ya'qub's renowned edifices. The construction projects having been completed, the Christian captives were then set free and allowed to form a valley settlement located somewhere between Fez and Marrakesh. On his deathbed Ya'qub lamented his decision to allow these Shibanis (as they came to be called) to form an enclave on Moroccan soil, thereby posing a potential threat to the stability of the Moorish empire: see Meakin, *Moorish Empire,* pp. 79–80, 278, 301–302.

139. *Lost Found Moslem Lesson No. 2, Q & A* 38. This passage raises the question, of course, as to who actually made the Devil—God or Yakub.

140. English Lesson No. Cl, Q & A 25–32. Three hundred seventy-nine years before 1934, the year in which this lesson was written, would be 1555, the mythical NOI date marking the arrival of African slaves on the North American continent. Recently Minister Louis Farrakhan sought to explain the disparity between this legendary date and 1619, the actual year in which the first African captives arrived in the Virginia colony. Rather than concede that W. D. Fard and Elijah Muhammad were both in error, Farrakhan recently canonized the period between the two dates as the "64 Lost Years." Skeptics may roll their eyes in disbelief, but even the least proficient numerologist understands that the combination of 6 and 4 yields 1, which stands for God . . .

141. Moorish *Holy Koran,* 10:22.

142. Moorish *Holy Koran,* 48:1.

143. *Lost Found Moslem Lesson No. 2,* Q & A 10, 11. See also Muham mad, *Message to the Blackman,* pp. 18–19; Strauss, *Life of Jesus,* pp. 293–96; Douglas R. A. Hare, *The Son of Man Tradition* (Minneapolis, MN: Fortress Press, 1990), passim.

144. Noble Drew Ali, "Moorish Leader's Historical Message to America," rpt. in *Moorish Literature* (n.p., n.d.), pp. 13–14.

145. Wilson, *Sacred Drift,* p. 37.

146. *Lost Found Moslem Lesson No. 2,* Q & A 11.

147. Prophet W. D. Fard, *This Book Teaches the Lost Found Nation of Islam,* Problem 13.

148. *Divine Constitution and By-Laws,* Act 7.

149. *Lost Found Moslem Lesson No. 1,* Q & A 12, 14.

150. *Lost Found Moslem Lesson No. 2,* Q & A 14; *English Lesson C1,* Q & A 9, 10; Beynon, "The Voodoo Cult," p. 901.

151. James Latimer, "Dusky 'Moors' Wear Turbans, Farm Nearby," *Richmond Times-Dispatch* 11 April 1943, p. 12; *Berkshire Eagle,* February 10, 1944; Clegg, *An Original Man,* p. 99.

152. Moorish *Holy Koran,* 48:3.

153. Beynon notes that Master Fard urged his followers to listen to radio broadcasts of Judge Rutherford, spiritual head of the Jehovah's Witnesses (Beynon, "The Voodoo Cult," p. 900). According to Witness doctrine, "The length of the period of Gentile supremacy or Jewish chastisement was discovered in Leviticus 26:18 and Daniel 4 to be 'seven times.' A time was taken to mean a symbolic year of 360 days, each one of which represents a calendar year. Seven times would denote, therefore, a period of 2520 years. The Gentile lease of power would legally cease to exist 2520 years after 606 B.C. [another predetermined "point in history from which all Gentile times" could be further calculated] so that Gentile supremacy would end in 1914 A.D. This date marked for them the end of the world, i.e. the end of present world organizations." Milton Stacey Czatt, *The International Bible Students: Jehovah's Witnesses* (New Haven: Yale University Press, 1933), p. 6.

154. Charles Taze Russell, *Studies in the Scriptures,* vol. 3, *Thy Kingdom Come* (1891), pp. 23, 59; cited in Barbara Grizzuti Harrison, *Visions of Glory: A History and a Memory of the Jehovah's Witnesses* (New York: Simon and Schuster, 1978), p. 43.

155. See Lee, *The Nation of Islam,* esp. pp. 91–105.

156. See Peter Lamborn Wilson, *Scandal: Essays in Islamic Heresy* (Brooklyn: Autonomedia, 1988).

9

African-American Muslims and the Question of Identity

Between Traditional Islam, African Heritage, and the American Way

YUSUF NURUDDIN

Ali Marzrui, in his 1986 televised PBS series, "The Africans," argued that Africans are the cultural heirs to a "triple heritage," consisting of (1) Africanity or traditional indigenous culture, (2) Islamic culture, and (3) Western culture. This triple cultural heritage, according to Mazrui, is at the center of all of the African continent's contemporary conflicts and predicaments.[1] I intend to argue here that African-American Muslims are also heir to this "triple heritage," but that vastly different historical circumstances between continental Africans and Africans in the diaspora (i.e., in the Americas) have resulted in entirely distinct patterns of interplay among these three cultural factors. In other words, the patterns of enculturation (socialization within the indigenous culture) and acculturation (adaptation to non-indigenous cultures) are vastly different in the African diaspora from what they are on the African continent, even though the basic cultural factors are similar, if not identical. Nevertheless, this "triple heritage" lies at the center of all of the African-American Muslim community's contemporary conflicts and predicaments, in much the same way that the "triple heritage" is at the center of Africa's conflicts.

Mazrui states that the "triple heritage" of the African continent actually consisted of two distinct phases: one of antiquity and the other modern. The modern phase began over a thousand years ago with the introduction of Islam into Africa in the seventh and eighth centuries. Western culture entered Africa much later, with the intrusion of colonialism beginning in the fifteenth century. However, during the phase of antiquity which dates back thousands of years to the dawn of civilization among Africans in Egypt, Africa was heir to both a Semitic (Hebraic and Arabian) culture which was the progenitor of the Islamic culture and a Graeco-Roman culture which was the progenitor of modern Westernism.

The "triple heritage" of diasporan Africans in the United States also has had two distinct phases. The modern phase is the post-emancipation phase; the pre-modern phase is the antebellum phase. During the antebellum or pre-Civil War phase, African slaves had not yet been completely Westernized. Although the institution of slavery was both a dehumanizing and de-Africanizing process, evidence of the widespread survival of Africanity (African cultural traits) abounds in the traditions and customs of the slave culture. Several historians have uncovered biographical information about the Islamic lifestyles of notable African-American Muslim slaves, indicating evidence (though not as widespread) of the survival of West African Islamic cultural traits also during the antebellum period.[2]

In the post-emancipation or post-Civil War phase of African-American history, a distinctly Westernized African begins to emerge. As long as the slave trade continued to thrive, newly arrived slaves would bring with them the customs and traditions of their homeland. With the abolition of slavery and the cessation of the slave trade, second- and third-generation Africans in America were cut off from the source of their African heritage, and those who were Muslim were cut off from the source of their Islamic heritage as well.

A dual or actually triple social process also began in the reconstruction era or early decades of the post-emancipation phase. As the newly emancipated African slave attempted to enter the mainstream of American society, he became more and more acculturated or assimilated into a Western way of life. Westernization, however, meant alienation from his African origins. Therefore, the process of Westernization was accompanied by an opposite process, a search for African identity—a quest for re-Africanization.

Because Islamic culture was an integral part of the West African heritage that was lost, the search for African identity frequently involved a search for Islamic identity. Therefore, the process of Westernization or Americanization (acculturation to Westernism or Americanism) and the processes of re-Africanization and re-Islamization (re-acculturation to Africanity and Islam) constituted the unique interplay of the "triple heritage" (Westernization, re-Africanization and re-Islamization) in the diaspora. This same interplay lies at the root of the current identity conflict and ideological conflict that plagues much of the African-American community. However, we cannot adequately address these issues—the psychological conflict of identity and, more importantly, the socio-cultural conflict of ideology—that exist in the African-American Muslim community before first addressing these same issues on the more general level of the African-American population as a whole. In other words, we should first understand how the "double heritage" of Westernization and re-Africanization creates identity conflict and ideological conflict within the general African-American community.

The celebrated African-American scholar, intellectual, and activist W. E. B. Du Bois commented eloquently upon this identity conflict when he said:

> One ever feels his twoness—An American, a Negro: two souls, two thoughts, two unreconciled strivings; two warring ideals in one dark body, whose dogged strength alone keeps it from being torn asunder.
>
> ... The history of the American Negro is the history of this strife—this longing to attain self-conscious manhood, to merge his double self into a better and truer self. In this merging he wishes neither of the older selves to be lost. He does not wish to Africanize America, for America has too much to teach the world and Africa. He does not wish to bleach his Negro blood in a flood of white Americanism, for he believes ... that Negro blood has yet a message for the world. He simply wishes to make it possible for a man to be both a Negro and an American without being cursed and spit upon. ... [3]

Thus the identity conflict which Du Bois personally experienced and struggled with is rooted in the ideological conflict which the African-American population has shared throughout its history of oppression in America. The ideals of re-Africanization as expressed in the nationalist-separatist philosophy of such African-American leaders as Marcus Garvey, Elijah Muhammad, Malcolm X, and Louis Farrakhan came into conflict with the ideals of Westernization as expressed in the integrationist-assimilationist philosophies of Du Bois (throughout most, though not all, of his life), Martin Luther King, Jr., and Elijah Muhammad's son, Wallace (or Warithuddin) Muhammad/Mohammed.

While the processes of Westernization and re-Africanization began, as noted, in the post-emancipation era, when ex-slaves attempted to enter the mainstream of American society as citizens, the roots of the ideological conflict reached into the era of slavery itself. Malcolm X, for example, poignantly reminded us of the profound differences in outlook that existed between the "house negroes" and the "field negroes," i.e., between the well-dressed, well-fed domestic servants and the plantation field hands who dressed in tattered rags and ate leftovers. Both of these groups were slaves, but the domestic servants were better assimilated into the slave master's system, while the plantation workers wanted nothing more than to separate themselves from that system.

The ideological conflict between integration-assimilation and nationalism-separatism is inherent in the multilayered system of social and racial stratification that was created and perpetuated by the historical circumstances of slavery and of legalized segregation, and by the contemporary reality of institutional racism. A system of intra-racial stratification initially based upon a hierarchy of color or skin complexion allowed an elite class of relatively well-educated mulattos (descendants of plantation owners and their domestic-servant mistresses) to play a decisive opinion-making and policy-making role in the early post-emancipation African-American community. Following this leadership, the majority of African-Americans have attempted to assimilate or integrate into the so-called melting pot of America. The system of segregation which more readily accepted mulattos than dark-complexioned African-Americans into the mix resulted in a rejection of Africanity and an embracing of Western standards. During the era of legalized segregation, the ultimate feat of assimilation was to be light-skinned enough to pass for white.

Historically and cross-culturally, this attitude of assimilationism has characterized members of oppressed groups, whether Jews in German concentration camps, Africans and Asians under South African apartheid or native Latin Americans under the Spanish conquistadors. There has always been a large faction of the vanquished who have either reluctantly or wholeheartedly embraced the culture of the conqueror. On the other hand, there has also been a sizable minority who have not. Such persons have resisted assimilation into the dominant culture and have, instead, rallied around themes such as ethnic solidarity, self-determination, territorial separation, and national independence. Nationalist-separatist ideologies and movements have appeared wherever one ethnic group has oppressed or dominated another. In fact throughout the world today we see evidence of nationalist-separatist movements that have gained allegiance not merely among a minority faction of the oppressed but among a majority faction, e.g., in British-occupied Northern Ireland, in the Israeli-occupied West Bank, in formerly Russian-occupied Afghanistan, and in Singhalese-controlled Sri Lanka. African-American nationalism, for the most part, has been an ideological position articulated by a small but vocal minority of blacks. However, according to historian John Bracy,[4] there have been four distinct periods of African-American history when nationalism gained a majority following: 1790 through 1820, the late 1840s through the 1850s, the near half-century stretching from the 1880s into the 1920s, and the middle 1960s to the middle 1970s. The two latter periods are of special interest both because they fall within the post-emancipation era when the ideological conflict came into full bloom and because it is during these two periods that we witness the birth and growth of Islamic movements among the African-American people.

African-American Islamic movements have been rooted historically in African-American nationalist-separatist movements. Movements toward re-Africanization, the return to Africa, and African identity provided the only real context in which re-Islamization movements were born. In this sense, Islamic movements among African-Americans were actually cultural nationalist movements to restore or revive a culture which had been lost or destroyed through the imposition of slavery and Westernization.

However, within the Islamic cultural nationalist ideology the seeds were sown for a new dimension of conflict, insofar as Islamic ideology and black nationalist ideology are both all-embracing. During the early decades of the post-emancipation era when the first Islamic cultural nationalist ideologies and movements were shaped by African-Americans, the Islamic Middle East was already in the throes of a nascent pan-Islamic movement pioneered by leaders such as Jamal al-Din al-Afghani. Furthermore, in the early decades of the twentieth century, the black nationalist movement was internationalized into a global pan-Africanist movement. Conflict was inevitable, because the two pan-ideologies were eventually to compete for the allegiance of the African-American Muslim. This conflict was not fully to emerge until the contemporary period. When it finally did, however, it further complicated the fundamental conflict between integrationism-assimilationism and nationalism-separatism which already existed in the African-American community.

In a racially stratified society where all social relationships are polarized into dichotomies of "we" versus "they," pan-Islamism (especially its modern radical variation, Islamic fundamentalism) was easily translated by some adherents into an ideology of Islamic separatism, i.e., a polarization of the world into the categories of Muslim and *kafir*, believers and unbelievers. For others, the universality of the pan-Islamic ideology, theoretically transcending factors such as race, nationality, or ethnicity, was easily translated into an ecumenical ideology fostering interreligious dialogue (all unbelievers are potential converts) along with an integrationist-assimilationist political stance. Neither of these positions was acceptable to the pan-Africanists, whose message was racial solidarity above all else. To mainstream integrationist-assimilationists, who viewed themselves as pragmatists and realists, none of the Islamic positions—Islamic cultural nationalism, Islamic separatism or Islamic ecumenicalism—was tenable. The African-American establishment viewed all Islamic movements as nothing more than sheer romanticism at best.

Finally, besides predictable conflicts with pan-Africanists (non-Muslim nationalists-separatists) and the African-American establishment (integrationists-assimilationists), the African-American Muslim movement began to develop some predictable and some not-so-predictable conflicts with the varying factions in the worldwide Muslim community.

Thus the African-American Muslim community has experienced ideological conflict in several directions. Externally, it has had to deal with the European-American and the African-American establishments in this country and with various factions of the global *umma* or worldwide Muslim community. Internally, it has come up against the ideologies of Islamic cultural nationalists, Islamic separatists, and Islamic ecumenicalists. These encounters, of course, form the social, cultural, and political underpinnings of the social-psychological conflict of identity that the African-American community continues to undergo. In the remainder of this chapter I shall attempt to address the above dimensions of conflict in their historical context, citing specific examples to illustrate my points.

Islamic Cultural Nationalism:
The Rich Legacy of the Past

The history of Islam in the post-emancipation era of the African-American experience can be divided into three periods: (1) the pre-Nation of Islam era, (2) the era of the Nation of Islam (under the leadership of W. D. Farrad (also known as Fard) and Elijah Muhammad), and (3) the contemporary era which begins with the excommunication of Nation of Islam's spokesman, Malcolm X.

A network of cosmopolitan intellectuals and activists was responsible for the spread of religious and political ideas throughout the African-American community. Islamic cults are often portrayed as but another variation of the many syncretistic and messianic movements that arose among the downtrodden superstitious negroes in the inner cities of America who were seeking escape or deliverance from their misery. Some historians insist that Islam—a heterodox or distorted version of Islam, at that—was introduced to African-Americans when mysterious self-styled street peddling prophets appeared in the Midwestern ghettoes and attracted large followings of gullible negroes in search of a messiah. On the contrary, my research reveals that the introduction of Islam to the African-American community was in the form of orthodoxy rather than heterodoxy. It did not arise in a vacuum but was the result of a series of international exchanges. Furthermore, it was initially propagated by a network of intellectuals rather than by one or two individual self-styled prophets. The claim is also made that the spread of Islam in the African-American community was due to the charisma of particular personalities.[5] The situation was in fact much more complicated. In addition to personalities and organizations, there was also a series of key events which led to the spread of Islam in America. One of them was the interaction of African-American soldiers with African troops stationed in Europe during the First World War. Many of the Africans, of course, were Muslim. Hence African-American troops returned home with an awareness of the faith that was practiced by their African brethren.

The pre-Nation of Islam (NOI) era is characterized by strong ideological links between Islam and pan-Africanism. Four key individuals and/or movements helped to forge these links: Edward Wilmot Blyden, Duse Muhammad Ali, Marcus Garvey and the Universal Negro Improvement Association (UNIA), and the Ahmadiyya Movement. A fifth, Noble Drew Ali and the Moorish Science Temple, acts as a transitional bridge between the Islamic pan-Africanist movement and the black supremacist Nation of Islam.

Blyden was the first architect of these links. A Virgin Islander of pure African stock who was well traveled and equally at home in the Caribbean, in the United States, and on the African continent, Blyden has been characterized by Hollis Lynch, his biographer, as the premiere black intellectual of the nineteenth century. In his collection of essays entitled Christianity,

Islam and the Negro Race,[6] he articulated an ideology of Islamic pan-Africanism which still reverberates today. In this work Blyden documented his impressions of some of his early travels in West Africa. He was favorably impressed by the industry and autonomy that he discovered in Islamic societies, yet was equally disturbed by the state of affairs that he discovered in West Africa where Western colonialists and Christian missionaries had made deep inroads. Having undertaken a regimen of Islamic and Arabic studies well over a decade before the publication of this book, in it Blyden advocated Islam as a way of life highly suited for the progress or advancement of the African race. The book received favorable reviews in Britain, in the United States, and in the Muslim world. Two years after its publication he toured the United States, lecturing extensively on the Qur'an and Islam in West Africa. One can only speculate on the number of African-Americans whom he favorably disposed toward Islam or actually influenced to the extent of conversion. He certainly created a climate for the successful propagation of the faith by later missionaries. The irony of all this, however, was that Blyden was actually a Christian minister. There is nonetheless reason to believe that he may have converted to Islam, since it is reported that when he died in Liberia his funeral bier was carried by Muslims, an honor reserved for their co-religionists. In any case, Blyden—or Abdul-Karim as he is rumored to have been named—was one of the first to be considered responsible for forging links between Islam and black nationalism.

When Blyden died in 1912, his life and achievements were lauded in the *African Times and Orient Review*, a paper with international circulation that was published in London by Duse Muhammad Ali (1866–1945), a Muslim activist and champion of African and Asian independence movements. An Egyptian national of Sudanese-Egyptian parentage, Duse Muhammad Ali was one of the most important and colorful figures in the global pan-Africanist movement. Although he lived in London he exercised a strong influence on the black nationalists movement in the United States, particularly on Marcus Garvey, the black nationalist/pan-Africanist leader who rallied masses of African-Americans around the nationalist cause in the 1920s.

Duse Muhammad Ali was the mentor of the Caribbean-born black nationalist and pan-Africanist Marcus Garvey. Garvey studied in London in the years 1912 and 1913 and quickly made the acquaintance of Ali, who was the leading figure in the London circle of West African and Caribbean pan-Africanists. Garvey immediately took a job working for Duse at the newspaper office of the *African Times and Orient Review*. The paper was an anti-colonialist/anti-imperialist journal that reported on significant persons, movements, and events in the third world. The journal not only championed the nationalistic political movements in the third world, but it also promoted African and Asian culture, religion, and philosophy. As its editor as well as publisher, Duse used the paper as a vehicle for the promotion of Islam. While working on the journal, Garvey gained an international perspective on significant events of the day. Two years after his arrival in the United States in 1916 Garvey began publishing his own pan-Africanist newspaper, *The Negro World*. The influence of Duse was apparent as Garvey printed several articles that were favorably disposed toward Islam.

Garvey never officially adopted Islam for either himself or his movement, preferring to keep the movement non-sectarian. However, a historian of Garvey's movement documents the fact that adherents of the Ahmadiyya established close contact with Garvey's UNIA (Universal Negro Improvement Association). According to Tony Martin, for example, Mufti Muhammad Sadiq, a missionary from northern India (now Pakistan), arrived in the United States in 1920 and established a mosque in Chicago.[7] By 1923, Sadiq was among the invited guests seated on the rostrum at a meeting in Liberty Hall, Garvey's New York headquarters. One of Sadiq's accomplishments at that time was his conversion of some forty Detroit UNIA members to Islam. The *Moslem Sunrise*, the official organ of the Ahmadiyya movement, reprinted pro-Islamic articles from the *Negro World*. The latter in turn published articles such as: "Has Christianity Failed and Has Islam Succeeded?" written by *Moslem Sunrise* editor Maulvi Muhammad Din.

The Ahmadiyya movement was declared heretical by the Pakistani ulama in the early 1970s, because of the Ahmadi belief that their founder Ghulam Ahmad was the messiah. Other than fervent Mahdism, however, this movement is well-grounded in Islamic orthodoxy and in fact was recognized as a large, significant, and legitimate sect with global adherents until the growing popularity and political influence of the movement in Pakistan was countered by a fatwa in 1974.[8]

The influences of Blyden, Ali, Garvey, and the Ahmadiyya movement, then, support the argument that the initial exposure of the African-American community to Islam was from orthodox rather than syncretistic or heterodox sources. Furthermore, this orthodox Islam was rooted in a nationalist or pan-Africanist tradition. Islam was viewed as a cultural alternative for black Americans who were awakening to their African identity and heritage. Hence we may characterize the early period of the spread of Islamic ideas in the African-American community as a time of Islamic cultural nationalism.

With Noble Drew Ali (1886–1929) and his organization, the Moorish Science Temple founded in Newark in 1913, we do encounter genuine heterodoxy. Noble Drew Ali's ideas seem clearly to have come from the Shriners or Ancient Arabic Order of Nobles of the Mystic Shrine. This is a fraternal organization, closely allied to Freemasonry, which uses a burlesque of Islam as its main ritual. William J. Florence, who was white, a member of the Masonic fraternity and a comedian by trade, had traveled in Europe and the Middle East where he was initiated in 1870 into a secret society whose rituals were based on Islam. He brought these rituals back to the United States, adapting them for the American public by developing them into elaborate comic routines. In 1872 the first Shriners' Temple, the Mecca Temple, was opened in New York. Eligibility for membership was restricted to those men who had become Thirty-Second Degree Masons in the Scottish rite or attained the equivalent level of Knights Templar in the York rite.[9] Although Masonry has always been segregated in the United States, with the majority of African-Americans being affiliated with the Prince Hall Lodges, by 1983 an Ancient Egyptian Arabic Order of Nobles of the Mystic Shrine had been incorporated under the Prince Hall jurisdiction.[10] Its ritual was also a burlesque of Islam that was not noticeably different form that of white Shriners.

It seems apparent that Timothy Drew became Noble Drew Ali when he joined a negro Shriner Temple. He took on the traditional Shriner title "noble" and an Arabic or Muslim name as all Shriners do within the confines of their lodge or temple. In fact, my research shows that the fez and bow tie that Elijah Muhammad adopted can be traced to the uniform of another Masonically affiliated organization called the Grotto, which is very similar to the Shriners in its parody of Islamic rituals.[11] Despite this, men like Drew Ali and Elijah Muhammad were evidently impressed with the seriousness of the Islamic religion and its relevance to the black man. Ali therefore left the Shrine and formed his own organization, the Moorish Science Temple, for the express purpose of "uplifting fallen humanity." Not having access to a real Qur'an, Drew Ali plagiarized large portions of a book entitled the *Aquarian Gospel of Jesus Christ* and called this plagiarized work, "The Holy Koran of the Moorish Science Temple of America." He combined large portions of two books, one entitled The Aquarian Gospel of Jesus Christ, the other entitled Unto Thee I Grant, under one cover and called this plagiarized work *The Holy Koran of the Moorish Science Temple of America.*[12]

In Drew Ali we see for the first time a move away from the factual documentation of African history, politics, culture, and religion that characterized the writings of Blyden, Duse, Garvey, and the Ahmadis. In its place we find mythology, legends, and parables about the lost or hidden history of the black man. This emphasis on mysteries and lost wisdom is consistent with the nature of the plagiarized scripture that the Moors were taught to believe in, and more important it is consistent with the emphasis on fraternal secrets and mysteries in the Shriners Temple from which the Moorish Science Temple descended. Hence it is in the Moorish Science Temple that we encounter fables about the "ancient Moabite kingdom now known as Morocco, which existed in northwest Amexem, which is now known as northwest Africa." We also discover that Moors (i.e., West Africans) arrived in the Americas before Columbus, a fact documented by Rutgers University anthropologist Dr. Ivan van Sertima's book, *They Came Before Columbus: The African Presence in Ancient America*, published in 1976.[13] However, we again encounter strange mythological names; where Van Sertima speaks of the Olmecs, a tribe of Indians in Mexico who intermarried and became intermixed with the West African settlers, the Moorish Scientists speak of the Yakubites, descendants of a Moor named Yakub who landed on the Yucatan peninsula.

Van Sertima documents the existence of Olmec sculpture, huge stone heads with recognizable African features, as just one of his many proofs. He was not the first to advance the theory of an African presence in pre-Columbian America, but was the first to prove conclusively a theory that had been advanced much earlier. The Moorish Scientists, to their credit, were aware both of these theories and of the stone heads themselves. But again they created an aura of unbelievable mythology around the sculptures. They said that the huge stone heads attested to the fact that the Yakubites evolved into a race of scientific geniuses with large heads (as depicted in the sculptures) and small bodies. This legend of Yakub—a big-headed scientist—finds its way into the mythology of the Nation of Islam, indicating that the founders of the NOI, W. D. Farrad and Elijah Muhammad, were influenced by the Moorish Science Temple, and were possibly even members. Several credible witnesses attest to the fact that photographs exist showing Farrad and Elijah in attendance at Moorish Science meetings led by Noble Drew Ali.[14] Another curiosity that emerged in my research in the private collections of memorabilia of Muslim senior citizens is an old, worn-out copy of a "sworn affidavit" by Christine Price-bey of Chicago, who "affirm[s] that during the 1929 Convention of Moorish Science Temples of America that I was the Registration Secretary and at that time registered the man Judson Houndes Bey, who later became known as Elijah Muhammad." Even if this is a copy of a true affidavit, I am uncertain about the validity of this legal document as irrefutable historical evidence. I am of the opinion, however, that Farrad was an Asian or Middle Eastern immigrant of Muslim background who found it comfortable to live and work among the black urban community and even to identify with its aspirations.[15] Documents and photographs exhibited at the Schomberg Research Library in New York show that Farrad and Elijah had joined the Garvey movement. It is therefore reasonable to believe that Farrad (and Elijah) may have been sincerely attracted to other movements such as the Moorish Science Temple. One plausible explanation is that Farrad stayed in the movement long enough to discover that, with his own authentic Muslim knowledge and background, he could develop a movement with even greater potential than the Moorish Temple.

It is interesting to note that when the Yakub fable found its way into the mythology of the Nation of Islam it had been changed considerably, yet enough original elements existed to suggest that it came directly from the Moorish Science Temple.[16] In narratives of the NOI, however, Yakub, the "big-headed scientist," was a member of a race of black God-like men who lived in the paradisiacal city of Mecca, which was the "root of civilization." Yakub was an evil genius who conducted genetic experiments and created the white race in his laboratory. He accomplished this feat by first isolating two genes in the black man, a strong (dominant?) black gene and a weak (recessive?) brown gene. From the brown gene he created the brown race. He then proceeded to isolate a brown gene and a weaker red gene, from which he created the red race. In this fashion he developed the yellow race from the red race and finally the white race from the yellow race. Since the genetic material became successively weaker, the white race was genetically constituted weak and evil. In fact, it was a race of devils who destroyed the paradise of Mecca by lying and stealing and engendering confusion and suspicion among the black race, eventually causing members of the black race to kill each other. As a punishment for sowing seeds of discord, Yakub and his "grafted devils" were "chased out of the Holy City of Mecca . . . across the burning sands of hot Arabian desert into the caves of West Asia which is now called Europe. While crossing the desert sands they went savage, losing everything except their language."[17] It is this type of mythology, with its assertion "that the black man is God and the white man is the devil," and the accompanying beliefs that Allah appeared in the person of Master W. D. Farrad Muhammad and that Elijah Muhammad was his Prophet, that led to a backlash against the NOI in the contemporary era (1965 through the present).

Whereas the predecessors of the NOI, notably Blyden, Ali, Garvey, and the Ahmadis, were black cultural nationalists and pan-Africanists, the NOI members were black supremacists. The precursors of the NOI were Islamic cultural nationalists who did not advocate black supremacy, but merely believed that the true disciplined practice of Islam would lead to political, economic, social and cultural "upliftment of fallen humanity," as Noble Drew Ali phrased it.[18] As the Nation of Islam deviated from this benign Islamic cultural nationalism and preached a philosophy of black supremacy which they blended with a heterodox theology (the un-Islamic notion of human incarnation of the divine, i.e., God appearing in the person of W. D. Farrad), the Sunni backlash against the NOI was strong and in opposition to any ideology that even remotely resembled the ideas of the NOI. This had direct implications for the benign black nationalist/Pan-Africanist ideas of the Islamic cultural nationalists; their ideas also became taboo in many African-American Sunni Muslim circles. There was a rush to embrace the strict Wahhabi interpretation of Islam brought to the U.S. by immigrant Muslims (especially Saudis) and to avow a universalism which holds that color, race, ethnicity, and national differences are inconsequential. *Asabiya* (nationalism) was considered *haram* (forbidden), and it was acceptable to proclaim loyalty only to the umma or community of Muhammad, the Messenger of God. This constituted a kind of extreme backlash to the extremist philosophy of the NOI. Such universalist adherents denied African identity and claimed an amorphous Muslim identity. These were the Sunni Islamic separatists who divided the world, conveniently, into Muslim and *kafir*. Their anti-nationalist posture created an anti-Sunni Muslim backlash in the overall black nationalist community. It also brought these Sunni Muslim Islamic separatists into conflict with the Sunni Islamic cultural nationalists, who were now reduced to a small dissident faction among the orthodox Muslims, even though they carried the legacy and philosophy of men like Blyden, Ali, and the early Ahmadiyya Garveyites, who were the pioneers of Islam in post-emancipation America.

Heterodox black supremacist cults began to spring up because there was no room to express nationalism in orthodox (Sunni) Islamic settings once the Sunni Islamic separatists had taken over the ideological leadership of the orthodox or Sunni African-American Islamic movement. The Ansaru Allah movement, for example, discarded much of the ideology of the NOI and adopted orthodox dress (thobes, *jallabiyas*, *hijab* or purdah, etc.) rather than suits and bow ties, yet maintained an extreme black supremacist position. Another NOI-splinter group, the Five Percenters, began to preach extremist black supremacy and a heterodox theology packaged in a hip African-American teenage slang "rhyme and rhythm" rap dialect that is especially appealing to adolescents.

Meanwhile, though anti-nationalist, some Sunni separatists were nevertheless radical in the sense that they called for jihad against the kafir. Sunni Muslim Islamic separatism took on the character of a radical "poor people's" movement, seeking to redistribute wealth, power, and prestige from the hands of the kafir (Western society) to the hands of the Muslims. According to this ideology, those among the poor (i.e., African-Americans) who do not become Muslim will unfortunately share the fate of the wealthy European-American kafirs. These radical ideas are not welcomed by the conservative middle-class immigrants who are attempting to assimilate into American society (especially, for example, Pakistanis who have entered such professions as medicine, pharmacy, accounting, finance, engineering, etc.). Tensions have continued to grow between the middle-class immigrant Muslims and the radical underclass Islamic separatists.

Elijah Muhammad's son Wallace (Warithuddin or Warith Din) became a major player in this scene by leading the NOI membership (which by 1975 had become an economically empowered middle-class community due to the self-help programs of Elijah) into a middle-class partnership with the immigrant community. His philosophy has been one of assimilation into America, American patriotism, and enhanced ecumenical relations among all Americans. Immigrant Muslim organizations such as the Muslim World League are comfortable with Wallace's middle-class assimilationist philosophy and recognize him as the representative of American Muslims.

Louis Farrakhan, along with other lesser-known Muslim leaders such as Silas Muhammad, have reacted against this kind of openness and tried to recreate versions of the old NOI movement. Some radical Islamic separatists have allied themselves with the Iranian revolution and become Shi'ite. Others remain Sunni but grow increasingly hostile in their relationships with middle-class immigrants. Meanwhile, Islamic cultural nationalists slowly try to regain strength and clout to reassert their voice in the fragmented movement and redirect it in the spirit of Blyden, Ali, and the early Ahmadiyya Garveyites. They are now no longer all Sunni, but include significant numbers of African-American Shi'as—and they attempt to make overtures to Ahmadiyyas as well—in an effort to regain control of the movement from Islamic separatists and Islamic ecumenicists.

Islam versus Afrocentricity: The Bitter Controversy of the Present

> When it is said to them:
> "Follow what God hath revealed":
> They say: "Nay we shall follow
> The ways of our fathers."
> What! even though their fathers
> Were void of wisdom and guidance?"
>
> (Qur'an 2:170)

In the past decade, relations between the African-American Muslim community and the African-American secular nationalist community have been strained.[19] This, however, has not always been the case. In the 1960s and early 1970s, Muslims were at the vanguard of the black power/cultural nationalist movement. The "Last Poets"[20]—Jalaluddin Mansur Nuriddin, Umar Bin Hassan, and Suliaman El Hadi—spread a fiery revolutionary nationalist message in their popular recorded albums of poetry during a period in which America witnessed one urban uprising after another. Muhammad Ahmad (Max Stanford) was a practicing Sunni Muslim and a high-ranking member of the Revolutionary Action Movement (RAM, a group that was disbanded after an alleged plot to blow up the Statue of Liberty was uncovered by the FBI), a political prisoner, and subsequently the chairman of the African People's Party, an organization which advocated revolutionary war as a means of achieving a black independent socialist nation in North America. Many of the members of this organization were also Sunni Muslims. Many political prisoners, those who were incarcerated for alleged involvement in underground black revolutionary activity, became Sunni Muslims during the period of their incarceration. Sekou Abdullah Odinga and Dhoruba bin Wahid, alleged members of the Black Liberation Army, are cases in point.

As the mood of the country shifted toward quietude in the mid-1970s, after Cointelpro's[21] infiltration and dismantling of radical movements, both the black nationalist organizations and the orthodox Muslim organizations veered away from activism to a preoccupation with intensive theorizing and ideological self-definition. It was during this period that Muslims and nationalists began to conclude that they were ideologically incompatible.

The stance adopted by Islamic separatists may have been the precipitating factor in the souring of relations. By sharply dividing the world into Muslim and kafir, they isolated and alienated themselves from the rest of the African-American community. An example of the extreme degree of the insularity of Islamic separatists is the fact that some have even considered their parents and next of kin as kafirs, and consequently have broken family ties, even though this behavior runs counter to an oft-quoted tradition of the Prophet.[22] On the receiving end of this Islamic separatist chauvinism during the 1970s, secular cultural nationalists launched an offensive against all variations of Islam.

Islam vs. Afrocentricity

The "Afrocentric Crusades," as I have named these offensives, began as early as 1971 with the publication of Chancellor Williams's *Destruction of Black Civilization*,[23] which stresses the historical role of Arabs as slave owners and cultural imperialists who forced Islam upon Africans. Publishing rights for this work were soon obtained by Third World Press, the publishing arm of the Institute of Positive Education, a Chicago-based black nationalist think-tank. This think-tank/publishing house, headed by author-publisher-educator Haki Madhubuti (Don L. Lee), became the chief disseminator of cultural nationalist anti-Muslim propaganda in the 1970s. For example, Madhubuti's own work, *Enemies: The Clash of Races* (1978), and Shawna Maglangbayan's *Garvey, Lumumba, Malcolm: Black Nationalists-Separatists* (1972) both mounted offensives against the African-American fervor for Islam. The latter was even critical of Malcolm's interpretation of his hajj experience.

The term "Afrocentricity" was coined and defined circa 1980 by Molefi Asante who currently chairs the Department of African American Studies at Temple University. Coining and defining the term is not the same as formulating the body of thought represented by the term. The corpus of Afrocentric thought was formulated by dozens of scholars. Asante, however, is often regarded as the Father of Afrocentricity because, in addition to coining the term, he provided a theoretical framework for this corpus.[24] In the seminal work, *Afrocentricity: The Theory of Social Change* (*1980*), Asante set the tone for the Afrocentrist attitude toward Islam.

In laying out the Afrocentric theoretical framework, Asante wastes no time in stating that Islam is "contradictory" to Afrocentricity. In fact, it is no exaggeration to state that the attack on Islam is the first item on the Afrocentric agenda—the second through the sixth pages of the Asante's text are devoted to discrediting Islam. Since Asante gives Islam such prominence in the opening pages of his text, one must assume that he views the Islamic ideology as the chief rival of Afrocentricity, in vying for the hearts of African Americans. Asante begins his tirade by stating bluntly that unlike the nationalistic emphasis of the Nation of Islam, "the present emphasis of Islam in America is cultural and religious. This is a serious and perhaps tragic mistake."[25] Diatribes follow about the cultural implications of Arabic being the language of the Qur'an, rather than Yoruba, Kiswahili, or Twi; Mecca being the direction prostration rather than the "sacred forest of Oshogbo" or Mount Kilimanjaro; and Muhammad, an Arab, being the seal of the Prophets. After roundly attacking Islam, Molefi moves next to a page-long attack on Black Hebrew Israelites.

Asante's assault was one of the initial salvos in the Afrocentric-Islamic cultural wars, but the Afrocentric Crusades did not reach a groundswell until the 1980s, when Harlem became the center for Afrocentric ideology. This may be attributed largely to three Harlem-based professors, Yosef ben Jochannan ("Dr. Ben"), John Henrik Clarke, and Leonard Jeffries, who reached beyond the confines of the university and went into the community to teach.[26] Here they attained celebrity status and nearly had cult followings. The trio were at the core of a local organization, the First World Alliance, and a national organization, the Association for the Study of Classical African Civilization (ASCAC), both of which aggressively promoted the view that African peoples and cultures had their historical origin in the Nile Valley civilizations of Kush, Nubia, and Kemet (respectively, ancient Ethiopia, Sudan, and Egypt). Furthermore, these organizations vehemently stated that many elements of the Western heritage, including philosophy and religion, are the "stolen legacy" of these black Nilotic civilizations.

These were not new ideas—Cheik Anta Diop, George G. M. James, and Chancellor Williams were among other scholars who had pioneered them[27]—but Ben Jochannan, Clarke, and Jeffries and their organizations became their popularizers. Television personality Gil Noble and radio personalities Bob Law and "Imhotep" Gary Byrd all hosted black talk shows which gave regular exposure to these professors and their cohorts.[28]

A network of cultural institutions throughout the five boroughs of New York such as the House of the Lord Church, the Slave Theatre in Brooklyn, and the African Poetry Theatre in Queens also gave support to the "missionary" activities of these Afrocentric "preachers," hosting lecture after lecture. Specialty bookshops catering to Afrocentric works, and ubiquitous street vendors hawking books as well as audio and video tapes of lectures, expanded this network of support. A great number of other Afrocentric forums, study groups and fraternal/sororal organizations began to spring up in the New York area, including the African Heritage Studies Organization, African People's Christian Organization, African Echoes, the Sons and Daughters of the Sun, the Ausar-Auset (i.e., Horus-Isis) Society, and the Jewels of Aton, later known as the Shrine of Ptah. Secular and religious distinctions began to fade as many of these groups called for a spiritual reawakening based upon a return to philosophies and cosmologies of ancient Egypt.

Afrocentricity, as shaped by these groups, bore a strong resemblance to the main themes of the Negritude movement pioneered by Leopold Senghor and Aime Cesaire in the 1940s: mysticism, the yearning for a utopian African past, and the celebration of racially "superior" African qualities.[29] Melanin, the biochemical agent causing skin pigmentation, was seized upon by the Afrocentrists as one of these superior African qualities, and local and national melanin conferences were held to extol the supposedly manifold virtues of this substance, e.g., increased propensity for intelligence, creativity, spontaneity, and cosmic consciousness.[30] In an attempt to find solutions for the contemporary problems of racism, class oppression, and urban decay via a romantic return to a utopian African past, leaders cried out for "the reclamation, reconstruction and resurrection" of Kemetic (ancient Egyptian) culture. The rituals and beliefs of the Kemetic African Mystery System were revived, the principle of Ma'at (balance, justice, and righteousness) was revered, the "neters" or Kemetic deities were invoked, ancient ancestors were called on, hieroglyphics were studied, the merits of the various Kemetic dynasties were debated, the names of illustrious pharaohs were adopted, and pilgrimages were made to the shrines and temples of Abu Simbel, Luxor, and Karnak.

"Hotep," the transliteration of the hieroglyphic word for "Peace," was the rallying cry of this neo-Negritude movement. It was as much a war cry as it was a greeting of peace, uttered in an aggressive manner to any newcomers or persons at the periphery of the movement to signal that any other cultural greeting, especially "As Salaamu Alaykum," was unwelcome. The adoption of Islam by African Americans was looked upon by these Afrocentrists as a gross ideological error, leading blacks into a false and neurotic sense of Arabocentric heritage and identity. The Arab slave trade and the Fulani jihads of Shehu Uthman dan Fodio, in which countless lives were lost, Africans pitted against Africans, are constantly cited by the Afrocentrists as evidence of the detrimental legacy of Islam. While Dr. Leonard Jeffries has taken a somewhat positive stance toward the role of Islam in African history, citing the era of the West African Islamic Mali and Songhai Empires as Africa's Second Golden Age, Drs. Yosef Ben Jochannan and John Henrik Clarke have become increasingly known for Islam-bashing in their public lectures. When cornered or pressed by Muslim members of the audience to elaborate, however, Clarke watered down his more vitriolic comments. In print both have been more cautious. Ben Jochannan's book, *African Origins of the Major Western Religions* (1973), contains diatribes against Arab and Persians, questions the authenticity of the Qur'anic revelation, and castigates members of the Nation of Islam for referring to themselves as Asiatic Black Men, yet gives praise to black historical figures such as Bilal, Mansa Musa, Ibrahim al-Mahdi, and al-Jahiz as the unsung "originators" and/or heroes of Islam. Clarke's collection of essays, *Africans at the Crossroads* (1991), warns against Arab-African alliances, stating that historically Africans "created" Islam and entered into a partnership with Arabs who eventually turned against Africans and used Islam as a justification for the slave trade.

Maulana Karenga, a West Coast cultural nationalist who is best known as the founder of Kwanzaa, a week-long African-American cultural nationalist holiday celebrated between Christmas and New Year's Day, is also a leading Afrocentrist and Islam-basher. His anti-Islamic stance stems as much from his personal history in the black nationalist movement as it does from purely ideological reasons. In the 1960s Karenga was the leader of US (pronounced like "us" and standing for United Slaves), a cultural nationalist organization which had a rivalry with the Black Panther party. The rivalry ended in bloodshed, a shoot-out that claimed the lives of two men from each organization. Karenga was accused by many of being an agent provocateur. As the inner-city California mosques are filled with many former Black Panthers or Panther sympathizers, Karenga has always had poor relationships with Muslims who derogatorily call his followers "Karengatans" (rhyming with orang-utans) and constantly battle with them for influence over the ideological direction of black student organizations on the California college campuses. A leading member of ASCAC and a nationally renowned lecturer, Karenga[31] has consistently made quick, fleeting, witty, but disparaging comments about orthodox Muslims. His hostility towards African-American Sunni and Shi'a Muslim activists is clearly evident in his speeches; yet his textbook, *Introduction to Black Studies* (1982), gives an objective assessment of the Nation of Islam and the historical role of the Moors in Spain.[32] More importantly, however, in translating and binding under one cover a selection of spiritual, moral, and ethical maxims drawn from various sacred ancient Egyptian manuscripts, he has provided the Afrocentrists with their own readily accessible religious text, *The Husia*,[33] which they can hold up as "superior" to and older than the Holy Qur'an.

The Afrocentric Crusades have also enlisted for their anti-Islamic arsenal the works of continental African authors and artists. *Ceddo*, a film by Senegalese director Ousmane Sembene, portrays a traditional African village ravaged by forced conversion to Islam. *Two Thousand Seasons* (1987), written by Ayi Kwei Armah and published by the Third World Press, is a novel with similar anti-Islamic themes as are *Segu* (1989), two novels by Maryse Conde, a Guadeloupean who traces her African roots to the Bambara people. Tayeb Salih's novel, *Season of Migration to the North* (1989), depicts the adolescent/young adulthood conflicts of a Sudanese youth of mixed Arab-African heritage who goes abroad to school and is seduced by European culture and lifestyle. The ensuing conflicts can be interpreted on many levels. The Afrocentric interpretation of the character's split personality and self-hatred is certainly unfavorable to Islam.[34]

In the realm of fiction one African-American work in particular stands out, Ishmael Reed's satirical novel *Mumbo Jumbo* (1972). Unlike the other works cited here, Reed's is not anti-Muslim. In a very careful and considered fashion it deals with the issue of Afrocentricity versus Islam, posing two protagonists against one another, Papa La Bas, a voudou hougan and Abd'ul-Hamid, a Muslim autodidact of prodigious knowledge. Thus, traditional African religion and culture is pitted against Islam. Reed opts in favor of traditional African religions but only after letting Abd'ul-Hamid build a very strong case for Islam. Because the novel is written on several levels in an improvisational literary style, with a number of themes and plots going on at once, it may prove daunting to some. I highly recommend it, however, for anyone seriously interested in the debate on Afrocentricity versus Islam.

Julie Dash's 1993 film, *Daughters of the Dust*, is also unique. It portrays a harmonious Gullah community in the Sea Islands off the coast of Georgia in 1902 consisting of at least one Muslim, Bilal Muhammad, several Christians, and a matriarch, Nana Peazant, who clings tenaciously to a traditional African religion.[35] There is a religious conflict in the film which is eventually resolved, but it takes place between the matriarch's Kongo-based rituals and beliefs and the strong Christian beliefs of one of her offspring.[36] The Muslim is respected and lives in peaceful coexistence with everyone, but he seems to be a lone or solitary figure. This character, Bilal Muhammad, is ignored or overlooked by most critics and fans of the film, who see its rich cinematography as heralding a new beginning for exploring and celebrating the relationships between black women and a new beginning for exploring and celebrating traditional African religion.

Muslim response to the Afrocentric onslaught has been slow in coming, largely because the ranks of African-American Muslim scholars are thin. Agadem L. Diara, author and publisher of *Islam and Pan-Africanism* (1973), makes one of the earliest known attempts to refute Dr. Ben Jochannan's analysis of Islam. Unfortunately, this mimeographed book was poorly circulated and is now out of print. Nai'm Akbar, a clinical psychologist, professor, author, and lecturer of national renown, is a member of the American Muslim movement. But he is also a member of ASCAC and his loyalties, which are divided, seem to lean towards the latter organization. When pressed by Afrocentrists about his continued involvement with Islam, Akbar seems unable or unwilling to mount any strong defense of his faith. Musa Abdul-Hakim, a writer and activist from Buffalo who has traveled extensively to West Africa, spoke at two ASCAC forums in the late 1980s—one national and one in the New York area—accusing the Afrocentrists of "Islamophobia." Without a more concentrated addressing of the issue, however, such single performances, no matter how well received, are quickly forgotten.[37]

Two prominent African Muslim professors of political science residing in the United States, Ali Mazrui, a Kenyan and editor of *The Africans* (1986), and Sulayman Nyang, a Gambian and author of *Islam, Christianity and African Identity* (1990), were roundly attacked by Molefi Asante, an African-American professor of black studies and leading exponent of Afrocentricity, in Asante's book *Kemit, Afrocentricity and Knowledge* (1990). Asante accuses both of inaccurately analyzing African culture because they are blinded by religious beliefs. Shahrazad Ali, author of the best-seller, *The Blackman's Guide to Understanding the Blackwoman* (1989), and a member of one of the splinter groups of the Nation of Islam, is routinely excoriated for her condemnation of black women and her unbridled support of black male supremacy. Some Afrocentrists have argued that her views on gender relations are distorted because they are derived from a patriarchal Arab-Islamic ideology rather than a gender-balanced Afrocentric ideology.[38] H. Khalif Khalifah, editor of the nationally distributed *Newport News and Commentator*, is also an NOI splinter group member, an avid supporter of Shahrazad

Ali, and a publisher of works by and about Elijah Muhammad. His periodical has influence in the Afrocentric community because it carries a widely read monthly book review section entitled "Your Black Books Guide." One of the few extant nationally circulated black book-review periodicals, the guide is simultaneously Afrocentric and oriented toward black Islam.

Rafiq Bilal, an African-American Muslim, and Thomas Goodwin, an Afrocentrist, are the joint authors of *Egyptian Sacred Science in Islam* (1987), a well researched but not widely distributed text which examines the evidence of Kemetic cosmology surviving in Qur'anic scripture. Afrocentrists and Muslims, however, are predisposed to interpret this evidence in very different ways. Muslims see the Qur'an as the perfect and universal culmination or completion of previous divine revelations that were sent to all tribes and nations, who unfailingly distorted or corrupted these early divine messages and thus were in need of one final scripture. Afrocentrists, on the other hand, are preoccupied with the idea of the primacy and originality of Egyptian contributions to civilization and the inferiority of cultures which "borrowed, copied or stole" Kemetic ideas. The book was an outcome of a weekly lecture series sponsored by Khalid Al-Mansour, a lawyer, lecturer, and author who has republished Blyden's long out of print *Christianity, Islam and the Negro Race* (1887) and published a number of his own evangelistic books on Islam and its relevance to black people. As he is an African-American who identifies himself as an "African Arabian," it is doubtful that he will have any impact on changing the perceptions of Afrocentrists.

Mustafa El-Amin's *Freemasonry, Ancient Egypt and the Islamic Destiny* (1988), a follow-up to his *Al-Islam, Christianity and Freemasonry* (1985), does not contain an in-depth examination of Kemetic culture or mystery systems but does offer many insights into the secrets of the Shriners. Adib Rashad (James Miller), author of *The History of Islam and Black Nationalism in America* (1991), does not directly address the issue of Afrocentricity, but does provide a fast-paced historical outline and polemic about Islamic cultural nationalism. Articles by Khalil Muhammed, Clyde Ahmad Winters, and Sulayman Nyang, booklets by Abdullah Hakim Quick (*Deeper Roots: Muslims in the Caribbean before Columbus to the Present*) and Abdulhakim Muhammad (*Seven Muslim Slaves*), and a chapter of my own manuscript in progress explore the Muslim roots of Africans in the Diaspora, as do Terry Alford's *Prince among Slaves* (1977) and Allan Austin's exhaustive *African Muslims in Ante-bellum America* (1984).[39] Ivan van Sertima, a renowned Afrocentrist author, lecturer, and professor of anthropology, makes a stunning contribution to African Islamic studies with his edited volume, *The Golden Age of the Moor* (1992). Khalid Fattah-Griggs of the Institute for Islamic Involvement is the editor/publisher of *Visions*, a newsletter whose black nationalist stance is reminiscent of the 1960s. The Admiral family proposes an agenda for nationalism-separatism in their book *Confronting America's Black-White Dilemma* (1992). K. Kazi-Ferrouillet, one of the authors of an article entitled "Afrocentricity, Islam and Al Hajj Malik Shabazz"

(1993), makes an attempt to address the shortcomings of the Afrocentricity movement, including the futility of its preoccupation with melanin and its inability or unwillingness to assess the many contributions of Islam to African and African-American history.

Since my original review of this literature in 1993, several new texts have been published.[40] Ameen Yasir Mohammed's *Afrocentricity, Minus Al-Islam, Cheats: Exposing The Conspiracy to Rob African-Americans of Their Most Precious Heritage* is, despite an awkward title, a very significant contribution to the literature. It is a comprehensive compilation of lengthy quotations, pro and con, on the subject of the impact of Islam on African civilizations. Mohammed first quotes the "allegations" of the leading Afrocentrists: Chancellor Williams, Yosef ben Jochannan, John Henrik Clarke, and Molefi Asante. He then proceeds to refute those "allegations" with "testimony" from other leading Africanist scholars: Cheik Anta Diop, W. E. B. DuBois, J. A. Rogers, Walter Rodney, Basil Davidson, Ivan van Sertima, and others. Mustafa El-Amin, whose works on Islam and Freemasonry were mentioned earlier, also takes on the Afrocentrists Williams, ben Jochannan, Clarke and Asante in *Afrocentricity, Malcolm X and Al-Islam,* a text which is directed towards a novice audience. Both Yasir Mohammed and Mustafa Al-Amin liberally quote from their leader Wallace (Warith Din) Mohammed, and the reference to "cheating" in Yasir Mohammed's title is actually drawn from a Wallace Mohammed speech.[41]

Two texts modeled after J. A. Rogers's *World's Great Men of Color,* a classic work which provided short biographical sketches of sung and unsung heroes, were recently published. While Joel Augustus Rogers's two-volume work surveyed heroic blacks, including several Muslims, Mohammad Abu-Bakr's *Islam's Black Legacy: Some Leading Figures* and Salim Abdul-Khaliq's *The Untold Story of Blacks in Islam* focus exclusively on Muslims of African descent. Drawing upon the description of the family of Abd al-Muttalib, the paternal grandfather of the Prophet Muhammad, both J. A. Rogers and Mohammed Abu-Bakr identify "Muhammad: The Great Ishmaelite Prophet of Islam" as a black man.[42]

Adib Rashad, whose text, *The History of Islam and Black Nationalism,* was mentioned earlier, has made major revisions in this text and retitled it *Islam, Black Nationalism and Slavery: A Detailed History.* This work is vastly superior to the original. There is no doubt that it contains the most comprehensive compilation on Muslim slaves in the New World to date. Rashad's chapters on contemporary communities tend to focus primarily on the Nation of Islam and its offshoots. Amina Beverly McCloud's *African American Islam* provides a skeletal survey or cursory look at the spectrum of contemporary African-American Muslim sects and communities. In this primer, McCloud continues her important work of painting the portraits of African-American Muslim women. In *American Jihad: Islam after Malcolm X,* a collage of short interviews, black journalist Steven Barboza, provides glimpses of Muslim personalities, African American as well as immigrant.

Yvonne Haddad and Jane Smith's *Mission to America* and their edited volume *Muslim Communities in North America* contain a number of important chapters on African-American Muslim communities. Several comprehensive studies of the African-American Muslim community are now in press or in preparation; hence, in the next several years the basic literature on African-American Muslims should be greatly expanded.[43]

With the increased availability of basic literature, the debates between Muslims and Afrocentrists will probably sharpen and deepen. Debates, in fact, intensified during the years 1993–1995. Samori Marksman, a black activist and talk show host on WBAI, a New York radio station which is the voice of the radical left, hosted two unaired symposiums in the black community in an effort to heal the rift between Muslims and Afrocentrists. On both occasions the dialogue between the panel of Afrocentrists and the panel of Muslims ended in acrimony.[44]

In 1995, Afrocentrists engaged in a relentless media campaign to make the African-American public aware of present-day Arab enslavement of Africans in the Sudan and Mauritania. They depicted an Arabized mulatto population in North Sudan as oppressing a dark-complexioned Christian and animist population in the south, subjecting them to all sorts of human rights violations in the name of Islam and Shari'a-based government. It was alleged that bedouin Muslims in Mauritania held in servitude a population of African Muslim houseboys, many of whom had been turned into eunuchs.[45] In 1995, a bitter exchange also took place in the black media between John Henrik Clarke and Imam Talib Abdur-Rashid of the Mosque of Islamic Brotherhood on the general issue of Afrocentricity versus Islam.[46]

Sahelian Thought, the Wave of the Future?

By 1996 African American Muslim intellectuals and scholars had yet to build a cohesive ideological system which is Meccacentric yet not Arabophile in content. I use the term "Meccacentric" metaphorically because Mecca is the qibla, but the terms Islamicentric and *tawhid*-centered are equally appropriate. African-American discourse, unfortunately, will be stuck at the present level until such African American Meccacentric model is firmly established. Such a Meccacentric model, or African Islamic model as some have termed it, must build upon the foundations of Islamic cultural nationalism and Islamic pan-Africanism. But it must be expanded into a comprehensive system without international tensions. This is the challenge with which African-American Muslims are faced.[47]

In late 1995, my colleague Sayeed Abdus-Samad coined the term "Sahelian thought" to describe the African Islamic ideological system. Sahelian refers to the Sahel region of western Africa (also known as the western Sudan) where classic African Islamic civilizations including Mali (1230–1494) and Songhai (1468–1591) were located. Another colleague, Muhammad Abdel-

Rahman, expands upon Abdus-Samad's idea by coining the term Andalus-Sahelian thought, which encompasses the legacy of the Moorish civilization of al-Andalus (711–1492) on the Iberian peninsula. In a lighthearted debate, Samad has insisted that Sahelian is a term which suffices because Moorish Spain and Portugal were merely the northernmost reaches of Sahelian civilization.[48] In any event, Sahelian or Andalus-Sahelian are both powerfully descriptive terms for this African Islamic ideological system. Thus armed with more crystalized concepts, Muslims may engage their ideological foes more successfully as the debate between Sahelian and Kemetic perspectives escalates.

Organization, of course, is the final key. While Afrocentrists have a host of interlocking organizations devoted to the advancement of Kemetic scholarship, African-American Muslim scholars to date have been working independently rather than collectively. Yet the formation of an Islamocentric school of thought, the advancement of African Islamic paradigms, and the production of a cohesive body of literature are only possible when there is a critical mass of scholars and intellectuals working on such a project. Competitive duplication of efforts could be minimized, and intellectual tasks could be divided so that many scholars contribute to one significant groundbreaking work. There has been much talk about rectifying this state of affairs, but real efforts to organize have been slow in coming. A few fledgling organizations exist such as the Ahmad Baba Research Center, the Center for the Advanced Study of Islam among African-Americans (CASIA), and the Uthman Don Fodio Institute. But much more organizing, merging of resources, and pooling of talents need to be done.[49]

Notes

1. *The Africans* was jointly produced by the British Broadcasting Corporation, London, and WETA Public Broadcasting Service, Washington, D.C. See the companion text, Ali Mazrui, *The Africans: A Triple Heritage* (Boston: Little Brown, 1986); or the telecourse textbook, Ali Mazrui and Toby Kleban Levine, eds., *The Africans: A Reader* (New York: Praeger, 1986). Also see three related cover-story articles: Ahmad Yahya, "Mazrui and I," Ali Mazrui, "Africa's Triple Heritage and I," and Sulayman Nyang, "The Scholar's Mansions," all in *Africa Events* 2, no. 7–8 (July–August, 1986): 32–43. Afrocentrists bitterly criticized Mazrui's "triple heritage" concept and made ad hominem attacks referring to his Arab-African ancestry, the Afrocentrists asserting that he was incapable of an African-centered analysis as he was either the victim of a confused identity or had a covert Arab agenda. The triple-heritage concept was attacked because it conveyed the false impression that Africa was a passive participant in world history and that alien societies and cultures had had a disproportionate impact on Africa. The Afrocentric perspective emphasizes the active role that Africa has played throughout history, influencing on other societies by disseminating its culture to the world. The Afrocentrists vehemently denied that there was any African heritage aside from the indigenous African one, and argued

that foreign cultures which were imposed upon Africans always met with re-sistance. John Henrik Clarke, of whom more will be said here, was the most prominent Afrocentrist leading the charge against Mazrui.

2. See the following sources: Philip D. Curtin's "Ayuba Suleiman Diallo of Bondu" and Ivor Wilks's two articles, "Salih Bilali of Massina" and "Abu Bakr Al-Saddiq of Timbuktu" in *Africa Remembered: Narratives by West Africans from the Era of the Slave Trade*, ed. Philip D. Curtin (Madison: University of Wisconsin Press, 1967), pp. 17–59, 145–69; Roger Bastide, *African Civilisations in the New World* (New York: Harper Torchbooks Publishers, 1971), pp. 104–5; Khalil Mahmud, Introduction to the second edition of H. M. Schieffelin, *The People of Africa* (Ibadan: Ibadan University Press, 1974), pp. v–xxiii; Harold Courlander, *A Treasury of Afro-American Folklore: The Oral Literature, Traditions, Recollections, Legends, Tales, Songs, Religious Beliefs, Customs, Sayings and Humor of Peoples of African Descent in the Americas* (New York: Crown Publishers, 1976), pp. 282–85, 288–90; Clyde-Ahmad Winters, "Roots and Islam in Slave America," *al-Ittihad* 13, no. 3 (October–November, 1976): 18–20; Clyde-Ahmad Winters, "Islam in Early North and South America, *al-Ittihad* 14, no. 3 (July–October, 1977): 57–67; Terry Alford, *A Prince among Slaves* (New York: Oxford University Press, 1977); Morroe Berger, "The Black Muslims," *Horizon* 6 (January, 1977): 49–59; Abdulhakim Muhammad, *Seven Muslim Slaves* [pamphlet] (Bronx, N.Y.: Bilalian Roots, 1979); Sulayman S. Nyang, "Islam in the United States: A Review of Sources," *Journal of the Institute of Muslim Minority Affairs* 3, no. 1 (1982): 189–98; Alan Austin, *African Muslims in Antebellum America: A Sourcebook* (New York: Garland Publishers, 1984); Alan Austin, "Islamic Identities in Africans in North America in the Days of Slavery, 1731–1865," *Islam et Sociétés au Sud du Sahara* 7 (Novembre, 1993): 206–19; Abdullah Hakim Quick, *Deeper Roots: Muslims in the Caribbean Before Columbus to the Present*, Occasional papers, no. 1, Association of Islamic Communities in the Caribbean, and Latin America (Nassau, Bahamas, 1990); Ronald A. T. Judy, *(Dis)Forming the American Canon: African-Arabic Slave Narratives and the Vernacular* (Minneapolis: University of Minnesota Press, 1993); Adib Rashad Islam, *Black Nationalism and Slavery: A Detailed History* (Beltsville, MD: Writers, Inc., 1995), pp. 30–100; see also n. 49.

3. W. E. B. DuBois, "Strivings of the Negro People," *Atlantic Monthly* 80 (August 1897): 194–95. The quotation gains more clarity and starkness if we substitute contemporary or "cutting edge" racial terms in the text for outmoded ones, i.e., substitute "African" for "Negro" and "African American" for "American Negro."

4. John H. Bracy, Jr., et al., eds., *Black Nationalism in America* (Indianapolis: Bobbs-Merrill, 1970), pp. xxv–xxvi.

5. See C. Eric Lincoln, *The Black Muslims in America* (Boston: Beacon Press, 1961), pp. 10–12. The following quotations are from Joseph R. Washington, "Negro Cults (in the United States)," Encyclopaedia Britannica, 15th ed. (1979), 12: 942–44. These quotations summarize the perceptions of many scholars concerning the origins of Islam among African Americans. "The main roots of Negro cults—Judaism, Islam, and Christianity—each have passed through a cult phase (an early stage of a religious movement), as did countless other groups in Western society that have failed to grow into a sect, denomination, universal church, or religion. Negro cults are, with few important exceptions, short-lived,

unstable, local, small in size, structureless, dominated by a charismatic leader, schism prone and mystically-oriented. . . ." The article goes on to state that after World War I, popular "race conscious leaders" were supplanted by a "talented tenth [sic?] or black bourgeoisie" creating a leadership "breach" among "the Negro masses." As a result: "[The Negro masses] were pressed by various forms of frustration, confusion, disillusionment and apathy. They clutched their only possessions: a primoridial race consciousness, religion, superstition, magic, rhythm, music, antiphonal singing, and improvisation. These floundering people, deprived both socially and economically, were forced to confront a leadership vacuum, which was filled by purveyors of voodoo (a religion of African origin), prophets, fortune-tellers, miracle workers, and such other personages who dealt with the aspirations of the Negro people. . . ."

6. Edward Wilmot Blyden, *Christianity, Islam and the Negro Race* (San Francisco: Julian Richardson, 1990 [1887]).

7. Tony Martin, *Race First: The Ideological and Organizational Struggles of Marcus Garvey and the Universal Negro Improvement Association* (Westport, CT: Greenwood Press, 1976), pp. 75–77.

8. Al-Islam: The Islamic Movement Journal, a publication of the Islamic Party of North America, carried the front-page headline: "Heretics Ruled Non-Muslim" on its Fall, 1974 issue (vol. 3, no. 1). An article on p. 6 of this issue states, "In an historic decision on September 7, 1974, the Senate and National Assembly of Pakistan unanimously passed a constitutional amendment that officially declared the Ahmadis (Qadianis) a non-Muslim minority community. The major clause of the amendment read: 'A person who does not believe in the absolute and unqualified finality of the Prophethood of Muhammad (peace be upon him) the last of the Prophets or claims to be a prophet in any sense of the word or any description whatsoever, after Muhammad (peace be upon him) or recognizes such a claimant as a prophet or a reformer, is not a Muslim for the purposes of the Constitution or law.'"

9. Three sources of information were consulted in regard to the origin of the Shriners: Aleppo Temple, *History of Aleppo Temple Ancient Arabic Order Nobles of the Mystic Shrine: Preceded by History of the Ancient Arabic Order and History of the Imperial Council Nobles of the Mystic Shrine for North America in Two Volumes* (Boston: Hall Publishing, 1916), 1:1–6; Charles W. Ferguson, *Fifty Million Brothers: A Panorama of American Lodges and Clubs* (New York: Farrar and Rinehart, 1937). pp. 234–36; and the Imperial Grand Council of the Ancient Arabic Order of Nobles of the Mystic Shrine, *The Secret Ritual of the Secret Work of the Ancient Arabic Order of Nobles of the Mystic Shrine* (New York: Masonic Supply Co., n.d.), pp. 5–8. According to the *History of the Aleppo Temple*, the Nobles of the Mystic Shrine trace the founding of the Order back to the "Kalif Alee, cousin-german and son-in-law of the Prophet Muhammad himself," who "conceived the idea of a superior court. This was in Mecca, and in the year of the Hegira 25 (A.D. 644). Strictly Arabian in its composition, this court was to deal out justice to violators of the law where the ordinary process would not reach, to break down corrupt influence, to form respect for and support of the law, to be an inquisition,—a vigilance committee, if you will, the founders of the unwritten Law" (p. 1). A long-winded, unsubstantiated "historical" narrative goes on to state that the triumphs of Islam in the areas of "establishing justice, and advancing the causes of learning and humanity" (p. 2) were all

attributable to this Mystic Shrine, that this secret order began to embrace Crusaders and other Christians as well as Jews. The narrative speaks of close relations with "the Bektash Order of Dervishes," splits between Egyptian and Arabian branches of the Shrine, establishment of the Shrine in Persia and Turkey, and periods of dormancy and revival. The modern revival begins in 1698 when the Shrine is introduced to Italy; in 1776 it is established in Bavaria where it is identified as being synonymous with Adam Weishaupt's infamous secret order, the Illuminati. Introduction of the order to the British and then the Americans soon followed. Here the narrative may be on more solid historical ground: "Credit for the introduction and spread of the order in the United States is due to the comedian and actor William J. Florence . . . and to Dr. Walter M. Fleming, 33, Sovereign Grand Inspector-General of the Ancient and Accepted Scottish Rite for the Northern Jurisdiction, who received the authority and instruction from Rizk Allah Hassoon Effendee. It was Dr. Fleming who was given complete jurisdiction by Hassoon, and it was Noble Florence who, having received the mysteries of the Order in the orient, brought them to this country" (p. 3).

In Ferguson's *Fifty Million Brothers* (chap. 16, "Allah Be Praised!: The Shriners"), the author states that "On a tour in 1870, William J. (Billy) Florence, American Comedian, made the acquaintance of Yusef Churi, and through him was presented to the Sultan, who at that time was head of the order in the East. The sultan was charmed by the geniality of the comedian, and he was incepted into the order at Cairo. Through Yusef Churi and Florence a translation of the ritual was made, first into French and then into English. Florence became cofounder in America with Dr. Walter M. Fleming. Those who brought the Shrine to North America required that the petitioners be either Knights Templar or Scottish Rite Masons only to insure a 'select class of men to compose its membership.' So while the Shrine is referred to variously as the 'playground of Masonry' and the 'golden rivet in the superstructure of Masonry,' it has no organic connection with the Ancient and Honorable Society" (pp. 234–35).

The Secret Ritual of the Secret Work of the Ancient Arabic Order of the Nobles of the Mystic Shrine states that "Wm. J. Florence, 33d deg., of New York City, while on a visit to Arabia was initiated in a temple of the Mystic Shrine in that country and the secret work of the order was brought by him to the United States in the Year 1871, and placed in the hands of Dr. Walter M. Fleming, 33d deg., Sovereign Grand inspector General of the Ancient and accepted Scottish Rite and eminent Commander of the Columbia Commandery, No. 1, Knights Templar of New York" (p. 5).

10. As to the origins of the Shrine among African Americans, Ferguson states in *Fifty Million Brothers* (chap. 13, "Blackface: The Lodges of the American Negro"), "One might think the Negro would be hard put to exceed in name and conception such a body as the Ancient Order of the Nobles of the Mystic Shrine for North America. Not at all. The Negroes assemble under the encircling banner of the Ancient Egyptian Arabic Order of the Nobles of the Mystic Shrine for North and South America. The Ancient Egyptian Arabic Order traces its apostolic succession as carefully as do the Negro Masons. It seems that Noble J. G. Jones and others received the mysteries from several members of the Shrine Council of Arabia when these members were visiting the Chicago World's Fair in 1893" (p. 189).

The Secret Ritual of the Secret Work of the Ancient Arabic Order of the Nobles of the Mystic Shrine states: "Noble John G. Jones, 33d deg., of Chicago, Ill., and who is the Sovereign Grand Commander of the United Supreme Council of the Southern and Western Masonic Jurisdiction, United States of America, after several years of correspondence, made application to the Grand Council of Arabia to be initiated into the work, and power and authority to institute Temples in the United States. His application, having been received and accepted, in June 1893, in the City of Chicago, Noble Rofelt Pasha, Deputy of the Grand Council of Arabia, and acting under the authority of the Grand Council of Arabia, and assisted with three other Nobles, with imposing ceremonies at the Masonic Hall, conferred the degree of Ancient Arabic Order of the Nobles of the Mystic Shrine upon him, and gave him the patent of power and authority to confer the degree of the Mystic Shrine, institute Temples and organize the Grand Imperial Councils, and be the Imperial Potentate of the Imperial Grand Council in the United States of America" (p. 7).

11. See the illustration of the grotto costume in Collier's *Encyclopedia* (1967 ed.) entry on "Fraternal Organizations," illustration, with caption "Organizations Allied to Freemasonry," is at the bottom of p. 339. Note that the fez, bow tie, and suit jacket are strikingly similar to the uniform adopted by the Honorable Elijah Muhammad. In subsequent editions of this encyclopedia, the entry on "Fraternal Organizations" is not accompanied by illustrations (Richard De Hann, "Fraternal Organizations" *Collier's Encyclopedia* 10: 334–43).

12. Levi H. Dowling, *The Aquarian Gospel of Jesus the Christ: The Philosophic and Practical Basis of the Religion of the Aquarian Age of the World: Transcribed from the Akashic Records by Levi* (Santa Monica, CA: DeVorss and Co., 1972); and Sri Ramatherio, ed., *Unto Thee I Grant* (San Jose, CA: The Supreme Grand Lodge of A.M.O.R.C., 1974). Though reputedly rare and only available to scholars in a few select libraries, in fact the paperback reprint of *The Holy Koran of the Moorish Science of America* has been available to the general public since the 1980s from small bookshops and street vendors in New York City—especially in Harlem and central Brooklyn—who specialize in selling collector's item reprints of early Nation of Islam literature. The central bookstore and street vendors of the then Brooklyn-based Ansaru Allah Nubian Islaamic Hebrew Community (now known as the Holy Tabernacle Ministries) also had copies of Drew Ali's *Koran* available for sale. As Yvonne Haddad and Jane Idleman Smith point out in *Mission to America: Five Islamic Sectarian Communities in North America* (Gainesville: University of Florida, 1993), p. 196, n. 54, many researchers have independently "discovered" the source of Drew Ali's *Holy Koran*. Here are my own independent "discoveries": chapter 1 and closing chapters 45–48 of Noble Drew Ali's *Holy Koran* appear to be original compositions of Drew Ali; chapters 2–19 are taken from *The Aquarian Gospel*; chapters 20–44 are taken from *Unto Thee I Grant*. These two spiritual books reputedly have strange origins and strange authors.

The Aquarian Gospel was allegedly revealed to Dowling when he was in a trance; the content of the scripture is concerned with the "hidden years" of Jesus Christ, i.e., the years before his public mission. The back inside cover of the first paperback edition (1972) of *The Aquarian Gospel* boasts that the cloth edition was then in its 45th printing and identifies the author, Levi Dowling (1844–1911), as "the son of a pioneer preacher among the Disciples of Christ in Ohio," a pastor at age eighteen, an Army Chaplain during the Civil War, "a graduate of two medical colleges" who practiced medicine for a number of years, and a lifelong student of world religions. In this latter capacity, Dowling became convinced of the existence of a domain of "superfine ethers" which were like "sensitized plates on which all history was recorded." Believing that he could solve the "the great mysteries of the heavens" by entering this etheric domain, Levi embarked upon forty years of study and meditation in order to reach the necessary state of spiritual consciousness. In this state, he purportedly entered the ethers and transcribed from the "akashic records" *The Aquarian Gospel.* The document allegedly is "a complete record of the 'lost' eighteen years" of Jesus Christ, "a period spent traveling and learning from the seers and wisemen in the temples and schools of Tibet, Egypt, India, Persia and Greece" (outer back cover).

One can only speculate on how widely *The Aquarian Gospel* was circulated, circa 1927, when Noble Drew Ali first published his *Holy Koran. The Aquarian Gospel* is now available for sale chiefly in "botanicas" or religious-article stores which specialize in the sale of candles, magic oils, powders and incantations to ward off evil spirits or bring back an estranged lover—or through mail-order houses which specialize in these aspects of the occult. Botanicas are located throughout African-American and Latino ghettoes and cater primarily to practitioners of New World variants of the Yoruba religion whose epicenter is Nigeria. These belief systems—taking peculiar forms and names, e.g., Santeria, Shango, Voudoun, Candomble, depending upon where in the Americas they first developed—are syncretistic blends of Yoruba and Christianity. Hence, alongside the African fetishes, one will find statues of saints (representing particular *orishas* or Yoruba gods) and strange "missing books" of the Bible such as the *Sixth and Seventh Books of Moses.* It is in this atmosphere that one will discover *The Aquarian Gospel.*

In the 1980s, the Ansaru Allah Nubian Islaamic Hebrew Community (for a description of this community, see Haddad and Smith, *Mission to America,* pp. 105–36) published a booklet entitled *Who Was Noble Drew Ali?* (Edition 109). This was in keeping with the tradition of claiming that the Ansaru Allah Community was the legitimate heir to all previous black nationalist Muslim sects. See Editions 100 and 101, *The Message of the Messenger is Right and Exact: The Book of the Laam,* parts I and II, which appropriate the legacy of Elijah Muhammad in an attempt to attract members of the Nation of Islam to the Ansar Community; and the very controversial Edition 195, *The Book of the Five Percenters,* which attempted to do the same for Five Percenters, but instead nearly precipitated a war between that group and the Ansaru Allah community. (For a description of the Five Percenters, see Yusuf Nuruddin, "The Five Percenters: A Teenage Nation of Gods and Earths," in Yvonne Haddad and Jane Idleman Smith, ed., *Muslim Communities in North America,* [Albany: SUNY Press, 1994], pp. 109–32.) In the booklet *Who Was Noble Drew Ali,* pp. 54–58, the Ansaru Allah community also reports about the plagiarism from *The Aquarian Gospel.*

The second source Drew Ali plagiarized for his *Koran* is even more esoteric than *The Aquarian Gospel* and very few researchers have discovered it (see Haddad and Smith, *Mission to America,* p. 196, n. 54; and Adib Rashad, *Islam, Black Nationalism and Slavery: A Detailed History* [Beltsville, MD: Writer's Inc. 1995], p. 168, n. 5). *Unto Thee I Grant* is a book of moral instruction and spiritual counsel published by the San Jose, California-based mail-order Rosicrucian fraternity, which calls itself the Ancient Mystical Order Rosae Crucis (AMORC, to distinguish itself from rival Rosicrucian organizations—all of which claim to be the sole and true heirs of a secret brotherhood whose origins stretch back to time immemorial).

Myths surround this book, just as they surround the Rosicrucian Fraternity. A preface appearing in the 1974 edition of *Unto Thee I Grant*, signed by "The Publishers" and dated May 20, 1925, is entitled "The Strange Story of this Book." It says that circa 1740–50, an unnamed British scholar and linguist commissioned by the Earl of Derby to gather works of historical interest, initiated contact with a Chinese prime minister, scholar, and linguist named Cao-Tsou who had translated some of the ancient manuscripts of the Tibetan lamas. The Englishman wanted to translate the most ancient Tibetan manuscript that Cao-Tsou had discovered, which had been in the possession of the lamas since 732, "which none of the lamas had been able to understand" (p. iv). Cao-Tsou translated the manuscript and discovered that it was a "complete system of mystical instruction, written in the language and the character of the ancient Gymnosophists or Brahmins" (p. iv). The preface goes on to say that the British scholar made his translation in 1749, that a limited number of copies were "distributed to the chief officers or executives of the several secret, mystic organizations then existing in Europe," and that "one of these copies has been preserved in the archives of the brotherhoods ever since and was used as the foundation for their teachings (p. v). According to the preface, scholars of the eighteenth century variously identified its author as Confucius, Lao-Tse, or the Brahmins, but "in light of modern research . . . there is every indication throughout the work . . . that most of it was written by Amenhotep IV, Pharaoh of Egypt, during the years 1360 to 1350 B.C. or thereafter, or by some of his successors in the great school of mysticism which he founded in Egypt" (pp. vii–viii). These ancient Egyptian teachings became available under the title *Unto Thee I Grant* when "the chief officer of this Brotherhood . . . finally granted official permission to the present publishers to reproduce the book in modern form" (p. vi).

That is the lore; here are some of the known facts. The book, regardless of its origins, was in its 29th edition as of 1974, and available at that time only through mail order to members of the Rosicrucian society. The imprint of that edition states that the first edition was published in 1925 by the Oriental Literature Syndicate of San Francisco, California (possibly a Rosicrucian body, if "The Publishers" of that 1925 edition were members of the "Brotherhood"). The San Jose-based Rosicrucian Press did not actually take over the copyright until the publication of the 18th edition in 1954. However, it is probable that the Rosicrucian Society recommended the book or made it available to their members at an earlier date, perhaps prior to 1927 when Drew Ali published his *Holy Koran*. According to H. Spencer Lewis, author of the AMORC publication, *Rosicrucian Questions and Answers: With Complete History of The Rosicrucian Order* (San Jose: AMORC, 1973), in 1916, branches of the Rosicrucian order "were established from coast to coast, and from Canada to Mexico. By the summer of 1917 there were so many branches of AMORC in existence and carrying on the work with such enthusiasm that a National Convention was called for one week in Pittsburgh, Penn. Here hundreds of delegates from the branches, and members of the order assembled to officially acknowledge the existence of the Order and to finally adopt a National Constitution" (p. 180). That Pittsburgh was a center of AMORC activity may be relevant, in light of the information supplied by Haddad and Smith (*Mission to America*, p. 87) that a Moorish Science Temple was established in Pittsburgh in 1925. I speculate that Drew Ali and the early African-American Muslim pioneers were probably not unlike many contemporary Muslim converts, including myself. As spiritual seekers, we were propelled by a wanderlust to travel a long and winding road through all sorts of secret societies and all sorts of arcane and occult literature before our spiritual search culminated in "taking *shahada*," or in Drew Ali's case, founding a sect. The Rosicrucian Order may have been one of the many "portals" through which Noble Drew Ali passed. According to H. Spencer Lewis (*Rosicrucian Questions and Answers*, p. 194), Rosicrucian correspondence courses were established shortly after the 1917 Pittsburgh Convention. Given a policy of mail-order recruitment and membership, Jim Crow would not have been a barrier preventing Drew Ali from joining AMORC or becoming acquainted with its literature.

13. Ivan van Sertima, *They Came before Columbus: The African Presence in Ancient America* (New York: Random House, 1976). The recently reprinted classic text on pre-Columbian African exploration of the Americas is Leo Weiner's *Africa and the Discovery of America* (Brooklyn: A & B Books, 1992 [1922]). See also Ivan van Sertima, ed., *African Presence in Early America* (New Brunswick: Transaction Books, 1987); Michael Bradley, *The Black Discovery of America* (Toronto: Personal Library, 1981) or the reprinted version, *Dawn Voyage: The Black African Discovery of America* (Brooklyn: A & B Books, 1992); R. A. Jairazbhoy, *Ramses III: Father of Ancient America* (London: Karnak House, 1992), and Alexander von Wuthenau, *Unexpected Faces in Ancient America: The Historical Testimony of Pre-Columbian Artists* (New York: Crown, 1975). For evidence of the plenitude and ethnic diversity of pre-Columbian explorers of the New World, see Barry Fell, *America B.C.: Ancient Settlers in the New World* (New York: Wallaby/Pocket Books, 1976); and Barry Fell, *Saga America* (New York: Times Books, 1983). For a debunker's point of view and accompanying bibliography, see Ronald Fritze, "Goodbye Columbus: The Pseudohistory of Who Discovered America," *Skeptic* 2, no. 4 (1994): 88–97.

14. I have seen some blown-up photographs of large Moorish Science gatherings, with the heads of those men purported to be Farrad and Elijah encircled, but these photos were not of convincing clarity. Other photos supposedly exist but I have not seen them.

15. The ethnic identity of W. D. Farrad (also known as W. D. Fard, Farrad Muhammad, Fard Muhammad, W. D. Muhammad, etc.) has been the subject of much speculation. See E. U. Essien-Udom, *Black Nationalism: A Search for an Identity in America* (1962), pp. 43–46 in the University of Chicago edition, and pp. 55–57 in the Dell/Laurel edition. See also C. Eric Lincoln, *The Black Muslims in America* (Boston: Beacon, 1961), pp. 10–12. My own speculations are not based on solid but circumstantial evidence. My question is a simple one: whose sociological profile would best fit the situation or circumstance of building an Islamic sect in a black community—a foreigner with a Muslim background or a foreigner with a non-Muslim background? The logical answer is obvious.

Solid evidence, initially, points in another direction. In *The Judas Factor: The Plot to Kill Malcolm X* (New York: Thunder's Mouth Press, 1992), Karl Evanzz provides FBI documentation which indicates that W. D. Farrad was born in Hawaii of a British father and New Zealander mother of dark-hued Polynesian Maori origin. This information was supplied to the FBI by Hazel Ford Osborne Evelsizer (nee Barton) who was W. D. Farrad's common-law wife in the late 1920s (see chap. 10, "Exposing Fard," pp. 131–146, esp. pp. 142–43).

The founder of another Islamic sect, Imam Isa (aka Dwight York, Malachi York, etc.) of the former Ansaru Allah Nubian Islamic Hebrew Community (now known as the Holy Tabernacle Ministries), sows seeds of doubt about this FBI information in several of his pamphlets and books. The Ansar literature, e.g., *The Message of the Messenger Is Right and Exact: The Book of Lamb 1* (Edition 100, Book 1 [1970])—this book opens from right to left and pages are unnumbered; see first question set numbered from 1–59; *Who Was Noble Drew Ali?* (Edition 109 [1980, rev. 1988]), pp. 98–102; *The Book of the Five Percenters* (Edition 195 [1991]), pp. 402–14, addresses the issue of Farrad's ethnic identity. The Ansar literature (with convincing photos provided in Editions 109 and 195) states that there were two men, one identified as Abdul Wali Farrad Muhammad, ethnically described as a Palestinian Arab and the second identified as Wallace Douglas (Dodd) Ford, "the Imposter" described as British and Polynesian.

According to the Ansar literature, Abdul-Wali Farrad Muhammad was once arrested and imprisoned, and the purported mug shots of this arrested man do not resemble the familiar photo of W. D. Farrad. This literature states that the imposter Wallace Douglas (Dodd) Ford replaced Abdul-Wali Farrad Muhammad, after the latter was murdered. Ansar literature is not a source for scholarly documentation, but the photos are enough to sow seeds of doubt and keep questions open for speculation and debate.

Elijah (Poole) Muhammad's identity has also been the subject of speculation and even wild rumors. The speculators point to the unusual "Asian-looking" facial features of Elijah Muhammad and, of course, the Nation of Islam's phrase, "Asiatic black man." One version of the rumor identified Elijah Muhammad as a Japanese spy, Major Takahashi. Another version identified him as the half-black, half-Japanese son of Major Takahashi. A Japanese Major Takahashi did exist, and he did have some influence on the Nation of Islam, though probably not to the extent of the wild rumors. Passing mention of Takahashi is made in C. Eric Lincoln's *Black Muslims in America*, pp. 16, 26; and in E. U. Essien-Udom's *Black Nationalism: A Search for an Identity in America*, p. 293, in the University of Chicago Press edition and p. 319 in the Dell/Laurel edition. A full account of the Japanese Major Takahashi and his impact on the Nation of Islam is reconstructed from "newspaper articles, FBI documents, military intelligence reports and court records" by the historian Ernest Allen, Jr., in his article "Satokata Takahashi and the Flowering of Black Nationalism," in *The Black Scholar* 24, no. 1 (Winter 1994): 23–46. Of related interest is Ernest Allen, Jr.'s, "Waiting for Tojo: The Pro-Japan Vigil of Black Missourians, 1932–1943," Gateway Heritage, Fall, 1994.

16. Hajji Talib Ahmad Dawud, a septugenarian bibliophile, personal friend, and mentor, and truly remarkable renaissance man who lists among his accomplishments that he was a jazz musician, martial artist, secret agent, and pioneer of the Ahmadiyya Muslim movement in America, lives in a Philadelphia row house amidst some ten thousand or more books. The Judson Hounds-Bey certificate is from the files of this enormous personal library. See Essien-Udom,

Black Nationalism, for more information on Hajj Talib Ahmad Dawud: pp. 313–17 and p. 280, n. 53 in the University of Chicago Press edition; pp. 338–342, pp. 415, n. 53, and 422, n. 30, in the Dell/Laurel edition. Also see Lincoln's Black Muslims in America, pp. 144, 170–71.

17. This quotation is taken from the fourth question and answer set of the Nation of Islam's Lost Found Muslim Lesson No. 1. This lesson is commonly referred to as "The 1 to 14," because it contains 14 questions and answers. The specific question and answer set, which is quoted below in full, is commonly known as "Number 4 in the 1 to 14."

4. Why did we run Yakub and his made devil from the root of civilization, over the hot desert, into the caves of West Asia, as they now call it Europe? What is the meaning of Eu and Rope? How long ago? What did the devil bring with him? What kind of life did he live? And how long before Musa came to teach the devil of their forgotten tricknology?

Ans.—Because they had started making trouble among the righteous people telling lies. They accused the righteous people causing them to fight and kill one another. Yacub was an original black man and was the father of the devil. He taught the devils to do this devilishment. The root of civilization is in Arabia at the Holy City, Mecca, which means where the wisdom and knowledge of the original man first started, when the planet was found. We ran the devils over the Arabian Desert. We took from them everything except the language and made him walk every step of the way. It was twenty-two hundred miles. He went savage and lived in the caves of Europe. Eu means hillsides and Rope is the rope to bind in. It was six thousand nineteen years ago. Musa came two thousand years later and taught him how to live a respectful life, how to build a home for himself and some of the tricknology that Yacub taught him, which was devilishment, telling lies, stealing and how to master the original man. Musa was a half original, a prophet, which was predicted by the twenty-three scientists in the year one, fifteen thousand nineteen years ago today.

With a few minor variations in the wording of text, such as "forgotten trick-knowledge" instead of "tricknology," the question and answer is the same in the "Five Percenter Lessons," although they will verbally "science out" or "break down" the meaning of the lesson so that it is a clarified, e.g., a sentence such as "Eu means hillside and Rope means rope to bind in" is somewhat cryptic or enigmatic without the proper "break down" or explanation: "Eu means the hillsides as Europe is a land full of mountains and Rope means the rope we used to bind the devils in the cave with."

As a minister for the Nation of Islam, Malcolm X made some extensive commentary on the above question and answer set. The speech which includes this commentary is recorded and available on a record album entitled *The Legend MALCOLM X: "Black Man's History"* (vol. 2, side two) on the Paul Winley Records label (LP 150 B). The date of the speech is not provided on the album. The speech, "Black Man's History," is also available in print in Benjamin Goodman, ed., *The End of White World Supremacy: Four Speeches by Malcolm X* (New York: Merlin House, 1971). In the introduction to this book, Goodman gives the date of this speech as December, 1962 (pp. 11–13).

In his commentary, Malcolm states that the casting of the devil out of Arabia was but another allegory comparable to the biblical allegory of Adam, the white man, being cast out of the Garden of Eden; both allegories refer to an actual historical event, the white man being cast out of the East and banished to the West. The white man was cast out of Paradise for causing disunity and starting confusion among the Original People, thereby "turning heaven into hell." According to the biblical legend, when Adam was cast out of the Garden, God placed an angel with a flaming sword at the East Gate of Eden, to prevent Adam's re-entry. Malcolm states that this angel was a metaphor for "the Turks who guarded the Straits of the Dardanelles," preventing Europeans from entering the Middle East. Malcolm also states that the rituals of the Masonic Order are reenactments of this historical event. When the white man was marched out of Arabia, he was stripped of everything except his language according to the "Lost-Found Lesson." Malcolm states that the Honorable Elijah Muhammad taught his followers that this meant that the white man was literally "stripped naked" as he was marched across the desert, and that a "lambskin apron" was draped around his loins to cover up his nakedness. He was also placed in chains or "cable-tows." The "lambskin apron" and the "cable-tow" are central elements in the Masonic ritual. In the higher orders of Masonry, e.g., the Shrine, once again this history is enacted, as Shriners are forced to cross "the hot burning sands of the desert."

18. In interviews and conversations, I have heard many Moors explain the mission of Noble Drew Ali with the succinct phrase "The Upliftment of Fallen Humanity." A famous illustration of Drew Ali pictures him stepping up on a shore labeled "Salvation," holding in his arms a woman, labeled "Humanity," whom he has rescued from drowning in an ocean, labeled "the Cares of the World." "Raising" or "uplifting" from "a dead level" is a well-known Masonic metaphor.

19. This chapter is excerpted from a longer work. There are many dimensions of conflicts which I am exploring in the longer work, including the conflicts between African-American Muslims and immigrant Muslims, particularly Arab and Pakistani immigrants, but increasingly Iranian immigrants as well. These racial and ethnic conflicts are exacerbated by class conflicts. For example, many Pakistani immigrants are professionals—medical doctors, engineers, accountants, pharmacists, etc., and have little in common with, say, the significant numbers of African-American Muslims who have converted to Islam while serving prison terms. Other tensions are fueled by the un-Islamic practices of Arab merchants who have monopolized the convenience-store trade in cities like New York. African-American Muslims complain that these merchants set up shop in ghetto communities and make a good living selling *haram* products such as beer and pork. I am exploring these racial, ethnic, and class conflicts in the American Islamic community with the same intensity that I have explored the religious and ideological conflicts between African-American Muslims and Afrocentrists.

20. "*The Last Poets* [are a] legendary ensemble of performing poets who emerged from the black cultural arts movement of the sixties as the undisputed masters of their craft.

Black pride, urban unrest and the search for both an African identity and a unique African American aesthetic spawned a number of notable black poets in the 60s, yet none of them touched such a raw nerve as *The Last Poets* did with their authentic anger, gripping passion and sharp insight about the oppressive conditions of ghetto life. Although their art form was born of the pangs of oppression, *The Last Poets* did not merely offer a dismal picture of stark social realism as many of today's rappers do. Indeed *The Last Poets* have been called the 'Grandfathers of Rap,' but their revolutionary message differed sharply from the nihilistic message contained in many (but not all) rap lyrics. *The Last Poets* offered a vision of nationhood, a vision of hope, a vision of new horizons and new possibilities towards which black people could aspire....

.... As relentless in their pursuit of artistic quality as they were in their opposition to oppression, *The Poets* continually experimented with new and different delivery styles and musical backgrounds including reggae, rap, and jazz. Each new recording was an adventure in the possibilities of creative expression with the spoken word.... (Yusuf Nuruddin, obituary for Suliaman El-Hadi, "An Internationally Renowned Poet and Performance Artist" October, 1995)

I should add to the statements above that the Last Poets were artistically, stylistically, and politically working in an entirely different genre from today's rappers. Theirs was truly revolutionary art—in the fullest sense of both words—not commercial doggerel. The name of the group itself was born of revolutionary inspiration. A South African poet, Little Wille Kgositile, provided this inspiration through a line in one of his poems about the struggle against apartheid. He warned that "these are the last days of the age of poems and essays," as the freedom struggle escalates, guns and rifles will replace poems and essays. In the context of American apartheid, the 1960s were a decade characterized by urban insurrections, which were merely "dress rehearsals for the things that are yet to come" according to the Last Poets. Their mission as poets was to wage war in the final stage of the ideological struggle—the war of words to win the minds and the hearts of the people—which would give birth to the armed struggle for liberation. For this reason, the Last Poets occupied a central place in the black cultural nationalist and black revolutionary movements of the late 1960s and early 1970s. They were as responsible as Stokely Carmichael, Huey P. Newton, H. Rap Brown, Amiri Baraka, or any other comparable figure for issuing a clarion call to revolution. Along with Gil Scott-Heron, another key recording poet, they helped to set a mood across black America of self-determination and uncompromising resistance to oppression. Theirs was a consciousness-raising message, with sharp and bitter insights into the system of racism in America. Young black people on college campuses as well as in ghetto tenements listened intently to this intelligent and artistic yet provocative, angry, and fiery message. No one was the same after hearing it. As is the case with all great art, their earliest compositions, now more than twenty-five years old, are as relevant today as they were in the late 1960s and early 1970s. Unfortunately, one of the factors in this equation is that racial conditions have not fundamentally changed.

The Last Poets have been making recordings consistently since 1969. These recordings, some originally issued as albums but now available on compact discs and tapes, include *The Last Poets* (1969), *This is Madness!* (1971), *Chastisement* (1972), *At Last* (1974), *Delights of the Garden* (1976), *O My People* (1984), *Freedom Express* (1988), and *Scatterap/Home* (1994). Selected poems by the Last Poets are also available in print, in a volume entitled *Vibes from the Scribes* (London: Pluto Press, 1985). The group originally consisted of poets Alafia Pudim (now known as Jalaluddin Mansur Nuriddin), Umar bin Hassen, and Abiodun

Oyewole and the percussionist Nilija. Tension existed within the group because Pudim and bin Hassen were Muslim, while Oyewole and Nilija were practitioners of Yoruba. The ensemble changed personnel over the years 1969–74, and dramatic changes in ideology were reflected in a 1974 album significantly given the title At Last, written in stylized calligraphy to resemble or convey the impression of Arabic script. In the album-cover photographs, Pudim, now Nuruddin, Suliaman El-Hadi, and Umar bin Hassen are all visibly Muslim because of their attire, their kufis and the *sajda* (prostration) marks on their foreheads. The obvious message in the title is "at last the Last Poets are all Muslim." Their fiery message, which was nothing less than a clarion call to black revolution, was broadened to a call for third world revolution, Islamic revolution, and spiritual transformation. Captivating audiences with their art form, they called the disenfranchised to Islam in a manner similar to the way reggae artist Bob Marley called disaffected people to the Rastafarian ideology. Bin Hassen, however, left the group shortly after the release of the *At Last* album, and Jaluddin Nuriddin and Suliaman El-Hadi were the mainstays of the group from 1974 until October of 1995 when Shaykh Suliaman El-Hadi died suddenly of a heart attack at age 59. Other Muslim musicians rounded out the group, most notably the percussionist Abu Mustapha. Former members of the group—including Oyewole and bin Hassen, and poets Felipe Luciano, Gylan Kain, and David Nelson who left the group before the first professional recording in 1969—have throughout the years attempted to perform and record under the name the Last Poets or the Original Last Poets. Some of these claims to the copyright are now being contested in court.

El-Hadi's poem "In Search of Knowledge" (At Last, 1973) was a major influence in my 1974 conversion to Islam; I met the Last Poets in 1977, beginning a friendship—and a collaboration—that became closer throughout the years. I am currently working with Jalaluddin Nuriddin and the El-Hadi family on a definitive biography of The Last Poets, a project initiated several years ago, and compiling and editing for publication thematic collections of El-Hadi's works, a project initiated shortly before Shaykh Suliaman's death.

21. Cointelpro was the FBI's acronym for its counterintelligence program. See Nelson Blackstock, *Cointelpro: The FBI's Secret War on Political Freedom* (New York: Vintage Books, 1976); Ward Churchill and Jim Vander Wall, *Agents of Repression: The FBI's Secret Wars against the Black Panther Party and the American Indian Movement* (Boston: South End Press, 1990), p. xii: "COINTEL PROs: FBI domestic Counterintelligence Programs designed to destroy individuals and organizations the FBI considers to be politically objectionable. Tactics included all manner of official lying and media disinformation, systematically leveling false charges against those targeted, manufacturing evidence to obtain their convictions, withholding evidence which might exonerate them, and occasionally assassinating 'key leaders.' The FBI says COINTELPRO ended in 1971, but all reasonable interpretations of FBI performance indicate it continues today, albeit under other code names."

See also Karl Evanzz, *The Judas Factor: The Plot to Kill Malcolm X* (New York: Thunder's Mouth Press, 1992); David J. Garrow, *The FBI and Martin Luther King, Jr.* (New York: Penguin Books, 1983); Kenneth O'Reilly, *Black Americans: The FBI Files* (New York: Carroll and Graf, 1994); Kenneth O'Reilly, *Racial Matters: The FBI's Secret File on Black America, 1960–1972* (New York: The Free Press,

1991); and Iris L. Washington, "The FBI Plot Against Black Leaders," *Essence* 9, no. 6 (October, 1978): 70–73, esp. p. 70:

> At the height of the civil rights and black power movements of the sixties the Federal Bureau of Investigation instituted a counterintelligence programmed at destroying the effectiveness of Black leaders and organizations that they termed Black nationalist hate groups. The bureau was reacting to what they believed were threats to national security. Fearful after one of the hottest summers of racial disturbance in United States history, the bureau ordered, on August 25, 1967, immediate and coordinated use of counterintelligence tactics against key Black leaders and groups. . . .

> The objectives of the plot against black leadership were spelled out in the August memo from the FBI director J. Edgar Hoover and in a subsequent one dated February 29, 1968; to expose, disrupt, misdirect, discredit or otherwise neutralize such groups and their leadership, spokesmen, members and supporters; counter their propensity for violence; frustrate efforts to consolidate their forces or to recruit new or youthful adherents; exploit conflicts within and between groups; use news media contacts to ridicule and otherwise discredit groups; prevent groups from spreading their philosophy publicly, and gather information on the backgrounds of group leaders for use against them. (p. 70)

The existence of Cointelpro was widely known and widely discussed in political activist circles in the African-American community. The plot of a popular black novel, John A. William's *The Man Who Cried I Am* (New York: Signet, 1967), which was published the same year that Cointelpro was initiated, exposes in an almost prescient manner a conspiracy coordinated by several government agencies (among them the FBI, CIA, National Security Agency) to destroy black leaders and organizations. This fictional conspiracy, which also detailed provisions for holding masses of African Americans in detention (concentration) camps in the event of continuing urban insurrections, was code-named the "King Alfred Plan" (pp. 307–12). The popularity of the novel and the discussion and research that it engendered made African-American activists acutely aware of Cointelpro and related repressive governmental policies and legislation.

22. The essence of the tradition is often paraphrased as, "Do not sever bonds of kinship." Jubair bin Mut'im said that he heard the Prophet (pbuh) saying: "The person who severs the bond of kinship will not enter Paradise." Bukhari and Muslim transmitted it (Sahih al-Bukhari, *The Book of Al-Adab* (good manners), vol. 8, bk. 72, chap. 11); the sin of the person who severs the bond of kinship (no. 13, p. 11). Variations of the same hadith in Sahih Muslim, *Kitab al-Birr wa'l-Salat-i wa'l-Adab* (Book of Virtue, Good Manners and Joining of the Ties of Relationship), vol. 4, bk. 30, chap. 1056; "Joining the Tie of Relationship and Prohibition to Break It," nos. 6199 and 6200, p. 1359.

Narrated Abu Huraira: "I heard Allah's Apostle (pbuh) saying, 'Whoever is pleased that he be granted more wealth and that his lease of life be prolonged, then he should keep good relations with his kith and kin.' Bukhari transmitted it." (Sahih al-Bukhari, ibid., vol. 8, bk. 72, chap. 12, no. 14, p. 11); Anas bin Malik, Bukhari and Muslim transmitted it (Sahih al-Bukhari, vol. 8, bk. 72, chap. 12, no. 15, p. 12; Sahih Muslim, vol. 4, bk. 30, chap. 1056, no. 6202 and no. 6203, pp. 1359 and 1360).

See also Qur'an 47:22–23 and related hadith: Sahih Bukhari, vol. 8, bk. 72, chap. 9, no. 11, pp. 9–10; chap. 10, no. 12, p. 10); chap. 13, no. 16, no. 17, no. 18, pp. 12–14; chap. 14, no. 19, p. 14; and chap. 15, no. 20, p. 15; Sahih Muslim, vol. 4, bk 30, chap. 1056, no. 6197 and no. 6198; cf. Muhammad Muhsin Khan, *The Translation of the Meanings of Sahih al-Bukhari* (Arabic-English, vol. 8) (Ankara: Hilal Yayinlari/ Crescent Publishing House, 1976); Abdul Hamid Siddiqi, trans., *Sahih Muslim: Being Traditions of the Sayings and Doings of the Prophet Muhammad as Narrated by his Companions and Compiled Under the Title "al-Jami'-us-Sahih" by Imam Muslim* (New Delhi: Kitab Bhavan, 1978).

23. Titles cited in the bibliographic essay are Salim Abdul-Khaliq, *The Untold Story of Blacks in Islam* (Hampton, VA: U.B.& U.S. Communication Systems, 1994); Mohammed Abu-Bakr, *Islam's Black Legacy: Some Leading Figures* (Denver: Purple Dawn Books, Inc., 1993); Terry Alford, *A Prince among Slaves* (New York: Oxford University Press, 1977); Shaharazad Ali, *The Blackman's Guide to Understanding the Blackwoman* (Philadelphia: Civilized Publications, 1989); Ayi Kwei Armah, *Two Thousand Seasons* (Chicago: Third World Press, 1987 [1979]); Molefi Asante, *Afrocentricity: The Theory of Social Change* (Buffalo, NY: Amulefi Publishing Co., 1980); Molefi Asante, *Kemit, Afrocentricity and Knowledge* (Trenton, NJ: Africa World Press, 1990); Alan Austin, *African Muslims in Antebellum America: A Sourcebook* (New York: Garland Publishers, 1984); Steven Barboza, *American Jihad: Islam After Malcolm X* (New York: Doubleday, 1994); Yosef ben Jochannan, *African Origins of the Major Western Religions* (New York: Alkebu-lan Books, 1973); Rafiq Bilal and Thomas Goodwin, *Egyptian Sacred Science in Islam* (San Francisco: Bennu Publishers, 1987); Eward Wilmont Blyden, *Christianity, Islam and the African Race* (original title: *Christianity, Islam and the Negro Race)* (San Francisco: First African Arabian Press, 1992 [1887]); John Henrik Clarke, *Africans at the Crossroads: Notes for an African Revolution* (Trenton, NJ: Africa World Press, 1991); Maryse Conde, *Segu* (New York: Viking/Penguin, 1987); Maryse Conde, *Children of Segu* (New York: Viking/Penguin, 1989); Agadem Lumumba Diara, *Islam and Pan-Africanism* (Detroit: Agascha Productions, 1973); Cheikh Anta Diop, *Civilization or Barbarism An Authentic Anthropology* (Brooklyn: Lawrence Hill Books, 1991); Mustafa El-Amin *Afrocentricity, Malcolm X, and Al-Islam* (Newark: El-Amin Productions, 1993); Mustafa El-Amin, *Al-Islam, Christianity and Freemasonry* (Jersey City, NJ: New Mind Productions, 1985); Mustafa El-Amin, *Freemasonry, Ancient Egypt and Islamic Destiny* (Jersey City, NJ: New Mind Productions, 1988); Khalid Abdul-Fattah Griggs, *Vision: Journal of the Institute of Islamic Involvement* (Winston-Salem, N.C.) 1980; Yvonne Haddad and Jane Smith, *Mission to America: Five Islamic Sectarian Communities in North America* (Gainesville: University Press of Florida, 1993); Yvonne Haddad and Jane Smith, ed., *Muslim Communities in North America* (Albany, NY: SUNY Press, 1994); George G. M. James, *Stolen Legacy* (San Francisco: Julian Richardson Associates, 1976 [1954]); Maulana Karenga, *Introduction to Black Studies* (Los Angeles: Kawaida Publications, 1982); Maulana Karenga, *Selections from the Husia: Sacred Wisdom of Ancient Egypt* (Los Angeles: Kawaida Pulications, 1984); K. Kazi-Ferrouillet, "Afrocentricity, Islam and El Hajj Malik Shabazz," *The Black Collegian*, January–February, 1993; K. Khalif Khalifah, ed., *The National Newport News and Commentator* (Newport News, VA: U.B. & U.S. Communications Systems); K. Khalif Khalifah, *Your Black Books Guide* (Newport News, VA: U.B. &

U.S. Communications Systems); Haki R. Madhubuti, *Enemies: The Clash of Races* (Chicago: Third World Press, 1978); Shawna Maglangbayan, *Garvey, Lumumba, Malcolm: Black Nationalist Separatists* (Chicago: Third World Press, 1972); Ali Mazrui, *The Africans: A Triple Heritage* (Boston: Little, Brown, 1986); Amina Beverly McCloud, *African American Islam* (New York: Routledge, 1995); Ameen Yasir Mohammed, *Afrocentricity, Minus Al-Islam, Cheats . . . : Exposing the Conspiracy to Rob African Americans of Their Most Precious Heritage* (Los Angles: Dawahvision, 1993); Abdulhakim Muhammad, *Seven Muslim Slaves* [pamphlet] (Bronx, NY: Bilalian Roots, 1979); Sulayman S. Nyang, *Islam, Christianity, and African Identity* (Brattleboro, VT: Amana Books, 1990); Quick, *Deeper Roots* (cited above); Adib Rashad, *History of Islam and Black Nationalism in Americas* (Beltsville, MD: Writers, Inc., 1984); Adib Rashad, *Islam, Black Nationalism and Slavery: A Detailed History* (Beltsville, MD: Writers, Inc., 1995); Ishmael Reed, *Mumbo Jumbo* (New York: Doubleday, 1972); J. A. Rogers, *World's Great Men of Color*, vols. 1–2 (New York: Collier Books, 1972 [1946]); Talib Salih, Season of Migration to the North (New York: Michael Kesend Publishers, 1989 [1969]); Ivan van Sertima, *The Golden Age of the Moors* (New Brunswick, NJ: Transaction Books, 1992); Chancellor Williams, *The Destruction of Black Civilization: Great Issues of a Race from 4500 b.c. to 2000 a.d.* (Chicago: Third World Press, 1987 [1971]); Imam A. S. Mahdi Ibn-Khalid Zayid, *Confronting America's Black-White Dilemma: The Admiral Family's Agenda and Strategy for American-American Political Autonomy* (New York: New Horizon Communications, 1992).

Films cited in the bibliographic essay: Ousmane Sembene, dir., *Ceddo* (1978, in Wolof with English subtitles), 120 minutes, 16mm/color. Made in Nigeria by Senegalese company, Dakkar Films; distributed in U. S. by New Yorker Films. Julie Dash, dir. *Daughters of the Dust* (1992), 113 minutes color. Made by American Playhouse Presentations in association with Geechee Girl Productions; distributed by Kino International Films.

24. Asante is widely published, but a trio of his works constitutes a sort of "Afrocentric canon": his self-published political manifesto, *Afrocentricity: The Theory of Social Change* (Buffalo, NY: Amulefi Publishing Co., 1980), and two scholarly works: *The Afrocentric Ideal* (Philadelphia: Temple University Press, 1987) and *Kemet, Afrocentricity and Knowledge* (Trenton, NJ: Africa World Press, Inc., 1990). In an article entitled "The Black Studies War: Multicuturalism versus Afrocentricity," *Village Voice* 40, no. 3 (January 17, 1995): 23–29, the author Greg Thomas quotes Molefi Asante as saying: "The only determination of who's Afrocentric or not is the definition of Afrocentricity—which I developed. It's kind of foolish to say, for example, that one is Marxist and yet does not believe in the principles established by Marx. Or that one is a deconstructionist and doesn't believe in the principles of Derrida. How can one say they are an Afrocentrist if one does not accept the fundamental basis of Afrocentricity as laid out in my works? That would be a contradiction in terms" (p. 29).

Asante's claims to being the creator of, sole authority on, and exclusive arbiter of what is or is not authentic Afrocentrism are widely disputed. He has been roundly criticized by his peers, especially John Henrik Clarke. Clarke's criticism can be summarized as follows: While the formalization of the concept and theory may have been Asante's contribution, the world view and the historical research which undergirds the world view were the result of the collective efforts of dozens of scholars working over decades. I am sharply inclined to agree with Dr. Clarke on this point. Furthermore, I would add that the modern origins (not the aged precursors) of Afrocentricity are rooted in (1) the cultural nationalist politics of the 1960s and (2) the related struggle to establish black studies as an academic discipline.

The clearest definition of Afrocentry, ironically, is not necessarily found in any of Asante's texts. In The Afrocentric Ideal, Asante states that his work "has increasingly constituted a radical critique of the Eurocentric ideology which masquerades as a universal view...." He then defines Afrocentricity: "The crystallization of this critical perspective I have named *Afrocentricity*, which means, literally, placing African ideals at the center of any analysis that involves African culture and behavior" (p. 6). In a footnote he adds: "To be Afrocentric is to place Africans and the interest of Africa at the center of our approach to problem solving" (p. 198, n. 3). One of Asante's colleagues at Temple, Abu Shardow Abarry, an associate professor of African American studies, offers a much more robust definition of Afrocentricity: "This concept as articulated by its main proponents—Diop, Asante, Karenga, Clarke, Carruthers, Keto and others—holds that any meaningful and authentic study of peoples of African descent must begin and proceed with Africa as the center, not periphery; as subject not object. Complex and multidisciplinary, the concept embodies a humanistic philosophy, a scholarly methodology, and a model of practical action. The main objective of its creators, however, is to liberate the research and the study of African peoples from the hegemony of Eurocentric scholarship, whose concepts, history, and traditions have been the absolute yardstick against which all other cultures are evaluated" (Abu Shardow Abarry, "Afrocentricity," *Journal of Black Studies* [December 1990], pp. 123–25). C. Tsehloane Keto, another of Asante's colleagues at Temple, consistently uses the term "African-centered" rather than "Afrocentric." See C. Tsehloane Keto's *The African-Centered Perspective of History* (Blackwood, NJ: K and A Associates, 1988). The terms Afrocentric and African-centered are often used interchangeably. However, in the lexicon of a skilled academician, African-centered has a different nuance or connotation from Afrocentric. It is a subtle put-down of Molefi Asante's claim to be the ultimate authority on Afrocentricity. In this context, African-centered means not dogmatically tied to Asante's theories and definitions.

25. Asante, *Afrocentricity: The Theory of Social Change*, p. 5: the text begins on page 4; the attack on Islam starts immediately (pp. 5–9). An attack on black Hebrew Israelites immediately follows on pp. 10–11.

26. Dr. John Henrik Clarke is professor emeritus of the Black and Puerto Rican Studies Department of Hunter College (CUNY) and a prolific scholar who is still writing though he is an octogenarian and blind; the infamous Dr. Leonard Jeffries was, until recently, chair of the Black Studies Department at the City College of New York (CUNY); he remains a faculty member there. Dr. Yosef ben Jochannan, a civil engineer by training who became an expert on the engineering and architectural feats of ancient Egypt and an expert on the history of the religious/philosophical systems which gave rise to those monuments, was a faculty member in the Department of History at Marymount College, a visiting professor in the Africana Studies Department at Cornell University, and an adjunct professor of history at several other colleges. Based upon his prodigious knowledge of Egyptology, he is now reputedly a visiting faculty

member or research associate at al-Azhar University in Cairo, but I cannot confirm this. [I use the word "Egyptology" for convenience; the Afrocentrists abhor the term, preferring instead Kemetic Studies, Nile Valley Civilization Studies, or the Study of Classical African Civilizations.] The three professors are Harlem-based in this sense: Dr. Yosef ben Jochannan and Dr. John Henrik Clarke live in Harlem; Dr. Jeffries teaches at a college located in Harlem. Commendably, they pooled their talents and with a cadre of over a dozen like-minded faculty (see following note), drawn from both a local and national base, and with administrators Bill Jones and Sister Khepra, they created the First World Alliance, an alternative educational institution in Harlem—a weekly lecture forum which meets on Saturday afternoons in the large auditorium of a Harlem church. At a rough estimate it holds about 250 people, and there were often standing-room-only crowds. Hence the institution (to my knowledge the classes have been meeting regularly since at least 1980 and possibly earlier, so it certainly is an institution) can be characterized as an "open university" or "university without walls." Jeffries has coined the term "communiversity"—community university—for this institution and others like it. I am not suggesting that students are able to pursue degrees through the First World Alliance, but there is a large and credentialed faculty pool and a student body numbering in the hundreds, thus the basis for building an accredited degree-granting institution exists. The name, First World Alliance, was at once a rejection of the term 'third world' for the economically underdeveloped sector of humanity who happened to be people of color, and a confirmation that culturally and historically, the first significant social developments in the world were the ancient African Nilotic civilizations.

The existence of independent institutions or organizations devoted to the study of African and African-American history is not a new phenomenon. In 1934, Dr. John Henrik Clarke joined the Harlem History Club (which in 1938 was renamed, ironically, the Blyden Society, after Edward Wilmot Blyden whom I cite in this text as one of the early pan-Africanist proponents of Islam). The instructor/head of the Harlem History Club/Blyden Society was Willis N. Huggins, a public high school history teacher, a position of some distinction for a black man sixty years ago. The club was a small circle of young bibliophiles and intellectuals, and it included some African foreign students; meetings were held at the local YMCA. Many of Huggins's students in the Harlem History Club went on to become luminaries. Between 1934–1940, in Huggins's class, the future historians John G. Jackson, J. A. Rogers, and John Henrik Clarke and the future African heads of state Nandi Azikwe of Nigeria and Kwame Nkrumah of Ghana all rubbed shoulders with one another. See John Henrik Clarke, "The Harlem History Club: My First University," the original draft, which I am citing from, has been reprinted in several publications including *The New American* and *The Black Collegian*, and Barbara Adams's biography, *Clark: The Early Years* (Hampton: UB & US Communications Systems, 1992).

27. At the World Festival of Arts, held in Dakar, Senegal, in 1966, Cheik Anta Diop (1923–86) and W. E. B. DuBois were honored as the writers "who had exerted the greatest influence on African people in the 20th century." See John Henrik Clarke, "Cheik Anta Diop and the New Concept of African History," in Ivan van Sertima, ed., *Great African Thinkers*, vol. 1: *Cheik Anta Diop* (New Brunswick, NJ: Transaction Books, 1986), p. 113. Yet the world knows who DuBois is, while few people outside of the field of African Studies recognize

the name of Diop. This is largely because Diop's major contribution to scholarship, the proof that the classical civilization which flourished in Ancient Kemet (Egypt) was a distinctly black African civilization, is still held to be controversial, untenable, preposterous, or nonsensical by mainstream Eurocentric scholars. Diop, born and raised in Senegal and educated in Paris, was a true polymath—a historian, physicist, and linguist—and he applied all of these skills to his groundbreaking research in Egyptology. For a detailed discussion of this, see Ivan van Sertima's introduction, "Death Shall Not Find Us Thinking That We Die," in his edited volume *Great African Thinkers*, 1:8–9. Diop was the author of several works, but the two most influential have been translated into English as *The African Origin of Civilization: Myth or Reality* (Westport, CN: Lawrence Hill, 1974) and *Civilization or Barbarism: An Authentic Anthropology* (Brooklyn, NY: Lawrence Hill Books, 1991). The collection of articles in Ivan van Sertima's edited work is the most comprehensive biography of this neglected towering genius.

George G. M. James (d. ca. 1955) is another iconoclast. His classic work, *Stolen Legacy* (San Francisco: Julian Richardson Associates, 1976 [1954]), with its front cover proclamation, "The Greeks were not the authors of Greek Philosophy, but the people of North Africa, commonly called the Egyptians," has been well known in certain circles of the African-American community for decades. It has recently gained the attention of Mary Lefkowitz who lambasts James's *Stolen Legacy*, along with Diop's *African Origins of Civilization*, and the works of Martin Bernal, Yosef ben Jochannan, and John G. Jackson in "Not Out of Africa: The Origins of Greece and the Illusions of Afrocentrists," *The New Republic*, February 10, 1992, pp. 29–36. Lefkowitz turns her full attention to James in "In Stolen Legacy (or Mythical History?): Did The Greeks Steal Philosophy From the Egyptians," *Skeptic* 2, no. 4 (1994): 98–103. The jury is still out on the James vs. Lefkowitz debate, because Mary Lefkowitz's arguments have come under sharp scrutiny and harsh criticism in a manuscript for publication that I have recently reviewed. Coincidently, as I make final revisions in this chapter, I am listening to this same debate raging on radio. Martin Bernal, the author of *Black Athena: The Afroasiatic Roots of Classical Civilization*, is making a strong defense of George G. M. James in a debate between Bernal and Lefkowitz aired on Utrice Leid's show *Talkbalk* on WBAI (New York). This January 1996 debate is centered on the release of Lefkowitz's new book, *Not Out of Africa: How Afrocentrism Became an Excuse to Teach Myth as History* (New York: Basic Books, 1996).

The late Chancellor Williams is also the author of a classic work in the Afrocentric canon, *The Destruction of Black Civilization: Great Issue of a Race from 4000 B.C. to 2000 A.D.*(Chicago: Third World Press, 1987 [1971]). Williams, a historian, was very good at reconstructing early African Nile Valley history. As a historian, however, he has a very ahistorical outlook on racism—which is viewed by most historians as a modern ideology and system of power relations initially developed by Westerners as a rationale for the African slave trade. Instead, Williams sees racism as endemic to the entire scope of human history. Thus black/non-black relations in the pre-modern world are viewed inaccurately through the lens of the modern world. Consequently, the vital lesson of history which he wishes to impart is essentially xenophobic: that all non-black peoples have always been the enemies of the African race and that none are to be trusted. In actuality, in the ancient world, culture and religion played a more central role than race in defining human antagonisms. Certainly, Africa was invaded by Asians in antiquity and Africans were enslaved by Arabs in the age of Islam, and no one should downplay the historical significance of these clashes of empire, culture, and religion. To suggest, however, that these conflicts were based on the same type of racial antagonisms that permeates the modern world is, in my estimation at least, an incorrect reading of history.

28. For a white neo-conservative reaction to black talk radio, see James Traub, "A Counter-Reality Grows in Harlem: Tuning in to the Gary Byrd Show," *Harper's Magazine*, August, 1991. Robin Pogrebin's "The Buzz on Black Radio," *New York Times*, January 28, 1996, section 13, p. 13, is a much shorter article written in the same vein.

The "cohorts" included local scholars such as Professor James Smalls, an administrator based at City College, who functioned as a "sidekick," i.e., assistant and understudy, to Dr. Leonard Jeffries; Dr. Rosalind Jeffries, an art historian and the wife of Leonard Jeffries; Dr. Edward Scobie, a member of the Department of Black Studies at City College and author of *Black Britannia: A History of Blacks in Brooklyn* (Chicago: Johnson Publications, 1972); the late Dr. Amos Wilson, author of *The Developmental Psychology of the Black Child* (New York: Africana Research Publications, 1978), *Black on Black Violence: The Psychodynamics of Black Self-Annihilation in Service of White Domination* (New York: Afrikan World InfoSystems, 1990), and *The Falsification of Afrikan Consciousness: Eurocentric History, Psychiatry and the Politics of White Supremacy* (New York: Afrikan World InfoSystems, 1993); Dr. Marimba Ani (Donna Richards), a protégé of Dr. John Henrik Clarke, a professor of Africana Studies at Hunter College and author of *Yurugu: An African-Centered Critique of European Cultural Thought and Behavior* (Trenton: Africa World Press, 1994); Dr. Adelaide Sanford, a member of the Board of Regents of the New York State Department of Education and an outspoken advocate of multiculturalism in the schools; and Dr. Charsee McIntyre, Professor Emerita of Humanities at SUNY at Old Westbury and the author of *Criminalizing a Race: Free Blacks during Slavery* (Queens, NY: Kayode, 1993). The national base included scholars such as Dr. Jacob Carruthers, a founder of ASCAC (Association for the Study of Classical African Civilizations), professor of inner-city studies and political science at Northeastern Illinois University and author of *Essays in Ancient Egyptian Studies* (Los Angeles: Sankore Press, 1989) and *African or American: A Question of Intellectual Allegiance* (Chicago: Kemetic Institute, 1994); Dr. Asa Hilliard, Fuller E. Callaway Professor of Urban Education at Georgia State University and author of *The Maroon Within Us: Selected Essays on African American Community Socialization* (Baltimore: Black Classics Press, 1995); Dr. Wade Nobles, author of *African Psychology: Toward Its Reclamation, Reascension and Revitalization* (Oakland: Black Family Institute, 1986); Dr. Oba T. Shaka, who was a professor of black studies at San Francisco State University and is the author of the *Art of Leadership*, 2 vols. (Richmond, CA: Pan Afrikan Publications, 1990); Dr. Kobi Kambon (Joseph Baldwin), professor of psychology at Florida A & M University and author of *The African Personality in America: An African Centered Framework* (Tallahassee: Nubian Nation Publications, 1992), and Dr. Tony Martin, professor of history at Wellesley College and author of *Race First: The Ideological and Organizational Struggles of Marcus Garvey and the Universal Negro Improve-*

ment Association (Westport, CT: Greenwood Press, 1976), and *The Jewish On-slaught: Dispatches from the Wellesley Battlefront* (Dover, MA: The Majority Press, 1993). This is a representative rather than exhaustive list in respect to both the individuals included and their publications. The network of Afrocentric scholars is comparatively large, well organized, credentialed, well positioned in academia, and productive in comparison to the network of African American Muslim scholars. Their tendency to publish with small presses should not be interpreted as a vanity-press phenomenon but as an economic empowerment initiative, an endeavor to build black-owned publishing businesses. The schol-ars listed above did not necessarily engage in a vilification campaign against Islam, but most advocated the philosophy embodied in the African term *sankofa*, the idea that people of African descent must return to the most ancient source of their culture (i.e., ancient Egyptian, Kemetic, or Nile Valley culture) in order to make progress.

29. Negritude initially was a literary movement among Caribbean and West African francophone writers who celebrated the black aesthetic. It was partially influenced by and comparable to the Harlem Renaissance. The pioneering fig-ures of the Negritude movement were the Martinique poet, Aime Cesaire, and the Senegalese poet and statesman, Leopold Senghor. Katherine Kemi Bandole in *The Afrocentric Guide to Selected Black Studies Terms and Concepts* (Long Beach, NY: Whittier Publications, 1995) ranks the Guianese writer Leon Damas alongside Cesaire and Senghor and links the Negritude movement to the jour-nal, *Presence Africaine*, which was launched in Paris in 1947. Negritude, how-ever, had a stronger voice in a shorter-lived publication *L'Etudiant Noir* launched in 1934 (see Senghor's "Preface Letter" and Benneta Jules-Rosette, "Conjugat-ing Cultural Realities: Presence Africaine," in Y. Y. Mudimbe's *The Surrepti-tious Speech: Presence Africaine and the Politics of Otherness 1947–1987* (Chicago: University of Chicago Press, 1992). Janheinz Jahn, in *Neo-African Literature: A History of Black Writing* (New York: Grove Press, 1968), states, "According to Senghor ["Rapport sur la doctrine et la propagande du parti," 1959], he and Cesaire 'launched' the word negritude in the years 1933–35. The first time it appeared in one of their works, however, was in Cesaire's poem, written in 1938, 'Cahier d'un retour au pays natal.' Since then it has come to bear different shades of meaning. . . ." The word has been used variously to denote style, quality, attitude, way of being, culture, essence, spirit, value sys-tem, skin color, and race. Inherent in all of these shades of meaning are the fol-lowing themes: rejection of Western ideas of civilization; embracing of primi-tivism; exoticism; and longing for an imaginary Africa (pp. 251–57). A. James Arnold in *Modernism and Negritude: The Poetry and Poetics of Aime Cesaire* (Cambridge: Harvard University Press, 1981), says: "The concept of negritude has known mixed fortunes in its forty-five year history. It has been successively a rallying cry, a modish literary label, and an ideology." Senghor, rather than Cesaire, was evidently responsible for fashioning negritude into a "political-cultural ideology" and committing other excesses which led Cesaire eventually to distance himself from Senghor's ideas. In a 1970 interview, Cesaire accused Senghor of constructing negritude into a "metaphysics," and "an essentialism as though there were a black essence, a black soul . . ." (p. 6). This has led some critics, such as Conde (1974) to make a distinction between Senghorian negritude and Cesairean negritude. Other critics have not made this distinction, seeing

both variants as reactionary, e.g., a Marxist scholar, Stanislaus Adotevi (1972) satirized the ideas denoted by negritude, and claimed that the ideas might be better described by the term "melanism" (Arnold, p. 7). Satire turns full circle to an attempt at serious scholarship when Afrocentrists began to use the concept of melanin (see following note).

30. Frances Cress Welsing's pamphlet, *The Cress Theory of Color Confrontation and Racism* (1970), reprinted in her collection of essays entitled *The Isis Papers: The Keys to the Colors* (Chicago: Third World Press, 1991), was the first popular work to introduce the concept of melanin into the Afrocentric discourse. Legrand Clegg's article "Melanin: The Key to Black Genetic Superiority," *Sepia*, June, 1980; Richard King's "Black Dot . . . Black Seed: Archetype of Humanity," pts. 1–2, *Uraeus: Journal of Unconscious Life* (1980, 1982); Carol Barnes's *Melanin: The Chemical Key to Black Greatness*, vol. 1 (Houston: C.B. Publishers, 1988); Richard King's *African Origin of Biological Psychiatry* (Hampton, VA: UB & US Communications Systems, 1994 [1990]); and Nur Ankh Amen's *The Ankh: African Origin of Electromagnetism* (Jamaica, NY: Nur Ankh Amen Co., 1993) all contributed to the discourse as did national and local melanin symposiums. For example, I have in my files a schedule for a "Third Annual Melanin Conference: April 6–9. 1989, Howard University Washington, D.C." and a collection of flyers for annual melanin symposiums at Medgar Evers College in Brooklyn, New York. In addition, Leonard Jeffries popularized the concept in his flamboyant lectures. See Michael Eric Dyson's "Melanin Madness," *Emerge*, February, 1992, pp. 32–37. T. Owens Moore's *The Science of Melanin: Dispelling the Myths* (Silver Spring, MD: Beckham House, 1995) purports to be a critical analysis of the African-centered research on melanin, yet the author provides nothing more than a gentle slap on the wrist to his colleagues for their theories of biological determinism, before espousing his own metaphysical theories about melanin acting as a "conduit between the material world and the spiritual world."

31. On various occasions, in his public lectures Karenga has sniped at Muslims obliquely, e.g., making derogatory remarks aimed at a target group: "You know who I mean—with your praying, practicing, fasting selves;" denigrated the emphasis that African-American Muslims have placed on the history of the Prophet and his companions instead of on African history, again with a characteristic indirect remark, "Your religious narrative, your narrative of faith is not your history;" and attempted to undermine Sunni Muslim claims to the legacy of Malcolm X, with a witty barb, "Do you think that if Malcolm were alive today that he would be an orthodox Islamic scholar?!" Dr. Maulana Karenga, as the creator of Kwanzaa—an African American holiday celebrated annually from December 26 to January 1—and a national lecturer, made the first two remarks during speeches at Kwanzaa celebrations in Brooklyn, New York, although I cannot immediately verify the exact dates or years without reviewing several videotapes of Karenga in my archives. The comment about Malcolm X was made in a speech entitled "The Moral Meaning of Malcolm X" delivered in Brooklyn during a Black History Month commemorating the February 21 assassination of Malcolm. Again verification of the date and year means hunting through a videotape collection that is not catalogued. I was, however, present in the audience on each of the three occasions. These were not isolated remarks but characteristic of the kind of anti-Muslim slurs that I have heard Karenga make on several other occasions. I will add that Onaje Abd'ul-Muid of the Admiral

(Amir'ul-Mu'minun) Family Circle in New Jersey, who generously reviewed this manuscript, cautions me that Maulana Karenga has ceased or at least softened these public attacks on Muslims as a result of his increasing interest in the area of social ethics. Karenga, who holds a Ph.D. in political science, is pursuing a second doctorate in social ethics; his focus is on the ancient Kemetic (Egyptian) principle of Ma'at (balance, reciprocity, justice, etc.).

32. Maulana Karenga, *Introduction to Black Studies* (Los Angeles: Kawaida, 1996). See summary accounts: "Moorish Empire in Spain," pp. 63–66, and "The Islamic Alternative," pp. 185–91; "Western Sudanic Civilization," pp. 57–63.

33. "The title of this text, *The Husia*, is taken from two ancient Egyptian words which signify the two divine powers by which Ra (Ptah) created the world, i.e., *Hu*, authoritative utterance and *Sia*, exceptional insight. Thus, I have put the two together to express the concept 'authoritative utterance of exceptional insight' . . . (Malauna Karenga, *Selections from the Husia: Sacred Wisdom of Ancient Egypt* [Los Angeles: Kawaida Publications, 1984], p. xiv). "The quest for spiritual enrichment among black people in the physical and cultural Diaspora has lead to the adoption of the Holy Books of other peoples; the Torah, the Bible and the Qur'an. Ironically, the sacred literature of ancient Egypt which predates those texts by thousands of years is the source of much of the wisdom in those Holy books, as Dr. Karenga points out. . . . [I]t is now time to return to the source" (Jacob Carruthers, Foreword to ibid., pp. ix–x). Karenga acknowledges his debt in preparing this volume to "existing translations and studies in English and French." He neglects to name his sources in the 1984 edition, but in the 1989 edition, he does include a bibliography. Some of the translators of ancient Egyptian texts included in this bibliography are James H. Breasted, E. A. Wallis Budge, R. O. Faulkner, Joseph Kaster, Miriam Lichtheim, Josephine Mayer, and Tom Prideaux, Alexandre Piankoff, and John Pritchard.

34. For an in-depth discussion of images of Islam as portrayed by African writers, see Kenneth W. Harrow, ed., *Faces of Islam in African Literature* (Portsmouth, NH: Heinemann, 1991).

35. African Americans living in the isolated Sea Islands retained strong African cultural and linguistic traits. Both the dialect and the native speakers became known as Gullah or Geechee. Bilal Muhammad seems to be crafted from an actual historical figure, Bilali Mohamet or Ben Ali Mohamet, a slave owned by Thomas Spaulding who lived on Sapelo Island off the coast of Georgia. In the movie, Bilal Muhammad is depicted as reading prayers from a small notebook, handwritten in Arabic. Again this is historically accurate. The Bilali or Ben Ali document is a thirteen-page document written in Arabic script by the slave Bilali Mahomet. The Georgia State Library received the document in 1930. After several failed attempts to decipher the work, in 1938 an anthropologist named Greenberg, with the assistance of Hausa religious scholars, identified a major portion of the document as excerpts from the *Risala*, a well-known work from the Malekite school of Islamic law. See Harold Courlander, *A Treasury of Afro-American Folklore* (New York: Crown Publishers, 1976), pp. 282–85, 288–90 and photo illustrations nos. 10 and 11 opposite p. 298.

36. See Robert Farris Thompson, *Flash of the Spirit: African and Afro-American Art and Philosophy* (New York: Vintage Books, 1983), pp. 108–9, 118–19 and 142–45, for Kongo cosmogram, nkisi-charm, and bottle tree which appear in this film.

37. Musa Abdul-Hakim, director of the Tarikh Research Institute in Buffalo, has written a paper which dissects the Afrocentric misperceptions and misrepresentations of Islam. The paper is entitled "The Cultural Unity of African Islamic Civilization: Neglected Dimensions in the Study of Classical African Civilizations." He is now working closely with CASIA and Ahmad Baba Research Center to publish his work (see below, n. 49).

38. See Osafo Akwesi Prempeh, "A Guide to Reject: 'The Blackman's Guide to Understanding the Blackwoman,'" in *The Alkebulanian*, 2, no. 8 (September 1990): 12–14. The title of the magazine comes from the term *alkebu-lan*, which Dr. Ben Jochannan states is the original name for Africa. For additional anti-Muslim and anti-Arab sentiment from this small press magazine which is published in Detroit, see Tarharqa's "Are You a Moslem? WHY!" in ibid., no. 2 (1992): 16–18, and Osafo Kwesi Prempeh's "The Arab and European Conflict: Africans Have No Business Participating," 2, no. 10 (October 1990): 3–5. A quotation attributed to Dr. Ben Jochannan on the back cover of ibid., vol. 3, no. 6 (June 1991), reads: "Your mother gave birth to you, your mother is the only thing you know gave birth to you. She is your God, your Goddess. She is your birth giver . . . she is bigger than Jesus, bigger than Jehovah, bigger than Allah."

39. For titles of works by Mahmud, Winters, and Nyang, see aboves, nn. 2 and 49.

40. One of the most prominent black nationalists to convert to Sunni Islam, H. Rap Brown, who is now known as Imam Jamil Al-Amin, recently published a work entitled *Revolution by the Book: The Rap is Live* (Beltsville, MD: Writer's Inc., 1993). Although al-Amin's conversion from a SNCC (Student Non-Violent Coordinating Committee) and Black Panther activist to a pious Muslim is duly narrated, there is no analysis in this *da'wa*-oriented book which would place it anywhere within the debate between Muslims and Afrocentrists. In his public speeches, al-Amin has disavowed any kind of nationalism, stating that "bonds of belief are stronger than bonds of blood."

41. Mohammed, *Afrocentricity,* p. 1. The quotation by Wallace D. Mohammed originally appeared in *Muslim Journal,* December 20, 1991, p. 15:

There is a new influence being promoted in the African family of people, especially here in America, called 'Afrocentricity'. . . . I am not against Afrocentricity, if it is honest and straight [but it] has not been honest and straight. . . .

Its promoters say we should make Africa the center, and all of us of the African family should look to Africa as center. But their Afrocentricity ignores Islam that has become the center and has been the center of Africa for many centuries. . . . But they want to ignore that and cheat us with idolatry and anything but true religion. . . .

That tells me that someone wants to sell me an Afrocentric belief to cheat me out of a brilliant and mighty page in the past. . . .

42. Rogers, *World's Great Men of Color,* 2: 539; Rogers, *Sex and Race,* 1: 95–96, 284; Muhammad Abu Bakr, *Islam's Black Legacy: Some Leading Figures* (Denver: Purple Dawn Books, 1993), pp. 1–19. "Abd'al-Muttalib [the paternal grandfather of the Prophet] fathered ten Lords, black as night and magnificent," according to *Kitab fakhr al-sudan 'ala al-bidan (The Book of the Superiority in Glory of the Black Race Over the White),* written by 'Uthman 'Amr Ibn Bahr (776–

868), the most prominent Muslim scholar of the ninth century, who was better known by the sobriquet al-Jahiz (the oggle-eyed); an English translation has been published under the title, *The Book of the Glory of the Black Race* (Los Angeles: France and William Preston, 1981); see p. 50 for the description of Abd'al-Muttalib. For a biography of al-Jahiz, described as "a very dark Negro . . . whose eyes seemed as if they were about to pop out of his head," see Rogers, *World's Great Men of Color*, 1:163–71.

43. As I make final editorial revisions on this manuscript, I am alerted that yet another book has been published. Abu Bakr bin Isma'il Salahuddin, a member of the Ahmadiyya Movement and the author of a newly released book, *The Afrocentric Myth: Or Islam, The Liberator of African American People*, published by New World Order Press, was interviewed on the *Tony Brown Show*, WLIB talk radio (New York), in late January 1996.

44. The two sessions of discussion were held within a two- or three-week interval, at the House of the Lord Church in Brooklyn. John Henrik Clarke was the main speaker for the Afrocentrists; Imam Siraj Wahhaj of Masjid al-Taqwa in Brooklyn, Adjunct Professor Marguerita Aisha Samad Matias of City College (CUNY), and Dr. Abdullah Hakim Quick of Toronto were speakers on the Muslim panel. I was not present at either of these sessions. I was, however, an active participant in a forum sponsored by CASIA (see final note) entitled "A Circle for the Advancement of African American Muslim Scholarship," which devolved into a fierce internal debate among African-American Muslim scholars on the issue of black nationalism. This heated session took place at Princeton University in late January of 1994. Presenters included Amir Al-Islam, Abdullah Hakim Quick, Musa Abdul-Hakim, Abdul-Hakim Jackson, Akil Kahera, myself, and others. There were approximately thirty key African-American Muslim activists/intellectuals in attendance. This forum was a significant event because it generated ideological debate and discussion among African-American Muslim scholars, activists, and intellectuals which continued for several months.

45. See February 1–February 7, 1995 issue of *The City Sun*, a New York City-based black weekly newspaper, which has the bold headline, "Arab Masters, Black Slaves." This issue contains Samuel Cotton's "The African Slave Trade: 1995" (p. 4); it was the first of a series of *City Sun* articles by him on this topic. This series ran every week or every other week for about four issues. Similar articles were run by *The Daily Challenge*, a New York-based black daily newspaper. *Village Voice* 40, no. 50 (December 12, 1995), has an article by Nat Hentoff entitled "Farrakhan and the Slave Masters" (p. 12) which questions how Farrakhan and the Nation of Islam, on the one hand, can go to great lengths to accuse Jews of involvement in the Atlantic slave trade in *The Secret Relationship between Blacks and Jews* (Chicago: Nation of Islam, 1991), yet, on the other hand, remain silent on the issue of contemporary slavery in the Sudan. This article was the first of a series on Arab enslavement of Africans by Hentoff in the *Village Voice*; it was followed by two or three others. Some African-American Muslims see the new Afrocentric abolitionists as the unwitting pawns of Zionists. Latif Sadiq, an African-American Sunni Muslim whom I interviewed, stated that the reports of human rights violations in the Sudan have been grossly exaggerated in order to create anti-Islamic government propaganda. In addition, he stated that the Israelis are covertly funding the secessionist forces in the southern Sudan in an effort to destabilize the Shari`a-based Sudanese gov-

ernment, which the Israelis regard as a terrorist state and a threat to Israeli security.

46. See Yusef Salaam's article "Imam's Lecture Cites Problem with 'Priests of Blackness'" in *The New York Amsterdam News*, 86, no. 36 (September 9, 1995): 21; and John Henrik Clarke's letter to the editor, "How Islam Came to Africa: Another Thought," ibid., 86, no. 38 (September 23, 1995): 13. Clarke's letter ends, "It might be hard for [Imam Talib Abdur-Rashid] to face the fact that the Arabs and Islam have been and still are the enemies of African people, but their behavior in Africa allows for no other conclusion."

47. My manuscript in progress, "Islam and the African American Experience," and the journal *Timbuktu* which I am co-editing along with Amir Al-Islam, an African-American activist and scholar in Islamic studies, will attempt to respond to this challenge.

48. There is little or no reference to the Sahel region of Africa in encyclopedias, on maps, or in atlases. Most people who have heard the name associate it with an area of starvation and devastation in Ethiopia which became a major focus of humanitarian concern fifteen or twenty years ago. Televised images of thousands of malnourished skeletal figures huddled in refugee camps triggered a massive relief effort complete with a benefit song, "We Are the World," sung by a all-star celebrity chorus. But this Oxfam image of the Sahel does not encompass the historical and cultural meanings of the term. Sayeed Abdus-Samad states that Sahel is actually an Arabic word known and used widely among West Africans. Literally, it means "the shoreline." Metaphorically, Arabs speak of the Sahara as a "sea of sand." The Sahel is the savannah or grassland region which begins at the southern edge of the Sahara, and is its metaphorical "shoreline." Geographically, it is a narrow band of savannah which stretches along the southern desert border from West Africa to East Africa. Historically and culturally, the Sahel was a trade and travel route linking the Arab north with sub-Saharan Africa. The western end of this savannah was the site of cities such as Kumbi-Saleh and Walata in ancient Ghana (300–1240) and the cities of Timbuktu, Jenne, and Gao, learning centers which were to flourish in the later West African empires of Mali and Songhai. The Sahel was thus a fertile zone and an African Islamic center of scholarship and enterprise. The Moorish civilization of al-Andalus bore many of the distinctive West African cultural traits in scholarship, music, and the arts that were peculiar to the Sahel region. It was in a very real way a northern extension of the Sahel.

Sayeed Abdus-Samad and Muhammad Abdel-Rahman are two of my very knowledgeable and hard-working colleagues on the staff of the Ahmad Baba Research Center. *Timbuktu: A Journal of Contemporary African American Muslim Thought* is the long-awaited major project of the center. Inadequate funding rather than a lack of talent or energy has delayed this project. Creative financing might be achieved through a recent cooperative effort with CASIA (see n. 49) and other Muslim organizations.

49. A Muslim research institute may vary in size from a network of scholars and intellectuals to a single lone scholar, with his personal library, and trusty typewriter or computer. Personal libraries, however, tend to be sizable and of unusual depth and quality, as there is a tradition of bibliophilia among African-American Muslims. Most institutes operate from a home-based library and home-based office, even when a network of individuals is involved. Resources are

simply not available to rent office space. Undoubtedly, there are many institutes in existence that I am unaware of, publishing small newsletters, pamphlets, and magazines of varying quality and limited circulation. Here are some of the intitutes that I do know.

The Uthman Don Fodio Institute is based in the Midwest and is headed by Clyde-Ahmad Winters, a scholar who has done significant pioneering research on Muslim slaves. Winters is the author of several articles and conference papers on this subject (see above, n. 2 for two of them). I have not yet seen Winters's "A Survey of Islam in the African Diaspora," *Pan African Journal*, 8, no. 4 (1975), which is cited by Sulayman Nyang (above, n. 2) "as one of the most interesting articles on Muslim slaves in the Americas." The Tarikh Research Institute in Buffalo, NY, is headed by Musa Abdul-Hakim. Abdul-Hakim has published several informative pamphlets under the auspices of his Bilalian Roots Institute in Bronx, NY. The Admiral (Amir'ul-Mu'minun) Family Circle is a think tank, publishing center, and activist group located in Teaneck, NJ. CASIA (Center for the Advanced Study of Islam in America) is based in New York City and is headed by Amir Al-Islam. This organization has begun to work collaboratively with an older New York-based institute, the Ahmad Baba Research Center, to produce a long overdue journal, *Timbuktu*. Yusuf Nuruddin is the executive director of the Ahmad Baba Research Center, whose founding members (1983) include Muhammad Abdel-Rahman, associate director, and Dawud Haneef Abeng, secretary-treasurer. There are over a dozen writers, scholars, and intellectuals actively affiliated with Ahmad Baba. The name of our organization commemorates the West African Muslim scholar and bibliophile, Ahmad Baba (1557–1627), who was the president of the famed University of Sankore at Timbuktu.

10

Understanding the Multi-Ethnic Dilemma of African-American Muslims

ROBERT DANNIN

The adoption of another people's god always entails the adoption of their space and system of measurement.

Henri Lefebvre[1]

In the autumn of 1990 the Rabita al-Alam al-lslami (Muslim World League and World Supreme Council of Masajid [mosques]) embarked upon a program to create worldwide consensus in favor of the Saudi-American military coalition against Iraq. In the United States this took the form of a concerted effort to mobilize support among both immigrant and African-American and other indigenous Muslims, since the Rabita sought to avoid the possibility that demonstrators would initiate an anti-war movement that would jeopardize political support for U.S. military action in Kuwait. By September 1990 activists had already organized marches and rallies against Operation Desert Shield. With the support of the Saudi kingdom and Washington, Rabita set about mollifying the Islamic community. A delegation of American Muslims led by Imam Warith Deen Muhammad (fig. 10.1) went to Mecca on September 10 to attend a special conference to discuss the events in the Persian Gulf. The assembly received assurances from Saudi religious officials that the Qur'an fully supported its decision to invite foreign infidel troops to defend the holy mosques of Mecca and Medina against Iraqi military aggression.[2] Steps were also taken to initiate a broad public relations campaign. When the delegation returned, Rabita invited African-American and immigrant Muslim imams throughout the United States and Canada to Chicago to participate in another conference. To ensure a good turnout, it paid for their airline tickets and booked a block of hotel rooms in downtown Chicago.[3]

Once the meeting convened, Rabita did not appeal directly to the many influential American imams from all corners of the country to support the

Figure 10.1. Imam Warith Din Muhammad, founder of the American Muslim Mission, internationally recognized as one of the principal American Muslim leaders. (Photo by Jolie Stahl)

war, but subsumed it under a more general petition calling for unity among the various branches of the American *umma*, and offered to make good on previously unfulfilled promises for material assistance to African-American Muslim communities. They proposed to revamp the *majlis al-shura*, the governing body, of the Islamic Society of North America by dividing it into five distinct regional groups and permitting the newly constituted regional councils to assume direct control over the waqf of the American Muslim community.[4] The idea was to ensure funds for communities too poor or too obscure to lobby at national conferences.

This gesture constituted tacit acknowledgment that it had been guilty of ignoring the persistent economic and social problems of indigenous Muslims and was meant to convince indigenous leaders that in the future they would have fewer problems in squaring their interests with those of immigrant Muslims. Allocation of resources was to be based on the criteria of need and proportional representation. While most of the participants favored the plan, some imams, particularly those from poor inner city mosques in desperate need of assistance for their schools and extracurricular programs, were skeptical.

This meeting marked one of the very few times that other American Muslim leaders convened in the company of Minister Louis Farrakhan of the Nation of Islam, making it a rare public demonstration of unity among the approximately 1.2 million African-American Muslims.[5] Anticipating the rancor of his most vociferous American Muslim critics, who maintain that he does not uphold the "five pillars" of the faith, Farrakhan delivered the keynote address and recited in Arabic the *kalima shahada*. He preached unity for all American Muslims and promised to institute orthodox worship among his followers in the Nation of Islam. As a concluding gesture of solidarity, he embraced Imam Warith Deen Muhammad and Imam Siraj Wahaj, a renowned black Sunni leader from Brooklyn.[6]

Several weeks after the meeting I asked Rabita's director for North America, Dr. Mohammed Qutbi,[7] if the meeting had been a pretext for mobilizing support against Iraq. He equivocated and tried to distance the Rabita's position on Desert Shield from that of the Saudi kingdom. Saudi religious leaders and the royal family did not see eye-to-eye on everything, he reported, particularly the sacrilege of the non-Muslim American soldiers traipsing around the holy lands of Mecca and Medina. As dissenting opinions go, it was mild, but nonetheless his diplomatic way of bridging the chasm that existed between the interests of the Saudi kingdom and grassroots feelings among African-American Muslims.

Qutbi was reluctant to challenge popular sentiment among African-American Muslims, suggesting that he grasped the complicated politics among American Muslims much better than Rabita officials back in Mecca, despite their great interest in the growing American Muslim population. This became evident when Operation Desert Shield became Desert Storm and American jets started raining bombs on Baghdad. By then, the divisions were clearly exposed in the pages of the two principal organs of the American Muslim press. On the one hand, *Muslim Journal*, the official weekly paper edited by the followers of Imam Warith Deen Muhammad, gave unequivocal support for the Saudi-American military alliance. From the beginning of the Gulf crisis onwards, the paper printed and reprinted verbatim statements issued by Rabita and the Saudi government.[8] It is conceivable that these positions reflected Imam Muhammad's traditionally cozy relationship with Saudi Arabia.[9] Nonetheless, it should not be forgotten that they also revealed his reformist attitudes about Islam and its role in American civil society, for he had moved 180 degrees from the position of his father, Elijah Muhammad, who had counseled draft resistance and even served a prison term for draft evasion during World War II.[10] Ironically, his major concern was seeing to the needs of Muslim-American military personnel by making certain that they got *halal* food rations and timely access to Muslim chaplains.

Many other Sunni Muslims, as well as the Nation of Islam, disagreed.[11] They opposed the war for both religious and political reasons, maintaining that there was no justification for the American army being anywhere near the holy sites of Mecca and Medina. Second, they felt that African-Americans, Hispanics, Native Americans, and poor whites should not be called upon to die in a foreign war when they were unable to get a decent education or job at home. They also believed that the only Islamic solution was for the Muslims to settle differences among themselves. Finally, it was suggested, the Kuwaiti sovereigns (and the Saudi prince, by extension) were not good Muslims anyway, since they withheld oil proceeds from needy Muslim nations and wasted their money on forbidden vices, thereby provoking Saddam's invasion. Citing the contradictions between U.S. diplomacy towards Iraqi military aggression against Iran in 1981 and Kuwait in 1990, *Final Call*, the official organ of the Nation of Islam, alleged that the Gulf Crisis was "orchestrated" by the United States. These arguments were promoted in headlines such as, "Send Your Son, Mr. Bush!"[12]

By the end of 1990, all semblance of unity and cooperation had evaporated. Farrakhan and the Nation of Islam continued to criticize Kuwait and Saudi Arabia as corrupt monarchies and to feature news supporting the antiwar movement, chronicling the conscientious objections of a Muslim soldier in the U.S. Air Force, and even calling upon General Colin Powell to resign.[13] For his part, Imam Warith Deen Muhammad's paper offered a withering denunciation of Farrakhan, accusing him of blasphemy and characterizing his reconversion in Chicago as a publicity stunt calculated to get money from "the Muslims of oil-rich states."[14]

Today, as then, the African-American Muslim community remains visibly divided over issues of national allegiance, ethnic identity, and religious orthodoxy. The mixed sentiments revealed by the Gulf War controversy constitute some of the underlying questions about Islam, the authenticity of African-American Muslims, and the incipient North American *jamuut* (community). How do these persons identify themselves simultaneously as Muslims and African Americans? Whether they prefer traditional Arabic culture to Afro-American folkways, whether they travel to Mecca via Cairo or Khartoum, or whether a man maintains one or several wives and sends his children to Qur'anic school in Senegal (fig. 10.2), an academy in Pakistan, or a mosque in Queens (fig. 10.3 & 4), African-American Muslims are caught in a dilemma. Whether one reenacts the Prophet's hijira by living and working in a Muslim enclave or pursues mixed company for family, residence, career, and social life, these choices seem to reflect something more than simple religious preference. They are the unmistakable insignia of a thirst for self-definition through the concatenation of innumerable spaces, intellectual pursuits, cultural activities, histories, and social relations opened to the believer by Islam.

The Islamic movement in the United States challenges the accepted conventions of social anthropology. Each time the anthropologist seems to have grasped the essence of a Muslim community defined in terms of its shared religious principles—the Qur'an, the hadith, worship—this unity disintegrates under the pressures of personal interpretation, ethnic controversy, linguistic diversity, and even nationalist preoccupations. The resulting fragmentation in its turn then provokes an incessant reclassification of the other Muslim as well as endless crises of identity. The African-American Muslims live these contradictions as a series of compound statuses reminiscent

Figure 10.2. Resident American Muslim students at Qur'anic school of the Tijaniyya Islamic Brotherhood in Medina Kaolack, Senegal. (Photo by Jolie Stahl)

of W. E. B. DuBois's theory of double-consciousness[15]—black and non-Christian, non-Arab and Muslim, indigenous American and religious convert, traditional Muslim woman and modern American feminist. The goal here is to elucidate the anthropological dimension of these contradictions and suggest some areas for future research in the context of sustained popular interest in Islam in North America.

Ethnohistory, the Qur'an and Islamic Unity

From a doctrinal viewpoint at least, unity is the *sine qua non* of Islamic communities. The concept of *tawhid* expresses this as the oneness of Allah; for all time He is everywhere and He rules all people, enveloping the universe in an indivisible singularity. Consequently, the Qur'an cautions Mus-

Figure 10.3. Islamic elementary school at Masjid Nuriddeen in Queens, New York. (Photo by Jolie Stahl)

lims against reifying ethnic or racial distinctions as contrary to the principles of montheisism and detrimental to the interests of the umma.

One can glimpse this ideal unity on Fridays at the big mosques in New York, Chicago, Los Angeles, and other American cities, where polyglot crowds jam the prayer halls, covering the antechamber floors haphazardly with piles of shoes whose styles range from expensive, hand-sewn Italian moccasins to Nike Air Jordans or even *babouches*, the pointy-toed clogs worn throughout the Mediterranean and Africa. Similar multi-ethnic, multi-racial crowds pray together at the Eid al-Fitr in municipal parks across the country. Each year as well, tens of thousands of African Americans make the hajj, donning the *ihram* (the white pilgrim's garment) to join the swirling humanity circumambulating the holy shrine at Mecca.

In addition to the demonstration of unity in ritual practice, American Muslims try to symbolize their religious solidarity on a civic level. For example, the first Qur'anic blessing ever performed to open a session of the U.S. Congress was recited by an imam from a mosque in the predominantly black neighborhood of Bedford-Stuyvesant in Brooklyn. Public appearances like this tend to reinforce the lofty representations of inter-ethnic harmony and social justice that are depicted in Islamic tradition and history. Nevertheless, it is important to understand that these gestures may well have more than symbolic impact. It is one thing to observe and listen to people inside their place of worship or to watch their leaders publicly embrace, but something else entirely to examine their relationships in the world outside their sacred domain.

Figure 10.4. Islamic Center of Southern California in Los Angeles. (Photo by Jolie Stahl)

An incident I witnessed in Los Angeles can serve to illustrate this point. During the 1988 presidential primary in California, Jesse Jackson was invited by the Muslim Political Action Committee to speak at the Islamic Center of Southern California not far from the Hollywood foothills. Over the years the center has served as a rendezvous point for Muslims from diverse backgrounds, including Sudanese medical students, Iranian refugees, an Egyptian army general (ostensibly there to visit his daughter but put in charge of security), and a few African Americans. The Jackson campaign appearance was scheduled for a Saturday afternoon in the center's rear parking lot. It was a beautiful June day with bright sunlight and deep shadows. Despite the candidate's tardiness, the atmosphere was festive. About 750 people had turned up, representing immigrant families of Arab, Persian, East Indian and Southeast Asian descent, mixed with a few African Americans. It was an assembly similar in ethnic composition to the worshipers attending Friday prayers at the center. The mood was one of calm anticipation and communal cheer (fig. 10.5).

Figure 10.5. Muslim-Americans awaiting Jesse Jackson at the Islamic Center of Southern California in June 1988. (Photo by Jolie Stahl)

Suddenly, an African-American Muslim wearing RayBans and a fez pushed open the rear fire door, tore through the crowd and ran to the vacant stage where he grabbed a microphone and shouted that he wanted to "expose the truth," before he was wrestled away by three strongmen from the candidate's Secret Service detail. A subdued murmur passed through the audience who then returned to their attentive ritual.

After Jackson's speech, I met the man who had shouted, one Dhanifu Karim-Bey, in front of the center on the sidewalk; there he recounted the events preceding his vaudevillian interlude on stage. First of all, he said, he could not have cared less about Jesse Jackson. He had come to the center that day to perform the noon prayer, after which he had propped himself against a pillar and begun reading the Qur'an. He languished there until shortly after two o'clock, the scheduled time for Jackson's speech. Several minutes later, the Egyptian general and another Arabic-speaking officer of the Islamic Center confronted him in the prayer hall. They inquired how much money it would take for him to leave the center immediately, insinuating that they did not want him around when Jackson showed up. Dhanifu was outraged, waited for them to disappear, and then made his emotional charge toward the podium to explain what he perceived as an un-Islamic racial affront.

Of the many stories I heard about inter-racial tensions among Muslims, the story of Dhanifu Karim-Bey best illustrates the complex considerations of race, class, and civil status, not to mention religious brotherhood involved and the problems caused by the conventional social attitudes of immigrants of many religious persuasions and national backgrounds. Normally, an immigrant may use ethnic or religious networks to learn the ropes of citizenship and increase socioeconomic mobility. In political terms, moreover, the identification of a constituency by ethnicity can benefit those who acknowledge each other as a national minority and thereby form powerful alliances. Jesse Jackson represented secular political power, and was there to address the immigrant Muslims about Palestine, a topic of broad concern. Although not Muslim himself, Jackson has been allied with Muslims often enough for them to believe that he can promote their interests. Therefore, he symbolized the business of inter-ethnic and interracial relations in the name of political goals. As a presidential contender, especially, his power transcended race (fig. 10.6).

By contrast Dhanifu Karim-Bey had no political capital upon which to draw. Black and powerless, he sported an identifiably "gangsta" look, suggesting his origins in Compton, an impoverished town adjacent the ghetto of South-Central Los Angeles. His fez was an underground symbol of defiance and militant nationalism dating back to the heyday of Noble Drew Ali's Moorish Science Temple of Islam, a forerunner of the Nation of Islam. When viewed against the background of a serious inter-ethnic political transac-

Figure 10.6. Jesse Jackson's campaign appearance for the Democratic presidential nomination at the Islamic Center was sponsored by the Muslim Political Action Committee. (Photo by Jolie Stahl)

tion. Dhanifu's appearance suggested militancy and violated the immigrants' understanding of civil conduct and politics (fig. 10.7). His very presence became a liability to the political alliance at stake in this event.

The Ethnography of Muslim Space

The ethnography of Muslims in America would have to include the various ways in which Muslims recognize each other and how they wish to be recognized within American society at large. This illustrates what is at stake in the situations just described in terms of the very complex fusion between scriptural ethics and the morality of daily life. In other words, the multiethnic dilemma can be analyzed by looking at the dichotomy between new Muslims (mostly of African descent) and new Americans (in this case, Middle Easterners and Asians). One can also attempt to explain how these identities determine the ways that non-Muslim Americans, or Muslims abroad, for that matter, view this dilemma.

Figure 10.7. Dhanifu Karim-Bey, Muslim and California community activist. (Photo by Jolie Stahl)

Henri Lefebvre's ideas about social space are helpful because we are dealing with situations relating to the cultural geography of contemporary Islam. Lefebvre might view this problem as one of interpenetrating or superimposed social spaces—the Dar al-Islam and Dar al-Harb, for example— where "each fragment of space subjected to analysis masks not just one social relationship but a host of them that analysis can potentially disclose."[16] Under this spatial optic then, we can juxtapose various inter-relationships and concomitant moralities among the Muslims in America.

For example, we might want to look at the new American who desires material success and recognition without having to cast off the rope of faith extended by Allah through the Prophet Muhammad. Immigrants, we assume, come to our shores in a fairly optimistic mood, at least in contrast to the desperation that marks the departure of refugees or exiles from home. They want to play by the rules, build networks, establish themselves in a nice community, and eventually achieve a modicum of the good life for themselves and their progeny. As part of the social practice essential to these goals, they stretch their networks as widely as possible in doing business, getting an education, and choosing a place to live. Even though adjusting to new ways of life presents intractable difficulties, first-generation immigrants usually manage to retain their native language, scriptures, and rites. Historically, in fact, traditions imported from various homelands were preserved in spaces like places of worship and parochial schools that enjoy constitutional protection. Over the course of time, the mother tongue sometimes disappears or ritual exercises change to conform with the surrounding environment. Nevertheless, revivals also occur as well, and traditions once thought of as lost are periodically regenerated.[17]

For Muslims, then, one might argue that the Dar al-Isam actually exists in immigrant communities. Certainly, there are several ways of thinking about this particular space, and the validity of such an assumption depends upon the many interpretations of where and under what conditions the Dar al-Islam prevails. In the simplest instance, this space might be defined as the sanctuary that lies within the power of a community to create and maintain.

Turning to the new Muslim or African American who converts to Islam, there exist sets of relationships concerning spatial divisions according to where one learned her/his religion—at home, abroad, perhaps in prison (fig. 10.8),[18] or from the one to whom one has pledged *bayat* (an oath of allegiance). Regarding time, some African Americans are very specific when categorizing fellow converts. New Muslims are recent converts; an elder Muslim is someone who deserves respect for her/his chronological age despite being a recent convert; a pioneer Muslim accepted Islam more than several decades ago. These variables already define a very complex set of interpenetrating social spaces and biographies.

There are also major doctrinal arguments separating Sunni from Shi'i; Muslims. Fundamentalists disdain assimilationists, reformers and especially

Figure 10.8. Shu 'aib Abdur Raheem, inmate imam (left) greet visitors to the 'id al-adha celebration as they enter the exercise yard at Wende Correctional Facility in upstate New York in August 1989. (Photo by Jolie Stahl)

Sufis[19] (fig. 10.9). Those schooled in the Black Church profess a different theology from Muslims who speak only of tawhid (the oneness of Allah), umma, and other strictly Islamic concepts. There are Arabophiles who identify with the Wahhabi sect, and those who prefer Islam with a Malaysian accent. Afrocentrists of varying persuasions identify with various tribes and states on the Mother Continent but disagree as to whether their cultural geography applies north of the Sahara. For virtually every nation on the map where Islam is practiced, it seems there is an African-American Muslim identifying with that community. For every doctrinal controversy in Islam, there are two or more African-American Muslims to recapitulate that argument. In Los Angeles, for example, there are African Americans who profess to follow the revolutionary Shi'ism of Iran's Ayatollah Khomeini; others who follow the Tabligh Jammaat, a Pakistani sect; or the Ahmadiyya movement in Islam, formerly based in Pakistan and now in London; or the Islamic Party of Sudan's Hassan al-Turabi; or the Muridiyya or Tijanniyya Sufi brotherhoods in West Africa.

Most new Muslims retain another set of spatial relationships having to do with the rural south, the urban north, the Christian dominion, and even farther back in time to the plantation, the tribe, and Africa. One can never assume that these spatial relations have been abandoned or transcended because one always has roots or family lore somewhere else.[20] Rather, they are superimposed onto new spaces by individuals who become Muslim, in search of the Dar al-Islam as a sanctuary from the Dar al-Harb a space often

Figure 10.9. An American Sufi lodge, al-Tareeqah al-Borhaniyya, in Brooklyn, New York. (Photo by Jolie Stahl)

synonymous with unhappiness and tragedy.[21] Thus, a multi-ethnic dilemma obtains when any of our subjects view each other. Without disputing their shared Muslim identity, whether they want to acknowledge a common Dar al-Islam in America or not, there are bound to be conflicts in matters of perception and practice. Some come to the United States optimistic about the prospects for a fresh start in a new place; others come to Islam with deep-seated pessimism about where they have been.

Stated another way, a Muslim does not dispute the representational space of the Qur'an which contains the divine revelations, its associated images and symbols, a sacred language, and a system of ethics toward which all Muslims strive. Not simply a matter of perception, the scripture defines the boundaries of a space within which every Muslim is summoned to live and think, and within whose constraints, if necessary, s/he may need to change. In their efforts to adhere to these principles, new Muslims learn Arabic and some even become hafiz, memorizing the Qur'an verse by verse. Others try to conduct business within the parameters of Islam, if not inside Muslim networks. Perennial bestsellers after the Qur'an and hadith in As-Suq book-store in Brooklyn, for example, are texts concerning the ethics of economic behavior in Islam.[22]

As far as practical matters and the nuts and bolts of everyday life are concerned, there are spatial exercises having little to do with Islam or any religion at all, thus implying a secular social space subdivided by race and class. For example, one may avoid certain areas of the city, regardless of one's religious beliefs, because the state inculcates many false ideas about personal safety. A salient example are the Islamic centers constructed in suburban areas as opposed to the inner city. Such choices do not exclude one or the other space from Dar al-Islam but suggest, nonetheless, conflicting ideas about which space will ultimately lend its characteristics to the general definition and perception of Islam in America. It is not so much that different ethics prevail in the suburban center as compared to the storefront mosque, but that a different emphasis, interpretation, or spin is given to the scriptures and traditions. Above all else, however, there is a difference in the prospects for assimilation, recognition, and personal gratification in the space of everyday life reflected in one's job, clothes, house, car, child's school, etc.

Anthropologists observe what happens in the course of rites of passage. This term can be understood as a spatial metaphor and applied to the ethnography of Muslim communities where action is often conceptualized in terms of spatial relations such as in pilgrimage or immigration. An excellent example of a rite of passage which I witnessed in August 1994 at the funeral of the late El Hajj Wali Akram, who founded the First Cleveland Mosque in 1934.[23] This event attracted over a thousand mourners from Cleveland's Muslim and African-American community. Waiting for the service to begin inside the sweltering Martin Luther King, Jr. Auditorium, I struck up a conversation with two of the very few representatives of the large immigrant Muslim community across town on the West Side. Both men stated their enduring admiration and affection for Wali Akram. He was the only "true American Muslim" according to one of the men. "When I moved here to work as an engineer in 1956, I looked in the phone book for mosques. I found Muhammad's Temple and went down there thinking I could make *salat* but it turned out to be Elijah Muhammad's people. They didn't like Arabs and wouldn't even let me in.[24] Afterwards someone told me about the First Cleveland Mosque."

In the many conversations I had with Wali Akram, he always contrasted himself to Elijah Muhammad by emphasizing the universality of Islam as opposed to a nationalistic or racially oriented doctrine. Moreover, he conceived his acceptance of Islam as a transition from a specific although maligned identity to a non-specific, universal Muslim identity. Once he abandoned "negro-ness" he never looked back, preferring, whenever necessary, to use the term "dark Americans" instead of Afro- or African Americans. This was a sincere act of religious faith that allowed him maximum freedom of action and movement in the Islamic world.

Clearly, not everyone was as enthusiastic about the First Cleveland Mosque as the two Arab mourners, judging by the weak representation of the umma at the funeral. Akram himself was very conscious of the schism and liked to ridicule it with his story of King Khalid's open-heart surgery at the Cleveland Clinic in the 1970s. When the monarch's entourage wanted to attend Friday prayer, they were admonished against venturing over to the

First Cleveland Mosque, not far from the clinic yet inauspiciously located inside the black ghetto. After contacting Imam Akram to discuss security precautions, they came to the First Cleveland Mosque anyway.

Despite this legacy, problems arose from time to time at the First Cleveland Mosque, as they do elsewhere. In April 1989, for instance, I met a young African-American man named Aqi (fig. 10.10), who had taken up temporary residence in the mosque itself. He explained that he had been a Muslim for ten years, that he had studied Islam in Pakistan and Bangladesh and was now part of the Tabligh Jamaat, which dispatches young missionaries to different Muslim communities in the United States. Many communities are targeted because they are thought to lack proper understanding of Islam. Aqi's first impression of the First Cleveland Mosque was ambivalent. His initial response was, "There's so much love here. Too much love. They're open to anybody. Things like this won't go on at other masajid. They create an opportunity for interactions between Muslims and non-Muslims. I will stay here all my life. I am so impressed with the feelings in this mosque." Several weeks later, he offered a more critical view. "There are different degrees of Muslims," he explained. "For example, some Muslims would look at the First Cleveland Mosque and say this isn't Islam. They need help here."

His attitude did not go unnoticed by members of the mosque. Yahya Muti, the young assistant imam remarked that "everyone is trying to emulate a culture—Arab culture—instead of the *din* [religion]. Wali Akram used to say,

Figure 10.10. Aqi, a young American missionary of the Tabligh Jammaat. Pictured at the First Cleveland Mosque. (Photo by Jolie Stahl)

'The Arabs left their robes at Ellis Island. We followed behind and put them on.' These *tablighi* are weird too. They're just spreading Pakistani culture. They've even got brothers eating on the floor with their fingers and telling them that using toilet paper is 'against the Prophet's tradition'" (fig. 10.11).

Aqi was eventually asked to leave First Cleveland, after which he relocated to another orthodox Sunni community. From an ethnographic point of view, it was difficult to interpret his moralizing on the character and conduct of Islam at the First Cleveland Mosque as an expression of racial or class prejudice. His attitude seemed to be based instead upon a dissonance between the identity of a convert who experienced Islam in a predominantly Muslim country (in this case, Pakistan) and that of a community of Muslim converts living in the predominantly Christian United States. In terms of Islamic identity, America has now become an arena for competing self-images where religious authority and cultural preferences are often conflated, if not altogether displaced and de-territorialized.

This was not the first time we heard cultural concepts expressed imperiously as part of the din. There is much confusion on this issue. It arises in many mosques on Fridays and erupts regularly every year at Ramadan, when American communities must decide whether to follow the observations of Saudi clerics or their own eyes for sighting the moon which signals the beginning and end of the fast. What was different about this instance was that, while such opinions usually divide along the rift between new Muslims and

Figure 10.11. Al-Hajj Wali Akram (d. 1994) with assistant imam, Yahya Muti (right), at the First Cleveland Mosque. (Photo by Jolie Stahl)

new Americans, here was a new Muslim, a migrant to an allegedly higher ground, challenging the practices of a pioneer Muslim with nearly seventy years experience in North America.

Aqi's allegiance to a missionary group from Pakistan had apparently given him license to reproach the practices at the First Cleveland Mosque. In return for this loyalty, he took advantage of his image as a pious, noble Muslim to decree what was permissible, good, and ultimately moral about the forms taken by Islamic worship and practice in America. In many cases it seems that the immigrants expect the new Muslims to absorb not only Islam but also their own national identities. One of the paradoxical tendencies of expatriate groups, Muslim or not, is that some members become unlikely yet dedicated cult—al advocates. Does this reveal a basic paradox of Islam, which wants to be wholly inter-communal but often finds itself torn as under by the sheer complexity of its ethnic components? Or is this also an effect of the multi-ethnic dilemma of African-American Muslims? Having defined themselves as Muslims, what is to be the basis of their participation in America's cultural stew?

These issues are deeper than mere self-reflection. The nature of the problems we have tried to illustrate does not show this to be the intention of African Americans who have simultaneously rejected the church and accepted the Qur'an. Rooted in the ritual of Islamic conversion for African Americans is not just a personal quest for self-identification but the perpetual search for a homeland where their differences can become a source of strength and proof of their humanity. In the current Islamic context, this signifies a great potential for alliances between immigrants and African Americans if the problems of cultural dissonance and prejudicial ideologies that we have illustrated can be overcome. Can Islam transcend these dilemmas of race and ethnicity? This is perhaps the greatest challenge facing American Muslims in the next century.

Notes

1. *The Production of Space* (Cambridge: Blackwell, 1991), p.11.

2. "U.S.A. Muslim Delegation in Saudi Arabia for Gulf Conference," *Muslim Journal*, 28 September 1990, and "Taking a Stand: Crisis in the Middle East," ibid., 14 September 1990, p. 3. In his statements to the conference, Imam Muhammad unequivocally condemned Iraq and offered support on behalf of American Muslims for Operation Desert Shield: "We respect and support the decision of the custodian of the Two Holy Mosques to unite the multi-national force for the defense of Saudi Arabia and the sovereignty of the countries in that region."

3. Referred to as the "Second Annual Meeting of the Continental Council of Masajid of North America," the conference took place 21–23 September 1990 at the Palmer House Hotel in Chicago. Participants included approximately 750 imams and religious leaders from the United States, Canada, Lebanon, Sudan, Jordan, and Saudi Arabia. Also attending were Dr. Omar Abdullah Naseef,

Secretary-General of Rabita, Shaikh Ali al-Hazafi, imam of the mosques of Mecca and Medina, and Khalil al-Khalil from the Department of Religious Affairs for the Royal Embassy of Saudi Arabia in Washington: "Muslim Unity Urged," *Final Call*, 31 October 1990, p. 2.

4. The history and organization of the Islamic Society of North America/ Muslim Students Association and its governing body, the Majlis al-Shura are described by Larry Poston, *Islamic Daw'ah in the West* (New York: Oxford University Press, 1992), pp. 104–5.

5. For a discussion of demographics, see Dannin, "African-American Muslims: From Slavery to the Present," Joint Center for Near Eastern Studies of New York University and Princeton University (typescript), pp. 18–19.

6. "Muslims Unite!" *Final Call*, 31 October 1990, p. 1.

7. Qutbi, born in the Sudan, served as an executive of the Muslim student Association of America, then studied in Saudi Arabia before returning to the United States with the Rabita.

8. See *Muslim Journal* weekly editions from 24 August to 23 November 1990. Particularly revealing was the printing of the official embassy portraits of King Fahd and Prince Bandar alongside a letter of support from Warith Deen Muhammad; ibid., 14 September 1990, p. 14.

9. Imam Muhammad and his followers were the beneficiaries of substantial Saudi largesse earlier that year when Prince Bandar bin Sultan al-Saud, the ambassador to the United States, attended groundbreaking ceremonies to donate money for the reconstruction of Masjid Felix Bilal in South Central Los Angeles. "From Mecca to Los Angeles, A Renaissance Begins," *Muslim Journal*, 10 August 1990, p. 1.

10. Elijah Muhammad was arrested in May 1942 and promptly convicted on two counts of draft evasion. He was sentenced to a five-year term at the Federal Correctional Institute in Milan, Michigan, and was released in 1946. See Malu Halasa, *Elijah Muhammad* (New York: Chelsea House Publishers, 1990), pp. 59–67.

11. A straw poll conducted by the *Muslim Journal* at the September conference in Chicago revealed that 89 percent of the 150 American Muslim leaders interviewed opposed any U.S. intervention in the Gulf. Reflecting apparent dissension within the paper's staff, the editors added a note to this report decrying the poll as "inconsequential" and "unrepresentative" of the 750 delegates in attendance; ibid., 12 October 1990, p. 14.

12. The paper quoted Libya's Col. Muamar Qadhafi in defense of Saddam Hussein, 7 September 1990, p. 16, as well as Farrakhan's charge that "King Fahd and the Saudi government [were] tied to American war-mongering" (10 December 20 1990, p. 13). Farrakhan also used the prospect of U.S. military action to reprise the theme of an impending Armageddon for U.S. power, citing a conversation with Elijah Muhammad (d. 1975) during an alleged UFO abduction in Mexico in 1985.

13. "Why War?" *Final Call*, 24 December 1990, p. 1.

14. Dr. M. Amir Ali, "Commentary: A Masterful Wordsman Should Be Studied Carefully," *Muslim Journal*, 19 October 1990, p. 21.

15. W.E.B. DuBois's characterization of the "double consciousness" remains an enduring key to understanding dilemmas of authenticity and self-identification of African Americans as well as those confronting many immigrants and

their descendants; DuBois, *Souls of Black Folk* (New York: New American Library, 1969), pp. 45, 221.

16. Lefebvre, "The Production of Space," p. 88.

17. To study this problem it may be necessary to assemble demographic information and analyze it in terms of thresholds and densities. The goal is to explain the periodic "awakenings" in American history; on the latest wave of revivals, see Robert Fogel, "The Fourth Great Awakening," *Wall Street Journal*, January 9, 1996.

18. For an ethnography of Islam in the prison system, see Robert Dannin, "Island in a Sea of Ignorance: Contours and Dimensions of the Prison Mosque" in Barbara Metcalf, ed., *Making Muslim Space* (Berkeley: University of California Press, 1996).

19. A new element in this equation is the growing number of Senegalese and other West African Muslims as immigrants. Many of them belong to the Tijane or Muride Sufi brotherhoods. In some places—the Malcolm Shabazz mosque in Harlem, once the pulpit of Nation of Islam ministers Malcolm X and Louis Farrakhan, now a Sunni masjid—is one, the Senegalese Murides often outnumber African-American Muslims at Friday prayers. These Sufi sects adhere to the Five Pillars and Sunni ritual to which they have appended the worship of local saints (marabouts) and lineages. To a large extent these religions represent the syncretization and popularization of Islam in Sahelian Africa. The Tijane Brotherhood, for example, is a transnational movement encompassing over 15 million Africans, Berbers, and Arabs throughout Sahelian Africa and surrounding regions. Is it possible that African-American Muslims will see these movements as appropriate solutions to the dilemma of their African heritage?

20. For the most important ethnographic work to date on the renaissance of rural traditions among urban blacks, see Carol Stack, *Call To Home: African Americans Reclaim the Rural South* (New York: Basic Books, 1996).

21. The most poignant summary of this sentiment were the words of Dizzy Gillespie commenting on the wave of conversions to Islam among jazz musicians. "They been hurt," he explained, "and they're trying to get away from it. It's the last resort of guys who don't know which way to turn . . . East . . . they turn east," quoted in Eric Hobsbawm, *The Jazz Scene* (New York: Pantheon, 1993) p. 181.

22. Another space which requires a great deal of study is the realm of economic and financial transactions among Muslims in America. Is it a definable space? Is it viable especially for those in the lower economic strata? Imam al-Amin Abdul Latif of Masjid Mu'minim on Atlantic Avenue in Brooklyn explained his economic strategy as one where cash would be exchanged six times within the Muslim community before flowing out to the Dar al-Harb.

Throughout the years indigenous Muslims always sought contacts with governments in Saudi Arabia, Egypt, Morocco, and elsewhere. Such contacts were based partly on fascination with the abundance of cultural materials in the umma and partly on hopes for finding business and financial opportunities. As far back as the 1940s groups like the Adenu Allah Universal Arabic Association in Philadelphia and the Arab-American Business Society in Detroit actively promoted Arabic culture and language as the basis for inter-ethnic cooperation and advancement. Historically, some African-American Muslim groups have asserted direct kinship links to the Quraish tribe, the lineage of the Prophet. This enables them to merge their ethnicity with that of Arabic-speaking People of the Book.

23. See Robert Dannin, "African American Muslims, From Slavery to the Present," The Joint Center for Near Eastern Studies of New York University and Princeton University, Seventeenth Annual Summer Institute (typescript), pp. 8–9.

24. Historically, the Nation of Islam (among other sects) rejects "the pale Arab" version of Islam. Elijah Muhammad once became BO enraged on being refused entry to Mecca that he not only ordered his temples to bar Arab-Muslim worshipers but decreed that his followers should orient their prayers toward Chicago instead of Mecca.

PART IV

AMERICANIZATION AND THE PRESERVATION OF CULTURAL IDENTITY

11

Muslims and the American Press

GREG NOAKES

Islam and Muslims have become American media mainstays in the decade and a half since the Islamic Revolution in Iran. Hardly a week goes by without news of some breaking event in the Muslim world, and with it reams of explanations of Islam and Muslims for Americans. In spite of the air time and column-inches devoted to Islam and Islamic themes, however, the performance of the mainstream American press in the coverage of Islam, Muslims, and events in the Muslim world has been little short of dismal.[1]

In order to understand why, it is important to answer several questions. How do the media cover Islam? What factors shape this coverage? If the performance to date has been lackluster, how can media coverage of Muslims be improved, and are these improvements likely to be made? When analyzing coverage of Muslims in the American press and the effects of that coverage on the Muslim community, it is important to keep in mind that "media" is a plural noun and remember that the media are not monolithic dispensers of information but rather a diverse array of outlets encompassing newspapers, magazines, journals, radio and television stations and networks, cable outlets, and such new technology as on-line information services. Given that diversity, it is neither useful nor illuminating to think in terms of conspiracy theories. This approach does have its adherents among critics, but ultimately it conceals much more than it reveals.

Nevertheless, the number of sources for reporting on the Middle East and the Muslim world is limited, and there is a great deal of overlap among media outlets. The three major broadcast networks (ABC, CBS, and NBC), in addition to the Cable News Network (CNN), maintain their own Middle East correspondents and special-assignment foreign correspondents. The American "newspapers of record," the *New York Times*, the *Washington Post*, the

Los Angeles Times, and the *Christian Science Monitor*, in addition to newsweeklies like *Time* and *Newsweek*, also have Middle Eastern correspondents. Most other outlets, however, rely on either one or more of the above sources or on wire services like the Associated Press, United Press International, or Reuters, who in turn often rely upon local stringers to report news.

In addition to the limited number of sources, one fairly standard editorial approach to news about Islam and Muslims has evolved over time, meaning that certain types of stories and analyses tend to be aired more often than others. This editorial line plays a dominant role in shaping the media's coverage of Islam, for good reporting and in-depth investigation and research are useless if they end up being cut for space or air time by a newspaper/magazine editor or a radio/television producer.

For the most part, American media coverage of Muslims and events in the Muslim world concentrates on the sensational. Standard media fare includes coverage of political upheavals, acts of violence carried out by extremist groups claiming to act in the name of Islam, perceived threats to American national interests, poor treatment of women, and outrageous human-rights abuses.[2] Admittedly, there are more than enough of these in the Muslim world, but they are extremes, and it is only these extremes that seem to attract the attention of reporters and editors.

In the hunt for the sensational, the media pass over the exciting variety of interpretation and expression among Muslims, who often profess very different ideas and attitudes while still remaining within the Islamic community. Constructive grassroots attempts to build up Muslim communities and the original, groundbreaking intellectual work being done across Islam are ignored, since they are neither photogenic nor particularly good for ratings or circulation numbers. The larger Muslim political, economic, and social context is largely ignored as well. One notable example that will be familiar to most Americans is the Iranian revolution of 1979. Very little mention was made in the American press of past American involvement in Iranian political and economic life, particularly the role of the Central Intelligence Agency in the 1953 overthrow of Iranian Prime Minister Muhammad Mossadegh and the restoration to the throne of Shah Muhammad Reza Pahlevi, or the impact of the American oil and arms industries on the Shah's ultimately disastrous domestic and foreign policies. Stripped of this background information, anti-American manifestations following the revolution seemed to most Americans to be irrational at best, fanatic at worst.

Media coverage can be characterized as sensationalist not just in the topics it addresses, but also in the imagery and language utilized in reporting those topics. Most egregious are recurring photographic or videotaped images that tend to dehumanize and depersonalize Muslims, such as pictures of hundreds or thousands of anonymous Muslims at prayer or the ubiquitous photos of a disembodied, upraised hand clutching a Qur'an high over the heads of a protesting crowd.

Other group shots which might show a different, less angry, and more human side of Muslims are hard to find. Funerals for Israeli dead, with crowds of sobbing mourners, are a staple of network newscast coverage of the Middle East, yet similar ceremonies for the more numerous Lebanese Muslim (and Christian) victims are almost never filmed, and the pain and suffering of their loved ones do not make the evening news.

When individual Muslims are shown, they are typically radicals. Few Americans could fail to identify a photo of the Ayatollah Ruhollah Khomeini or Shaikh 'Umar 'Abd al-Rahman, whose images come to represent all Muslims for the uninformed reader and viewer.

The media's use of terminology is similarly reductive, relying on certain ill-defined words both to convey certain concepts to an audience and to avoid closer scrutiny or definition of groups, individuals, and events. The most obvious example is, of course, "Islamic fundamentalism." The term "fundamentalism" was first applied to a strain of nineteenth-century evangelical Protestant Christian thought which upholds the inerrancy of the Bible. The term is meaningless when applied in its strictest sense to Islam (since all Muslims believe, as an article of faith, that the Qur'an is the Word of God revealed to the Prophet Muhammad), and yet it has assumed great currency.[3] Even those who object to the term find themselves falling back on it at times to make themselves understood. "Fundamentalist" is a loaded term, pregnant with sinister overtones and imbued with fanaticism and radicalism, which again obscures more than it reveals. Even some Muslim activists— the "fundamentalists" themselves—have adopted the term through their invention of the Arabic word *usuliyyin*, which can be roughly translated as "those of the roots". But loaded terms such as these are of little use when trying to pick out small details, one of the main tasks of a good journalist.

One recent example demonstrates how quickly and easily such nonsensical buzzwords come into being, and how they can shape and at times dominate public debate. "Ethnic cleansing" is a term that grew out of the war in Bosnia-Herzegovina, and it is used constantly in reference to the tragic events in that nation. The media picked up on the term and have used it to describe the Bosnian conflict without having to dig too deeply into messy details (such as who is doing the "cleansing" and to whom). It enables journalists to gloss over subtle trends and breaking events, lumping one horrible atrocity in with all of the others. The question remains unasked and unanswered by the media: is there any difference between "genocide" and "ethnic cleansing"? The latter, like "fundamentalism," is reductive, ultimately non-descriptive and, alas, used constantly.

A good deal of the media's coverage of Muslims, particularly as one moves away from hard political or economic reporting into feature and background pieces, is quirky and idiosyncratic. There are the funny anecdotes of Saudi women having to pose for passport photos under a veil, inordinate attention paid to the Turkish Islamist Refah Party's plans to paint Istanbul's curbs green after their victories in that city's 1994 municipal elections, and numerous pieces on such malevolent and retrograde practices as female circumcision and the slave trade, which reinforce the notion of the Muslim as "other" and the idea that Islam subscribes to a different and rather lower standard of humanity than does the West.

There is also an unhealthy reliance by the American media on editorial pieces to convey information about Islam and Muslims. The op-ed page too often is the only place to find in-depth analysis of the Islamic world. By definition, persuasive writing is designed to convey only one side of an argument; seldom is it the Muslim perspective that graces the editorial pages of the *Times* or *Post*. The debate on Islam and the Muslims viewed in light of the American media tends to be somewhat lopsided.[4]

Given this kind of coverage, it is apparent that the media are presenting only one part of the story when it comes to Islam—and a small part at that. The media often hit only the highest of the high points, without any discussion of one event's relationship to another or the ties which bind (or the issues which divide) one organization or personality from the next. The reader or listener is left to make sense of such a situation; like an archipelago, above the water the myriad islands seem to be scattered haphazardly across the surface, but seen from below they form part of a single geological body, and are clearly interrelated.

The average news consumer is presented with an image of Muslims as irrational and confused, and vaguely threatening in their unpredictability. Iran enforces the Shari'a, Saudi Arabia enforces Shari'a, and Sudan enforces Shari'a. Why then is Sudan so different from Saudi Arabia, and why are the "fundamentalist" governments in Riyadh and Tehran so often at one another's throats? Why does the United States count one of these countries as a close ally and brand the other two as international pariahs?[5] There are justifications for these seeming inconsistencies, but they are complicated and thus judged to be beyond the scope of straight journalism. It is not the media's job, it is thought, to chart the archipelago.

The media present Americans with a simplistic view of Islam and then leave them to press that fifth of humanity which is Muslim into this over-simplified mold. It is no doubt unrealistic to expect the mainstream media to convey the Muslim world in all of its rich diversity, yet their present performance falls well short of even reasonable—and achievable—expectations of accuracy and fairness.

The reasons for this substandard coverage can be broken into subjective factors, which are relatively easy to overcome, and objective factors, which have grown up over time, are much less susceptible to change, and in a sense set the parameters for what realistically can be expected from the media in terms of improved reporting on Islam and the Muslim community in the future. The first of these subjective factors is the political sensibility of the Muslim world. The Arab-Israeli conflict, while easily the most sensitive topic for the American media, is only one of several contentious issues: Bosnia, Kashmir, and Cyprus are all subject to vigorous debate among sectors of the

American public, as are the larger topics of north-south economic relations and the so-called clash of civilizations between Muslim and non-Muslim societies, cultures, and economies.[6] Because so much of the Muslim world is so politically sensitive, coverage of Islam can be a minefield into which reporters and editors venture with caution—some would say timidity.

In extreme cases, "impolitic" coverage of events in the Muslim world can result in economic (and in a very few cases, physical) threats directed against media outlets or personnel. The most intense pressure is exerted by well-organized special interests who can mobilize important groups of consumers or advertisers. Since newspapers depend on advertising revenue for their survival, and much of any daily paper's advertising business comes from a few select customers, such as local car dealerships, grocery chains, and department stores, decisions by a few of them to pull their ads can be devastating to a paper. Veteran journalist Charles Arnot, for example, wrote that he once asked his boss, press mogul William Randolph Hearst, why his reports from Cairo never received the same favorable treatment as those from his colleague in Tel Aviv. "Well, Charlie, look at it this way," Hearst replied, "just how many Arabs own big department stores that spend money advertising in our papers?"[7]

Broadcast outlets are more susceptible to boycotts, not of their shows, but of their advertising customers, who in turn are encouraged to withdraw their advertising dollars from the offending show or station. The implications can be disastrous, particularly in a small or competitive market.

Under such circumstances a kind of self-censorship quickly develops. An editor who receives a toughly worded opinion piece packed with solid, factual information must decide whether to run it knowing it will offend important people in the community who could inflict economic losses on the newspaper or station in question. The editor's decision probably depends on the subject at issue, the financial state of her/his business, her/his relations with the owners, the power of the special-interest group and the editor's past experience in similar situations. A little controversy sells papers and attracts an audience, but too much can sink one, or at least its editor.

A second and even more common problem is the subtle manipulation of media outlets by interested parties. The problem is compounded by the narrowly restricted pool of "experts" who turn up time and again on both the televison screen and the editorial pages. Fouad Ajami, for instance, writes regularly for *Newsweek*, the *New Republic* and *Foreign Affairs*; he is the in-house Middle East expert for CBS News, and he appears often on the "MacNeil/Lehrer News Hour." One talking head who has drawn considerable criticism for his comments about Muslims is self-styled terrorism expert Steven Emerson, who traffics in innuendo and unprovable accusations, yet continues to enjoy ready access to both the airwaves and the newspapers. Emerson's broadcast commentary in the two days following the April 19, 1995, bombing of the federal building in Oklahoma City, when he relentlessly (and incorrectly) pounded away at the presumed involvement of "Muslim terrorists," was particularly egregious and drew criticism from Muslims and non-Muslims alike. Emerson's replies to his critics was uncontrite.[8] Another good example of an often-used but biased commentator is former Secretary of State Lawrence Eagleburger, who once served as United States Ambassador to Yugoslavia and has longstanding professional, financial, and personal ties with Serbian strongman Slobodan Milosĕvic. Despite these links to the Serbian president, Eagleburger regularly offered his views on events in the former Yugoslavia in the American media (on the "McNeil/Lehrer NewsHour," for instance) with no mention or disclaimer of his personal interests and involvement.[9]

Related to the problem of a limited band of commentators is the lack of credible Muslim voices among this coterie. Ajami, a Lebanese Shi'i, is hardly a typical Muslim voice in the views he espouses, and despite a number of articulate thinkers and analysts in both the Muslim world and the American-Muslim community, representative Muslims are seldom allowed to speak for themselves on issues that concern them. Working journalists with little background in the Middle East too often turn to this narrow band of experts, many of whom are personally or professionally involved in the situations on which they are commenting, though this often is unknown to the news consumer.

Most journalists assigned to the Middle East beat have no particular background or training in the area; have no personal contacts in the region; and do not speak Arabic, Farsi, Urdu, Turkish, or Hebrew. Thus they must spend their first twelve to eighteen months on the job simply getting their bearings and painstakingly building up a network of reliable sources. By the time this is in place, they often are reassigned to other beats, since media outlets also want to move fresh faces into sensitive postings periodically. Some journalists use a foreign correspondent's posting simply as a step up the professional ladder, and not because they have any interest in the region. There is good precedent for this. Both Dan Rather of CBS and Peter Jennings of ABC, for example, first gained prominence as foreign correspondents— Rather in his reporting from Vietnam and Jennings as ABC's London bureau chief. They are now among the highest paid and highest profile newsmen in the world.[10]

To practice law or medicine, build a bridge, design a building, or even cut hair requires professional certification; there are no special requirements to be a journalist or editor. Print journalists must be able to write and radio and television reporters should have some kind of "presence" on the air, but neither are expected to meet particular educational, professional, or ethical standards before they can practice their craft. Yet these reporters and editors are the sole source of knowledge and understanding of Islam and the Muslim world for most Americans. Some journalists, such as Judith Miller and Thomas Friedman, both of the *New York Times*, have been elevated to the status of Middle East scholar, complete with books and journal articles to their credit.[11]

Put unprepared journalists in touch with sources with axes to grind or interests to protect and the product is substandard journalism. Reporters expect their sources to put some kind of spin on the information they provide; a "high-ranking State Department official," for example, is supposed to give the State Department's official line, even if it is not his or her own opinion or if it fails to jibe with reality. In most cases the official simply puts out the official view of events, but sometimes the "spin" can even involve outright disinformation. One such instance was the 1986 story of Libyan hit teams in the United States who allegedly were targeting President Ronald Reagan and members of his cabinet. In reality, there were no Libyan assassins; the stories were planted for political purposes by the administration.[12]

High-ranking officials have several cards they can play in their dealings with journalists. The ability to pick up the phone and get through to high officials in the White House, the Pentagon, or the State Department, or to have a reserved seat on official travel junkets, is pretty heady stuff for most journalists. The ability to tap into these highly placed sources of information also brings about a measure of prestige among a journalist's colleagues and the general public. A series of scoops can literally make a reporter's career. Thus, the journalist's quest for access and prestige—or later the fear that they may be lost—can be a powerful tool in the hands of a well-placed source who wishes to publicize a particular version or interpretation of events. To counter such tactics, a good journalist relies upon both background knowledge and a network of informed, credible, and diverse sources of information. Many American journalists covering the Muslim world lack precisely these basic resources, rendering them more susceptible to subtle—or blatant—"spin."

The net result of these factors—self-censorship and ouside pressures, a small number of "experts" and commentators, and a heightened susceptibility to disinformation—is what is regarded as "conventional wisdom." Inexperienced reporters who are able to draw on only a few recognized sources for information about a topic where the ideological stakes are high—and the potential professional and personal costs to be paid for rocking the boat are similarly high—are unlikely to stray very far from this conventional view of people and events. Thus, the parameters of the debate on Islam, Muslims, and the Muslim world are very narrow, and very difficult for most individuals and organizations within the mainstream American media to transgress without fear.

All of these factors could be changed or countered with relatively simple reforms, but others are more difficult to move and have at least as strong an impact on the American media and their approach to Islam and Muslims. These objective factors can be divided into two categories: first, the historical relations between Islam and the West, and second, the nature of the contemporary American news media.

The historical differences, misunderstandings, and biases that have divided Islam from the West continue to influence how the American media perceive Islam (and how Muslims see the West, it should be added). These conflicts date back to the time of the Prophet Muhammad in the seventh century and run through the Byzantine Empire, the Crusades, the Spanish Reconquista, the fall of Constantinople, the eras of colonialism and national independence, up to today.[13] It is clearly impossible to put an end to fourteen centuries of mutual hostility and distrust overnight. Everything dealing with Islam and the Muslim world will be colored to one degree or another by this history: the manner in which the journalist views the story, the way a source responds to a question, the language the writer will use, the process an editor uses to approve and place the article and, ultimately, the reader's understanding of the information contained within the finished piece.

Most Americans are singularly uninformed about Islam and Muslims. A 1993 poll conducted by the *Los Angeles Times*, for example, asked 1,273 individuals four general questions about Islam. The number one response to three of those questions was "don't know," including 64.9 percent of the responses to the query, "What is your impression of the religion called Islam?" These dismal results illustrate the media's failure to inform the American public about Islam and the Islamic world, despite the tremendous amount of coverage devoted to those topics over the last fifteen years.[14] Add to that the fact that basic American education neglects the Middle East (aside from a bit on Pharaonic Egypt, which is included in the sweep of "Western Civilization" in most school curricula) and lacks foreign-language teaching and that Americans have little or no professional or personal contact with the region and little exposure to the religious and ethical teachings of Islam and one is not surprised to discover a public devoid of knowledge of the area. Journalists are, of course, drawn from the general American population, and where that population lacks knowledge and understanding of a subject it is not surprising that journalists as a group will suffer from the same deficiencies. These factors—the history of antagonism between Islam and the West and the lack of basic background knowledge of Islam and Muslims—are the two most important factors affecting the American media's ability adequately to cover Islam and Muslims.

Other factors inherent in the American media structure itself also have an impact on the media's coverage. First, the media give highest priority to immediate action and current events, particularly if these are deemed to constitute a threat to Americans or American interests. Historical background or probing analyses of future events fall rather lower on their list of priorities. Algeria, for instance, has received more media attention in the three years since the January 1992 cancellation of parliamentary elections and the outbreak of the country's low-level civil war than it did in the previous three decades of its existence as an independent nation. Yemen was front-page news in the summer of 1994 when it went through its own civil war; since that time it has vanished from the media's radar screen.

This phenomenon is not limited to the Middle East. To repeat one commonly cited example, thousands of jet airliners take off and land safely every day; it is only when one crashes that it becomes news. The result is a serious error of perception: although air travel is among the safest forms of transportation, thousands of people are afraid of flying.

In the case of the Muslim world, the fact that the media generally limit their coverage to violence and upheaval gives Americans the impression that these calamitous events are the rule, rather than the exception of daily life in the region. The American media provide the public with very little evidence to contradict that widely held, yet baseless assumption.

Second, news events are reported in terms of American interests, severely affecting not only the point of view of a story but also which stories are considered to be of interest. Muslims are news when they impinge on American interests—usually negatively. Sectarian and ethnic violence resulted in the loss of thousands of lives in Karachi, Pakistan, over the winter of 1994–95, yet coverage of the civil strife was extremely limited in the American press until an attack on a U.S. Consulate vehicle killed two American diplomats in the spring of 1995. Afterward, Karachi again slipped from the pages, although the violence in that port city continued.

Third, the American media are undergoing financial changes that are dictating shrinking resources. Newspapers and networks operate fewer foreign bureaus, employ reduced staffs, limit expenses for travel, accommodation, and other expenditures, and have generally scaled back their operations. As in politics, "all news is local," and expensive, far-flung foreign operations are therefore among the first targets of cost-cutting. Faced with declining revenues, the media are trimming budgets—and their ability to cover the news—to maintain their profitability. This is a growing problem for daily newspapers in small to medium-sized markets. Two decades ago most local newspapers were owned by an individual, family, or company with roots in the community. Today, very few dailies have escaped the trend toward corporate ownership. Large media conglomerates such as Gannet, Hearst, Scripps-Howard, and the New York Times Corporation now own the overwhelming majority of papers in the United States. These papers must remain profitable to please stockholders, sometimes at the expense of good journalism.

Fourth, the American mainstream media simply are not proficient at reporting on religious issues. There are individual journalists who are very adept at covering them, particularly for mainstream Protestant denominations and the Roman Catholic Church. Religious News Service, a wire service which provides a number of denominational and non-religious papers and newsletters with copy, boasts an extremely talented staff of writers and editors. But coverage of religion generally is relegated to one or two pages in the Sunday paper, and of the three major broadcast network news divisions, only ABC News maintains a full-time religion reporter.[15] Most reporters and editors on the main news or foreign desks see religion as an overly sensitive and specialized topic, and not normally as a source of "hard" news.[16]

Finally, most Americans are getting their news from television rather than a daily paper or a weekly magazine. Television often gives viewers a better sense of place than written journalism; it is more vibrant and attractive to the eye, and reports of events are often almost instantaneous. Televion news is, however, more ephemeral than print journalism. It is more difficult to use broadcasts for research purposes or for fact-checking, for instance. In addition, the amount of information contained in a ninety-second television report is substantially less than in a ten- or twelve-paragraph newspaper story. Nightly network news shows tend to cover fewer foreign stories than do daily papers, and only a handful of these overseas reports are more than two minutes long.

The growth in the importance of television news has had its impact on print journalism as well. The trend in both newspapers and newsweeklies is toward shorter stories with information increasingly being transmitted visually through charts and graphs. A decade ago *USA Today* seemed garish; today, nearly all local and national dailies use color photos and graphics in their layouts. Even "the Gray Lady," *The New York Times*, is slowly introducing color into its pages, beginning with inside feature sections and moving over time to the front page. Such graphics can help sell papers, but they seldom provide in-depth information, particularly about complex subjects. They reduce information to easy-to-read visuals, rather than expanding on information to provide greater or clearer understanding.

Taken together the various objective and subjective factors which affect the portrayal of Islam in the media make the situation seem rather bleak. The media now have fewer resources and provide less news and information to an audience which already has very little understanding of Islam and Muslims, and is unlikely to be exposed to new or substantially better sources of information in the future.

Muslim individuals, organizations, and nations must also bear some responsibility for this sad state of affairs, however. In the Muslim world there is a great deal of suspicion of the West in general, and of the Western media in particular. With the advent of CNN and satellite television, Muslim populations are able to see how they are portrayed in the West (both in the news and in entertainment), and they don't like it. Governments say they and their countries are neglected, but they want media coverage only so long as it is positive and furthers their goals and/or self-image. Unfortunately for these officials, it is impossible to dictate to the international press as they often can to local media outlets. This creates resentment and suspicion on both sides. As a result, Muslim countries have hurt themselves by restricting access to Western journalists, who must then rely on second-hand information for their stories. It is difficult for heads of state or ministers of information to complain about inaccurate reporting if they refuse to talk to reporters or allow them to do their jobs. On the other hand, it is unclear that simply allowing journalists to come to a Muslim country and providing them with access to local and national officials and other personalities will necessarily make media coverage more sympathetic. A case in point is Saudi Arabia which, when faced in 1994–95 with a series of news stories in the American and European press which predicted gloom and doom for the Kingdom both economically and politically, organized several press junkets for foreign journalists. The resulting coverage continued to focus on perceived problems (declining petroleum revenues, a young and expanding labor force, depleted cash reserves, regional instability, the age and health of King Fahd, etc.) rather than on the Kingdom's strengths and remarkable development, as Saudi officials had hoped.

The same unrealistic expectations can be found among American Muslims. Most of them believe their community has been ill-treated at the hands of the media, but not many are willing to speak up or take steps to change things. There are few American Muslim institutions in place that are equipped to deal with media coverage. Among those American Muslim organizations who have made inroads in media relations are the American Muslim Council (AMC) and the Council on American-Islamic Relations (CAIR) in Washington, D.C., and the Los Angeles-based Muslim Public Affairs Council (MPAC). In 1994 I gave a presentation at a mosque in northern Virginia on Islam in the media. When asked how many had seen something in the mainstream media over the last year which they felt insulted Islam or Muslims, over 90 percent of the roughly 250 Muslims in attendance raised their hands. Asked if they had written a letter to the editor or called a radio or television station to complain, only two Muslims raised their hands.

American Muslims agree that media coverage is a pressing concern for the community, yet many still want their sons and daughters to become doctors and engineers, not journalists, editors, and producers. These attitudes are changing, but the pace of change is slow. There is also a marked ambivalence in the attitudes of journalists who write for Muslim publications when they try to balance their professional duties against their duties as Muslims. They are reluctant to criticize when reporting on Muslim organizations, because to do so is often seen, not as good investigative or analytical journalism, but as a breakdown in etiquette or a violation of taboos. Yet if the Muslim community wants to produce journalists of note (and to be well informed in the process), these perceptions must change as well.

Finally, Muslims are unrealistic to expect that they will receive positive coverage even in light of violent attacks committed by radicals claiming to act in the name of Islam. As long as wayward Muslims blow up parking garages, skyjack airliners, or fire all manner of munitions at one another, there will be news stories which reflect negatively on Muslims. Coverage of Muslims will not become any more positive until the behavior of some Muslims around the world improves. This is not to argue that the radical fringe of Muslim extremists is anything but a tiny minority among the world-wide Muslim community, but that fact does little to affect the rational assessment of the American media and their relation to Islam.

There are ways to improve American media coverage, however, and most of them are relatively easy to implement and would not disrupt the smooth operation of a newsroom, but they do require the initiative of reporters, editors, producers, and owners if they are to succeed. Three of the easiest and most far reaching suggestions are described below.

First, the quality, knowledge, and understanding of the journalists in the field and the editors in the office of topics related to Islam and Muslims must be improved. They must be acquainted with the geography, history, politics, economics, social mores, and religious beliefs found in the Muslim world if they are to report accurately and convincingly on these topics. This suggestion raises the question of bias, however, since informed journalists inevitably will form their own opinions. Is it better to have an informed but opinionated reporter, or one who has no point of view but is also ignorant? This is not to argue that an informed reporter cannot be critical of the subject covered; in the United States, for example, much of the best and most critical reporting and editorializing on Israel and U.S.-Israeli relations can be found in the pages of Jewish weeklies like the *Washington Jewish Week*, the *Jewish Week* of Queens, New York, and New York City's excellent *Forward*. Crucial to the process are well-informed editors, who could and should strike a balance between their knowledgeable if opinionated writers and thus provide a continuum of news and views about Islam and Muslims.

A second curative measure would be to expand the range of sources being consulted about Islam to obtain a real diversity of views.[17] It is a daunting task to seek out, interview, and analyze the statements of a diverse and unfamiliar set of sources, and then make sense of those statements for a non-specialist audience. This is a job for informed journalists; without them, including more sources will likely only produce more confusion.

Writers and editors should allow Muslims to speak for themselves, and thus allow their readers or listeners to be exposed to the varied points of view and opinions found within the Muslim community on a wide range of topics. This in itself would constitute a new challenge for the American Muslim community, which has articulate spokespeople but has not been given the opportunity for them to be widely heard. Only time will tell how successful American Muslims will be in facing up to this new responsibility, but at least if they do so they will have no one to credit or blame but themselves.

Finally, media executives must make a commitment of resources to the reporting of Islam and Muslims. Stories on Islamic issues are found throughout the media, but quantity must be better supported by a commitment to quality. This means putting more and better journalists on the story and keeping these journalists on the Middle East beat for a longer period of time. One journalist who has acquired a deep understanding of Muslims and the

Muslim world and has continued to cover those topics rather than moving on to a higher-profile position is Robin Wright of the *Los Angeles Times*. Like the *Monitor*'s Peter Ford, Wright is adept at bringing together a diversity of views in her reporting and allowing Muslim sources to have their say. Another journalist who concentrates on one region and is able to convey its complexity with great subtlety is the British Broadcasting Corporation's former India correspondent Mark Tully, who set the standard for reporting on the Subcontinent.

Writers and editors should also be allowed to break away from crisis-driven coverage and turn their attention to background features which delineate the larger context of the Muslim community. This would allow the introduction of alternative images and models of Muslims and Islam—perhaps the single most important ingredient in shattering long-held American myths about Muslims and allowing a more realistic and accurate portrayal of the worldwide Muslim community to emerge. That, in the end, should be the goal of American journalism when it turns its attention to Islam.

Will these prescriptions actually be implemented, and will they actually work? In the short term, probably not. The subjective and objective factors which shape media coverage are very strong, the media can be very defensive and resistant to change, and there is little in the way of immediate economic returns to encourage such transformations. Redirecting media practice is like turning a battleship—a slow, tedious and cumbersome process. It is unlikely that substantial reforms will be implemented anytime soon, and little prospect of improved coverage of Islam and Muslims in the near future. In the long run, however, improvement is likely to be forced by factors quite beyond the control of the media. There already are some one billion Muslims in the world, boasting some of the globe's highest birthrates and inhabiting a considerable portion of the earth's most economically and politically important real estate. Sometime in the next century, Islam will become the second largest religion in the United States, as it already is throughout much of Western Europe. If anything, Islam is becoming increasingly important and newsworthy as both an international and a domestic story, and ultimately Islam and Muslims will demand a higher standard of journalism than the American media have achieved up to this point. The media can take steps now to turn this challenge into an exciting opportunity to broaden their perspectives and those of their readers and listeners, or American journalism can play catch-up later, with all of the displacement and disappointing results that course entails.

Notes

1. For a somewhat dated but still trenchant book-length critique of American media coverage of Islam, see Edward Said, *Covering Islam* (New York: Pantheon Books, 1981). See also Richard Curtiss, *A Changing Image: American Perceptions of the Arab-Israeli Dispute* (Washington, D.C.: American Educational

Trust, 1986), particularly chapter 31, "The Media—Copout or Conspiracy?" pp. 307–26.

2. One such example is "Women of the Veil," a 12-page special supplement written by Deborah Scroggins which appeared in the *Atlanta Journal-Constitution* on June 28, 1992. It provoked national criticism from American Muslim individuals and organizations displeased with its biased and simplistic portrayal of women in the Muslim world.

3. For a discussion of the term, see John Esposito, *The Islamic Threat: Myth or Reality?* (Oxford: Oxford University Press, 1992), pp. 7–8; and Bernard Lewis, *The Political Language of Islam* (Chicago: University of Chicago Press, 1988), pp. 117–18, n.3.

4. See Curtiss, *Changing Image*, pp. 309–12.

5. John Esposito raises this point in his *Islamic Threat: Myth or Reality?* and notes that the very different regimes governing Iran, Pakistan, and Libya also have been labeled "fundamentalist"; see Esposito, *Islamic Threat*, p. 8.

6. For the article which began the "clash of civilizations" debate, see Samuel Huntington, "The Coming Clash of Civilizations," *Foreign Affairs* 72, no. 3 (Summer 1993): 22–49.

7. Charles Arnot, *Don't Kill the Messenger: The Tragic Story of Wells Hangen and Other Journalistic Combat Victims* (New York: Vintage Press, 1994), p. 186.

8. For a critique of Steven Emerson's work by a fellow investigative journalist, see Robert I. Friedman, "One Man's *Jihad*," *The Nation* 260, no. 19 (May 15, 1995): 656–57.

9. As detailed in Khalid Duran, "Bosnia: Genocide 1992," *International Report*, February 1993, pp. 6–7.

10. Both *The New York Times* and *The Washington Post* generally replace their Jerusalem correspondent after two or three years, and a similar situation has arisen vis-à-vis the papers' correspondents in Sarajevo.

11. See, for example, Thomas Friedman, *From Beirut to Jerusalem* (New York: Anchor Books, 1989), and Judith Miller's various contributions to *Foreign Affairs*, including "The Challenge of Radical Islam" in 72, no. 2 (Spring 1993): 43–56; and "Faces of Fundamentalism" in 73, no. 6 (November–December 1994): 123–42. For a critique of Friedman's work, see Edward Said's review, "The Orientalist Express: Thomas Friedman Wraps Up the Middle East" in the anthology *The Politics of Dispossession: The Struggle for Palestinian Self-Determination, 1969–1994* (New York: Pantheon Books, 1994): 360–65.

12. For a discussion of the Reagan administration's use of Libya as a scapegoat for domestic political advantage, see Noam Chomsky, "Middle East Terrorism and the American Ideological System" in Edward Said and Christopher Hitchens, eds., *Blaming the Victims: Spurious Scholarship and the Palestinian Question* (New York: Verso, 1988): 138–39.

13. For a provocative and balanced examination of this history of perception, see Maxim Rodinson, *Europe and the Mystique of Islam* (Seattle: University of Washington Press, 1987). For more polemical critiques, consult Edward Said, *Orientalism* (New York: Pantheon Books, 1978) and Bernard Lewis's response in his *Islam and the West* (Oxford: Oxford University Press, 1993). All of these works focus on Western intellectual approaches to Islam, yet many of their criticisms hold true for today's American media as well.

14. "Islam Rising," *Los Angeles Times*, April 6, 1993.

15. This position (filled by Peggy Wehmeyer, formerly a religion reporter for WFAA-TV, ABC's Dallas-Fort Worth affiliate) reportedly was created at the insistence of anchorman Peter Jennings.

16. For an interesting discussion of the American media's approach to religion in general, see the liberal Catholic magazine *Commonweal*'s special issue on "Religion and the Media," February 24, 1995.

17. An excellent example of this kind of reporting can be found in a six-part series in the *Christian Science Monitor* written by Peter Ford on "Islam and Democracy: Redefining Arab Rule." The articles, which appeared on April 21–23 and 26–28, 1993, included quotations and statements from a variety of Muslim and non-Muslim thinkers, politicians, and activists from across the political and ideological spectrum.

12

Economic Security and Muslim Identity

A Study of the Immigrant Community
in Durham, North Carolina

ELISE GOLDWASSER

The purpose of a study of Muslim immigrants in Durham, North Carolina, conducted over two years was to determine the reasons behind the decision to immigrate and see if those reasons had any correlation with the religious identity and practices of the immigrants involved. The study compared the experience of middle-class immigrants to those with little or no economic security. The findings were that the more prosperous ones were intent on retaining their Muslim way of life, while the poor were trying to transform themselves to fit into an American mold; both groups, however, adopted some aspect of the host culture and rejected others.

Since the 1970s immigrant Muslims have been settling in the so-called Triangle area of Raleigh, Durham, and Chapel Hill.[1] According to local community leaders, approximately 5,000 Muslims now live in the region: 3,000 in Raleigh and more than 30 families or about 500 Muslims in Durham. The majority are Sunni, but there are also some Shi'a. The group is also ethnically diverse: about 35 percent is native-born, both African American (30 percent) and white (5 percent) who have converted to Sunni Islam; about 60 percent is foreign-born; 10 to 15 percent is Arab, primarily from Egypt and North Africa or from the Saudi peninsula and the Gulf states. Asians from Bangladesh, India, and Pakistan comprise about 10–15 percent; the remainder are from Iran or Asians from Malaysia and Indonesia, and Africans, primarily from Nigeria, Eritrea, and the Republic of South Africa.

The group is also economically diverse. Refugees from Eritrea arrived impoverished; some of the other groups were well situated in the middle class—research scientists, medical professionals, educators, or owners of small businesses. The native-born Muslims also spanned the economic spectrum from minimum-wage jobs to high-paying positions in the city and county governments.

Over the past twenty years, the Durham community has developed institutions to serve both its native- and foreign-born members, fulfilling traditional functions as well as the new ones needed for cultural survival in the United States. The community has built a mosque which is both a meeting place for communal prayers and a social and educational center. It hosts typically American institutions such as monthly potluck suppers, prayer breakfasts during Ramadan and weekly women's study programs and lectures. In addition, in 1990 the community founded an Islamic day school with room for seventy students; its student body is drawn from all national groups represented. These programs and institutions foster a community identity for this otherwise diverse population.[2]

The study was supplemented by interviews with 25 Muslims from 10 countries. Of these 25 subjects, 5 were from Egypt, 4 from Indonesia, 3 from Ethiopia, 3 from Pakistan, and 3 from the United States; 2 were from Bangladesh, and 1 each from Dubai, India, Saudi Arabia, and Syria. All were Sunni (none of the small number of Shi'a I contacted was available for interviews, though they were not unwilling—arrangements simply did not work out). Their responses revealed certain patterns connecting economic security to both cultural marginality and preservation of an Islamic world view. Well-educated, financially secure Muslims who have settled in the United States to take advantage of the freedom this society offers maintain their Islamic world view and are continuing to practice their religious observances. Though economically secure, they choose to remain marginalized culturally. On the other hand, the Eritreans immigrants, fleeing life threatened by political unrest, came to the United States for security more than for freedom. As refugees with no financial resources, they face obstacles to the maintenance of their native traditions, and though they have tried to Americanize themselves, they have found that poverty impedes assimilation.

Economic security is the pivotal factor influencing the degree to which immigrants preserve their Islamic ways of life. In Durham, assimilation is related to financial security and socioeconomic status.[3] The important role of economics, however, does not diminish the crucial part that other factors such as ethnicity play in preserving cultural and religious identity. Attending exclusively to economic factors, as early and influential immigration historians have, is to ignore the significance of the efforts immigrants have made to shape their own lives.[4] For example, financially secure Muslims in Durham, indifferent to efforts by the dominant culture to assimilate them, use their socioeconomic status to establish Islamic lives in their new home. Responding to questions about cultural and ethnic differences in a community as multinational as Durham's, most informants maintained that a Muslim's primary allegiance is to God, and since Islam is their central concern, ethnic differences are less important than the harmony of the community.[5] They use the freedom economic security allows to maintain their identity as Muslims and also to criticize many aspects of the dominant consumer-oriented culture and its emphasis on individualism. Their Islamic world view emphasizes a holistic analysis that informs their perceptions of their new homeland. For instance, one topic that came up frequently in the interviews was the difficulty of carrying out daily Islamic ritual in the United States. In keeping with their Islamic world view, they did not attribute these problems to individual shortcomings, but rather as a result of living in a culture whose socioeconomic system makes ritual practice difficult.

The Eritreans came from an Islamically centered culture, but began life in the United States not only penniless but without the kinds of skills that would provide economic stability. In Ethiopia, the women did not work outside the home; their husbands were mainly tailors who owned small shops. Having fled violence and starvation, they were entirely dependent on the vagaries of the American economic system to reestablish their lives. To compensate for their lack of power they attempted cultural assimilation; religious practice and an Islamic world view were secondary to earning a living in a foreign economic and social system. They have tried to embrace American ways and they are encouraging their children to grow up as Americans.

While being a Muslim immigrant in Durham in the late twentieth century is a unique experience, immigrating to the United States is not. The project therefore drew on labor history and history by and about Muslims (primarily Arabs) in the United States to place their situation into the larger context of American labor immigration and assimilation over the centuries. Historians of Arab and Muslim labor immigration agree that up to now, assimilation and the rise to the middle class go hand in hand. In fact, labor scholarship strongly suggests that for working-class immigrants of all nationalities, the price of economic security has been to sacrifice some part of one's ethnic identity. Labor historians debate the degree to which entry into the middle class entails a reconstruction of ethnic identity or its replacement with "Anglo-Saxon" (i.e., American) models of social convention and political habit.[6] Arab and Muslim literature suggests that for earlier immigrants, assimilation was particularly thorough. Haddad, Naff, and Orfalea document second- and third-generation Arabs and Muslims who have anglicized names, intermarried with non-Muslims, know nothing of traditions, rituals, and the Arabic language, and have entirely embraced the dominant culture, all of which, they argue, coincide with their ascent to middle-class status.[7] The Eritrean refugees seem also to be following this pattern of assimilation.

Little of the scholarship, however, discusses immigrants who arrive in the United States already belonging to the middle class, and the literature rarely mentions middle-class immigrants who choose to remain unassimilated. This, however, is the situation of the well-educated, English-speaking Muslims who have arrived in Durham since the 1970s. White-collar Muslims in Durham have set their own terms for assimilation and it includes the ability to retain their Muslim way of life.

This study suggests that everyone lives within parameters but that money makes the space within those parameters larger. The freedom to determine the kind of life they will live in the United States is available primarily for those immigrants who can afford those choices. Others, however, must live within the rules their economic situation sets for them.

Economic Marginality and Cultural Assimilation

To represent the Eritrean group, I interviewed a woman, her husband, and his brother.[8] The couple has two elementary-school-aged children; the brother and his wife have three children all under the age of seven and all born in Durham. Having fled Ethiopia in 1979 and having lived in refugee camps in Sudan for years, the two families had come to Durham in 1983 and have lived there ever since. The women came from relatively wealthy families; in fact, one is the daughter of a shaykh. In their birthplace of Asmara, neither woman worked outside her home and both had household servants. Their husbands owned tailoring businesses in Asmara and in Sudan; however, they did not immigrate with enough capital to restart their businesses in the United States, or with any degrees or marketable skills. For these reasons, all four adults are now working to make enough money to provide basic necessities. Their first jobs were low paying menial positions: three washed dishes and bussed tables at a restaurant; the other cleaned hotel rooms. Even now that they speak English more fluently and are making more money, they work for hourly wages with very few health benefits. One woman cooks at an expensive restaurant in the evenings and takes care of other peoples' children during the day; her husband works at the Duke University Medical Center laundry facility. The other man does menial work at a restaurant and a hotel. His wife works at the Duke University Medical Center as well.

In Eritrea three of the four adults prayed daily and all of them led what they considered Islamically centered lives. They have tried to preserve their cultural and religious identity because it is important to them. They have given their children Arabic names that reflect their Muslim heritage; they have taught the children bedtime prayers and mealtime customs. They have requested that the school not make their children eat pork. These efforts are, however, minor compared to the enormous changes they have had to make.

Their lack of economic security has forced them to put economic survival above all other concerns. They try to compensate for their insecure economic situation by mooring themselves to the dominant culture which brings them closer to the mainstream and fosters a feeling of physical and psychological security, both in terms of food, shelter and physical safety and in control, however limited, over their daily lives.

They all work more than forty hours a week. The limited amount of free time that results means that they have given up many of their Islamic practices and they have not sought out other Muslims in the area. During the interviews, each expressed frustration at having to choose between using time to observe Islamic rituals or to go to work—in other words, their precarious economic position pits job security against Islamic practice. For example, although Islam forbid Muslims to drink or to serve alcohol, the woman who cooks in a restaurant must prepare recipes that call for wine or sherry. Her brother-in-law works in a beer garden, where he is making more money than he had earned at any other job in Durham.

Lack of time also pushes the Eritreans to choose which Islamic customs to observe and which to disregard. Work schedules keep then from praying at the five assigned times of day and from attending Friday communal prayers at the mosque. Each deals with this problem differently: one woman prays as close to assigned times as possible; one of the men prays three times daily; the other man simply does not pray. The physical difficulty of their work is also a factor in the decline of their religious practice. For example, in Ethiopia, all of the adults observed the month-long Ramadan fast from sunrise to sunset. In Durham, however, none fast because they cannot perform their strenuous jobs without sustenance. All say that taking time off without pay is not a choice.

Just as working long hours and forgoing various Islamic practices ensures their physical and financial survival, taking part in the dominant culture bolsters their psychological security. Each separately reported that fitting in is very important to their family. "In America, we are Americans," the woman said. All of the family members try hard to be what they consider typical Americans; they dress in Western clothing, though none did in Ethiopia. The woman explained that she and her husband did not want strangers to stare at their unusual clothing; they also wanted to shed some of the characteristics that made them feel self-consciously different from their neighbors. When she worked as a motel maid, the woman found that her African-American coworkers looked down on her; they would talk about her behind her back and taunt her to her face. They told her to cut her long hair or wear it tied up because otherwise it would dirty her uniform. Within earshot, they would whisper, "Look at her, she's African! She's African! She's so primitive."

Their children, too, are self-conscious about standing out and have thrown themselves into the dominant culture. The children understand Tigre, but will speak only English. The elder daughter of the older brother, born in Africa, speaks fluent English with the accent of a gentrified lady from northeastern North Carolina. After three months in the first grade, she also read English fluently. With distinct voices for various characters, she would read stories to her younger sister. The girls' younger cousins show signs of growing up as Americans as well. They are completely comfortable with the things American boys value. When he was four, the six-year-old already associated the adults in his life by the cars they drove; neighbors became Laurie

Datsun and Danny Celica. Often it was possible to hear him correct his older friends, "That's not a Datsun wagon. It's a Toyota hatchback." Like most school-age boys in the United States, now he and his four-year-old brother play at being Teenage Mutant Ninja Turtles. They greet each other and everyone else with a raised fist and the cry, "Turtle Power." Aside from their Arabic names, these children are nearly indistinguishable from their non-immigrant peers.

While children raised in the United States adapt to the dominant culture fairly easily, their Ethiopian-raised parents find the process complicated by their pressing need for safety and security—in fact, the two are inextricably linked. As refugees, their primary goal was to reestablish a safe home for their families. In Ethiopia, where government-sanctioned, military-sponsored midnight killings were commonplace, they had reason to fear for their lives. They see their escape to the United States as their salvation and the foundation for economic security. They are grateful to be alive even if they are struggling. Though by economic standards they are not successful, they do not criticize the system or the dominant culture. Rather, they blame themselves, their foreignness, and their inability to speak English fluently. They say their lives in Durham are difficult because rent, food, utilities, and clothing are expensive and their hard work does not cover all of their expenses; they need to work harder.

Despite these hardships they believe they have chosen the best of their limited options. Because they are able to live without the threat of execution or starvation, there is always the possibility of regaining what they have given up. All three parents pinned their aspirations for the future on their children, for whom they wish an Islamic life. A college education which will help the children find secure jobs is, they suggest, one way to ensure the maintenance of this Muslim identity. One parent has started a college fund into which she makes a monthly $25 payment for each of her two daughters.

Freedom, Financial Security, and Cultural Marginalization

In the Muslim world, political and economic changes combined with technological advancements have created a scientifically literate middle class[9] and have allowed scientists, medical doctors, and other intellectuals to pursue research opportunities in Europe and the United States, where these domestic changes coincided with the relaxation of discriminatory immigration laws.[10]

A well-educated group of sixteen immigrants in this category were interviewed for this survey. Three held Ph.D.s, four were medical doctors, and eight had master's degrees in various fields. All spoke English before their arrival in Durham; nine studied in Great Britain or in another part of the United States. All chose to live in Durham because they had jobs at the local educational and research institutions, Durham Technical Instate, the Institute for Parapsychology, North Carolina Central University, the University of North Carolina, Duke University, its medical center, or its engineering school.

What they have in common is their determination to preserve their Islamic way of life, including the primacy of their relationship to God and identification with the Muslim community through practices defined in the Qur'an and the Sunna.[11] In Durham, as in every Muslim community, there is disagreement over interpretation of some Islamic codes. Community members often disagree in particular over what constitutes appropriately modest dress for women and ritually fit meats. Some women cover themselves completely; others wear nonrevealing clothes but do not cover their heads; still others dress modestly but in Western skirts and blouses.[12] Because Muslims, Jews, and Christians believe in the same God, Muslims may eat kosher meat, and meat from Christian suppliers, so long as it is not pork; all the informants would prefer to buy their meat from a Muslim butcher, but there is none in the area. Anticipating the lack of *hallal* meat in Durham, one Indonesian informant had consulted the religious authorities in Jakarta. Their ruling was that since the United States was a "Christian" country, its businesses were Christian as well, and therefore meat in any supermarket was fine.[13] A Syrian, a Pakistani, two Egyptians and an informant from Dubai echoed this sentiment; but other Pakistanis, Egyptians, and an informant from Saudi Arabia eat either kosher meat or meat that they slaughtered themselves on a farm 95 miles to the east in Rocky Mount. These differences, however, were minor compared to the convictions they held in common.

Since they had left their native countries not for economic survival but for the lack of opportunities for career advancement, the freedom that financial security affords them allowed them to preserve their Islamic way of life. They also had social prestige that allowed them to live as they wished. They were able to maneuver their work schedules to accommodate individual daily prayer, attendance at Friday prayer, fasting during Ramadan. When they encountered obstacles to religious observance, they simply distanced themselves from elements of the dominant culture that they perceived as un-Islamic or chose some acceptable way to compromise.

They maintained Islamic practices even when they conflicted with the rhythms of the Western business world. Although it takes considerable time out of the day, thirteen Muslims who prayed in their native countries continued to do so in Durham since they had at work both the autonomy and the privacy to structure prayer sessions into their work routine. It is not surprising then that most who attended *jum'a* prayers at either of the two mosques in Durham are either professionals or students, in other words, people with control over their time. An anesthesiologist from Pakistan forewent his lunch hours during the week to accumulate enough time to attend the lengthy prayers on Fridays. One woman said that when she accepted her research position, she explicitly requested time off for Friday prayers and mentioned that several professionals from Research Triangle Park belonged to the same weekly group.

Even more demanding than daily and weekly practices is the month-long observance of Ramadan which requires schedule changes that these financially secure Muslims can accommodate. All of the financially secure Muslim informants followed the prohibitions of Ramadan. To abstain from food and drink for eighteen or more hours they chose tasks that were possible as the day wore on and arranged their work accordingly. They gave themselves time to focus on the spiritual aspects of the fast. To allow himself time for prayer and reflection, the Pakistani anesthesiologist took his vacation in Ramadan.[14]

Financial security permitted these Muslims not only to observe their practices, but to declare their presence as Muslims in the public realm. In May 1985, during a visit to her family in Durham, a Pakistani woman was diagnosed with sinus cancer and was admitted as a patient to Duke University Medical Center; she remained in Durham until her death in August 1986. During her frequent hospital visits, the woman's family permitted medical personnel to treat her illness only within the parameters of Islamic law, even when those rules were inconvenient for her doctors. For example, because Islam sets proscriptions on contact between men and women who are not relatives, the family made sure that no male doctor was alone with the woman. They insisted that at least one of the woman's daughters remain in the examination room during all meetings with male doctors; the doctors complied with the rule against touching by performing more expensive, noninvasive tests, though they took longer to yield results. To preserve their mother's dignity as a law-abiding Muslim, the daughters breached the hospital's policy of one overnight guest in a patient's room, and both would stay so that if one daughter needed to leave the room, someone would be with their mother should a male doctor come in.

The woman's death in the emergency room heightened the stakes for control for both her family, which insisted on following Islamic law, and the hospital administration, which at first refused to change its policies to accommodate the family's desires. In the middle of the night, the four sisters and their brother brought their dying mother to the emergency room. When she died, the family refused to send her body to the morgue. While the family members attended to their mother's body, the woman's doctor, an Asian Buddhist sensitive to the problems of carrying out non-Christian religious practices at Duke Hospital, insisted to hospital administrators that the body remain out of the morgue and with the family in the emergency room. For many hours, the five children remained with the body and read a designated chapter of the Qur'an until it was possible to transport the body to a funeral home.

The family found that the funeral-home management and staff, though unfamiliar with the proscriptions, were willing to work within the tenets of

Islamic law. They familiarized themselves with the Islamic laws concerning death and permitted the Muslims to carry out preburial rituals such as bathing and perfuming the body without using alcohol, forbidding men to see the nude body, permitting only women to touch the body, and having a Muslim with the body at all times. Because there were no women on the funeral-home staff, the daughters and other women from the Muslim community bathed the body. When no female embalmer was available, a Muslim doctor performed the embalming with instructions from a male embalmer who stood within earshot but out of sight of the body. Once the body was bathed, perfumed, embalmed, and clothed in a shroud that the daughters had made, the family and community members waited in the funeral home for three days for the arrival of legal permits to fly the body back to Pakistan.

The woman's death made it possible for the community to institute Islamic practice at the funeral home and at Duke University Medical Center. Now when a Muslim dies at Duke, the staff knows not to send the body to the morgue but alerts community members who arrange for the preburial rituals and, when necessary, for permits to transport the body. The funeral home is also prepared. The staff has stored the appropriate equipment for bathing and perfuming the body. Its staff is aware of the existence of Islamic burial practices and the possibility that family and community members may spend a few nights in the building.[15]

Manipulating their work schedules and pressuring institutions have allowed these financially secure Muslims both to preserve their Islamic heritage and to keep themselves from un-Islamic influences in the dominant culture; however, some obstacles are insurmountable. When faced with impediments, this group complains, sometimes even going so far as to state that instituting an Islamic way of life would improve Western society morally. The Muslims condemn the dominant culture's need for immediate gratification which they believe erodes spirituality by encouraging materialism and immoral behavior. They criticize both materialism and sexual permissiveness as signs that the society promotes freedom without responsibility and fosters greed and selfishness.[16] Most of their complaints revolve around the prevalence of pornography, casual sex, illegal drugs, violence, and money as indications of the society's numerous weaknesses. While their criticisms ranged from simplistic to sophisticated, all attributed society's problems to its prevalent secular world view and thought that implementing religious and moral strictures could mend the society. A research scientist from Pakistan commented that the "standard of success in this culture is based on material accumulation" instead of on the Islamic standard of spiritual and moral achievement. The Pakistani anesthesiologist and a Syrian engineer suggested that religious practice would remedy many social problems. If more Americans believed in God and followed moral and religious principles, the doctor suggested, there would be fewer problems involving sex, alcohol, drugs, and debt. An informant from Saudi Arabia castigated non-

God-fearing individuals for causing others to behave immorally, declaring that women who wear bikinis and other revealing clothes are responsible for provoking sexual assault. As they see it, the socioeconomic system, geared to immediate gratification through material enticements and permissive pleasures, leads people away from spirituality toward wrongful behavior. The consensus of this group is that without responsibility to a higher power, such as the Islamic accountability to God, this society will never alter its morally corrupt ways. Refusing to accept the stipulations of consumer culture uncritically and adhering to their own moral code, they set their own terms for participating in mainstream society.[17]

As these examples have shown, each day members of this group find themselves mediating between the demands of the host culture and their responsibilities as Muslims. A psychiatry resident from India is a case in point: we will call her here Latifa Ahmad; she is typical of how Muslim professionals use their freedom to set the terms of cultural assimilation. Dr. Ahmad's interview responses[18] suggest that her family's emphasis on strict religious adherence and affirmation of her intellectual capabilities shaped her belief that she could practice medicine within an Islamic framework. Even after her graduation from medical school in 1978, she remained in her parents' home in southern India and neither dated nor socialized in mixed-sex groups. In 1979 she married a Pakistani Muslim whom her sister's husband had recommended. Chaperoned by her sister and her aunt, she met with her prospective husband accompanied by her brother in-law. After fifteen minutes in an ice cream parlor, they concluded their meeting with positive results. After all she stated, "[Our] common tie is the religion. In Islam you marry and begin to love that person."

Arriving in August 1979, Dr. Ahmad and her husband transplanted their strict religious orientation and their medical careers to Durham. They established the foundations of a multigenerational Islamic home; Dr. Ahmad's parents in-law live with them. Her husband practiced anesthesiology; Dr. Ahmad stayed home with their first child, born in November 1979, but used the time to study for her medical licensing examinations in radiology and oncology. From 1982 to 1985, she practiced radiology and oncology at Duke University Medical Center, but because she found dealing with pediatric cancer patients too depressing and too stressful she turned to psychiatry as a resident in 1985.

Dr. Ahmad's daily life shows that she is serious not only about maintaining Islamic practices but also about raising her children as devout Muslims. She and her husband allow only *hallal* meat into their home. They are considering building a swimming pool because Dr. Ahmad will not swim in mixed-sex groups nor will she allow her children to do so when they reach their teens. Dr. Ahmad and her husband insist on their parental responsibility to be models of Islamic behavior. They have taught their children to begin each meal by invoking God's name. The older children, aware of the Islamic prohibitions on pork and pork products, check labels on cookies and sweets before they lobby for treats during family trips to the food store. Dr. Ahmad and her husband also plan Islamic-oriented family activities. During summer evenings, they discuss hadith and its meaning for their lives and the importance of prayer as one of the mainstays of Islam. In the mornings and the evenings, when everyone is home together, three generations of Ahmads perform their prayers as a family. Since he was five, the seven-year-old son has been chanting the *adhan* (call to prayer) in Arabic, both for his family and for community gatherings. The parents are equally proud of their daughter, who under the guidance of her grandfather, has been reading the Qur'an in Arabic since she was four and a half years old.

The parents' Islamic pedagogy extends to their children's relationships with the Muslim community as well. Dr. Ahmad calls her children's socializing with other Muslims children "group therapy" because the play time reaffirms their good feelings about themselves as Muslims and allows them to share those feelings with non-Muslim classmates and acquaintances. During the interview, their Urdu- and English-speaking daughter, then a public-school second grader, told about taking a book on Islam for show and tell: "It's called *Hadith for Children*, and it's in Arabic," she explained, careful to differentiate between Arabic and Urdu. The children have an awareness and knowledge of their ethnic and religious heritage and ritual practices that is rare for such young children.

Although she can successfully run her household and raise her children according to Islamic tradition, Dr. Ahmad has found that in her professional life, she must make compromises with religious practice. Although she prays in her office during the week, her schedule prohibits her attending jum'a prayers on Fridays, but it is in any case optional for women. She has had to alter her attire, since saris and head covers were impractical in the hospital. She Westernized her wardrobe in stages, first wearing the Pakistani women's outfit of a long-sleeved tunic over loose trousers, then turning to loose, longsleeved shirts and baggy pants that comply with Islamic stipulations for women to cover themselves and hide their form. At first she found meeting alone with men even more troublesome. As a psychiatrist, she not only meets one-on-one with male patients, but in the preliminary interview, she must ask them questions about their sexual habits, a subject which as a devout Muslim, she would normally not discuss with any man other than her husband. "On the other hand," she explained, "this is the art of medicine," and in her role as a doctor she has a responsibility to help her patients which she can do only by learning pertinent information about them.

In other ways, she has been more successfully Muslim. She believes, for example, that her residency in psychiatry has fortified her already strong commitment to Islam. For centuries Islam has been concerned with the consequences of alcoholism, gluttony, and promiscuity. She believes in the therapeutic value of religious faith for her patients who feel they have no control over their lives.

She is raising her children as Muslims not just because she is a Muslim, but because, she says, "I want my children to be Muslims for their emotional well being." She is making the most of her skills as both a practicing Muslim and a psychiatrist. The Pakistani woman who died in the emergency room had been both Dr. Ahmad's patient on the oncology ward and a family friend. Dr. Ahmad therefore took part in organizing support for the grieving family and in the pre-burial bathing preparations. She was also the only Islamically qualified person available to embalm the lady, so for the honor of her dead friend, Dr. Ahmad performed her first embalming. It took her eight hours instead of the normal one. Thus was Dr. Ahmad's determination to use her professional skills to maintain her Islamic heritage.

The Eritreans' need for security and the Muslim professionals' desire for freedom led these two groups to very different patterns of adapting to life in the United States. The Eritreans feel compelled to relinquish Islamic practices that impede their ability to fit safely into the mainstream. The professionals, regardless of their nationality, use their socioeconomic status to preserve their Islamic heritage and thereby choose to remain on the cultural margins. Their lack of economic security pushes them to seek psychological security by identifying with the dominant culture. They dress in Western clothing; women as well as men even wear blue jeans. Their children, products of Head Start and the Durham County public schools, speak English with a southern accent. The parents regard these signs of successful Americanization as a harbinger of their future security in their new homeland. The professionals, on the other hand, have taken advantage of their prosperity, status, and skills to set limits on what and how much of the dominant culture they will accept and as a result have been able to preserve their Islamic traditions even in the quintessentially un-Islamic environment of Durham, North Carolina.

Notes

1. I wish to thank Shaykh Abdenasser Zouhri, Imam of Masjid al-Rahman, for assistance with the recent demographic data.

2. A community of the followers of Warith Deen Muhammad, all native-born converts, also reside in Durham, but the two communities interact very little. This study, however, focuses solely on the immigrants. For an overview of native-born Muslims, see C. Eric Lincoln, "The American Muslim Mission in the Context of American Social History" in *The Muslim Community in North America*, ed. Earle H. Waugh, Baha Abu-Laban, and Regula B. Quershi (Alberta: University of Alberta Press, 1983).

3. According to the literature on immigration and assimilation in the United States, those immigrants in the upper- and middle-income categories are usually the most likely to strive for cultural assimilation. The actions of the financially secure Muslims in Durham, however, contradict the notion. For examples of this argument, see Leonard Dinnerstein and David M. Reimers, *Ethnic Americans: A History of Immigration* (New York: New York University Press, 1977);

S. N. Eisenstadt, *The Absorption of Immigrants* (Glencoe, IL: Free Press, 1955); Nathan Glazer and Daniel P. Moynihan, *Ethnicity: Theory and Experience* (Cambridge: Harvard University Press, 1975.); Milton M. Gordon, *Assimilation in American Life* (New York: Oxford University Press, 1964); Andrew M. Greely, *Ethnicity in the United States* (New York: John Wiley & Sons, 1974), and Peter Isaac Rose, ed., *Nation of Nations* (New York: Random House, 1972).

4. In two ways, the findings and the focus of this study differ from the work of Oscar Handlin (*The Uprooted* [Boston: Little, Brown and Company, 1951]). First, focusing only on general economic trends, he ignores specific ethnic and cultural differences that shape the immigrant experience. Second, his emphasis on economics reduces the immigrants to pawns of the economic system instead of actors in their own lives. This study, however, explores not only the relationship of culture and economics but also the ways immigrants control their lives within socioeconomic and cultural limitations.

5. See, in particular, interviews 6, 14, 15, and 18 in the possession of the author.

6. For examples of labor historiography, see John Bodnar, *The Trans planted: A History of Immigrants in Urban America* (Bloomington: University of Indiana Press, 1985), and *Immigration and Industrialization: Ethnicity in an American Mill Town, 1870–1940* (Pittsburgh: University of Pittsburgh Press, 1977). See also Rudolf J. Velcoli's critique of Oscar Handlin's argument, "Contadini in Chicago: A Critique of *The Uprooted*" in *Journal of American History* 51 (1964): 404–17. For other refutations of Handlin's argument with details on other ethnic groups, see Ewa Morawska, Humbert S. Nelli and Judith Smith below. See also, Josef J. Barton, *Peasants and Strangers: Italians, Rumanians and Slovaks in an American City* (Cambridge: Harvard University Press, 1975); Rowland Tappan Berthoff, *British Immigrants in Industrial America, 1790–1950* (Cambridge: Harvard University Press, 1953); John Bodnar, Roger Simon, and Michael P. Webb, *Lives of Their Own: Blacks, Italians and Poles in Pittsburgh, 1900–1960* (Chicago: University of Illinois Press, 1980); Kathleen Neils Conzen, "Immigrants, Immigrant Neighborhoods and Ethnic Identity: Historical Issues," *Journal of American History* 66 (1979): 603–15. Jay P. Dolan, *The Immigrant Church: New York's Irish and German Catholics* (Baltimore: The Johns Hopkins University Press, 1975); Donna Gabbaccia, *Militants and Migrants: Rural Sicilians Become American Workers* (New Brunswick, NJ: Rutgers University Press, 1988); Victor Greene, *For God and for Country: The Rise of Polish and Lithuanian Ethnic Consciousness in America* (Madison: University of Wisconsin Press, 1975); Joan M. Jensen, *Passage from India: Asian Indian Immigrants in North America* (New Haven: Yale University Press, 1988). Ewa Morwraska, *For Bread With Butter: The Lifeworlds of East Central Europeans in Johnstown, Pennsylvania, 1890–1940* (New York: Cambridge University Press, 1985); Humbert S. Nelli, *From Immigrants to Ethnics: The Italian-Americans* (New York: Oxford University Press, 1983); Theodore Salontos, "Causes and Patterns of Greek Emigration to the United States," *Perspectives in American History* 7 (1973): 381–437; Alexander Saxton, *The Indespensible Enemy: Labor and the Anti-Chinese Movement in California* (Berkeley: University of California Press, 1971); Judith E. Smith, *Family Connections: Italians and Jews in Providence, 1900–1940* (Albany: SUNY Press, 1985), and Yasuo Wakatsuki, "The Japanese Emigration to the United States, 1866–1924," *Perspectives in American History* 12 (1979): 389–516.

7. Alixa Naff, *Becoming American: The Early Arab American Immigrant Experience* (Carbondale, IL: Southern Illinois University Press, 1985). Gregory Orfalea, *Before the Flames: A Quest for the History of Arab Americans* (Austin: University of Texas Press, 1988). See also Yvonne Y. Haddad, "Arab Muslims and Islamic Institutions in the United States" in *Arabs in the New World: Studies on Arab-American Communities*, ed. Sameer Y. Abraham and Nabeel Abraham (Detroit: Wayne State University Press, 1983), pp. 64–81; Ayad al-Qazzaz, "The Changing Characteristics of the Arab American Community in the U.S.," *Arab Perspectives* 2 (February 1981): 4–8; Joseph G. Jabbra and Nancy W. Jabbra, "An Arab Family in Transition from Marj-ar-Tahin, Lebanon to Littleton, Nova Scotia," *Arab Perspectives* 2 (February 1981): 17–19. The earliest studies of Arab and Muslims assimilation include Abdo A. Elkohloy, *The Arab Moslems in the United States* (New Haven: College and University Press, 1966.); Afif S. Tannous, "Acculturation of an Arab Syrian Community in the Deep South," *Sociological Review* 8 (1943): 264–70; and Atif A. Wasfi, *An Islamic-Lebanese Community in the U.S.A.: A Study of Cultural Anthropology* (Beirut: Beirut Arab University Press, 1971). Specifically on Shi`a communities in the United States, see Farah Gilanshah, "Iranians in the Twin Cities," *Journal of the Institute of Muslim Minority Affairs* 7, no. 1 (January 1986): 117–23; Azim Nanji, "The Nizari Ismaili Community in North America: Background and Development," *The Muslim Community in North America*, ed. Earle H. Waugh et al. (Alberta: University of Alberta Press, 1983); and Laurel D. Wigle, "An Arab Muslim Community in Michigan," *Arabic Speaking Communities in American Cities*, ed. Barbara Aswad (Staten Island, NY: Center for Migration Studies of New York, 1974).

The literature about middle-class immigration is primarily the work of sociologists. See for example, S. S. Nyang and Mumtaz Ahmad, "The Muslim Intellectual Émigré in the United States," *Islamic Culture* 57, no. 3 (1985): 277–90, which emphasizes the Muslims' successful cultural assimilation and their many social contributions. See also the statistical compilations of Yvonne Y. Haddad and Adair T. Lumis, *Islamic Values in the United States* (New York: Oxford University Press, 1987).

8. No real names are used here, since most of the respondents requested anonymity. The Eritreans were particularly difficult to interview since many did not speak English well, and they refused to have their interviews recorded—taking it for granted that the recording would end up in the hands of the authorities—and most were reluctant to answer questions about their political beliefs, involvement in the civil war, or reasons for leaving.

9. On the immigration of well-educated, English-speaking Muslims with scientific research skills, see Arif A. Ghayur, "Ethnic Distribution of American Muslims and Selected Socio-Economic Characteristics," *Journal of the Institute of Muslim Minority Affairs* 1 (1983–84): 47–59. See also Lafi Ibrahim Jaafari, "The Brain Drain to the United States: The Migration of Jordanian and Palestinian Professionals and Students," *Journal of Palestine Studies* 3, no. 1 (1973): 119–31; and S. S. Nyang and Mumtaz Ahmad, "The Muslim Intellectual Émigré in the United States," *Islamic Culture* 57, no. 3 (1985): 277–90.

10. On changes in U.S. immigration laws and their effect on Muslim immigrants, see Arif M. Ghayur, "Muslims in the United States: Settlers and Visitors," *The Annals of the Academy of Political and Social Sciences* 45, no. 4 (1981):

151–63; Mohammed Sawaie, *Arabic-Speaking Immigrants in the United States and Canada* (Lexington, KY: Mazda Publications, 1985), and Waugh et al., *Muslim Community in North America*.

11. For a clear explication of Islamic law and customs for non-Muslims, see Mustafa Yusuf McDermott and Muhammad Manzir Ahsan, *The Muslim Guide: For Teachers, Employers, Community Members and Social Administrators in Britain* (Leicester, U.K.: The Islamic Foundation, 1980), p. .

12. Interview no. 1, side 2.

13. Interview 19, side 1. In favor of eating meat from the supermarket, interviews 9, 12, 13, 14, and 25; against eating non-*hallal* or non-kosher meat interviews 1, 6 and 10.

14. Information for this section on personal Islamic practice comes from interviews 1, 3, 6–22. The Pakistani anesthesiologist on *jum'a* prayers and Ramadan are in interview 10, tape 2, side 1.

15. Information for this section from interviews 1 and 22.

16. On the transformation of U.S. culture to a secular, consumer-oriented society, see Susan Porter Benson, "Women's Rites: Consumption, Class and Gender," paper presented at the annual meeting of the American Historical Association, Cincinnati, Ohio, December 1988; T. J. Jackson Lears and Richard W. Fox, eds., *Culture of Consumption: Critical Essays in American History, 1880–1920* (New York: Pantheon Books, 1983); T. J. Jackson Lears, *No Place of Grace: The Transformation of American Culture, 1880–1920* (New York: Pantheon Books, 1981), and Warren I. Susman, *The Transformation of American Society in the Twentieth Century* (New York: Pantheon Books, 1984).

17. While every informant in the group of professionals mentioned these ideas in some form, interviews 3, 6, 7, 8, 9, 10, 14, 15, 16, and 22 discuss these issues in detail.

18. Interview 22.

13

Approaches to Mosque Design in North America

OMAR KHALIDI

In North America, unlike long-established Muslim societies, a majority of mosques are buildings originally constructed for other purposes—abandoned churches, Masonic lodges, fire stations, funeral homes, theaters, warehouses, and shops. A survey conducted in 1992–95 showed that of the nearly one thousand mosques and Islamic centers in the United States, fewer than one hundred were designed as mosques. Here, however, we will be concerned only with those structures specifically designed and erected as mosques and their relationship to the subject of identity.

Although a Muslim presence in North America has been documented for at least a century, liberalization of American immigration laws in 1965 led to the first large-scale influx of Muslims from many different countries. Simultaneously, the conversion to Islam of Americans, especially of African Americans, vastly increased the Muslim population in the United States. Lack of funds had prevented the earliest Muslim immigrants from constructing mosques; most of them in any case did not come to the United States to settle permanently. Their primary purpose was economic. Then a number of nondescript structures were built as mosques in Highland Park, Michigan (1919), Michigan City, Indiana (1924), Cedar Rapids, Iowa (1925), Ross, North Dakota (1926), Quincy, Massachusetts (1930), and Sacramento, California (1941). Many of these were multipurpose structures used as cultural or community centers—for example, the Albanian Cultural Center, Arab Banner Society, Indian/Pakistani Muslim Association, and the like—and not simply mosques. They had a room for prayer, but they also served as clubs, with a social hall for weddings and parties, and a basement for bingo games.

Although the mosque had been developing for fourteen centuries it was still certainly an architectural novelty in North America and most of the rest of the Western world. The thematic and visual characteristics of mosque architecture in North America had therefore to deal with an alien environment, one that had its own deeply embedded historical and visual vocabulary. The architectural characteristics of these North American mosques were in some conflict with their context, a result of both religious and cultural factors. While the building had to respond to its own inner formal cultural and functional determinants, it could not ignore its regional setting.

The stylistic features of the more elaborate mosques built over the last few decades vary considerably, but one of three basic themes turn up in the aesthetic content of all of them. Some are the result of traditional design wholly transplanted from Islamic lands: examples are the Islamic Cultural Center in Washington, D.C. (1957); the Islamic Center of Toledo, Ohio (1983); the Islamic Center of Charleston, West Virginia, and any number of smaller mosques which reflect a transplanted notion of a traditional mosque. Others represent a reinterpretation of tradition, sometimes combined with elements of American architecture. Examples are the Islamic Cultural Center in Manhattan (1991); Dar al-Islam Mosque in Abiquiu, New Mexico (1981), and the mosque in Jonesboro, Arkansas. Still others are entirely innovative. Examples of these are the Islamic Society of North America headquarters in Plainfield, Indiana (1979), the Islamic Center of Albuquerque, New Mexico (1991), the Islamic Center of Edmond, Oklahoma (1992), and the Islamic Center of Evansville, Indiana (1992). Most of these structures also do not operate strictly as places of worship alone, but rather as Islamic centers with facilities for a variety of activities: an Islamic school on Sunday, library, conference center, bookshop, kitchen, social hall, recreational facilities, residential apartments, and sometime even a funeral home.

The Islamic Center of Washington, D.C. (fig. 13.1) was the first of these large traditionally based structures and architecturally still the most significant building that Muslims have built in this country (it is listed, and therefore protected, as a historical American building). This stone-finished building was designed by Mario Rossi (d. 1961), an Italian architect practicing in Cairo, with the help of engineers from the Egyptian Ministry of Awqaf. The conceptual design was modified and built for the actual site by the firm of Irvin S. Porter, a Washington, D.C. firm which is no longer in business.

The building took its inspiration in part from the Mamluk architecture of Cairo, but it also includes Ottoman Turkish and Andalusian decorative motifs. It was completed in 1957, but its planning went as far back as 1944 when a wealthy Palestinian real estate developer and the Egyptian ambassador to the United States organized the building of a mosque to serve the immediate need of conducting a funeral service for the Turkish ambassador who had died in Washington. The final mosque was financed by the diplomatic missions of the Islamic countries and such wealthy Muslim potentates as the Nizam of Hyderabad who donated $50,000, a grand sum in those days. It represented a new cooperation among Muslim countries in support of a U.S. mission and became a symbol of Muslim unity and identity in the United States.[1]

Figure 13.1. Islamic Center; Washington, D.C. (Photo by O. Khalidi)

This is one of the first cases in which an Islamic community center in America presented what the community considered its best image to the American public and to their own fellow Muslims. In its historic references and in the international and diplomatic context in which it is located, this building is reminiscent of the "exotic" pavilions Islamic countries erected to represent their national architecture in the great international expositions of the late nineteenth century. Conceptually and spatially, the building is closer to the images of the "mysterious and exotic Orient" than it is to any particular historic structure in the Islamic world.

The Albanian Islamic Center in Harperwood, Michigan, is another example of transplanted Islamic architecture in America. Designed and built in 1962 by an American architect, Frank Beymer, the mosque (fig. 13.2) makes a clear and unambiguous statement of its national character in its Ottoman exterior represented by sleek, pointed arches, dome, and color scheme. Although all Muslims are welcome there, its façade proclaims the identity of its original founders, the Albanian Muslim immigrants of Michigan.

A number of mosques similar to the one in Harperwood, Michigan, and the Washington, D.C. Islamic Center, varying only in size and scale, were built in the 1980s. Two other transplantations of traditional mosque architecture onto an American site are the Islamic centers near Toledo, Ohio, and in Charleston, West Virginia (figs. 13.3, 13.4). The Turkish architect Talat Itil designed and built the striking Ottoman-style mosque in the cornfields of Ohio in 1983. Its 135 foot-high minarets and large spherical dome (60 feet

Figure 13.2. Albanian Islamic Center; Harperwood, Michigan. (Photo by O. Khalidi)

in diameter) are visible from the interstate highway. On top of one of the two minarets is a *ma'dhana* for calling the faithful to prayer, but it has never been used as its congregation live too far from the mosque. The architecture of the mosque was not received well by the local community, as the "farmers initially thought the Muslims were trying to build a Middle East conglomerate and spoil the landscape."[2] One woman claimed that, waking in

Figure 13.3. Islamic Center; near Toledo, Ohio. (Photo by O. Khalidi)

Figure 13.4. Islamic Center; Charleston, West Virginia. (Photo by O. Khalidi)

the middle of the night, she looked out her window, saw the white, sparkling domed buildings amidst the cornfields, and thought she was having a nightmare in which she has been kidnapped and taken to the Middle East! Two truckers on first sighting the Toledo mosque are said to have wondered if it wasn't a new Middle Eastern restaurant. While these anecdotes may be exaggerated, it is undeniable that the architect violated the basic principal of good design that a building should be site-bound. Itil seems to have believed instead that a design is sight-bound! The tall Ottoman minarets stand out as an exotic bit of Middle Eastern culture in an otherwise Midwestern environment. In addition to the obvious disregard for its surroundings, the architect appears to also to have disregarded the spirit, if not the letter, of Islam that the material culture (including architecture) of Muslims is bound by space and time and can therefore be both varied and diverse.

In the design process it has hardly made a difference whether the architect happened to be a Muslim or not. The transplanted mosque approach has been used by Muslim and non-Muslim architects alike: in Washington, D.C. and Toledo, Ohio, they were Muslim; the Harperwood, Michigan, architect was not. The guiding principles, not the religious background of the architect, produced the design. In Charleston, West Virginia, a non-Muslim architect William Preston, the designer of the mosque, said he was modeling it "after a famous Islamic house of worship, the Badshahi Mosque, in Lahore, Pakistan. The Badshahi Mosque is larger than the Taj Mahal, and is considered to be the largest house of worship in the world."[3] The Charleston mosque (1989) is far from its source of inspiration, however, but judging from conversations with the architect, his clients, and many of the worshipers at the mosque, the final architectural product does not seem to disappoint them. For them imitation was "capturing the flavor" of the old, the familiar, or at the most the "blending" of the old and new. Although in fact close to parody, for this nostalgic community it was regarded by a generation who in the words of Preston "have lost faith in the future, and seek for the present the stability and humanness embodied in vernacular and premodern architectures."[4]

In this context the role of the architect is to bring back the past, the familiar, to make the users of the building feel at home, and to reinterpret its vocabulary in everyday language which can be easily understood. In post-modern America this is the language of the commercial strip, with the result that the clients and their architects consider with pride the "capturing the essential symbols of Islamic architecture." But these same symbols (minarets, domes, arches) have been found throughout America in Masonic temples, gambling casinos, Shriner halls, vaudeville theaters, and restaurants. In the 1920s an American aviator and millionaire named Glenn Curtiss designed a city outside Miami, called Opa Locka, to satisfy his visions of Arabia and the Orient; in it every major building had a dome and a minaret. It provided a fantastic setting to an otherwise sandy area that Americans thought looked like the Arabian desert. Similar architectural fantasies have since turned up in Hollywood productions and in Disneylands.

Mosques and Islamic centers that try to replicate the original mosques of the Islamic world lack both the qualities and materials of traditional architecture. The distorted expressions of many of these buildings, their garish colors, and use of prefabricated industrial materials all deny the authenticity of the old monuments they aspire to imitate. Their generally crude aesthetics is also related to the low esteem in which a professional architect is held among American Muslims. Since the cost of re-creating a monumental mosque is beyond the financial means of the community, the clients will settle for a rough replica that any architect can provide simply by referring to photographs. As the Pakistani-Canadian architect Gulzar Haidar explains: "When Muslim groups set out to build an Islamic center or a mosque, they consider professional architectural services quite redundant. An architect is 'not needed' because 'who does not know what a mosque looks like,' and 'we need only a few drawings for fund raising' and 'later' any draughtsman under an engineer's advice can draw them up for a building permit."[5] The results are always imitative and unimaginative buildings passing for "authentic" Islamic architecture and they can be found in the United States from coast to coast.

In the cases of transplanted mosques, the design simply depends on some feature such as a dome or minaret to provide the Islamic affinity. Mosques that have attempted a reinterpretation of the traditional mosque architecture in American landscape have had mixed results. The Islamic Cultural Center of Manhattan (ICC) is one example (fig. 13.5). It was designed by the presti-

Figure 13.5. Islamic Cultural Center of Manhattan, New York. (Photo by O. Khalidi)

gious firm of Skidmore, Owings and Merrill (SOM) and completed in 1991 on a site in uptown Manhattan at the intersection of Third Avenue and 96th Street. The project represents an effort to find an image that would please both Muslims and the larger society. It also highlights the relationship between architectural production and the cultural politics of identity. The mosque was designed for the use of Muslims in the New York City metropolitan area, which includes a group of high-profile influential Muslim diplomats and others attached to the United Nations, consulates, and trade offices.

The idea of the mosque project goes back to 1966 when the governments of Kuwait, Saudi Arabia, and Libya bought the site. Since 1981, the prime financier of the project has been the State of Kuwait, whose U.N. ambassador Muhammad Abulhasan is now chairman of the Board of the Trustees of ICC. Initially, the project was given to the Iranian American architect Ali Dadras, who drew up a traditional mosque plan with a courtyard and gardens. By the mid 1980s, however, its Board of Trustees had come out in favor of a more contemporary style, and Dadras was replaced by SOM. SOM's long architectural involvement in the Islamic world included the Hajj Terminal at the Jeddah airport and King Abdulaziz University and the National Commercial Bank in Jedda as well as many other large building projects in Saudi Arabia, Kuwait, and Bahrain. The appointment of SOM for the ICC project was logical in that it was based on its previous experience in designing buildings for Muslims.

During the design stage of the project, the ICC Board appointed two advisory committees, one composed of "prominent members" of the Muslim community in New York, the other of architects, mostly non-Muslims, led by Michael McCarthy of SOM, and of Islamic art historians such as Oleg Grabar (then at Harvard University), Renata Holod (University of Pennsylvania), and Marilyn Jenkins (then a curator of Islamic art at the Metropolitan Museum); there was also one architectural critic, Mildred Schmertz of the *Architectural Review*. The debate between the two committees centered on the image of the mosque. The practitioners and scholars wanted "a mosque that belonged to the 21st century."[6] The Muslims on the other committee wanted the architects to reproduce the style of a traditional mosque with literal versions of historic motifs. Their conception was not very different from the original plan designed by Ali Dadras.

The scholars urged the architects to exercise complete freedom in forms and motifs while respecting Islamic beliefs, and Michael McCarthy, the SOM architect, chose to follow them. He justified his decision by pointing out that "Islam in its vast conquests absorbed the best of local building techniques and materials under an overall umbrella of careful geometric ordering of mass, enclosures, and finishes. Why not meld this tradition with the best that the twentieth-century technology has to offer?"[7] After a long and thoughtful debate the two groups agreed on a "modernist" building, but with the Muslim committee forcing the inclusion of both a minaret and a dome, neither of them favored by the architects and scholars. The conflicting perceptions of what a mosque ought to look like brought into high relief the salience of "old and familiar" for Muslims that Western scholars and Westernized, non-practicing Muslims tend to disregard.

When it was completed in 1991, the ICC mosque consisted of a 90-foot clear span structure roofed by a system of four trusses supporting a steel and concrete dome, from which is suspended the women's gallery beneath. The plan is composed of a domed cubical area in the center, with four square corners roofed by skylights in the form of quarter pyramids. Light pours in from these skylights and through the decorative square openings of the trusses beneath the dome.

Islamic decorative features include a modern adaptation of Kufic used here as ornament over the main entry portal, the mihrab, and the apex of the dome, and a modern circle of steel-wire-supported lamps, somewhat reminiscent of the circle of lamps in Ottoman mosques. Interior decoration adapts the square module of the screens located within the large square openings of the trusses to the entrance screen, the carpet pattern, and the ceiling tiles. The walls of pastel green have almost no decoration. Green was the clients' choice. Green has traditionally symbolized fertility and hope everywhere, but is also particularly associated with Islamic culture and used extensively in the Muslim world, though not in the pastel tone applied in the ICC mosque. The square module has been consistently used throughout the building at various scales and in a variety of materials and expressions. The external walls are divided into large square modules of light granite panels, each outlined by a strip of glass and supported by a concealed grid of tubular steel. The abstract nature of this geometric form has lent the design of the mosque a simple rational appeal and given the project a contemporary character, while allowing continuity of association with traditional Islamic architecture through the use of abstract geometry.

The building's link with traditional mosque architecture, however, goes deeper than subtle references through geometry, or the obvious use of architectural icons and calligraphy. As Oleg Grabar pointed out, the drawings for the final design of the mosque prepared by the SOM team were quite reasonably within the conventional Ottoman tradition. The SOM reference to the Ottoman mosque type also inspired the skylights in roof corners and patterned glass in walls that bathed the prayer area with light. The interior of the mosque is broadly divided into three vertical zones: the part between the floor of the main prayer hall and the soffits of the peripheral areas, the large screen trusses that define the middle part of the interior, and the dome to mark the upper part. The stepped, pendentive-like beams at the corners of the middle part, in addition to their structural role in supporting the dome, help visually to connect the trusses to the dome, thus allowing a smooth transition between the square and the dome. This inspiration from traditional structural and aesthetic systems seems to unify the middle and upper parts of the interior of the mosque. The steel-ribbed structure of the dome expresses its modernity, and the tectonic expression of the supports of these ribs, with their minimum proportions reinforced by the light penetration, creates a distinctively modern floating effect. Although the dome is used as a traditional form, it is effectively and successfully expressed in a contemporary language.

The structural system of the screen trusses that support the dome appears to be cantilevered from the external walls, creating a truly modern expression. This cantilevering of the middle part of the interior is illusionary, created by the ambiguity of the relationship between the trusses and their vertical supports in the outer walls, and by the fact that the soffits of the trusses are merged with the ceiling of the peripheral areas. All this seems to create discontinuity between the lower and middle parts of the interior of the mosque and to give visual weight to the trusses. The intersection of the main trusses is emphasized by the creation of the corner skylights which allow this intersection to be seen as a point on which all the upper part of the building is supported. This dematerialization of the corner seems to be in contradiction with the tectonic emphasis on the support system of the dome above. By contrast, in an Ottoman mosque such as the Suleymaniye, the effect of the enormous columns leading up to the large central dome creates a graceful, uninterrupted upward thrust, while increasing the lightness of the ceiling and the slenderness of the support system. The reversal of this arrangement in the Manhattan mosque is a clear statement of the modern technology employed, but it sacrifices the organic lightness and "spirituality" of the Ottoman prototype for the sake of creating a column-free space, to satisfy the clients' desire for a progressive image.

The ICC mosque assimilates traditional design elements in at least three other places. Few mosques in America have been able to solve the problem of providing a women's prayer area in a sophisticated and architecturally sound manner. Mosques in Muslim societies were rarely entered by women, though they were not forbidden to pray there, so they supplied no precedent. The solution the architects arrived at was to divide the mosque into two levels: the main prayer hall on the ground level, and the women's gallery suspended by rods from trusses above. This is undoubtedly an innovative way of integrating women and men under one roof. Access to the upper gallery is gained from two staircases that act as free-standing sculptural elements directly accessible from the main floor. The complete visual transparency of the women's area, its direct link to the men's area, and the fact that it is located above the men's prayer hall, all represent bold innovations.

While the architect-scholar committee had disapproved the inclusion of the minaret, some outsiders were more enthusiastic. Among them was the philanthropist David Rockefeller, who donated a large sum toward the financing of a minaret when he was told it was in danger of being excluded for reasons of economy as well as design. With this encouragement the design for the minaret was given to Swanke, Hayden, Connel (SHC) of New York; the chief designer was Alton Gursel, a Turkish-American architect. According to Gursel he was faced with the unenviable task of having to satisfy the perception of what a minaret should look like to the nearly fifty Muslim countries represented in the New York community. Gursel designed nine models of minarets ranging in appearance from sharp pencils to ballpoint pens before eventually choosing one that was sufficiently abstract and de-historicized; the final design was more in the ballpoint pen mold, as the pencil image was so strongly Ottoman Turkish in appearance. In contrast to the massiveness of the mosque proper, the minaret's slenderness, sheer height (one and a half times the height of the dome), and simple articulation makes it an elegant addition to the project.

In view of its astounding cost ($1.5 million) and its uselessness in functional terms, however, the minaret also demonstrates to what lengths some are willing to go to express their identity. Significant parts of the mosque project, such as the school and the library had to be delayed so that the minaret's construction could go ahead. Image-making in this case took precedence over providing services to the community. The architects and the chief financial patrons of the project, however, had a different view. Because of the mosque's location in one of the world's financial and cultural capitals, the architects conceived it as a "welcoming image which includes, rather than excludes the public." Since its completion in 1991, the mosque has become a landmark in the area. One New Yorker remarked, "It is nice to have something of every denomination represented in the city." For some Muslims (particularly immigrants), it provides a welcome familiarity in an area of high-rise development along Third Avenue. This building, like its counterpart, the London Central Mosque, is an unusual feature in the landscape, but it is generally seen as an improvement rather than a detraction.

Similar to the Washington, D.C. mosque in conceptual framework, but differing in scale and location is the Dar al-Islam mosque in Abiquiu, New Mexico, designed by the leading Egyptian architect, the late Hasan Fathy. It was built in 1981 and is used predominantly by native-born Muslims (fig. 13.6). The 2,260-square-foot mosque sits on a reinforced concrete foundation, upon which a concrete block stem wall has been built to create a uniform edge at ground level. The mosque's dramatic form, as sculptural as anything in the surrounding landscape, derives from combining a Byzantine and Sasanid dome, barrel vaults, and large, pointed arches. The Dar al-Islam mosque grew out of the same romanticized regional style that Fathy created for New Gourna in Egypt and uses the same earth construction. Because of New Mexico's cultural links to Spain, which produced a local

Figure 13.6. Dar al-Islam Mosque; Abiquiu, New Mexico. (Photo by O. Khalidi)

mudbrick building tradition quite similar to that used in New Gourna, Fathy's Dar al-Islam is certainly appropriate to its context. Three criticisms can be made of the Dar al-Islam project, however. One is its disregard of the local climate resulting in water seepage from the roof and the dome. The second is that its physical isolation from population centers avoids having to deal with the conflicts and diversities of modern life. The other is that, by refusing to engage in a dialogue with the dominant culture, the mosque and its community are in danger of reinforcing Western views about the "otherness" of Islam.

A decisive departure from both the approach of transplanting traditional architecture and the approach of modern reinterpretation can be found in the designs of two architects: Gulzar Haidar, the Pakistani-Canadian and Bart Prince, an American. Their projects represent the innovative, the creative, and the unprecedented mosque. Haidar advocates a design approach that is "environmental," "morphological" and "semiotic." His notable example is the mosque in the Islamic Society of North America (ISNA) headquarters in Plainfield, Indiana. According to Haidar,

> Islamic architecture should be expressive and understandable to all. It should employ a form language which invokes in immigrant Muslims a sense of belonging in their present and hope in their future. To the indigenous Muslims it should represent a linkage with Muslims from other parts of the world and should underscore the universality and unity of Islam. To the new Muslim this architecture should invoke confidence in their new belief. To non-Muslims it should take the form of clearly identifiable buildings which are inviting and open, or at least not secretive, closed or forbidding.[8]

In 1979, the Muslim Students Association of the United States and Canada (MSA), the parent organization of the Islamic Society of North America (ISNA), decided to consolidate its numerous activities by establishing a headquarters in Plainfield. Haider was engaged to design the building complex, with detailed construction documents prepared by the associated architect Mukhtar Khalil, an Indian Muslim. The headquarters was never completed, and in early 1996 plans were afoot to move the ISNA offices to Washington, D.C. The buildings that were constructed included a mosque, library, and some office space, all collectively known as the ISNA headquarters. The headquarters is set amidst elaborate landscaping with formal front plaza (fig. 13.7). The three units of this building, the mosque, the library, and the office block, form a unified scheme in which the mosque and the office block are placed on an axis and the library is located on an axis perpendicular to the first axis. The architect describes the symbolism of this design thus:

> A mosque is a space celebrating man's servitude to God. The office building is an arena of work for Islam and its society in North America. The library is a research facility upholding the Qur'anic ideal that only through knowledge, intellect, and contemplative thought does man ascend to higher levels of belief and action.[9]

Figure 13.7. Islamic Society of North America Headquarters; Plainfield, Indiana. (Photo by O. Khalidi)

The ISNA mosque has an austere contemporary character that is entirely without iconic references to traditional Islamic architecture. The solid walls of the exterior give little clue as to what is inside the building and narrow, vertically slit, widely spaced, windows add to the building's sense of impenetrability. This is in contrast to the large dome in the mosque hidden behind the high walls and parapets, which comes as a pleasant surprise as one ventures from outside to the inside of the building. Haidar justifies this contrast between outside and inside as embodying two of the ninety-nine beautiful names of God: al-Batin (the hidden) and al-Zahir (the manifest). Haidar sees these attributes of God as "of special interest to architects in pursuit of the silent eloquence of space and the quintessential presence of form."[10] Through his experience of Islamic architecture he became very intrigued by these divine attributes: "And in all the beautiful names of God, I searched for a special wisdom to guide the designer who must create but not confront, offer but not attack, and express profoundness in a language understandable and pleasing to the listener. . . . I chose to distinguish the exterior from the interior. I chose to veil the mosque."[11] According to Haidar, the ISNA mosque addresses itself to Muslims through the concept of the al-Zahir and al-Batin, through mystical geometry, and particularly through the cubic form of the mosque as a subliminal reminder of the Ka'ba, the symbol of unity. He relates his decision to contrast the inside and the outside to the context of Muslims being in a minority living in a predominantly non-Islamic America. He sees this contrast as symbolic of the fact that Islam in this country is restricted to a private matter of faith rather than a state religion as is the case in much of the Islamic world. "If the dome is symbolic of the esoteric and the divine, and the cube that of the esoteric and of the Earth, then we consider it a befitting gesture to make the dome internally manifest and externally veiled."[12] Moreover, the exterior of the building, its choice of materials, details, and fenestration is intended by Haidar to be "sympathetic to North American indigenous architecture rather than any historic or modernized Islamic style."[13]

The architectural character of the ISNA mosque reflects the architect's fascination with the mystical interpretation of Islamic architecture. The adoption of abstract geometry in the building can be seen as Haidar's search for universal architectural solutions, with which he can identify as a Muslim, because of the roots of these solutions in Islamic architectural tradition. This architectural character may also be viewed as an attempt at addressing complex cross-cultural issues, and the difficult question of expressing identity through form without having to resort to traditional imagery which does not appeal to his modern design sensibilities. Many would regard Haidar as working within the prevalent architectural thinking to which he was exposed in North America, particularly in the work of Louis Kahn. The ISNA headquarters is one of the significant examples of Islamic centers in America; it is regrettable that it was unable to flourish in the Midwest due no doubt to a lack of a significant Muslim population in the area for whom it could serve as a focal point.

Conceptually related to the ISNA headquarters in terms of innovative mosque design are a number of other Islamic centers. One is the Islamic Center of Albuquerque, New Mexico, designed by Bart Prince, a leading exponent of organic architecture, which as completed in 1991 (fig. 13.8). From a distance, the building resembles a giant set of bleachers reaching skyward in tiers topped by towers that contain tall, narrow windows. Inside, the mosque is essentially one large hall divided at prayer times by a temporary partition to separate men from women. The ceiling steps up with the tiers, supported by thick wooden beams and rafters made of bronze-colored pipe. Daylight pours through the narrow windows. It is a simple, elegant building, functional, and completely at home in its environment.

The work of the New Mexican architect resists easy translation into words. Dramatic and often unusual forms characterize this project, along with his other buildings in New Mexico. His style is rooted in the peculiarly American tradition of organicism. Defined by the Midwestern architect Frank Lloyd Wright (1867–1959) and the Oklahoman architect Bruce Goff (1904–1982), the organic tradition argues for the necessary individuality of each architect and each architectural design. The tradition's individualism makes it difficult to classify its work with a coherent set of stylistic characteristics. Coherence comes instead from a shared attempt to create an organically integral architecture that rethinks the possibilities of geometry, space, structure, and material.

Figure 13.8.   Islamic Center of Albuquerque, New Mexico. (Photo by O. Khalidi)

The building project began in 1986 during a time of extremely negative press about Islam owing to events in the Middle East, the architect designed a climatically sound building unencumbered by historical precedent. There is no dome, no minaret, nor any other readily identifiable sign of "Islamic architecture." There is, however, a projection in the qibla wall marking the mihrab and pointing the believers toward Mecca.

Akin to the Albuqurque mosque is the Islamic Center of Evansville, Indiana. Built in 1992, this is a bungalow-like building (fig. 13.9) with no reference whatsoever to traditional Islamic architecture. Inside is a large rectangular room with a barn-like roof. Minimum effort is made in this building to relate the interior of the prayer hall to the conventional image of a mosque, and no architectural elements have been added as direct visual iconic references to a mosque. The only exception in this otherwise domestic, suburban design is the projection in the qibla wall, just like the one in the Albuquerque project.

Practically the same design is found in the Masjid al-Salam in Edmond, Oklahoma, which was completed in 1992 (fig. 13.10). According to Siddiq A. Karim, the architect of this mosque, the local authorities required the mosque be in harmony with the context of single-family homes amidst which it is located.

What do these various mosque projects tell us about the nature and direction of mosque design in North America? New and insecure Muslim communities at first often construct mosques that are architecturally nondescript, of the kind seen in Michigan, North Dakota, Pennsylvania, and

Figure 13.9. Islamic Center; Evansville, Indiana. (Photo by O. Khalidi)

California. Since then a large number of mosques have been built in the purely traditional style found in the Muslim countries with little regard to their surroundings in North America, and still less to the resulting negative consequences. Some architects have experimented with reinterpreting traditional design with mixed designs of uneven quality. The innovative mosques of Haidar, Prince, and Karim have not always been well received by the immigrants because they do not match up to their particular image of what a mosque should be. Given the extreme diversity of Muslims in America, the logical choice would seem to be to favor the unprecedented mosque with maximum regard to the strictly Islamic requirements and minimum regard for ethno-national taste or historical style, whether it be Ottoman, Mamluk, or Mughal. We have already seen such a compromise reached in the case of the minaret of the Manhattan mosque.

Attachment to traditional design principles is, however, by and large restricted to first-generation immigrant Muslims. Their descendants and American converts, who will eventually constitute the majority of the Muslim population, will probably tip the scales in favor of more innovative architecture. Many Muslims of all backgrounds may even see it as responding to a prime Islamic imperative: to live in harmony with the total natural and historical environment of a place.

A kind of Islamic architectural representation is familiar to the American public through pavilions in exhibitions or entertainment and recreational centers. As long as they represented a culture remote from the experience

Figure 13.10. Masjid al-Salam; Edmond, Oklahoma. (Photo by O. Khalidi)

of the viewers, they remained harmless fantasy. But since Muslims are now part of the American population, these images become critical for cross-cultural communication. As Haidar writes, "Muslims in the United States and Canada should recognize the basic fact that the images of Islamic architecture and culture they carry with them from their original countries or from their history are well recognized in North America but in very different contexts and visually with grossly different meaning."[14] Thus any design based solely on traditional principles will retard creativity. The unwillingness of some Muslims—either as clients or architects—to innovate, experiment or rethink design in a new context reflects a lack of confidence, and reaffirms the perceptions that Muslims are either resisting or acquiescing to Western influences and therefore incapable of changing from within their own tradition.

Notes

1. E. Allen Richardson, *East Comes West* (New York: Pilgrim Press, 1985), p. 154.

2. Steve Wilson, "Mosques Goes All Out in Tradition," *USA Today*, February 17–19, 1984.

3. Conversation with William Preston, June, 1993.

4. Ibid.

5. Gulzar Haidar and Muhammad Mukhtar, "Islamic Architecture in Non-Muslim Environments," *Places of Public Gathering in Islam*, Fifth Aga Khan Award for Architecture Seminar (Geneva: Aga Khan Award, 1980), p. 164.

6. Stephen Kliment, "Manhattan Mosque," *Architectural Record*, August 1992, p. 93.

7. Ibid.

8. Haidar and Mukhtar, "Islamic Architecture in a Non-Muslim Environment," p. 166.

9. Ibid.

10. Ibid.

11. Ibid.

12. Interview with Haidar at MIT in 1993.

13. Ibid.

14. Ibid.

Selected Bibliography

Abdul-Khaliq, Salim. *The Untold Story of Blacks in Islam.* Hampton: U.B. & U.S. Communication Systems, 1994.

Abdul-Rauf, Muhammad. "The Future of the Islamic Tradition in North America." *The Muslim Community in North America.* Eds. Earl H. Waugh, Baha Abu-Laban and Regula B. Qureshi. Edmonton: University of Alberta Press, 1983: 271–278.

———. *History of the Islamic Center: From Dream to Reality.* Washington, DC: The Center, 1978.

Abedin, Syed Z. and Saleha M. Abedin. "Muslim Minorities in Non-Muslim Societies." *The Oxford Encyclopedia of the Modern Islamic World.* Ed. John L. Esposito. Oxford: Oxford University Press, 1994: 112–117.

Abell, Aaron Ignatius. *The Urban Impact on American Protestantism, 1865–1900.* Cambridge: Harvard University Press, 1943.

Abou El Fadl, Khaled. "Islamic Law and Muslim Minorities: The Juristic Discourse on Muslim From the Second/Eighth to the Eleventh/Seventeenth Centuries." *Islamic Law and Society* 1, #2 (1994): 140–187.

———. "Legal Debates on Muslim Minorities: Between Rejection and Accommodation." *Journal of Religious Ethics* 22, #1 (1994): 127–162.

Abrams, Kathryn. "Title VII and the Complex Female Subject." *92 Michigan Law Review* (1994): 2481.

Abu-Bakr, Mohammed. *Islam's Black Legacy: Some Leading Figures.* Denver: Purple Dawn Books, Inc., 1993.

AbulJobain, Ahmad. *Islam Under Siege: Radical Islamic Terrorism or Political Islam?* Annandale, VA: United Association for Studies and Research Inc., Occasional Papers Series No. 1, June 1993.

AbuSulayman, A. A. *Towards an Islamic Theory of International Relations.* Herndon, VA: International Institute of Islamic Thought, 1993.

Ackerman, Bruce. "What Is Neutral About Neutrality?" *Ethics* 93 (1983): 372–390.

Adams, Barbara. Clark: *The Early Years*. Hampton: UB & US Communications Systems, 1992.

Addison, James Thayer. "The Ahmadiya Movement and Its Western Propaganda." *Harvard Theological Review* 22, #1 (January 1929): 1–32.

Ahmad, Akbar. *Postmodernism and Islam: Predicament and Promise*. London: Routledge, 1992.

Ahmad, Ghulam. *Jesus in India: Being an Account of Jesus' Escape from Death on the Cross and His Journey to India*. Rabwah, West Pakistan: Ahmadiyya Muslim Foreign Missions Dept., 1962.

Ahmad, Mirza Bashir-ud-din Mahmud. "Sign of a Living Religion." *Moslem Sunrise* 2 (January 1923): 159.

Ahmad, Mumtaz. "Islamic Fundamentalism in South Asia: The Jamaat-i-Islami and the Tablighi Jamaat." *Fundamentalisms Observed*. Eds. Martin E. Marty and R. Scott Appleby. Chicago: University of Chicago Press, 1991: 457–530.

Ahmad, Qutbi. "Muslim Organizations in the United States." *The Muslims of America*. Ed. Yvonne Y. Haddad. Oxford: Oxford University Press, 1991: 11–25.

al-Ahsan, Abdullah. *OIC: The Organization of the Islamic Conference*. Herndon, VA: International Institute of Islamic Thought, 1988.

Alford, Terry. *Prince Among Slaves*. New York: Harcourt Brace Jovanovich, 1977.

Ali, M. Amir. "Commentary: A Masterful Wordsman Should Be Studied Carefully." *Muslim Journal*, 19 October, 1990: 21.

Ali, Shaharazad. *The Blackman's Guide to Understanding the Blackwoman*. Philadelphia: Civilized Publications, 1989.

Allen, Ernest. "Religious Heterodoxy and Nationalist Tradition: The Continuing Evolution of the Nation of Islam." *Black Scholar* 26, #3–4 (Fall-Winter 1996): 2–34.

———. "Satokata Takahasi and the Flowering of Black Nationalism." *The Black Scholar* 24, #1 (Winter 1994): 23–46.

———. "Waiting for Tojo: The Pro-Japan Vigil of Black Missourians, 1932–1943." *Gateway Heritage* (Fall 1994): 38–55.

———. "When Japan Was 'Champion of the Darker Races': Satokata Takahashi and the Flowering of Black Messianic Nationalism." *Black Scholar* 24, #1 (Winter 1994): 23–46.

al-Alwani, Taha J. "Taqlid and Ijtihad." *American Journal of Islamic Social Sciences* 8, #1 (Spring 1991): 129–142.

———. "The Crisis in Fiqh and the Methodology of Ijtihad." *American Journal of Islamic Social Sciences* 8, #2 (Summer 1991): 317–337.

———. "Taqlid and the Stagnation of the Muslim Mind." *American Journal of Islamic Social Sciences* 8, #3 (Fall 1991): 513–524.

———. "Taqlid and Ijtihad." *American Journal of Islamic Social Sciences* 9, #2 (Summer 1992): 233–242.

———. "The Scope of Taqlid." *American Journal of Islamic Social Sciences* 9, #3 (Fall 1992): 383–386.

———. "Missing Dimensions in Contemporary Islamic Movements." *American Journal of Islamic Social Sciences* 12, #2 (Summer 1995): 240–254.

Amanat, Abbas. *Resurrection and Renewal: The Making of the Babi Movement in Iran, 1844–1850.* Ithaca: Cornell University Press, 1989.

Amen, Nur Ankh. *The Ankh: African Origin of Electromagnetism.* Jamaica, NY: Nur Ankh Amen Co., 1993.

al-Amin, Jamil. *Revolution By the Book: The Rap is Live.* Beltsville, MD: Writer's Inc., 1993.

el-Amin, Mustafa. *Afrocentricity: Malcolm X and Al-Islam.* Newark: El-Amin Productions, 1993.

———. *Al-Islam, Christianity and Freemasonry.* Jersey City: New Mind Productions, 1985.

———. *Freemasonry, Ancient Egypt and Islamic Destiny.* Jersey City: New Mind Productions, 1988.

Ani, Marimba. *Yurugu: An African-Centered Critique of European Cultural Thought and Behavior.* Trenton: Africa World Press, 1994.

Ansari, Zafar Ishaq. "Aspects of Black Muslim Theology." *Studia Islamica* 53 (1981): 137–176.

———. "W. D. Muhammad: The Making of a 'Black Muslim' Leader (1933–1961)." *American Journal of Islamic Social Sciences* 2, #2 (Summer 1985): 245–262.

Anway, Carol L. *Daughters of Another Path.* Lee's Summit, MO: Yawna Publications, 1996.

Armah, Ayi Kwei. *Two Thousand Seasons: Ayi Kwei Armah.* London: Heine mann, 1979.

Arnold, A. James. *Modernism and Negritude: The Poetry and Poetics of Aime Cesaire.* Cambridge: Harvard University Press, 1981.

Arnot, Charles. *Don't Kill the Messenger: The Tragic Story of Wells Hangen and Other Journalistic Combat Victims.* New York: Vintage Press, 1994.

Asante, Molefi. *The Afrocentric Idea.* Philadelphia: Temple University Press, 1987.

———. *Afrocentricity: The Theory of Social Change.* Buffalo: Amulefi Publishing Co., 1980.

———. *Kemit, Afrocentricity and Knowledge.* Trenton: Africa World Press, 1990.

Assad, Dawud. "Holy Prophet." *Majallat al-Masajid* 2, #2 (February 1981): 4.

Austin, Alan, ed. *African Muslims in Antebellum America: A Sourcebook.* New York: Garland Publishers, 1984.

———. "Islamic Identities in Africans in North America in the Days of Slavery, 1731–1865." *Islam et Sociètès au Sud du Sahara.* Paris: Foundation de la Maison des Sciences de L'Homme, 1993: 206–219.

al-Azmeh, Aziz. *Islams and Modernities.* London: Verso, 1993.

Baer, Hans A. *The Black Spiritual Movement: A Religious Response to Racism.* Knoxville: University of Tennessee Press, 1984.

Baer, Hans A. and Merrill Singer. *African-American Religion in the Twentieth Century: Varieties of Protest and Accommodation.* Knoxville: University of Tennessee Press, 1992.

Baldick, Julian. *Mystical Islam: An Introduction to Sufism.* New York: New York University Press, 1989.

Baldwin, James. *The Price of the Ticket: Collected Nonfiction, 1948–1985.* New York: St. Martin's, 1985.

Baldwin, Joseph. *The African Personality in America: An African Centered Framework.* Tallahassee: Nubian Nation Publications, 1992.

Bandole, Katherine Kemi. *The Afrocentric Guide to Selected Black Studies Terms and Concepts.* Long Beach: Whittier Publications, 1995.

Bannerman, J. P. "OIC: Structure and Activities." *The Oxford Encyclopedia of the Modern Islamic World.* Ed. John L. Esposito. Oxford: Oxford University Press, 1996. 262–266.

Barboza, Steven, ed. *American Jihad: Islam After Malcolm X.* New York: Doubleday, 1994.

Barnes, Carol. *Melanin: The Chemical Key to Black Greatness.* Vol. 1. Houston: C.B. Publishers, 1988.

Barrett Sr., Leonard E. *The Rastafarians: Sounds of Cultural Dissonance.* Boston: Beacon Press, 1988.

Barton, Josef J. *Peasants and Strangers: Italians, Rumanians and Slovaks in an American City, 1890–1950.* Cambridge: Harvard University Press, 1975.

Bastide, Roger. *African Civilizations in the New World.* Trans. Peter Green. New York: Harper & Row, 1971.

Bayunus, Ilyas. "On Terrorism and the Bandwagons." *The Message,* June 1995: 25.

Beckley, Gloria T. and Paul Burstein. "Religious Pluralism, Equal Opportunity, and the State." *Western Political Science Quarterly* 44 (1991): 185–208.

Benson, Susan Porter. "Women's Rites: Consumption, Class and Gender." Paper presented at the Annual Meeting of the American Historical Association, December 1988.

Berger, Graenum. *Black Jews in America: A Documentary With Commentary.* New York: Commission on Synagogue Relations, Federation of Jewish Philanthropies of New York, 1978.

Berger, Morroe. "The Black Muslims." *Horizon* 6, #1 (Winter 1964): 48–65.

Bernal, Martin. *Black Athena: The Afroasiatic Roots of Classical Civilization.* London: Free Association Books, 1987.

Bernal, Martin., Yosef ben Jochannan and John G. Jackson. "Not Out of Africa: The Origins of Greece and the Illusions of Afrocentrists." *The New Republic* (10 February 1992): 29–36.

Berthoff, Rowland. *British Immigrants in Industrial America, 1790–1950.* Cambridge: Harvard University Press, 1953.

Betts, Robert Brenton. *The Druze.* New Haven: Yale University Press, 1988.

Beynon, Erdmann Doane. "The Voodoo Cult Among Negro Migrants in Detroit." *American Journal of Sociology* 43, #6 (May 1938): 894–907.

Bilal, Rafiq and Thomas Goodwin. *Egyptian Sacred Science in Islam.* San Francisco: Bennu Publishers, 1987.

Biobaku, S. O. *The Origin of the Yoruba.* Lagos: University of Lagos, 1971.

Blackstock, Nelson. *Cointelpro: The FBI's Secret War on Political Freedom.* New York: Vintage Books, 1976.

Blavatsky, H. P. *Isis Unveiled: A Master-Key to the Mysteries of Ancient and Modern Science and Theology*. 2 vols. Pasadena, CA: Theosophical University Press, 1988.

Blyden, Edward Wilmot. *Christianity, Islam and the Negro Race*. San Francisco: First African Arabian Press, 1992.

Bodansky, Yossef. *Target America: Terrorism in the US Today*. New York: S.P.I. Books, 1993.

Bodnar, John E. *Immigration and Industrialization: Ethnicity in an American Mill Town, 1870–1940*. Pittsburgh: University of Pittsburgh Press, 1977.

———. *The Transplanted: A History of Immigrants in Urban America*. Bloomington: University of Indiana Press, 1985.

Bodnar, John E., Roger Simon and Michael P. Weber. *Lives of Their Own: Blacks, Italians and Poles in Pittsburgh, 1900–1960*. Urbana: University of Illinois Press, 1982.

Bontemps, Arna and Jack Conroy. *Anyplace But Here*. New York: Hill and Wang, 1966.

Bousquet, G. H. "Moslem Religious Influences in the United States." *Moslem World* 25, #1 (January 1935): 40–44.

Bracey Jr., John H., August Meier and Elliott Rudwick. "Black Ideologies, Black Utopias: Afrocentricity in Historical Perspective." *Contributions in Black Studies* 12 (1993–1994): 111–116.

———. eds. "Introduction." *Black Nationalism in America*. Indianapolis: Bobbs- Merrill, 1970: xxv–lxvii.

Bradley, Michael. *The Black Discovery of America*. Toronto: Personal Library, 1981.

Breasted, James H. *The Conquest of Civilization*. New York: Harper, 1926.

Brent, George Wilson. "The Ancient Glory of the Hamitic Race." *A.M.E. Church Review* 12 (October 1895): 272–275.

Brooke, John L. *The Refiner's Fire: The Making of Mormon Cosmology, 1644–1844*. Cambridge: Cambridge University Press, 1994.

Brotz, Howard M. *The Black Jews of Harlem: Negro Nationalism and the Dilemmas of Negro Leadership*. New York: Schocken, 1970.

———. "Negro 'Jews' in the United States." *Phylon* 13, #4 (December 1952): 324–337.

Brown, John P. *The Dervishes; or Oriental Spiritualism*. Philadelphia: Lippincott, 1868.

Bruce, John Edward. *The Selected Writings of John Edward Bruce: Militant Black Journalist*. Ed. Peter Gilbert. New York: Arno Press, 1971.

Burgess, Ebenezer. *What Is Truth? An Inquiry Concerning the Antiquity and Unity of the Human Race: With an Examination of Recent Scientific Speculations on Those Subjects*. Boston: I. P. Warren, 1871.

Burkett, Randall K. *Garveyism as a Religious Movement: The Institutionalization of a Black Civil Religion*. Metuchen, NJ: Scarecrow Press and American Theological Library Association, 1978.

Buttar, Zahra. "American Female Muslim Conversion Survey." Unpublished paper presented to the University of Nevada Las Vegas Sociology Department, 3 September, 1993.

Calhoun, Craig. "Social Theory and the Politics of Identity." *Social Theory and the Politics of Identity.* Ed. Craig Calhoun. Oxford: Blackwell Publishers, 1994: 9–35.

Calverley, Edwin E. "Negro Muslims in Hartford." *Moslem World* 55, #4 (October 1965): 340–345.

Campbell, Bruce F. *Ancient Wisdom Revived: A History of the Theosophical Movement.* Berkeley: University of California Press, 1980.

Carruthers, Jacob. *African or American: A Question of Intellectual Allegiance.* Chicago: Kemetic Institute, 1994.

———. *Essays in Ancient Egyptian Studies.* Los Angeles: Sankore Press, 1989.

Cheridan, Chris. "Islamophobia." *Mirror* 10, #52 (1 June, 1995): 11–12.

Chicago Commission on Race Relations. *The Negro in Chicago: A Study of Race Relations and a Race Riot in 1919.* New York: Arno Press, 1968.

Chirenje, J. Mutero. *Ethiopianism and Afro-Americans in Southern Africa, 1883–1916.* Baton Rouge: Louisiana State University Press, 1987.

Chomsky, Noam. "Middle East Terrorism and the American Ideological System." *Blaming the Victims: Spurious Scholarship and the Palestinian Question.* Eds. Edward W. Said and Christopher Hitchens. London: Verso, 1988: 97–147.

Churchill, Ward and Jim Vander Wall. *Agents of Repression: The FBI's Secret War Against the Black Panther Party and the American Indian Movement.* Boston: South End Press, 1988.

Churchward, Albert. *The Origin and Evolution of Freemasonry Connected With the Origin and Evolution of the Human Race.* London: G. Allen & Unwin, 1920.

———. *Origin and Evolution of the Human Race.* London: G. Allen & Unwin, 1921.

Clark, Elmer T. *The Small Sects in America,* rev. ed. New York: Abingdon-Cokesbury Press, 1949.

Clarke, John Henrik. *Africans at the Crossroads: Notes for an African World Revolution.* Trenton: Africa World Press, 1991.

———. "How Islam Came to Africa: Another Thought." *The New York Amsterdam News* 86, #38 (23 September, 1995): 13.

Clegg III, Claude A. *An Original Man: The Life and Times of Elijah Muhammad.* New York: St. Martin's Press, 1997.

Close, Upton [Josef Washington Hall]. *The Revolt of Asia: The End of the White Man's World Dominance.* New York: G. P. Putnam's Sons, 1927.

Coil, Henry Wilson. *Coil's Masonic Encyclopedia.* Richmond, VA: Macoy Publishing and Masonic Supply Co., 1996.

Coleman, Henry R. *Light from the East: Travels and Researches in Bible Lands in Pursuit of More Light in Freemasonry.* Louisville, KY: by the author, 1881.

Conde, Maryse. *Children of Segu.* New York: Penguin, 1989.

———. *Segu: A Novel.* Trans. Barbara Bray. New York: Viking, 1987.

Connoly, William. *Identity/Difference: Democratic Negotiations of Political Paradox.* Ithaca: Cornell University Press, 1991.

Conzen, Kathleen Neils. "Immigrants, Immigrant Neighborhoods and Ethnic Identity: Historical Issues." *The Journal of American History* 66 (1979): 603–615.

Coomaraswamy, Ananda K. *The Message of the East.* Masras: Ganesh & Co., n.d. [after 1909].

Cooper, Mary H. "Muslims in America." *Congressional Quarterly Researcher,* 30 April, 1993: 365–366.

Courlander, Harold. *A Treasury of Afro-American Folklore: The Oral Literature, Traditions, Recollections, Legends, Tales, Songs, Religious Beliefs, Customs, Sayings and Humor of Peoples of African Descent in the Americas.* New York: Marlowe & Co., 1996.

Crenshaw, Kimberle. "Beyond Racism and Misogyny: Black Feminism and 2 Live Crew." *Words That Wound: Critical Race Theory, Assaultive Speech and the First Amendment.* Eds. Mari J. Matsuda, Charles R. Lawrence III, Richard Delgado and Kimberle Williams Crenshaw. Boulder: Westview Press, 1993: 111–132.

———. "Mapping the Margins: Intersectionality, Identity Politics, and Violence Against Women of Color." *After Identity: A Reader in Law and Culture.* Eds. Dan Danielsen and Karen Engle. New York: Routledge, 1995: 332–354.

Cuba, Prince A., *Before Adam: The Original Man,* rev. ed. Hampton, VA: United Brothers Communications Systems, 1992.

Culp Jr., Jerome McCristal. "Neutrality, The Race Question, and the 1991 Civil Rights Act: The 'Impossibility' of Permanent Reform." *Rutgers Law Review* 45 (1993): 965–1010.

Curtin, Philip D. "Ayuba Suleiman Diallo of Bondu."*Africa Remembered: Narratives by West Africans From the Era of the Slave Trade.* Ed. Philip D. Curtin. Madison: University of Milwaukee Press, 1967: 17–59.

Curtiss, Richard H. *A Changing Image: American Perceptions of the Arab-Israeli Dispute.* Washington: American Educational Trust, 1982.

Czatt, Milton Stacey. *The International Bible Students: Jehovah's Witnesses.* New Haven: Yale University Press, 1933.

Daftary, Farhad. *The Ismailis: Their History and Doctrines.* New York: Cambridge University Press, 1990.

Dannin, Robert. "African-American Muslims: From Slavery to the Present." The Joint Center for Near Eastern Studies of New York University and Princeton University, Seventeenth Annual Summer Institute, transcript.

———. "Island in a Sea of Ignorance: Contours and Dimensions of the Prison Mosque." *Making Muslim Space in North America and Europe.* Ed. Barbara Daly Metcalf. Berkeley: University of California Press, 1996: 131–146.

DeCock, Liliane and Reginald McGhee, eds. *James Van Der Zee.* Dobbs Ferry, NY: Morgan & Morgan, 1973.

Delany, Martin R. *The Origin of Races and Color.* Baltimore: Black Classic Press, 1991.

DeLorenzo, Yusuf Talal. "The Search for God's Law: Islamic Jurisprudence in the Writings of Sayf al-Din al-Amidi." *American Journal of Islamic Social Sciences* 11, #4 (Winter 1994): 579–582.

Denny, Frederick M. "The Legacy of Fazlur Rahman." *The Muslims in America.* Ed. Yvonne Y. Haddad. New York: Oxford University Press, 1991: 96–110.

Deveney, John Patrick. *Paschal Beverly Randolph: A Nineteenth-Century*

Black American Spiritualist, Rosicrucian, and Sex Magician. Albany, NY: State University of New York Press, 1997.

Diara, Agadem Lumumba. *Islam and Pan-Africanism.* Detroit: Agascha Productions, 1973.

Dinnerstein, Leonard and David M. Reimers. *Ethnic Americans: A History of Immigration and Assimilation.* New York: New York University Press, 1977.

Diop, Cheikh Anta. *The African Origin of Civilization: Myth or Reality.* Trans. Mercer Cook. New York: L. Hill, 1974.

——. *Civilization or Barbarism: An Authentic Anthropology.* Trans. Yaa-Lengi Meema Ngemi. Brooklyn: Lawrence Hill Books, 1991.

Dobrin, Arthur. "A History of the Negro Jews in America." Schomburg Center for Research in Black Culture, 1965.

Dolan, Jay P. *The Immigrant Church: New York's Irish and German Catholics, 1815–1865.* Baltimore: The John Hopkins Press, 1975.

Dowling, Levi H. *The Aquarian Gospel of Jesus the Christ: The Philosophic and Practical Basis on the Religion of the Aquarian Age of the World: Transribed from the Akashic Records by Levi.* Santa Monica: DeVorss and Co., 1972.

Douglas, J. Archibald. "The Chief Lama of Himis on the Alleged 'Unknown Life of Christ.'" *Nineteenth Century* 39 (April 1896): 667–678.

Drake, St. Clair. *Black Folk Here and There.* 2 vols. Los Angeles: Center for Afro-American Studies and the University of California, 1987–1990.

——. "Negro Americans and the African Interest." *The American Negro Reference Book.* Ed. John P. Davis. Englewood Cliffs, NJ: Prentice-Hall, 1966: 629–665.

——. *The Redemption of Africa and Black Religion.* Chicago: Third World Press, 1970.

DuBois, W.E.B. *The Souls of Black Folk.* New York: Kraus-Thomson Organization, 1973.

——. "Strivings of the Negro People." *Atlantic Monthly* LXXX (August 1897): 194–195.

Duncan, Isabella. *Pre-Adamite Man: Or, The Story of Our Old Planet and Its Inhabitants Told by Scripture and Science,* 2nd ed. London: Saunders, Otley and Co., 1860.

Duran, Khalid. "Bosnia: Genocide 1991." *International Report,* February 1993: 6–7.

Dyson, Michael Eric. "Melanin Madness." *Emerge* (February 1992): 32–37.

Easton, Hosea. *A Treatise on the Intellectual Character and Civil and Political Condition of the Colored People of the United States and the Prejudice Exercised Towards Them.* Philadelphia: Historic Publications, [1837], 1969.

Ehrman, Albert. "Black Judaism in New York." *Journal of Ecumenical Studies* 8, #1 (Winter 1971): 103–114.

Eickelman, Dale. "Ethnicity." *The Oxford Encyclopedia of the Modern Islamic World.* Ed. John L. Esposito. Oxford: Oxford University Press, 1995: 447–451.

Eickelman, Dale and James Piscatori. *Muslim Politics.* Princeton: Princeton University Press, 1996.

Eisenstadt. S. N. *The Absorption of Immigrants: A Comparative Study Based on the Jewish Community in Palestine and the State of Israel.* Westport, CT: Greenwood Press, 1975.

Elkohloy, Abdo A. *The Arab Moslems in the United States.* New Haven: College and University Press, 1966.

Emerson, Steven. "The Other Fundamentalists." *The New Republic*, 12 June, 1995: 21–30.

———. "Testimony of Steven Emerson: Subcommittee of Africa House International Relations Committee," US House of Representatives, 6 April, 1995.

Essien-Udom, Essien Udosen. *Black Nationalism: A Search for an Identity in America.* Chicago: Chicago University Press, 1962.

Esposito, John L. "American Perceptions of Islam and Arabs." *The Diplomat*, October 1996: 10–11.

———. *The Islamic Threat: Myth or Reality.* New York: Oxford University Press, 1995.

———. "Ismail R. Al-Faruqi: Muslim Scholar-Activist." *The Muslims of America.* Ed. Yvonne Y. Haddad. New York: Oxford University Press, 1991: 65–79.

———. ed. *Voices of Resurgent Islam.* New York: Oxford University Press, 1983.

Evanzz, Karl. *The Judas Factor: The Plot to Kill Malcolm X.* New York: Thunder's Mouth Press, 1992.

Ewick, Patricia and Susan S. Silbey. "Subversive Stories and Hegemonic Tales: Toward a Sociology of Narrative." *Law and Society Review* 29 (1995): 197–226.

Fard, Prophet W. D. *This Book Teaches the Lost Found Nation of Islam: A Thorough Knowledge of Our Miserable State of Condition in a Mathematical Way, When We Were Found By Our Saviour W. D. Fard.* n.p.: n.d., c. 1934.

Farrakhan, Louis. *The Secret Relationship Between Blacks and Jews.* Chicago: Nation of Islam, 1991.

al-Faruqi, Ismail R. "Islamic Ideals in North America." *The Muslim Community in North America.* Ed. Earl H. Waugh, Baha Abu-Laban and Regula B. Qureshi. Edmonton: University of Alberta Press, 1983: 259–270.

Fauset, Arthur Huff. *Black Gods of the Metropolis: Negro Religious Cults in the Urban North.* Philadelphia: University of Pennsylvania Press, 1944.

Fell, Barry. *America B.C.: Ancient Settlers in the New World.* New York: Quadrangle/New York Times Books Co., 1976.

———. *Saga America.* New York: Times Books, 1980.

Ferguson, Charles W. *Fifty Million Brothers: A Panorama of American Lodges and Clubs.* New York: Farrar and Rinehart, 1937.

Flournoy, H. W., ed. *Calendar of Virginia State Papers and Other Manuscripts from January 1, 1799 to December 31, 1807.* Preserved in the Capitol, at Richmond, 11 vols. Richmond, 1890.

Fogel, Robert. "The Fourth Great Awakening." *The Wall Street Journal*, 9 January, 1996: A12.

Fox, Richard Wightman and T. J. Jackson Lears, eds. *The Culture of Con-*

sumption: Critical Essays in American History, 1880–1920. New York: Pantheon Books, 1983.

Friedman, Robert I. "One Man's Jihad." *The Nation* 260, #19 (May 15 ,1995): 656–657.

Friedman, Thomas. *From Beirut to Jerusalem.* New York: Farrar Straus Giroux, 1989.

Friedmann, Yohanan. *Prophecy Continuous: Aspects of Ahmadi Religious Thought and Its Medieval Background.* Berkeley: University of California Press, 1989.

Fritze, Ronald. "Goodbye Columbus: The Pseudohistory of Who Discovered America." *Skeptic* 2, #4 (1994): 88–97.

Frug, Mary Joe. "A Postmodern Feminist Legal Manifesto." *After Identity: A Reader in Law and Culture.* Eds. Dan Danielsen and Karen Engle. New York: Routledge, 1995: 7–23.

Fuller, Graham and Ian Lesser. *A Sense of Siege: The Geopolitics of Islam and the West.* Boulder, CO: Westview Press, 1995.

Gabbaccia, Donna. *Militants and Migrants: Rural Sicilians Become American Workers.* New Brunswick: Rutgers University Press, 1988.

Galeotti, Anna Elizabetta. "Citizenship and Equality: The Place for Toleration." *Political Theory* 21 (1993): 589.

Gall, James. *Primeval Man Unveiled: or, the Anthropology of the Bible.* London: Hamilton, Adams & Co., 1871.

Gardell, Mattias. *In the Name of Elijah Muhammad: Louis Farrakhan and the Nation of Islam.* Durham, NC: Duke University Press, 1996.

———. "The Sun of Islam Will Rise in the West: Minister Farrakhan and the Nation of Islam in the Latter Days." *Muslim Communities in North America.* Eds. Yvonne Y. Haddad and Jane I. Smith. Albany: State University of New York Press, 1994: 15–50.

Garrow, David J. *The FBI and Martin Luther King, Jr.* New York: Penguin Books, 1983.

Gennep, Arnold van. *The Rites of Passage.* Chicago: University of Chicago Press, 1960.

Gerber, Israel J. *The Heritage Seekers.* Middle Village, NY: Jonathan Publishers, 1977.

Ghayur, Arif M. "Muslims in the United States: Settlers and Visitors." *The Annals of the Academy of Political and Social Sciences* 45, #4 (1981): 151–163.

Gilanshah, Farah. "Iranians in the Twin Cities." *The Journal of the Institute of Muslim Minority Affairs* 7, #1 (January 1986): 117–123.

Glazer, Nathan and Daniel P. Moynihan, eds. *Ethnicity: Theory and Experience.* Cambridge: Harvard University Press, 1975.

Glendon, Mary Ann. *Rights Talk: The Impoverishment of Political Discourse.* New York: Free Press, 1991.

Gliozzi, Giuliano. *Adamo e il Nuovo Mondo: La Nascita dell'Anthropologia Come Ideologia Coloniale: Dalle Genealogie Bibliche alle Teorie Razziali (1500–1700).* Florence: La Nuova Italia, 1977.

Gobineau, Comte Arthur de. *Les Religions et Les Philosophies dans l'Asie Centrale.* 2 vols. Paris: G. Cres, 1923.

Godbey, Allen H. *The Lost Tribes A Myth: Suggestions Towards Rewriting Hebrew History*. New York: KTAV Publishing House, 1974.

Godement, Francois. *The New Asian Renaissance: From Colonialism to the Post-Cold War*. New York: Routledge, 1997.

Goodspeed, Edgar J. *Famous "Biblical" Hoaxes*. Grand Rapids, MI: Baker Book House, 1956.

Gordon, Milton M. *Assimilation in American Life: The Role of Race, Religion, and National Origins*. New York: Oxford University Press, 1964.

Gottschalk, Stephen. *The Emergence of Christian Science in American Religious Life*. Berkeley: University of California Press, 1973.

Gramsci, Antonio. *Il Materialismo Storico e la Filosofia di Benedetto Croce*. Turin: Giulio Einaudi, 1944.

Greely, Andrew M. *Ethnicity in the United States: A Preliminary Reconnaissance*. New York: John Wiley & Sons, 1974.

Greenawalt, Kent. *Religious Convictions and Political Choice*. New York: Oxford University Press, 1988.

Greene, Victor R. *For God and Country: The Rise of Polish and Lithuanian Ethnic Consciousness in America, 1860–1910*. Madison: State Historical Society of Wisconsin, 1975.

Hadar, Leon. "What Green Peril," *Foreign Affairs* 72, #3 (Spring 1993): 27–42.

Haddad, Yvonne Yazbeck. "American Foreign Policy in the Middle East and Its Impact on the Identity of Arab Muslims in the United States." *The Muslims of America*. Ed. Yvonne Y. Haddad. New York: Oxford University Press, 1991: 217–235.

———. "Arab Muslims and Islamic Institutions in the United States." *Arabs in the New World: Studies on Arab-American Communities*. Eds. Sameer Y. Abraham and Nabeel Abraham. Detroit: Wayne State University Press, 1983: 64–81.

———. "The Challenge of Muslim 'Minorityness': The American Experience." *The Integration of Islam and Hinduism in Western Europe*. Eds. W. A. R. Shadid and P. S. van Koningsveld. Kampen, The Netherlands: Kok, 1991: 134–153.

———. "Current Arab Paradigms for an Islamic Future." *Religion and the Authority of the Past*. Ed. Tobin Siebers. Ann Arbor: University of Michigan Press, 1993: 119–160.

———. "Islamic 'Awakening' in Egypt." *Arab Studies Quarterly* 9, #3 (1987): 234–259.

———. "Muslim Revivalist Thought in the Arab World: An Overview." *The Muslim World* 76, #3–4 (1986): 143–167.

———. ed. *The Muslims of America*. New York: Oxford University Press, 1991.

———. "The 'New Enemy'? Islam and Islamists After the Cold War." *Altered States: A Reader in the New World Order*. Eds. Phyllis Bennis and Michel Moushabeck. New York: Olive Branch Press, 1993: 83–94.

———. "Operation Desert Shield/Desert Storm: The Islamist Perspective." *Beyond the Storm: A Gulf Crisis Reader*. Eds. Phyllys Bennis and Michel Moushabeck. New York: Interlink Books, 1991: 248–260.

————. "The Qur'anic Justification for an Islamic Revolution: The Views of Sayyid Qutb." *Middle East Journal* 38, #1 (January 1983): 14–29.

————. "Sayyid Qutb: Ideologue of Islamic Revival." *Voices of Resurgent Islam*. Ed. John L. Esposito. New York: Oxford University Press, 1983: 67–98.

Haddad, Yvonne Y. and Adair T. Lummis. *Islamic Values in the United States: A Comparative Study*. New York: Oxford University Press, 1987.

Haddad, Yvonne Y. and Jane I. Smith, eds. *Mission to America: Five Islamic Sectarian Communities in North America*. Gainesville: University Press of Florida, 1993.

————. eds. *Muslim Communities in North America*. Albany: State University of New York Press, 1994.

Halasa, Malu. *Elijah Muhammad*. New York: Chelsea House Publications, 1990.

Halsell, Grace. *Journey to Jerusalem*. New York: Macmillan, 1981.

————. *Prophecy and Politics: Militant Evangelists on the Road to Nuclear War*. Westport, CT: Lawrence Hill & Co., 1986.

de Hann, Richard. "Fraternal Organizations." *Collier's Encyclopedia*. Vol. 10. New York: Collier-Macmillan Books, 1967: 334–343.

Hare, Douglas R. A. *The Son of Man Tradition*. Minneapolis: Fortress Press, 1900.

Harlan, Louis R. *Booker T. Washington: The Wizard of Tuskegee, 1901–1915*. New York: Oxford University Press, 1983.

Harris, Joseph E. *African-American Reactions to War in Ethiopia, 1936–1941*. Baton Rouge: Louisiana State University Press, 1994.

Harris, Sara. *Father Divine*. New York: Collier Books, 1971.

Harrison, Barbara Grizzuti. *Visions of Glory: A History and a Memory of the Jehovah's Witnesses*. New York: Simon and Schuster, 1978.

Harrow, Kenneth W., ed. *Faces of Islam in African Literature*. Portsmouth, NH: Heinemann, 1991.

Hart, H. L. A. *The Concept of Law*. Oxford: Clarendon Press, 1961.

Hashmi, Sohail. "Is There an Islamic Ethic of Humanitarian Intervention?" *Ethics and International Affairs* 7 (1993): 55–73.

Hay, Denys. *Europe: The Emergence of an Idea*. New York: Harper & Row, 1966.

Hay, Stephen N. *Asian Ideas of East and West: Tagore and His Criticcs in Japan, China and India*. Cambridge: Harvard University Press, 1970.

Hayne, Joseph Elias. *The Negro in Sacred History: or, Ham and His Immediate Descendants*. Charleston, SC: Walker, Evans & Cogswell Co., 1887.

al-Haytami, Ibn Hajar. *al-Fatawa al-Kubra al-Fiqhiyya*. Vol. 4. Beirut: Dar al-Kutub al-'Ilmiyya, n.d.

Helm, Carl. "Negro Sect in Harlem Mixes Jewish and Christian Religions." *New York Sun*, 29 January, 1929: 6.

Hentoff, Nat. "Farrakhan and the Slave Masters." *The Village Voice* 40, #50 (12 December, 1995): 12.

Herder, Johann Gottfried. *Outlines of a Philosophy of the History of Man*. New York: Berman, 1966.

Hermansen, Marcia K. "Two-Way Acculturation." *The Muslims of America*. Ed. Yvonne Y. Haddad. New York: Oxford University Press, 1991: 188–201.

Higgins, Godfrey. *Anacalypsis: An Attempt to Draw Aside the Veil of the Saitic Isis or An Inquiry Into the Origin of Languages, Nations and Religions.* 2 vols. Brooklyn: A&B Books, 1992.

Higginson, Thomas Wentworth. *Black Rebellion.* New York: Arno Press, 1969.

Hill, Adelaide Cromwell and Martin Kilson, eds. *Apropos of Africa: Sentiments of Negro American Leaders on Africa From the 1800s to the 1950s.* London: Cass, 1969.

Hill, Robert A., ed. *The Marcus Garvey and Universal Negro Improvement Association Papers.* Berkeley: University of California Press, 1983.

Hilliard, Asa. *The Maroon Within Us: Selected Essays on African American Community Socialization.* Baltimore: Black Classics Press, 1995.

Hippler, Jochen. "The Islamic Threat and Western Foreign Policy." *The Next Threat: Western Perceptions of Islam.* Eds. Jochen Hippler and Andrea Leug. London: Pluto Press, 1995: 117–153.

History of Aleppo Temple Ancient Arabic Order Nobles of the Mystic Shrine: Preceded by History of the Ancient Arabic Order and History of the Imperial Council Nobles of the Mystic Shrine for North America in Two Volumes. Boston: Hall Publishing, 1916.

Hobsbawm, Eric. *The Jazz Scene.* New York: Pantheon, 1993.

Hoffert, A. T. "Moslem Propaganda: The Hand of Islam Stretches Out to Aframerica." *Messenger* 9, #5 (May 1927): 141, 160.

Hourani, Albert H. *Arabic Thought in the Liberal Age, 1798–1939.* London: Oxford University Press, 1962.

House Republican Research Committee. "Iran's European Springboard?" Unpublished report by the Task Force on Terrorism and Unconventional Warfare, 1 September 1992.

Houston, Drusilla Dunjee. *Wonderful Ethiopians of the Ancient Empire.* Baltimore: Black Classic Press, 1985.

Hudson, Winthrop S. *Religion in America.* New York: Charles Scribner's Sons, 1965.

Hunter, Monica. *Reaction to Conquest: Effects of Contact With Europeans on the Pondo of South Africa.* 2nd ed. London: Oxford University Press, 1961.

Huntington, Samuel. "The Coming Clash of Civilizations." *Foreign Affairs* 72, #3 (Summer 1993): 22–49.

Ibn Bahr, Uthman Amr. *The Book of the Glory of the Black Race.* Los Angeles: France and William Preston, 1981.

Ibn Tahir al-Baghdadi, Abd al-Qahir. *Kitab Usul al-Din.* Beirut: Dar Kutubal-Ilmiyah, 1981.

Infinite Wisdom. Chicago: de Laurence, 1923.

Israeli, Raphael. "Muslim Minorities Under Non-Islamic Rule." *Current History* 78, #456 (April 1980): 159–160.

Jaafari, Lafi Ibrahim. "The Brain Drain to the United States: The Migration of Jordanian and Palestinian Professionals and Students." *Journal of Palestine Studies* 3, #1 (1973): 119–131.

Jabbra, Joseph G. and Nancy W. Jabbra. "An Arab Family in Transition from Marjar-Tahin, Lebanon to Littleton, Nova Scotia." *Arab Perspectives* 2 (February 1981): 17–19.

Jackson, Carl T. *The Oriental Religions and American Thought: Nineteenth-Century Explorations*. Westport, CT: Greenwood, 1981.

Jackson, John G. "The Empire of the Moors." *Golden Age of the Moor*. Ed. Ivan Van Sertima. New Brunswick, NJ: Transaction, 1992: 85–92.

Jacobs, Sylvia M., ed. *Black Americans and the Missionary Movement in Africa*. Westport, CT: Greenwood Press, 1982.

Jahn, Janheinz. *Neo-African Literature: A History of Black Writing*. New York: Grove Press, 1968.

Jairazbhoy, R. A. *Ramses III: Father of Ancient America*. London: Karnak House, 1992.

James, George G. M. *Stolen Legacy: Greek Philosophy Is Stolen Egyptian Philosophy*. Trenton, NJ: Africa World Press, Inc., 1992.

Jenkins, Clarke. *The Black Hebrews of the Seed of Abraham—Isaac and Jacob of the Tribe of Judah-Benjamin and Levi After 430 Years in America*. Detroit: n.p., 1969.

Jensen, Joan M. *Passage From India: Asian Indian Immigrants in North America*. New Haven: Yale University Press, 1988.

ben Jochannan, Yosef. *African Origins of the Major Western Religions*. New York: Alkebu-Ian Books, 1973.

Johnson, Steve. "Political Activity of Muslims in America." *The Muslims of America*. ed. Yvonne Y. Haddad. Oxford: Oxford University Press, 1991: 111–125.

Jonas, Hans. *The Gnostic Religion: The Message of the Alien God and the Beginnings of Christianity*. 2nd ed. Boston: Beacon Press, 1963.

Jones, Elias Fanayeye. "Black Hebrews: The Quest for Authentic Identity." *Journal of Religious Thought* 44 (Winter–Spring 1988): 35–49.

Jones, William R. *Is God a White Racist? A Preamble to Black Theology*. Garden City, NY: Anchor Press/Doubleday, 1973.

Judy, Ronald A. T. *(Dis)Forming the American Canon: African-Arabic Slave Narratives and the Vernacular*. Minneapolis: University of Minnesota Press, 1993.

Jules-Rosette, Benneta. "Conjugating Cultural Realities: Presence Africaine." *The Surreptitious Speech: Presence Africaine and the Politics of Otherness 1947–1987*. Ed. Y. Y. Mudimbe. Chicago: University of Chicago Press, 1992: 14–44.

Kaplan, Sidney. "Blacks in Massachusetts and the Shays' Rebellion." *Contributions in Black Studies* 8 (1986–1987): 5–14.

Kapur, Sudarshan. *Raising Up a Prophet: The African-American Encounter with Ghandhi*. Boston: Beacon Press, 1992.

Karenga, Maulana. *Introduction to Black Studies*. Los Angeles: University of San Kore Press, 1993.

———. *Selections from the Husia: Sacred Wisdom of Ancient Egypt*. Los Angeles: Kawaida Publications, 1984.

Kashmeri, Zuhair. *The Gulf Within: Canadian Arabs, Racism and the Gulf War*. Toronto: James Lorimer & Company, 1991.

Kearney, Reginald. "Afro-American Views of Japanese, 1900–1945." Ph.D. diss., Kent State University, 1991.

———. "Japan: Ally in the Struggle Against Racism, 1919–1927." *Contributions in Black Studies* 12 (1993–1994): 117–128.

Kerruish, Valerie. *Jurisprudence As Ideology.* New York: Routledge Press, 1991.

Keto, C. Tsehloane. *The African-Centered Perspective of History.* Blackwood, NJ: K and A Associates, 1988.

Kettani, M. A. *Muslim Minorities In the World Today.* London: Mansell, 1986.

Khadduri, Majid. *War and Peace in the Law of Islam.* Baltimore: Johns Hopkins University Press, 1955.

Khan, Mohammed A. Muqtedar. "Dialogue of Civilizations?" *The Diplomat* (June 1997): 45–49.

———. "Islam and an Ethical Tradition of International Relations." *Islam and Christian-Muslim Relations* 8, #2 (Summer 1997): 173–188.

———. "Sovereignty in Modernity and Islam." *East West Review* (Summer 1995): 43–57.

———. "Tribalism the Historical Nemesis of Islam." *The Message* (March 1996): 15–18.

Khan, Muhammad Muhsin. *The Translation of the Meanings of Sahih Al-Bukhari.* Ankara, Turkey: Hilal Yayinlari/Crescent Publishing House, 1976.

Khan, Sheema. "The Root of the Hijab Controversy in Quebec." *Muslim Voice* 2, #2: 4.

"King Fahd and the Saudi Government Were Tied to American War-Mongering." *Muslim Journal*, 10 December, 1990: 13.

King, K. J. "Some Notes on Arnold J. Ford and New World Black Attitudes to Ethiopia." *Journal of Ethiopian Studies* 10, #1 (January 1972): 81–87.

King, Richard. *African Origin of Biological Psychiatry.* Hampton, VA: U.B. & U.S. Communications Systems, 1994.

Knox, R. Buick. *James Ussher: Archbishop of Armagh.* Cardiff: University of Wales Press, 1967.

Kobre, Sydney S. "Rabbi Ford." *Reflex* 4, #1 (January 1929): 25–29.

Koran Questions for Moorish Americans. Chicago: n.p., 1928.

Kramer, Martin. "Islam vs. Democracy." *Commentary* (January 1993): 35–42.

Kurd, Rahat. "My Hijab Is an Act of Worship—and None of Your Business." *The Globe and Mail*, 15 February, 1995: A20.

Kymlicka, Will. *Multicultural Citizenship: A Liberal Theory of Minority Rights.* New York: Oxford University Press, 1995.

Landes, Ruth. "Negro Jews in Harlem." *Jewish Journal of Sociology* 9, #2 (December 1967): 175–189.

Lane-Poole, Stanley. *The Story of the Moors in Spain.* Baltimore: Black Classic Press, 1990.

Latimer, James. "Dusky 'Moors' Wear Turbans, Farm Nearby." *Richmond Times-Dispatch*, 11 April, 1943: 12.

Layman, Emma McCloy. *Buddhism in America.* Chicago: Nelson-Hall Publish ers, 1976.

Lears, T. J. Jackson. *No Place of Grace: Antimoderism and the Transformation of American Culture, 1880–1920.* New York: Pantheon Books, 1981.

Lee, Griffin [Paschal Beverly Randolph]. *Pre-Adamite Man: The Story of the Human Race, from 35,000 to 100,000 Years Ago.* New York: Sinclair Tousey, 1863.

Lee, Martha F. *The Nation of Islam: An American Millenarian Movement.* Syracuse: Syracuse University Press, 1996.

Lefebvre, Henri. *The Production of Space.* Cambridge: Blackwell Press, 1991.

Lefkowitz, Mary. "In Stolen Legacy (or Mythical History?): Did the Greeks Steal Philosophy From the Egyptians." *Skeptic* Vol. 2, #4 (1994): 98–103.

———. *Not Out of Africa: How Afrocentrism Became an Excuse to Teach Myth as History.* New York: Basic Books, 1996.

Lemon, Michele. "Understanding Does Not Always Lead to Tolerance." *The Globe and Mail*, 31 Janury, 1995: A2.

Levi. *The Aquarian Gospel of Jesus the Christ.* Marina Del Rey: DeVorss, 1991.

Levine, Lawrence W. *Black Culture and Black Consciousness: Afro-American Folk Thought from Slavery to Freedom.* Oxford: Oxford University Press, 1977.

Lewis, Bernard. "Islam and Democracy." *The Atlantic* (February 1993): 87–98.

———. *Islam and the West.* New York: Oxford University Press, 1993.

———. *The Political Language of Islam.* Chicago: University of Chicago Press, 1988.

———. *Race and Color in Islam.* New York: Harper & Row, 1971.

———. "The Roots of Muslim Rage." *The Atlantic Monthly* (September 1990): 47–60.

Lewis, H. Spencer. *Rosicrucian Questions and Answers: With Complete History of the Rosicrucian Order.* San Jose: Supreme Grand Lodge of AMORC, 1981.

Lewis, Robert Benjamin. *Light and Truth: Collected from the Bible and Ancient and Modern History, Containing the Universal History of the Colored and the Indian Race, from the Creation of the World to the Present Time.* Boston: A Committee of Colored Gentleman, 1844.

Lincoln, C. Eric. "The American Muslim Mission in the Context of American Social History." *The Muslim Community in North America.* Eds. Early H. Waugh, Baha Abu-Laban and Regula B. Qureshi. Alberta: University of Alberta Press, 1983: 215–233.

———. *The Black Muslims in America.* Boston: Beacon Press, 1961.

Lindsey, Hal. *Countdown to Armageddon.* New York: Bantam Books, 1980.

Lomax, Louis E. *When the Word is Given: A Report on Elijah Muhammad, Malcolm X, and the Balck Muslim World.* Westport: Greenwood Press, 1979.

Lowrie, Arthur. "The Campaign Against Islam and American Foreign Policy." *Middle East Policy* 4, #1–2 (September 1995): 210–219.

Mackenzie, Kenneth. *The Royal Masonic Cyclopaedia.* New York: 1877.

Madhubuti, Haki R. *Enemies: The Clash of Races.* Chicago: Third World Press, 1978.

Maglangbayan, Shawna. *Garvey, Lumumba, Malcolm: Black Nationalist Separatists.* Illinois: Third World Press, 1972.

Magubane, Bernard Makhosezwe. *The Ties That Bind: African-American Consciousness of Africa.* Trenton, NJ: African World Press, 1987.

Mahmud, Khalil. "Introduction to the Second Edition." *The People of Africa.* Ed. H. M. Schieffelin. Ibadan: Ibadan University Press, 1974: v–xxiii.

Malcolm, Noel. *Bosnia: A Short History.* New York: New York University Press, 1994.

Mamiya, Lawrence H. "Minister Louis Farrakhan and the Final Call: Schism in the Muslim Movement." *The Muslim Community in North Africa.* Ed. Earle H. Waugh, Baha Abu-Laban and Regula B. Qureshi. Edmonton: University of Alberta Press, 1983: 234–255.

Marcus, Abraham. *The Middle East on the Eve of Modernity.* New York: Columbia University Press, 1989.

Martin, Tony. *The Jewish Onslaught: Dispatches from the Wellesley Battlefront.* Dover, MA: The Majority Press, 1993.

———. *Race First: The Ideological and Organizational Struggles of Marcus Garvey and the Universal Negro Improvement Association.* Westport: Greenwood Press, 1976.

Marty, Martin E. and R. Scott Appleby, eds. *Fundamentalisms Observed.* Chicago: University of Chicago Press, 1991.

al-Mawardi. *Kitab Qital Ahl al-Baghy min al-Hawi al-Kabir.* Ed. Ibrahim Sandaqji. Cairo: Matbaʿat al-Madani, 1987.

al-Mawdudi, Abul Aʿla. *The Process of Islamic Revolution.* Lahore: Islamic Publications, 1977.

Mazrui, Ali. *The Africans: A Triple Heritage.* Boston: Little Brown, 1986.

———. "Africa's Triple Heritage and I." *Africa Events* 2, #7–8 (July–August 1986): 32–43.

Mazrui, Ali A. and Toby Kleban Levine, eds. *The Africans: A Reader.* New York: Praeger, 1986.

McBride, Eve. "The Hijab's Contradictions: A Form of Freedom Without Choice." *The Gazette,* 6 October, 1994: A2.

McCann, Michael W. *Rights At Work: Pay Equity Reform and the Politics of Legal Mobilization.* Chicago: University of Chicago Press, 1994.

McCloud, Aminah Beverly. *African American Islam.* New York: Routledge, 1995.

———. "Racism in the Ummah." *Islam: A Contemporary Perspective.* Ed. Mohammad Ahmadullah Siddiqi. Chicago: NAAMPS, 1994: 73–80.

McDermott, Mustafa Yusuf and Muhammad Manazir Ahsan. *The Muslim Guide: For Teachers, Employers, Community Members and Social Administrators in Britain.* Leicester, UK: The Islamic Foundation, 1993.

McIntyre, Charsee. *Criminalizing a Race: Free Blacks During Slavery.* Queens, NY: Kayode, 1993.

McIlroy, Ann. "Hijab: Politically Charged Piece of Cloth." *Ottawa Citizen* 2 November, 1994: B2.

Meakin, Budgett. *The Moorish Empire: A Historical Epitome.* New York: Macmillan, 1899.

Meckes, Catherine. "Wearing a Uniform of Oppression." *The Globe and Mail,* 5 July, 1993: A12.

Mehden, Fred R. von der. "American Perceptions of Islam." *Voices of Resurgent Islam.* Ed. John L. Esposito. Oxford: Oxford University Press, 1983: 18–32.

Meier, August. "The Emergence of Negro Nationalism: A Study in Ideologies." *Along the Color Line, Explorations in the Black Experience*. Ed. August Meier and Elliott Rudwick. Urbana: University of Illinois Press, 1976: 189–216.

Melton, J. Gordon. *Biographical Dictionary of American Cult and Sect Leaders*. New York: Garland, 1986.

———, ed. *The Encyclopedia of American Religions*. 3 vols. Tarrytown, NY: Triumph Books, 1991.

Merguii, Raphael and Philippe Simonnot. *Israel's Ayatollahs: Meir Kahane and the Far Right in Israel*. London: Saqi Books, 1987.

Miller, Judith. "The Challenge of Radical Islam." *Foreign Affairs* 72, #2 (Spring 1993): 43–56.

———. "Faces of Fundamentalism." *Foreign Affairs* 73, #6 (November/December 1994): 123–42.

Minault, Gail. *The Khilafat Movement: Religious Symbolism and Political Mobilization in India*. New York: Columbia University Press, 1982.

Minow, Martha. *Making All the Difference: Inclusion, Exclusion, and American Law*. Ithaca: Cornell University Press, 1990.

Mitchell, Richard P. *The Society of the Muslim Brothers*. London: Oxford University Press, 1969.

Mohammed, Ameen Yasir. *Afrocentricity, Minus Al-Islam, Cheats . . . : Exposing the Conspiracy to Rob African Americans of Their Most Precious Heritage*. California: Dawahvision, 1993.

Moore, T. Owens. *The Science of Melanin: Dispelling the Myths*. Silver Spring: Beckham House, 1995.

"A Moorish Temple Catechism." *Moslem World* 32, #1 (January 1942): 55–59.

Moruzzi, Norma Claire. "A Problem With Headscarves: Contemporary Complexities of Political and Social Identity." *Political Theory* 22 (1994): 653–672.

Morwraska, Ewa. *For Bread With Butter: The Life-worlds of East Central Europeans in Johnstown, Pennsylvania, 1890–1940*. New York: Cambridge University Press, 1985.

"Mosque Council Condemns Reagan's Attack on Islam." *Majallat al-Masajid* 2, #2 (February 1981): 17–18.

Muhammad, Abdulhakim. "Seven Muslim Slaves." Pamphlet. Bronx: NY: Bilalian Roots, 1979.

Muhammad, Akbar. "Muslims in the United States: An Overview of Organizations, Doctrines and Problems." *The Islamic Impact*. Eds. Yvonne Y. Haddad, Byron Haines and Ellison Findly. Syracuse: Syracuse University Press, 1984: 195–218.

Muhammad, Elijah. *Message ot the Blackman in America*. Chicago: Muhammad's Temple No. 2, 1965.

———. *The Secrets of Freemasonry*. Cleveland: Secretarius Publications, 1994.

———. *The Theology of Time*. Hampton, VA: U.B. & U.S. Communications Systems, 1992.

Muhammad, Isa. *Al Imam Isa Vs. the Computer*. Brooklyn: Isa Muhammad, 1982.

————. *The Message of the Messenger Is Right and Exact*. Brooklyn: Isa Muhammad, 1979.

————. *365 Questions to Ask the Orthodox Sunni Muslims*. Brooklyn: n.p., 1989.

————. *Racism in Islam*. Brooklyn: Isa Muhammad, 1982.

Muhammad, Warith D. *Challenges That Face Man Today*. Chicago: W. D. Muhammad Publications, 1985.

————. *Focus on Islam*. Chicago: Zakat Publications, 1988.

Muller, Max. "The Alleged Sojourn of Christ in India." *Nineteenth Century* 36 (October 1894): 515–522.

Muslim Communities in Non-Muslim States. London: Islamic Council of Europe, 1980.

"Muslim Unity Urged." *Final Call*, 31 October, 1990: 2.

"Muslims Unite!" *Final Call*, 31 October, 1990: 1.

Mustafa, Naheed. "My Body is My Own Business." *The Globe and Mail*, 29 June, 1993: A26.

————. "The Fear of Hijab." *The Message Canada*. January 1995: 15.

The Mystic Shrine: An Illustrated Ritual of the Ancient Arabic Order, Nobles of the Mystic Shrine. Chicago: Ezra A. Cook, 1975.

Naff, Alixa. *Becoming American: The Early Arab Immigrant Experience*. Carbondale, IL: Southern Illinois University Press, 1985.

Nagel, Joane. "Constructing Ethnicity: Creating and Recreating Ethnic Identity and Culture." *Social Problems* 41, #1 (February 1994): 152–176.

Nanjel, Azim. "The Nizari Ismaili Community in North America: Background and Development." *The Muslim Community in North America*. Eds. Earle H. Waugh, Baha Abu-Laban, and Regula B. Qureshi. Alberta: University of Alberta Press, 1983: 149–164.

Nasrulla, Amber. "Educators Outside Quebec Mystified by Hijab Ban." *The Globe and Mail*, 13 December, 1994: A1–4.

————. "Their Canada Includes Hijab." *The Globe and Mail*, 22 August, 1994: A1–2.

al-Nawawi, Muhyyi al-Din. *Riyad al-Salihin*. Beirut: Muassasat al-Risalah, 1982.

al-Nazawi, Abu Bakr al-Kindi al-Sammadi al-Nazawi. *al-Musannaf*. Vol. 10. Oman: Wazarat al-Turath al-Qawmi, 1983.

Nelli, Humbert S. *From Immigrants to Ethnics: The Italian-Americans*. New York: Oxford University Press, 1983.

Nicolaevsky, B. "Russian, Japan, and the Pan-Asiatic Movement to 1925." *Far Eastern Quarterly* 8, #3 (May 1949): 259–295.

Nietzsche, Friedrich W. *On the Genealogy of Morals*. Cambridge: Cambridge University Press, 1994.

Nobles, Wade. *African Psychology: Toward Its Reclamation, Reascension and Revitalization*. Oakland: Black Family Institute, 1986.

Norris, Alexander. "Lemieux Blasted for Remarks Attacking Hijab." *The Montreal Gazette*, 24 November, 1994: A1.

Notovich, Nikolai. *The Unknown Life of Jesus Christ*. Chicago: V. R. Gandhi, 1894.

Nuruddin, Yusuf. "The Five Percenters: A Teenage Nation of Gods and Earths." *Muslim Communities in North America*. Eds. Yvonne Y. Haddad and Jane I. Smith. Albany: State University of New York Press, 1994: 109–132.

Nyang, Sulayman S. "Convergence and Divergence in an Emergent Community: A Study of Challenges Facing U.S. Muslims." *The Muslims of America*. Ed. Yvonne Y. Haddad. Oxford: Oxford University Press, 1991: 236–249.

———. *Islam, Christianity, and African Identity*. Brattleboro, VT: Amana Books, 1984.

———. "Islam in the United States: A Review of Sources." *Journal of the Institute of Minority Affairs* 3, #1 (1982): 189–198.

———. "The Scholar's Mansions." *Africa Events* 2, #7–8 (July–August 1986): 32–43.

Nyang, Sulayman S. and Mumtaz Ahmad. "The Muslim Intellectual Emigre in the United States." *Islamic Culture* 57, #3 (1985): 277–290.

Odum, Howard W. *Social and Mental Traits of the Negro*. New York: Columbia University, 1910.

"One Year's Moslem Missionary Work in America." *Moslem Sunrise* 1 (July 1921): 13.

"The Only Solution of Color Prejudice." *Moslem Sunrise* 1, #2 (October 1921): 41–42.

O'Reilly, Kenneth. *Racial Matters: The FBI's Secret File on Black America, 1960–1972*. New York: The Free Press, 1989.

Orfalea, Gregory. *Before the Flames: A Quest for the History of Arab Americans*. Austin: University of Texas Press, 1988.

Ottley, Roi. *New World A-Coming*. New York: Arno Press, 1968.

Padover, Saul K. "Japanese Race Propaganda." *Public Opinion Quarterly* 7, #2 (Summer 1943): 191–204.

Painter, Nell Irvin. *Exodusters: Black Migration to Kansas After Reconstruction*. New York: Alfred Knopf, 1977.

Parker, George Wells. *Children of the Sun*. Baltimore: Black Classic Press, 1978.

Perry, Glen E. "Caliph." *The Oxford Encyclopedia of the Modern Islamic World*. ed. John L. Esposito. Oxford: Oxford University Press, 1995: 239–243.

Perry, H.F. "The Workingman's Alienation From the Church." *American Journal of Sociology* 4 (March 1899): 621–629.

Perry, Rufus L. *The Cushite; or, The Children of Ham, (The Negro Race) As Seen by the Ancient Historians and Poets*. Brooklyn: Literary Union, 1887.

Peters, Rudolph. *Islam and Colonialism: The Doctrine of Jihad in Modern History*. The Hague: Mouton, 1979.

Peterson, Thomas Virgil. *Ham and Japhet: The Mythic World of Whites in the Antebellum South*. Metuchen, NJ: Scarecrow Press, 1978.

Philips, Abu Ameenah Bilal. *The Evolution of Fiqh*. Riyadh: International Islamic Publishing House, 1996.

Pipes, Daniel. "Fundamental Questions About Muslims." *Wall Street Journal*, 30 October, 1992: A11.

———. "Fundamentalist Muslims." *Foreign Affairs*, Summer 1986: 939–959.

———. *In the Path of God: Islam and Political Power*. New York: Basic Books, 1983.

————. "The Muslims Are Coming! The Muslims Are Coming!" *National Review* 42, #22 (November 19, 1990): 28–31.

Piscatori, James. "International Relations and Diplomacy." *The Oxford Encyclopedia of the Modern Islamic World.* Ed. John L. Esposito. Oxford: Oxford University Press, 1995: 216–220.

————. *Islam in a World of Nation-States.* Cambridge: Cambridge University Press, 1986.

Pogrebin, Robin. "The Buzz on Black Radio." *New York Times* (28 January 1996): 13.

Popkin, Richard H. *Isaac La Peyrere (1596–1676): His Life, Work and Influence.* New York: E. J. Brill, 1987.

Post, Ken. *Arise Ye Starvelings: The Jamaican Labour Rebellion of 1938 and Its Aftermath.* The Hague: Nijhoff, 1978.

Poston, Larry. *Islamic Da'wah in the West: Muslim Missionary Activity and the Dynamics of Conversion to Islam.* New York: Oxford University Press, 1992.

Prempeh, Osafo Akwesi. "The Arab and European Conflict: Africans Have No Business Participating." *The Alkebulanian* 2, #10 (October 1990): 3–5.

————. "A Guide to Reject: 'The Blackman's Guide to Understanding the Blackwoman.'" *The Alkebulanian* 2, #8 (September 1990): 12–14.

al-Qaradawi, Yusuf. *Al Fatwa Bayn al Indibat wa-al-Tasayyub.* Cairo: Dar al Sahwa, 1988.

al-Qazzaz, Ayad. "The Changing Characteristics of the Arab American Community in the U.S." *Arab Perspectives.* Vol. 2 (February 1981): 4–8.

Quick, Abdullah Hakim. "Deeper Roots: Muslims in the Caribbean Before Columbus to the Present." Nassau, Bahamas: Occasional Paper, No. 1, Association of Islamic Communities in the Caribbean and Latin America, 1990.

Qutb, Sayyid. *Milestones.* Indianapolis: American Trust, 1990.

Raboteau, Albert J. *A Fire in the Bones: Reflections on African-American Religious History.* Boston: Beacon Press, 1995.

————. *Slave Religion: The "Invisible Institution" in the Antebellum South.* Oxford: Oxford University Press, 1978.

Raisin, Jacob S. *Gentile Ractions to Jewish Ideals, with Special Reference to Proselytes.* New York: Philosophical Library, 1953.

Rashad, Adib. *Islam, Black Nationalism and Slavery: A Detailed History.* Beltsville, MD: Writers Inc., 1995.

Reade, W. Winwood. *Savage Africa.* New York: Harper, 1864.

Redkey, Edwin S. *Black Exodus: Black Nationalist and Back-to-Africa Movements, 1890–1910.* New Haven: Yale University Press, 1969.

Reed, Ishmael. *Mumbo Jumbo.* New York: Doubleday, 1972.

Reid, Ira De A. "Let Us Prey!" Opportunity (September 1926): 274–278.

Renteln, Alison Dundes. *International Human Rights: Universalism vs. Relativism.* Newbury Park: Sage Publications, 1990.

Richardson, E. Allen. *East Comes West: Asian Religions and Cultures in North America.* New York: Pilgrim Press, 1985.

Rida, Rashid. *Fatawa al-Imam Muhammad Rashid Rida.* Vol. 1–6. Beirut: Dar al-Kitab al-Jadid, 1970–71.

Roberson, B. A. "Islam and Europe: An Enigma or a Myth?" *Middle East Journal* 48, #2 (Spring 1994): 288–308.

Roberts, B. H. *The Mormon Doctrine of Deity: The Roberts-Van der Donckt Discussion, To Which is Added a Discourse, Jesus Christ, the Revelation of God: Also a Collection of Authoritative Mormon Utterances on the Being and Nature of God.* Bountiful, UT: Horizon Publishers, 1976.

Rodinson, Maxim. *Europe and the Mystique of Islam.* Seattle: University of Washington Press, 1987.

Rogers, J. A. *World's Great Men of Color.* Vol. 1–2. New York: Macmillan, 1972.

———. *Sex and Race.* Vol. 1. New York: Helga Rogers, 1967.

Root, George Livingston. *Ancient Arabic Order of the Nobles of the Mystic Shrine for North America.* San Antonio, TX: n.p., 1916.

Rose, Peter Isaac, ed. *Nation of Nations.* New York: Random House, 1972.

Rousseau, Jean-Jacques. *Du Contrat Social: Ou, Principes du Droit Politique.* Paris: Garnier Freres, n.d.

Roux, Edward. *Time Longer Than Rope: A History of the Black Man's Struggle for Freedom in South Africa.* 2nd ed. Madison: University of Wisconsin Press, 1964.

Sabbagh, George and Mehdi Bozorgmehr. "Secular Immigrants: Religiosity and Ethnicity Among Iranian Muslims in Los Angeles." *Muslim Communities in North America.* Ed. Yvonne Y. Haddad and Jane I. Smith. Albany: State University of New York Press, 1994: 445–474.

Sabih, Hatim A. "The Nation of Islam." M.A. thesis, University of Chicago, 1951.

Said, Edward W. *Covering Islam: How the Media and the Experts Determine How We See the Rest of the World.* New York: Pantheon Books, 1981.

———. *Orientalism.* New York: Pantheon Books, 1978.

———. *The Politics of Dispossession: The Struggle for Palestinian Self-Determination, 1969–1994.* New York: Pantheon Books, 1994.

Salaam, Yusuf. "Imam's Lecture Cites Problem With 'Priests of Blackness'." *The New York Amsterdam News* 86, #36 (9 September, 1995): 21.

Salih, al-Tayyib. *Season of Migration to the North.* New York: Michael Kesend Publishers, 1989.

Salontos, Theodore. "Causes and Patterns of Greek Emigration to the United States." *Perspectives in American History* 7 (1973): 381–437.

Saxton, Alexander. *The Indispensable Enemy: Labor and the Anti-Chinese Movement in California.* Berkeley: University of California Press, 1971.

Sawaie, Mohammed. *Arabic Speaking Immigrants in the United States and Canada.* Lexington, KY: Mazda Publications, 1985.

Schechtman, Marya. *The Constitution of Selves.* Ithaca: Cornell University Press, 1996.

Schlesinger, Arthur Meier. "A Critical Period in American Religion, 1875–1900." *Proceedings of the Massachusetts Historical Society* 64 (October 1930–June 1932): 523–547.

Scobie, Edward. *Black Britannia: A History of Blacks in Brooklyn.* Chicago: Johnson Publications, 1972.

Scott, Emmett. *Negro Migration During the War.* New York: Arno Press, 1969.

Scott, William R. "Rabbi Arnold Ford's Back-to-Ethiopia Movement: A Study of Black Emigration, 1930–1935." *Pan-African Journal* 8, #2 (Summer 1975): 191–202.

————. *The Sons of Sheba's Race: African-Americans and the Italo-Ethiopian War, 1935–1941*. Bloomington: Indiana University Press, 1993.

Seager, Richard Hughes. *The World's Parliament of Religions: The East/West Encounter, Chicago, 1893*. Bloomington: Indiana University Press, 1995.

The Secret Ritual and the Secret Work of the Ancient Arabic Order of Nobles of the Mystic Shrine. New York: Masonic Supply Co., n.d.

al-Shafi'i, Abu Abd Allah. *al-Umm*. Ed. Muhammad al-Najjar. Vol. 4. Beirut: Dar al-Ma'rifa: n.d.

————. *al-Umm*. Ed. Muhammad al-Najjar. Vol. 7. Beirut: Dar al-Ma'rifa: n.d.

Shafiq, Muhammad. *Growth of Islamic Thought in North America: Focus on Ismail Raji al Faruqi*. Brentwood, MD: Amana Publications, 1994.

Shaka, Oba T. *Art of Leadership*. Vol. 1–2. Richmond, CA: Pan Afrikan Publications, 1990.

Shaltut, Mahmud. *al-Fatawa*. Beirut: Dar al-Shuruq, 1986.

Shapiro, Deanne. "Factors in the Development of Black Judaism." *The Black Experience in Religion*. Ed. C. Eric Lincoln. Garden City, NY: Anchor Press/Doubleday, 1974: 254–272.

Shepperson, George. "Ethiopianism Past and Present." *Christianity in Tropical Africa*. ed. C. G. Baeta. London: Oxford University Press, 1968: 249–264.

————. "Nyasaland and the Millennium." *Millennial Dreams in Action: Studies in Revolutionary Religious Movements*. Ed. Sylvia L. Thrupp. New York: Schocken, 1970: 144–159.

al-Shirazi, Abu Ishaq. *al-Muhadhab*. Vol. 2. Cairo: Mustafa al-Babi al-Halabi, 1971.

Siddiqi, Abdul Hamid. Trans. *Sahih Muslim: Being Traditions of the Sayings and Doings of the Prophet Muhammad as Narrated by His Companions and Compiled Under the Title Al-Jami'-us-Sahih by Imam Muslim*. New Delhi: Kitab Bhavan, 1978.

Silvestre de Sacy, Antoine-Isaac. *Expose de la Religion des Druzes*. 2 Vols. Paris: L'Imprimerie Royale, 1838.

Simpson, Frank T. "The Moorish Science Temple and Its 'Koran'." *Moslem World* 37, #1 (January 1947): 56–61.

Singer, Merrill. "The Southern Origin of Black Judaism." *African Americans in the South: Issues of Race, Class, and Gender*. Eds. Hans A. Baer and Yvonne Jones. Athens: University of Georgia Press, 1992: 123–138.

Smith, Jane I. "Seyyed Hossein Nasr: Defender of the Sacred and Islamic Traditionalism." *The Muslims of America*. Ed. Yvonne Y. Haddad. New York: Oxford University Press, 1991: 80–96.

Smith, M. G., Roy Augier and Rex Nettleford. *The Rastafari Movement in Kingston, Jamaica*. Mona, Jamaica: University of the West Indies, 1978.

Smith, Theophus H. *Conjuring Culture: Biblical Formations of Black America*. New York: Oxford University Press, 1994.

Snowden, Frank M. *Blacks in Antiquity: Ethiopians in the Greco-Roman Experience*. Cambridge: Belknap Press of Harvard University Press, n.d.

Sollors, Werner. *Beyond Ethnicity: Consent and Descent in American Culture*. New York: Oxford University Press, 1986.

Somers, Margaret R. and Gloria D. Gibson. "Reclaiming the Epistemological 'Other': Narrative and the Social Constitution of Identity." *Social Theory and the Politics of Identity*. Ed. Craig Calhoun. Oxford: Blackwell Publishers, 1994: 37–99.

Spear, Allan H. *Black Chicago: The Making of a Negro Ghetto, 1890–1920*. Chicago: University of Chicago Press, 1967.

Stack, Carol B. *Call To Home: African Americans Reclaim the Rural South*. New York: Basic Books, 1996.

Strauss, David Friedrich. *The Life of Jesus, Critically Examined*. Trans. Marian Evans. St. Clair Shores, MI: Scholarly Press, 1970.

Susman, Warren I. *The Transformation of American Society in the Twentieth Century*. New York: Pantheon Books, 1984.

Tannous, Afif S. "Acculturation of an Arab Syrian Community in the Deep South." *Sociological Review* 8 (1943): 264–270.

Taylor, Charles. *Human Agency and Language*. Cambridge: Cambridge University Press, 1989.

———. *Multiculturalism and "The Politics of Recognition."* Princeton: Princeton University Press, 1992.

Thomas, Greg. "The Black Studies War: Multiculturalism Versus Afrocentricity." *The Village Voice*. 40, #3 (January 17, 1995): 23–29.

Thomas, Wendell. *Hinduism Invades America*. New York: Beacon Press, 1930.

Thompson, Robert Farris. *Flash of the Spirit: African and Afro-American Art and Philosophy*. New York: Random House, 1983.

Tibi, Bassam. "The Worldview of Sunni Arab Fundamentalists: Attitudes Toward Modern Science and Technology." *Fundamentalisms and Society: Reclaiming the Sciences, the Family and Education*. Chicago: University of Chicago Press, 1993: 73–102.

"True Salvation of the American Negroes." *Moslem Sunrise* 2, #2–3 (April–July 1923): 184.

Turgay, A. Uner. "Nation." *The Oxford Encyclopedia of the Modern Islamic World*. Ed. John L. Esposito. Oxford: Oxford University Press, 1995: 231–235.

Turner, Bryan S. *Religion and Social Theory*. London: Sage Publications, 1991.

Turner, Richard B. "The Ahmadiyya Mission to Blacks in the United States in the 1920s." *Journal of Religious Thought* 44, #2 (Winter-Spring 1988): 50–66.

Turner, Richard Brent. *Islam in the African-American Experience*. Bloomington: Indiana University Press, 1997.

Tweed, Thomas A. *The American Encounter with Buddhism, 1844–1912: Victorian Culture and the Limits of Dissent*. Bloomington: Indiana University Press, 1996.

Unto Thee I Grant. San Jose, CA: Supreme Grand Lodge of AMORC, 1968.

Uthman, Muhammad Rafat. *Mahr al Zawjah*. Cairo: Dar al-Kitab al-Jamii, 1982.

Van Loon, Hendrick Willem. *The Story of Mankind*. New York: Liveright, 1984.

Van Sertima, Ivan., ed. *African Presence in Early America*. New Brunswick: Transaction Books, 1987.

——. *The Golden Age of the Moors.* New Brunswick: Transaction Books, 1992.

——. *They Came Before Columbus: The African Presence in Ancient America.* New York: Random House, 1976.

Vatralsky, Stoyan Krstoff. "Mohammedan Gnosticism in America: The Origin, History, Character, and Esoteric Doctrines of the Truth-Knowers." *American Journal of Theology* 6, #1 (January 1902): 57–78.

Velcoli, Rudolf J. "Contadini in Chicago: A Critique of The Uprooted." *The Journal of American History* 51 (1964): 404–417.

Venturi, Richard. "Integration Or Assimilation in Montreal's Schools." *McGill Tribune,* 15 November, 1994: 10.

Vidal-Naquet, Pierre. "Atlantis and the Nations." *Questions of Evidence: Proof, Practice, and Persuasion Across the Disciplines.* Eds. James Chandler, Arnold I. Davidson, and Harry Harootunian. Chicago: University of Chicago Press, 1994: 325–357.

Voll, John O. "Fundamentalism in the Sunni Arab World: Egypt and the Sudan." *Fundamentalisms Observed.* Eds. Martin E. Marty and R. Scott Appleby. Chicago: University of Chicago Press, 1991: 345–402.

——. "Islam as a Special World-System." *Journal of World History* 5, #2 (Fall 1994): 213–226.

Wagner, Donald E. *Anxious for Armageddon.* Scottdale, PA: Herald Press, 1995.

Waitzkin, Howard. "Black Judaism in New York." *Harvard Journal of Negro Affairs* 1, #3 (1967): 12–44.

Wakatsuki, Yasuo. "The Japanese Emigration to the United States, 1866–1924." *Perspectives in American History* 12 (1979): 389–516.

Waldman, Marilyn Robinson. "Reflections on Islamic Traditions, Woman and Family." *Muslim Families in North America.* Eds. Earl H. Waugh, Sharon McIrvin Abu-Laban, Regula Burckhardt Qureshi. Edmonton: University of Alberta Press, 1991: 309–325.

Walbridge, Linda S. "The Shia Mosques and their Congregations in Dearborn." *Muslim Communities in North America.* Eds. Yvonne Y. Haddad and Jane I. Smith. Albany: State University of New York Press, 1994: 337–358.

al-Wansharisi, Ahmad. *al-Miyar.* ed. Muhammad Hajj. Vol. 2. Beirut: Dar al- Gharb al-Islami, 1981.

Wasfi, Atif A. *An Islamic-Lebanese Community in the U.S.A.: A Study of Cultural Anthropology.* Beirut: Beirut Arab University Press, 1971.

Washington, Booker T. *The Booker T. Washington Papers.* Eds. Louis R. Harlan and Raymond W. Smock. Urbana: University of Illinois Press, 1972–1989.

Washington, Iris L. "The FBI Plot Against Black Leaders." *Essence* 9, #6 (October 1978): 70–73.

Washington, Joseph R. *Black Sects and Cults.* Garden City, NY: Doubleday, 1972.

——. "Negro Cults (in the United States)." *Encyclopedia Britannica.* Vol. 12, Part 3 (1970): 942–944.

Washington, Peter. *Madame Blavatsky's Baboon: A History of the Mystics, Mediums, and Misfits Who Brought Spiritualism to America.* New York: Schocken Books, 1995.

Watts, Jill. *God, Harlem U.S.A.: The Father Divine Story*. Berkeley: University of California Press, 1992.

Waugh, Earl H. *The Muslim Community in North America*. Edmonton: University of Alberta Press, 1983.

Way, Frank and Barbara J. Burt. "Religious Marginality and the Free Exercise Clause." *American Political Science Review* 77 (1983): 652–665.

Webb, James Morris. *The Black Man, the Father of Civilization*. Seattle: Acme Press, Printers, 1910.

Weiner, Leo. *Africa and the Discovery of America*. Brooklyn: A & B Books, 1992.

Weiss, Bernard. *The Search for God's Law: Islamic Jurisprudence in the Writings of Sayf al-Din al-Amidi*. Salt Lake City: University of Utah Press, 1992.

Whalen, William J. *Christianity and American Freemasonry*. Huntington, IN: Bruce Publishing, 1987.

Whyte, Abbie. "Christian Elements in Negro American Muslim Religious Beliefs." *Phylon* 25, #4 (Winter 1964): 382–388.

Wilks, Ivor. "Abu Bakr al-Saddiq of Timbuktu." *Africa Remembered: Narratives by West Africans From the Era of the Slave Trade*. Ed. Philip D. Curtin. Madison: University of Milwaukee Press, 1967: 145–169.

———. "Salih Bilali of Massina." *Africa Remembered: Narratives by West Africans From the Era of the Slave Trade*. Ed. Philip D. Curtin. Madison: University of Milwaukee Press, 1967: 17–59.

William, John A. *The Man Who Cried I Am*. Boston: Little, Brown, 1967.

———. *The Destruction of Black Civilization: Great Issues of a Race from 4500 B.C. to 2000 A.D.* Chicago: Third World Press, 1987.

Williams, Walter L. *Black Americans and the Evangelization of Africa*. Madison: University of Wisconsin Press, 1982.

Wilmore, Gayraud S. *Black Religion and Black Radicalism: An Interpretation of the Religious History of Afro-American People*. Maryknoll, NY: Orbis Books, 1983.

Wilson, Amos. *Black on Black Violence: The Psychodynamics of Black Self-Annihilation in Service of White Domination*. New York: Afrikan World InfoSystems, 1990.

———. *The Developmental Psychology of the Black Child*. New York: Africana Research Publications, 1978.

———. *The Falsification of Afrikan Consciousness: Eurocentric History, Psychiatry and the Politics of White Supremacy*. New York: Afrikan World InfoSystems, 1993.

Wilson, Dwight. *Armageddon Now*. Tyler, TX: Institute for Christian Economics, 1991.

Wilson, Peter Lamborn. *Sacred Drift: Essays on the Margins of Islam*. San Francisco: City Lights Books, 1993.

———. *Scandal: Essays in Islamic Heresy*. Brooklyn: Autonomedia, 1988.

———. "Shoot-Out at the Circle Seven Koran: Noble Drew Ali and the Moorish Science Temple." *Gnosis* 12 (Summer 1989): 44–49.

Winchell, Alexander. *Preadamites; Or, A Demonstration of the Existence of Men Before Adam: Together With a Study of Their Condition, Antiquity, Racial Affinities, and Progressive Dispersion Over the Earth*. 5th ed. Chicago: Scott, Foresman, 1901.

Winters, Clyde-Ahmad. "Islam in Early North and South America." *Al-Ittihad* 14, #3 (July–October, 1977): 56–67.

———. "Roots and Islam in Slave America." *Al-Ittihad* 13, #3 (October–November 1976): 18–20.

Woolman, David S. *Rebels in the Rif: Abd El-Krim and the Rif Rebellion.* Stanford: Stanford University Press, 1968.

Work, Monroe, ed. *Negro Year Book, 1931–1932.* Tuskegee, AL: Negro Year Book Publishing, 1932: 257–258.

———, ed. *Negro Year Book, 1937–1938.* Tuskegee, AL: Negro Year Book Publishing, 1938: 218–219.

World's Parliament of Religions (1893: Chicago, Ill). *The Dawn of Religious Pluralism: Voices From the World's Parliament of Religions, 1893.* Ed. Richard Hughes Seager. La Salle, IL: Open Court, 1993.

Wuthenau, Alexander von. *Unexpected Faces in Ancient America (1500 BC–AD 1500): The Historical Testimony of Pre-Columbian Artists.* New York: Crown, 1975.

X, Malcolm. *The End of White World Supremacy: Four Speeches by Malcolm X.* Ed. Benjamin Karim. New York: Arcade Publications, 1989.

Yahya, Ahmad. "Mazrui and I." *Africa Events* 2 #7–8 (July–August 1986): 32–43.

Yusuf, Ahmad. "Al-Hajma al-Sihyoniyya ʻala al-Muslimin fi al-Wilayat al-Muttahida. Mawjat al-Tahrid al-Thalitha: al-Jihad fi America." *Filastin al-Muslima,* January 1995: 38–40.

Zarcone, Thierry. *Mystiques, Philosophes et Francs-Macons en Islam: Riza Tevfik, Penseur Ottoman (1868–1949): Du Soufisme a la Confrerie.* Paris: Institut Francais d'Etudes Anatoliennes, 1993.

Zaretsky, Eli. "Identity Theory, Identity Politics: Psychoanalysis, Marxism, Poststructuralism." *Social Theory and the Politics of Identity.* Ed. Craig Calhoun. Oxford: Blackwell Publishers, 1994: 198–216.

Zayid, Imam A. S. Mahdi Ibn-Khalid. *Confronting America's Black-White Dilemma: The Admiral Family's Agenda and Strategy for American-American Political Autonomy.* New York: New Horizon Communications, 1992.